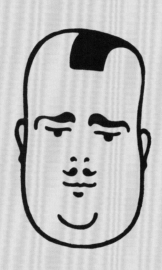

JAMES LAYTON

DAVID PIERCE

KING of JAZZ
PAUL WHITEMAN'S TECHNICOLOR REVUE

Edited by Richard Koszarski

Foreword by Michael Feinstein

Appendix by Crystal Kui and James Layton

MEDIA
HISTORY
PRESS

Published by Media History Press, an imprint of Media History Digital Library, Inc.
1725 Grande View Ave., Severn, MD 21144

Generously supported by

Distributed in North America by Cardinal Publishers Group

Distributed in Europe by Gazelle Book Services Ltd.

Edited by Richard Koszarski
Copyedited by Catherine A. Surowiec
Appendix, image research, and project management by Crystal Kui
Designed by Christian Zavanaiu
Cover photograph colorized by Tom Maroudas

Typeset in Grunion LT, Frutiger, and Market Deco
Printed on 128 gsm Chinese matte art paper
Printed and bound by C&C Offset Printing Co., Ltd., China

Library of Congress Control Number: 2016935177
ISBN 978-0-9973801-0-1

CONTENTS

FOREWORD

For those who wish to experience an authentic time capsule of 1930, *King of Jazz* remains a gaudy and resonant depiction of American cultural expression. With an audacious co-mingling of film, art, Broadway, vaudeville, mixed music, and social attitudes, it's striking in the way it evokes both the sophistication and innocence of the era. The film is a fascinating and jumbled cinematic excursion, but it preserves a slice of good old-fashioned show business, combined with new and exciting technology of its time.

By 1930 the bandleader Paul Whiteman had fallen victim to his own publicity, having been crowned leader of the Jazz movement. That he was not a true purveyor of authentic jazz mattered not to a public that had embraced the title, thus catapulting Whiteman to a level of fame and fortune that was previously unheard of. He formed Whiteman "ghost bands" that toured the country to fulfill the demands of audiences who wanted to hear his brand of music in person. Paul Whiteman remains the best-remembered popular bandleader of his time, and many competitors were left in the dust, green with envy.

Perhaps it was inevitable that a film would be made to celebrate this fascinating larger-than-life figure, for he had a kind of bravado that richly entertained his public and delivered a first-rate musical show. His savvy at hiring the best musicians and arrangers paid off handsomely, and it did not matter that such high costs of operation far exceeded those of any other band of the time. Paul always wanted and got the best, including some of the most talented jazz performers of the era, like Bix Beiderbecke, Joe Venuti, Frankie Trumbauer, Eddie Lang, and singer Bing Crosby.

Despite its initial financial failure, *King of Jazz* is now recognized for, among other things, the memorialization of Whiteman's legendary collaboration with the greatest American composer in history: George Gershwin. The producers of the film paid the composer an astonishing $50,000 for the rights to use *Rhapsody in Blue* in the movie because a film called *King of Jazz* simply had to include it.

The genesis of the *Rhapsody in Blue*, quaintly dramatized in the film, owes "Pops" a deep debt of gratitude, because six years earlier he casually commissioned it by announcing in an interview that George Gershwin was composing a work for his band's upcoming concert at Aeolian Hall. George, who was 25 at the time, learned about it in the newspaper. Rather than simply dismissing the commission, he took up the challenge, and created his jazz concerto for the Whiteman band in less than a month. The impact of the *Rhapsody in Blue* (with the composer at the piano) was instantaneous when it premiered on February 12, 1924. The trajectory of American music was forever changed that day, and Gershwin and Whiteman soared to even greater heights, their careers inseparably intertwined for the rest of their lives.

Due to its rapturous reception, the concert featuring the *Rhapsody* was repeated multiple times (with Gershwin again as piano soloist), prompting Victor to record the work four months later, and Harms to publish the score, all to the amazement of the composer, who had regarded the *Rhapsody in Blue* more as special material composed expressly for the Whiteman band. It became clear though that he had touched a nerve, creating a work that not only caught the public's imagination but immediately came to symbolize the pulse of the Jazz Age: people could not get enough of this new combination of jazz and concert music.

Shortly afterwards, however, Gershwin and Whiteman started clashing on the way the work was interpreted. Whiteman eventually made the ubiquitous Andante section of the *Rhapsody* his orchestra's signature theme, while Gershwin played it in concert and on radio innumerable times, but without Whiteman. They didn't play together again until *King of Jazz* premiered in 1930 at the Roxy in New York, as part of the live stage show featuring Whiteman and the orchestra.

The piano soloist in the film is Roy Bargy, but the *New York Times* movie critic mistakenly identified him as Gershwin himself. Ironically, some twenty years later Roy Bargy stood in for Whiteman, when he conducted a recording of *Rhapsody in Blue* in 1951 that was released as "Whiteman Conducts Gershwin," even though pianist Leonard Pennario told me Paul was sequestered at home in Pennsylvania during the Los Angeles recording session. It still became a best-selling record, because the combination of Gershwin and Whiteman retained its luster through the 1950s, and unsuspecting record buyers wanted to experience the authenticity of the Whiteman touch.

Now that *King of Jazz* has been lovingly restored, we can truly experience that "Whiteman touch" at the height of his powers. Equally exciting is this landmark book, giving us a detailed account of how it all came to happen, along with an amazing array of eye-popping illustrations.

Enjoy, and appreciate the achievement of one time that lives again, in another that sorely needs what it has to offer.

Michael Feinstein

PREFACE

The founder of Universal Pictures, Carl Laemmle, was a gifted promoter and consummate showman, perfect for the larger-than-life world of motion pictures. His grand vision was to create Universal Studios in Universal City, California—an entire city dedicated to motion pictures. He publicized the completion of Universal Studios with a New York to Los Angeles whistle-stop train tour culminating in the opening of the then 230-acre facility on March 15, 1915. Fifteen thousand people attended Opening Day. The studio grew into a fantastical land of medieval castles, Wild West towns, and exotic cities, complete with its own zoo and encampments of movie extras. As the head of the studio, Carl Laemmle Jr. built on his father's vision by producing prestige films such as *Broadway* (1929), *All Quiet on the Western Front* (1930), and, of course, *King of Jazz* (1930). It is this magnificent vision that is embodied in the breathtaking set pieces and musical numbers in *King of Jazz*.

Recognizing the need to protect the legacy of Universal's filmmakers, active film preservation work at the studio began in the 1950s. We are grateful for these early pioneers who instituted the climate-controlled vaulting processes that are the foundation of our work today. In the late 1970s, Universal began a policy of geographically separating duplicate sets of elements on both East and West Coasts. Since then, we have established an on-going maintenance and protection program that ensures the long-term viability of the Universal library. In 2012, Universal announced an expanded commitment to film restoration as part of the company's Centennial celebration. To date, more than 50 titles have been restored, including *All Quiet on the Western Front*, *The Birds* (1963), *Buck Privates* (1941), *Dracula* (1931), the Spanish-language version of *Dracula* (1931), *Frankenstein* (1931), *Jaws* (1975), *Schindler's List* (1993), *Out of Africa* (1985), *Pillow Talk* (1959), *Bride of Frankenstein* (1935), *The Sting* (1973), *To Kill a Mockingbird* (1962), *Touch of Evil* (1958), *Double Indemnity* (1944), *High Plains Drifter* (1973), *Holiday Inn* (1942), *Spartacus* (1960), *One-Eyed Jacks* (1961), and *King of Jazz*. In 2015, the Studio announced the silent film initiative to preserve and restore 15 of Universal's classic silent films. The first of these restored titles, *The Last Warning* (1929), premiered at the San Francisco Silent Film Festival on June 4, 2016.

Film, by its nature, is a collaborative art. Film preservation and restoration is no different. We want to express our deep appreciation to our collaborators on this project, especially the

Cohen Film Collection, the Packard Humanities Institute at the UCLA Film & Television Archive, and the Danish Film Institute. We would like to thank the authors of this book, who provided key historical information that was invaluable to the process, as well as our laboratories, YCM Laboratories, Cineric, and Prasad Corp. We also want to acknowledge the talented teams at NBCUniversal Content Management and NBCUniversal StudioPost, including vault managers, researchers, project managers, colorists, sound mixers, engineers, restoration artists, and archivists. Dozens of individuals with decades of experience do the painstaking, frame-by-frame work that makes restorations such as *King of Jazz* possible.

We are delighted that James Layton and David Pierce have written this book about *King of Jazz*. It thoroughly documents the studio's new restoration, and the breadth of research and fascinating illustrations offer incredible new insight into the film and the studio that made it. Carl Laemmle's goal was "to make people laugh or cry or sit on the edge of their chairs the world over!" By preserving, restoring, and sharing these classic films, we hope they continue to delight audiences for generations to come.

Michael Daruty
Senior Vice-President, Global Media Operations
NBCUniversal

Peter Schade
Vice-President, Content Management
NBCUniversal

ACKNOWLEDGMENTS

We wish to thank our families for their support and encouragement: Jade Pierce, Crystal Kui, Elizabeth Layton, and Peggie and Terence Kui.

The book would not have been possible without the groundwork laid by Diane and Richard Koszarski, and their continuing passion for the film and seeing this book realized. Our research and writing has benefitted immensely from the knowledge of many friends and associates, including: Eric Aijala, Rob Bamberger, Malcolm Billingsley, Robert S. Birchard, Kevin Brownlow, Joe Busam, Michael Feinstein, Will Friedwald, Ron Hutchinson, Miles Kreuger, Scott MacQueen, Tom Maroudas, Steve Massa, John McElwee, Robert McKay, Peter Mintun, Jon Mirsalis, Don Rayno, David Stenn, Catherine Surowiec (also our tireless and enthusiastic copyeditor), Karl Thiede, Marc Wanamaker, Edward Watz, and George Willeman. We are especially grateful to Peter Schade, Emily Wensel, Janice Simpson, Seanine Bird, Cassandra Wiltshire, Aaron Rogers, Mike Feinberg, and Michael Daruty at NBCUniversal for inviting us to participate in the restoration of *King of Jazz* and assisting us in the production of this book. The Paul Whiteman and Herman Rosse collections at the Williams College Archives and Special Collections and the George Gershwin and Ferde Grofé collections at the Library of Congress were the source for many previously unpublished illustrations and documents. We thank the curators at these institutions for allowing us to use these to provide insight into the creative process of these artistic collaborators.

Many individuals and institutions contributed research, illustrations, and much more to the book, and we are very grateful for their contributions of time and effort: Academy Film Archive, Los Angeles (Tessa Idlewine), Clara Auclair, Robert S. Bader, Anna Batistová, Matías A. Bombal, Geoff Brown, Don Casper, Ralph Celentano, Gary Chapman, Vanessa Cherry, K. Y. Cheung, Cinémathèque suisse, Lausanne (Thomas Bissegger), Ned Comstock, Danish Film Institute, Copenhagen (Thomas Christensen), Nancy Dantzig, Deutsche Kinemathek, Berlin (Andrea Ziegenbruch), Gloria Diez, Graham and Patricia Donohoe, Almudena Escobar López, Filmmuseum Austria, Vienna (Alejandro Bachmann and Oliver Hanley), Florida State University, Tallahassee (Avis Berry and Laura Gayle Green), Mark Forer, Rob H Freriks, Adam Gershwin, Vince Giordano, Gosfilmofond of Russia, Moscow (Peter Bagrov, Yulia Belova, and Oleg Botchkov), Ferde Grofé Jr., James Harrison, Daisuke Kawahara, Robert

J. Kiss, Pancho Kohner, Teodor Leff, Library of Congress, Washington, DC / Culpeper, VA (Mike Mashon, Zoran Sinobad, Josie Walters-Johnston, George Willeman), Neil Lipes, Cindy Magill, Jeffery Masino, Margaret Herrick Library, Los Angeles (Jenny Romero and Faye Thompson), Tom Maroudas, Stephen Morgan, The Museum of Modern Art, New York (Dave Kehr, Ron Magliozzi, Peter Oleksik, and Ashley Swinnerton), Museo Nazionale del Cinema, Turin (Roberta Basano and Fabio Pezzetti), Národní filmový archiv, Prague (Veroslav Haba, Tomáš Lachman, Ivan Svoboda, and Tomáš Žůrek), National Film Center, Tokyo (Hitomi Matsuyama), Sabrina Negri, Christoph Nestel, John Newton, Jonas Nordin, Shota Ogawa, Jelena Rakin, Brian Real, David Robinson, William H. Rosar, Ulrich Ruedel, Alicia Seymour, Shari Skye, Natalie Snoyman, Carlos Roberto de Souza, Petr Szczepanik, Swedish Film Institute, Stockholm (Ola Torjas), Lupita Tovar Kohner, Brandon Tung, Frank van Nus, Williams College, Williamstown, MA (Wayne G. Hammond and Katie Nash), Milan Wolf, Joseph Yranksi, Balint Zagoni.

This book has been a costly undertaking, and would not have been possible without the generous financial contributions of the following: Rob and Chris Bamberger, Joe Busam, Fons Castermans, Vince Giordano, Tracey Goessel, Dudley Heer, Guenter Knorr, Peggie and Terence Kui, Rachel Kui, John McElwee, Trevor Nicholls, Mark Rosse, and 272 additional backers on Kickstarter.

INTRODUCTION

Eighty-six years after *King of Jazz* premiered in 1930, enthusiastic crowds gathered for a series of sold-out screenings at The Museum of Modern Art in New York City. Newly restored by NBCUniversal, Paul Whiteman's spectacular Technicolor revue was reborn for new audiences, after years of being available in only substandard copies. As the first digital restoration from a two-color Technicolor negative, the remarkable clarity and color reproduction came as a revelation—like seeing the film for the first time. Many in the audience spotted details they had never been able to see before—the Paul Whiteman "potato-head" caricature on the Rhythm Boys' twin pianos or the cable raising the lid of the giant piano during *Rhapsody in Blue*. The excited audiences cheered and clapped throughout the screenings, and were carried away by the film's careful balance of music, comedy, and impressive song and dance talent.

This book tells the full story of this 1930 motion picture, from its pre-history and genesis, through its lengthy, troubled production and disappointing reception, and up to the film's rediscovery in the 1970s and the recent restoration. *King of Jazz* brought together leading figures in film, theater, and music, and this book is equally ambitious, mixing parallel stories related to these different mediums, along with recent archival history. The narrative follows the careers of bandleader Paul Whiteman, Universal Pictures founder Carl Laemmle and his son, and theater director John Murray Anderson, until they convened at Universal City in November 1929 to make this film. Additionally, the book gives further background on the tradition of Broadway revues, early Hollywood musicals, film exhibition practices in 1930, and how some of the first sound films were distributed around the world in multiple language versions.

Cinema was going through a period of experimentation in 1930, with filmmakers incorporating new technologies and new techniques of storytelling in the face of rapidly changing audience tastes. *King of Jazz* is remembered as the last of a short-lived film genre—the revue—and one of the last of another, the two-color Technicolor musical. But this film is much more than that; it was an attempt to meld a theatrical form into a motion picture, and *King of Jazz* is completely successful on those terms. The film also represents a musical crossroads. The definition of the term "jazz" was still evolving in 1930, and the film is conflicted in its acknowledgment of jazz's African and European roots.

Few know the full background to the making of *King of Jazz*, and even fewer are aware of the diverse influences that informed the film. Historians have discussed the film in reference to Paul Whiteman's career, and as part of the early musicals boom, or as a footnote in the history of Universal Pictures, but none have ever tackled *King of Jazz* as the main focus of study. Learning more about the film only enhances the viewing experience. Once familiar with the backstory and the antecedents of what went into the film, the end result on the screen becomes much richer.

Our research for this book was broad and interdisciplinary. The manuscript benefitted from firsthand access to the personal collections of Paul Whiteman and the artist Herman Rosse, who designed the Academy Award-winning costumes and sets for *King of Jazz*. Both of these collections are housed at Williams College in Williamstown, Massachusetts, and we are grateful to the staff there for their cooperation and collaboration. We are also fortunate to be able to work closely with Richard and Diane Koszarski, and their support and friendship have been among the greatest rewards of this project. Together they undertook comprehensive research into Universal's studio files in the 1970s and interviewed several participants in the production of *King of Jazz*. They generously shared their notes, photocopies, and memories with us. We are also very indebted to Richard for agreeing to come on board to guide the project as editor.

Just as this eye-opening restoration will allow audiences to reinterpret and engage with the film in new ways, so will this book. As historians and archivists, we are not only interested in the story of the film's production, but also what happened to the film in the intervening years. We hope that this book may present a model for future scholars to investigate the production history and public response to other important, but less well-known, films. We have gone to great lengths to research every aspect of the film and to put it into context. This is matched with an incredible selection of never-before-published illustrations, and a detailed appendix that should become an indispensable reference guide to the film. This book is the first publication from Media History Press, an imprint of the non-profit Media History Digital Library. Profits from the sale of this book will support the mission of the Media History Digital Library to digitize public domain media periodicals and provide free online access to the histories of cinema, broadcasting, and recorded sound.

James Layton and David Pierce

Chapter 1

PAUL WHITEMAN
AND SYMPHONIC JAZZ

Paul Whiteman, the man who became known as the "King of Jazz," was born in Denver, Colorado, in 1890, and grew up during the ragtime era. Ragtime predated jazz and incorporated the formalism of European music, with a rhythmic syncopation from African American traditions. Neither ragtime nor jazz were welcome in the Whiteman household. Paul's father, Wilberforce Whiteman, was superintendent of music education for the Denver schools, musical director at the local Methodist church, organized amateur orchestras, and gave private music lessons, as did Paul's mother Elfrida, a skilled singer.

Paul showed musical interest and aptitude from an early age, but his father was a strict disciplinarian. Compelling his son to sign a contract requiring regular practice sessions in return for a violin removed the boy's joy of music at the same time that it provided the means. When Paul contracted typhoid fever at the age of 12, the resulting hair loss and increased appetite for food plagued him the rest of his life. Despite this and other challenges, Paul qualified as a viola player with the Denver musicians' union at age 16, and after jobs in local hotel and theatre orchestras joined the Denver Symphony after graduating from high school. In 1914 he headed to San Francisco, violin and viola in hand, in a successful attempt to join one of the orchestras at the Panama-Pacific International Exposition. That led to three years playing viola for the San Francisco Symphony. In the popular music field in 1917, the raucous ragtime was being supplanted by a new syncopation and older dances by the fox trot.

"Jazz was beginning to be popular," Whiteman recalled, "and I made the surprising discovery that, while I was able to earn only $40 a week in the symphony, I could get $90 playing what was then called 'jazz' fiddle" in hotel orchestras and other ensembles.[1]

After a stint as a bandmaster during World War I, Whiteman established a dance orchestra, serving as manager, arranger, and leader, first at a San Francisco hotel, then in Santa Barbara and Pasadena, finally settling into the Alexandria Hotel in Los Angeles for $650 per week. The nine-member "Paul Whiteman's Jazz Classique" consisted of piano, trumpet, trombone, tuba, two on saxophone, drums, and banjo, plus Whiteman conducting and on violin. Soon after the band's Alexandria opening, Whiteman brought in Ferde Grofé on piano. Grofé had played with the Los Angeles Symphony, and in addition to his fluency with piano, viola, and composition, Whiteman admired Grofé's ability as an arranger for what he called "jazzing the classics"—adapting classical works into dance numbers. Among Grofé's many arrangements of this type, he took a theme from Rimsky-Korsakov's 1898 opera *Sadko* and created "Song of India," a hit for the orchestra.[2] As manager, Whiteman held frequent rehearsals, and worked with Grofé to find new songs to expand their repertoire. The engagement attracted the Hollywood crowd, and Whiteman's band was invited to private parties, first as musicians and then as guests. It was at this engagement that Whiteman first acquired the informal title "King of Jazz."

The owner of the Alexandria Hotel, S. W. Straus,

Whiteman's orchestra at the opening of the Alexandria Hotel, Los Angeles, December 1919. Left to right: Henry Busse (trumpet), Harold McDonald (drums), T. E. "Buster" Johnson (trombone), J. K. "Spike" Wallace (string bass), Paul Whiteman (violin), Charles Caldwell (piano), Leslie Canfield (saxophone), Charles Dornberger (saxophone), and Mike Pingitore (banjo).

offered Whiteman $1,200 per week to open his new Ambassador Hotel in Atlantic City, New Jersey. Audiences built slowly in the East Coast resort hotel after they opened there on June 1, 1920, but the orchestra quickly reached the same level of success they had enjoyed in Los Angeles.

Recording with Victor

The Whiteman orchestra began to make recordings during the Ambassador Hotel engagement. Representatives of the Victor Talking Machine Company, which was based in Camden, New Jersey, were in Atlantic City at the end of June for a convention of the distributors for Victor's phonographs and discs. Most of the meetings were held in a nearby hotel, but as Whiteman recalled, "a representative of theirs, Calvin Childs, happened to lunch at the Ambassador and heard us play."[3] That represent-

ative was the manager of Victor's artists and repertoire department, and he liked what he heard. Victor already offered recordings from 21 other orchestras in its catalog, but Childs recognized that Whiteman's sound was different. A few days later, Whiteman signed a two-year contract; for each song recorded, Paul would receive $50 and the musicians $25 each, with no further royalties.

The recording process at that time was an art form in itself. Acoustic recording, the standard until electrical microphones were introduced in 1925, required performers to direct their performance to the open end of a large horn, which concentrated the sound waves to a diaphragm, transferring them to a vibrating needle which etched grooves into a wax disc. Satisfactory recording using this entirely mechanical process was achieved by the selection of horns of different design and thickness, the type of diaphragm, and the arrangement of performers in front of the horn. It took Whiteman and the Victor engineers several sessions to work this out

Sheet music for Ferde Grofé's arrangement of Rimsky-Korsakov's "A Song of India." Whiteman recorded the song in 1921, and it was a hit again in 1937 for bandleader Tommy Dorsey.

satisfactorily, with three recording sessions in two weeks during August 1920, at the company's studios in nearby Camden, New Jersey.

Certain instruments such as the soprano saxophone did not record effectively, and substitutes (such as tuba for the double bass) were used. To replace the regular drum, Whiteman experimented with using the banjo to keep time, moving it to the forefront of the orchestration. "As a rule we made two records at a time," Whiteman recalled, "though once I believe we made nine in three days. Each [recording session] averages about an hour and a half or two hours, for there must first be a rehearsal and a test before the perfect record is passed upon by the company 'hearing committee.'"[4] Starting with their first release in November 1920, Victor aimed for one Whiteman release per month.

To the Palais Royal

The New York nightlife scene was already familiar with a less stylized, more raucous jazz. Jazz music was introduced to New York in January 1917, when the Original Dixieland Jazz Band, a five-member, all-white ensemble (cornet, trombone, clarinet, piano, and drums) from New Orleans (by way of Chicago) opened at Reisenweber's Cafe on Columbus Circle. While John Murray Anderson choreographed entertainment for afternoon tea dances for the Paradise supper club on the third floor, the jazz band was booked for the second-floor cabaret. Its success started a craze for jazz music, and the group's first record for Victor, "Livery Stable Blues," a novelty number with the instruments mimicking barnyard animals, became a surprise hit after its release that March. Jazz was then smoothed and popularized by the California bandleader Art Hickman, who included two saxophones in his nine-piece band, which spent much of 1919 in New York, returning the following year to perform in the *Ziegfeld Follies of 1920*.

As the Atlantic City summer season was concluding, Whiteman considered many offers to move his orchestra to one of Manhattan's cafes or hotels. The owners of the Palais Royal restaurant at 48th and Broadway in New York City tried to hire Art Hickman, but he preferred to return to San Francisco. Whiteman chose the Palais Royal over other offers because the orchestra, billed as "Paul Whiteman and His Band Classique," would be the main attraction for dining and dancing. A limited booking at $1,600 per week, beginning in September 1920, became a four-year engagement, with the ensemble renamed "Paul Whiteman's Palais Royal Orchestra." The reputation of the orchestra grew rapidly, and the following autumn the orchestra was added to the bill at the Palace Theatre, the flagship vaudeville house of the Orpheum Circuit, despite concerns about booking a dance orchestra in a location with no dance floor. "After listening to the Paul Whiteman Orchestra [at the Palace], you will understand why the Palais Royal restaurant is doing a $3,000 nightly gross business," noted *Variety*. "There is something about the Whiteman band that makes young people dance—and not altogether only the young."[5] The initial week was extended by another four, and when Whiteman returned to the Palace the following April, his fee went from $900 per week to $2,750.

The reputation of Whiteman and his orchestra was growing. In 1921, Whiteman acceded to the entreaties of his business manager and his agent to create satellite bands—smaller groups using Whiteman's name and Grofé's arrangements to perform out-of-town engagements and at private events. By the next year there were 19 Whiteman orchestras at clubs, cabarets, and on transatlantic steamers. In the summer of 1922 Whiteman got royal fever when the vacationing Lord Louis Mountbatten (cousin of the Prince of Wales) and his wife Lady

The Palais Royal restaurant, on Broadway at West 48th Street, New York City, ca. 1920.

Edwina were regulars at the Palais Royal.

The 1922 edition of *George White's Scandals* featured Whiteman's orchestra (also performing later in the evening a few blocks away at the Palais Royal). George Gershwin provided the score for five consecutive editions of the *Scandals*, starting in 1920, and the rehearsals began the professional association of the composer and the conductor. The first-act finale was a performance of "I'll Build a Stairway to Paradise," sung by Winnie Lightner, with Whiteman's orchestra on stage, along with fifty chorus girls clad in black patent leather dancing on two circular white staircases. It was a true showstopper. Critic Alexander Woollcott noted this gave the "stage over for a little while to such a festival of jazz as sets the audience to swaying like a wheat field touched by the wind."[6] The number's impact remained vivid to Gershwin, recalling it years later: "I'll never forget the first time I heard Whiteman do it. That was one of those thrills that come once in a lifetime. Paul made my song live with a vigor

that almost floored me."[7]

Working for Whiteman—or any top-flight orchestra of the day—was no picnic. A typical day in 1922 consisted of rehearsal or recording dates at noon and again at 3 p.m., performances at the Palace Theatre at 2 and 8:30 p.m., and then to the Palais Royal restaurant to play until 3 a.m.[8] And the players were expected to use every free moment for individual practice. Later in the decade touring included endless travel by train, with daily performances. Whiteman was there every minute, and was responsible for the business and music.

By 1923, there was no doubt that the recording industry's top act was Paul Whiteman and His Orchestra. Their first hits were songs that Whiteman popularized and refined in live performance.

"Whispering," coupled with "The Japanese Sandman," released in November 1920, set Victor's record, with 1,185,000 discs sold. It was common for competing companies to release their own recordings of a popular song, but Whiteman's polished performances outshone—and outsold—all competitors.[9] And soon enough, Whiteman became the brand. One New York department store had over 1,000 standing orders from customers for home delivery of each new Whiteman record.[10]

And yet this success in live performance, vaudeville, and recordings wasn't enough to satisfy Whiteman. This was partly from ambition, but it also reflected his childhood rebellion against his father, who never accepted his son's work as serious music. Even as the toast of New York, "we had a hankering to be taken seriously. We even believed that there was something worthwhile about jazz, danceable as it was," Whiteman recalled. "But no one took us seriously. At that stage, it wouldn't have done to say anything about jazz being an art."[11]

Whiteman accepted an engagement in a British stage revue, *Brighter London*, starting in March 1923, for $7,500 per week. The show featured comedian Lupino Lane, but the reviews and audiences went for the music. "Paul Whiteman and his band have turned London upside down," wrote *Variety*'s London correspondent. "He is the biggest hit ever registered by an American importation."[12] After approval from the British musicians union, the orchestra was able to add late-night performances at a London nightclub for £400 weekly, plus the same or more from a percentage of the cover charge. Lord Mountbatten held a party to present Whiteman and his music to the Prince of Wales, who soon became a regular at the nightclub and invited the orchestra to perform at his private parties.

Named as "King of Jazz"

Paul Whiteman's coronation as the "King of Jazz" was more press event than public acclamation. Whiteman was first called "King of Jazz" in a newspaper article in 1919. Bandleader Ted Lewis used the term more than Whiteman in the early 1920s, and there were innumerable "Jazz Kings." But Whiteman "was intelligent enough to recognize a good publicity idea when he heard it and adventurous enough to go along with it," recalled Mary Margaret McBride, the co-author of his 1926 autobiography, *Jazz*.[13]

For Whiteman's return from England on the ocean liner *Leviathan*, a committee of his business associates planned a celebration. On August 13, 1923, the ship was met at the quarantine station by a yacht displaying a banner emblazoned "Paul Whiteman Welcome Home Committee." While the ship took on the harbor pilot, an eight-man band in life preservers played from the water.

Paul Whiteman endorsed instruments from the Buescher Band Instrument Co. The company sold a full line of musical instruments, including tens of thousands of saxophones in nine distinct models. 1924 magazine advertisement.

As the ship headed into port, it was serenaded by a band on the guest boat, while another played from an army bombing plane overhead. On arrival at the West 46th Street pier, a fourth band emerged to welcome Whiteman and his orchestra to America.

Once ashore, Whiteman was crowned "King of Jazz" by the head of the Buescher Band Instrument Co. (endorsed by Whiteman) using a crown with miniature replicas of band instruments, including their heavily promoted saxophone. The following evening Whiteman and the band were guests of honor at a banquet and reception held at the Waldorf-Astoria Hotel, feted by guests including Broadway's Irving Berlin, Victor Herbert, George S. Kaufman, George M. Cohan, and Marc Connelly. Both the welcome on the pier and the banquet were broadcast by RCA's station WJZ, with extensive nationwide press coverage.[14]

Its prestige increased by five months away, the Whiteman band returned to the Palais Royal, and to Broadway for the *Ziegfeld Follies of 1923* in October. By the end of the year, the orchestra had completed more than 70 recording sessions for Victor.

While Whiteman had been conquering England, his friend George Gershwin was adding critical respect-

Musicians welcome Whiteman on his return from Europe, while waiting for his ship to dock, August 13, 1923.

ability to his commercial success. Gershwin's first step toward the respectability of the concert hall came the year after *Scandals of 1922*. Between tours of North America and Europe, Canadian mezzo-soprano Éva Gauthier presented an annual recital in New York with new material.[15] During 1923, her friend, French composer Maurice Ravel, recommended that she include American jazz compositions. She asked the multi-talented Carl Van Vechten, whose many careers included music criticism, to recommend a musician to act as her guide, and he directed her to George Gershwin, "whose compositions I admired and with whose skill as a pianist I was acquainted."[16] "Recital of Ancient and Modern Music for Voice," presented the evening of November 1, 1923 at Aeolian Hall, began with the pantheon of serious music, followed by works from 20th-century composers including Béla Bartók, Paul Hindemith, Arnold Schoenberg, and Arthur Bliss. The modern section began with arrangements of songs by Jerome Kern and Irving Berlin, concluding with three by George Gershwin—"I'll Build a Stairway to Paradise," "Innocent Ingenue Baby," and

"Swanee"—with Gershwin at the piano, his first onstage appearance as part of a serious concert program.[17]

In the audience was Paul Whiteman, impressed at how Gershwin's "Stairway to Paradise" had moved from Broadway to the concert stage.

Jazz, or at least the term "jazz," had become a straightjacket for Whiteman, and he was moving away from it as rapidly as possible. There was much talk about the "Jazz Age" and its effects upon morals, and Whiteman reflected "it is a little disconcerting to wake up one fine morning and find headlines acclaiming [me] 'King of Jazz'." If anyone was corrupting America's youth, it wasn't him—"the truth is that I have never played jazz, and neither, to my knowledge, has any member of my band." Instead, he told *Variety*, "what we have played is 'syncopated rhythm,' quite another thing. And our orchestrations have always been worked out with all the color and beauty of symphonies."[18]

Yet for critic Gilbert Seldes, the band was almost too perfect. "It is a real perfection of the instrument, a mechanically perfect organization which pays for its

Composer George Gershwin was a key participant in Whiteman's plan to elevate jazz to the concert hall. Gershwin's *Rhapsody in Blue* subsequently became the signature tune of Whiteman's orchestra.

perfection by losing much of the element of surprise; little is left to hazard and there are no accidents. Whiteman has been clever enough to preserve the sense of impromptu and his principal band—that of the Palais Royal in New York—is so much under control (his and its own) that it can make the slightest variation count for more than all the running away from the beat which is common *chez* [bandleader Ted] Lewis."[19]

The Éva Gauthier recital crystallized Whiteman's decision to distinguish his music from jazz and raise the reputation of the musical qualities of his orchestra and its dance music. Whiteman booked the same venue, the 1,100-seat Aeolian Hall, for a date three months later. By late December, a *Billboard* columnist wrote: "Paul is serious in this project and is going to give a mixed program of jazz and classic in his well-known style and sincerely hopes to convince the critics that there is something of value in popular music if it is done right."[20] Whiteman commissioned new pieces from Victor Herbert and George Gershwin. The twelve-person ensemble used at the Palais Royal expanded to 23 players to provide a fuller sound in the large hall, with extra violinists and French horns and a string bass/tuba player. Gershwin's contribution was written rapidly; once he had the composition worked out, he prepared it as a reduced score for two pianos (with annotations for specific instrumentation), with Ferde Grofé stopping by his apartment house daily throughout January to pick up additional pages. Grofé completed his orchestration to fit the expanded orchestra and piano barely a week before the performance.

In preparation for the event Whiteman carefully cultivated the critics and selected his audience. As he recalled, "while we were getting ready for the concert, we gave a series of luncheons for the critics, took them to rehearsals and explained painstakingly what we hoped to prove, at the same time displaying our orchestral tools for the enterprise."[21] The audience that came to hear "An Experiment in Modern Music" at Aeolian Hall on the afternoon of February 12, 1924 included Leopold Godowsky, Jascha Heifetz, Fritz Kreisler, Sergei Rachmaninoff, and Leopold Stokowski from the concert world, and luminaries of equal stature from opera, the legitimate theatre, the art world, and the critical community.

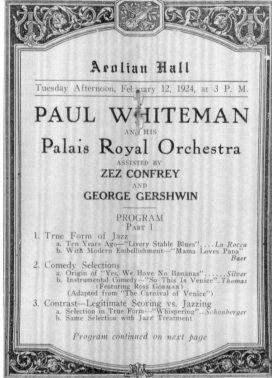

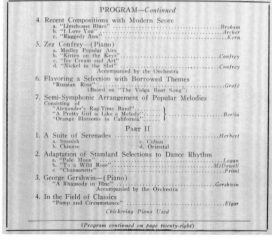

Paul Whiteman presented his first concert program to demonstrate
how jazz had moved from its roots to what he called "symphonic jazz."
Program, Aeolian Hall, New York, February 12, 1924.

Whiteman hoped to use the concert to position himself and his orchestra as not only a highly successful dance band but the presenter of a new musical form, which, while different from the classical repertoire, was worthy of equal consideration. This was risky; as the *New York Times* reviewer noted, "when a program consists almost entirely of modern dance music, that is naturally a danger, since American dances of today do not boast a great variety of step or character."[22]

Before his appearance on stage, the concert opened with a raucous performance of "Livery Stable Blues," performed by five musicians, as *Billboard* noted, "to demonstrate the work of an orchestra of the original jazz type, namely, all the noise and vulgarity musically possible."[23] Other selections contrasted the original jazz style with "modern scoring"—"Whispering" was performed in both styles. Then the entire second half of the concert consisted of popular songs and new works presented in symphonic style. The highlight of the concert, positioned next to last on the program, was the first public performance of Gershwin's *Rhapsody in Blue*, with Whiteman conducting and the composer at the piano.

The audiences and most reviewers agreed that the concert was a triumph, though they differed on how. For the *New York Times* reviewer Olin Downes, it was Whiteman who caught his eye. "He does not conduct. He trembles, wobbles, quivers—a piece of jazz jelly, conducting the orchestra with the back of the trouser of the right leg and the face of a mandarin the while." Meanwhile, Downes thought the music compared favorably with "the pitiful sterility of the average production of the 'serious' American composer," while the New York *Evening World*'s critic Frank H. Warren hoped that Gershwin's *Rhapsody* might become the basis of the longed-for American school of music.[24]

The *New York Herald* reviewer W. J. Henderson enjoyed the concert, reserving his highest praise for *Rhapsody in Blue*: "Mr. Gershwin's composition proved to be a highly ingenious work, treating the piano in a manner calling for much technical skill and furnishing an orchestral background in which saxophones, trombones, and clarinets were merged in a really skillful piece of orchestration." Other reviewers felt the middle of the piece was weaker, but the *Evening Sun*'s critic Gilbert Gabriel thought "the beginning and the ending of it were stunning. The beginning particularly, with a flutter-tongued, drunken whoop of an introduction that had the audience rocking. Mr. Gershwin has an irrepressible pack of talents."[25]

Nearly every critic agreed that *Rhapsody in Blue* identified Gershwin as a composer of merit, with greater works in his future. It also raised Grofé's profile, giving him the confidence to compose his own concert works. And overnight Paul Whiteman and His Orchestra became a force in the concert field.

Whiteman spent over $11,000 staging and promoting the concert, and even though the hall was full, he admitted a loss of about $7,000, while his business manager estimated it at $12,000. The orchestra returned to its Palais Royal and *Ziegfeld Follies* engagements, while testing the waters for a concert tour. The entire concert was repeated four times in March and April, including at Carnegie Hall, to equal acclaim. A concert management company, the Metropolitan Music Bureau, booked the expanded orchestra on an 18-day tour, with Gershwin on piano for the first seven cities. Whiteman was to receive $2,000 per week plus 70% of the net after expenses. It was just as well that they were out of town on tour, as after their departure the Palais Royal was raided by federal agents and shut down for violating the Volstead Act.

The response to Whiteman's concert tour and the closure and then sale of the Palais Royal changed the nature of the orchestra. The loss of a home base for its performances turned the orchestra into a touring ensemble, and the success of the Aeolian presentation reshaped their public profile to a popular orchestra that presented concerts, not dances. Ferde Grofé became a full-time arranger, and Whiteman hired a business manager to coordinate the orchestra's complex booking and travel arrangements.

September 1924 saw the start of a 55-day tour, followed by concerts in New York and Boston. That summer Whiteman added vocalist Morton Downey, and spotlighted players within musical numbers. Trombonist Wilbur Hall had refined a comedy routine playing "Pop Goes the Weasel" with a fiddle and a bow that kept jumping out of his hands, capping it with a finale playing Sousa's march "The Stars and Stripes Forever" on a bicycle pump. He often stopped the show, as did Mike Pingitore's intricate and rapid banjo solos.

In January, they left for a four-month tour, reaching Los Angeles and San Francisco, and a concert in Denver, where Whiteman's father heard his son's orchestra in live performance for the first time. The orchestra returned to New York in May 1925 for a triumphant three-week engagement at the Hippodrome Theatre, returning to the theater again after Labor Day. The expanded membership used for the Aeolian Hall concerts and first tour remained in place, reaching 28 musicians. The orchestration was six violins, two violas, two cellos, one string bass, three trumpets, three trombones, four saxophones, two pianos, and one each of banjo, guitar, bass, and drums. Many of the players could play multiple instruments,

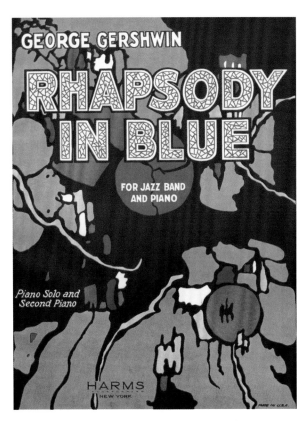

An arrangement of George Gershwin's *Rhapsody in Blue* for two pianos was published in 1925, and a solo piano edition and arrangement for theater organ in 1927. Ferde Grofé's orchestral arrangement was published in 1926.

which provided more flexibility in arrangements and the variety of the band's sound.

In September 1925, on break from their engagement at the New York Hippodrome, where he received $7,500 weekly, Whiteman received $8,500 for a one-week engagement. The previous summer, Whiteman had turned down an offer from vaudeville's competitor, motion pictures. The building boom of lavish new downtown theaters with thousands of seats led to ferocious competition, where the film sometimes mattered less than the live acts on the program. Famous Players-Lasky (producer of Paramount pictures) had bid for Whiteman's services for the next two years, at $10,000 per week. Whiteman turned it down; he was going to gross $19,000 per week from his upcoming cross-country tour. *Variety* calculated that there were only four vaudeville theaters remaining that could offer any act more than $5,500 weekly, while beyond Paramount (and its recently acquired Balaban & Katz chain) there were at least 75 to 100 motion picture theaters "east of Omaha" that had effectively no limit on what they could pay for an engagement of a week or longer.[26]

Paramount had also pursued other options—the front page of the same issue of *Variety* noted that Famous Players had hired musical comedy director John Murray Anderson to produce stage musicals for presentation in its Broadway motion picture theaters and then on tour.

The Whiteman orchestra's fall 1925 tour was a marathon, with 80 bookings in 12 weeks, concluding with 38 consecutive concerts, each day in a new city. Upon returning to New York City, the band was rewarded with three days off, and then recording dates, rehearsals, or concerts occupied every day (including a benefit concert on Christmas Day) until they departed on January 2, 1926 for a three-month cross-country concert tour, featuring Grofé's tone poem *Mississippi Suite*. By March 1926 they were back in New York, to leave on the orchestra's second European tour.

Whiteman and Jazz

The modern definition of jazz is very closely tied to music featuring improvisation, syncopation, and rhythm. Whiteman excelled in a bouncy, danceable beat, but the opportunities for improvisation were limited and controlled. Whiteman's goal was arranged jazz in a symphonic style. "Brought up as I was in the symphonic field, I could never understand why jazz had to be a haphazard thing," he wrote, recalling jazz bands in San Francisco that sometimes hit the mark and other times were just "jamming."[27]

Whiteman's popular success was attributable to careful choice of material with excellent, innovative arrangements, extensive rehearsal of his ensemble of top-flight players, the high quality of his musicianship, and the ability to reinvent the band when he saw that their previous direction was going stale. His arrangers would take a song and fit it to Whiteman's style and his band's instrumentation, which allowed for tonal variety and innovative rhythms, with very precise, repeatable performances. For many years Whiteman made a practice of hiring symphony-trained musicians—one jazz musician left the band because he was afraid he would lose his ability to improvise. Starting around 1926, with band members who were more experienced with improvisation, the arrangements allowed for more solos, using smaller ensembles for the more jazz-inspired numbers.

Whiteman's primary arranger until the late 1920s was Ferde Grofé, and it was Grofé who set the Whiteman sound. He served as orchestrator—assigning different parts of the song to the players—as well as the arranger—adding color and harmony. "Mr. Grofé considers the orchestra a sort of quartette, ranging from

During the tour that followed the premiere of "An Experiment in Modern Music," the orchestra stopped off at Niagara Falls on May 16, 1924 *en route* from Rochester to Buffalo, and posed for a photograph along with their instruments. Kneeling: Wilbur Hall, Lyle "Eddie" Sharpe, Oscar Adler, Aldo Ricci, Jack Eaton, Phil Boutelje, Henry Busse, Mario Perry. Standing: John Bouman, Edward Stannard, Kurt Dieterle, Frank Siegrist, Roy Maxon, Milton Rettenberg, Al Armer, Gus Helleberg, Max Barr, George Torde, Charles Strickfaden, Ross Gorman, unidentified, Paul Whiteman, Elfrida Whiteman, Al Corrado, George Marsh, George Gershwin, Arturo "Arthur" Cerino, Mike Pingitore.

soprano to bass," Whiteman noted. "In the separate instrumental groups, he also divides the parts from high to low. If you give the highest voice and the lowest to the saxophone and the middle voices to the brass, you will get a singularly rich effect."[28] For each new piece, Whiteman would discuss every aspect with Grofé, who would then spend several days preparing the arrangement. During rehearsals Whiteman would work out the details of additional musical effects to make the performance innovative and memorable.

For example, the melody might be played straight at first, followed by a key change between each chorus, with a change of instrumentation at the beginning and middle. The instrumentation might change from saxophones in the lead to oboe and clarinets, then brass and saxophones playing staccato, with violins in the background. Then muted brass, solo clarinet, trumpets, followed by violins and saxophones. The arrangements were "marvels of orchestrational ingenuity," composer and historian Gunther Schuller noted, making "full use of the coloristic variety of Whiteman's basic instrumentation of nineteen or twenty players, augmented by from four to seven strings."[29]

The "jazz" that Whiteman introduced during the first phase of his success was popular syncopated music in a symphonic style performed by a top-notch dance band. He then went fully into the symphonic style, with pieces more lively than most of the traditional symphonic repertoire. But when he shifted to a more recognizable jazz around 1925, like his contemporaries, Whiteman appropriated African American music style, traditions, and music, transposing them into a European musical framework. As Whiteman put it, "I never stopped wanting to go into concert halls and in some measure remove the stigma of barbaric strains and jungle cacophony from jazz."[30]

Paul Whiteman's second "Experiment in Modern Music" concert, at Carnegie Hall on December 29, 1925, featured George Gershwin's jazz opera *135th Street* (a slightly modified version of *Blue Monday*, which was written for the 1922 edition of *George White's Scandals*), Ferde Grofé's *Mississippi Suite*, and the premiere of Deems Taylor's *Circus Day*. Left to right, the major participants in the 1925 concert: Deems Taylor, Ferde Grofé, Paul Whiteman, vocalist Blossom Seeley, and George Gershwin.

Gilbert Seldes recognized that in this musical transformation jazz's rough edges were eliminated. "All the free, the instinctive, the wild in negro jazz which could be integrated into his music, he has kept; he has added to it, has worked his material, until it runs sweetly in his dynamo, without grinding or scraping. It becomes the machine which conceals machinery."[31]

Whiteman had an endless curiosity for music and musical styles, and frequented the Harlem clubs that featured African American performers for a mostly white clientele. Duke Ellington and his band performed at the Kentucky Club near the Palais Royal, and he noted that "Whiteman came often as a genuine enthusiast, said his words of encouragement, very discreetly slipped the piano player a fifty-dollar bill, and very loudly proclaimed our musical merit."[32]

Whiteman was friends with Fletcher Henderson, Duke Ellington, and Eubie Blake, yet found that their

sound could not be reduced to notes on a page. According to his biographer Thomas DeLong, Whiteman considered integrating his band to capture some of the energy and style, but would have had to give up touring, as there would have been too many impediments to a mixed ensemble for performances, travel, and hotels. Whiteman added African Americans to his payroll in other ways, performing songs by Andy Razaf and Thomas "Fats" Waller and recruiting William Grant Still as an arranger. Fletcher Henderson and His Orchestra recorded "Whiteman Stomp," a raucous Fats Waller/Jo Trent number arranged by Don Redman. "The piece comes across as a tour de force of nervous energy, rich in timbral and textural variety," noted Joshua Berrett. Recorded by the Whiteman band three months later at a slightly faster pace, the recording lost some of the spirit of the original. "The piece was both a bona fide symphonic jazz composition and a parody of the whole style," Jeffrey Magee

While in Berlin for the band's second European tour, Paul Whiteman and his orchestra participated in a promotion by the newspaper *Berliner Zeitung* and airline Deutsche Luft Hansa for rides in a triple-engine Junkers G 24 aircraft over the city. June 1926.

noted. "It also suggests a role reversal. Now, the orchestra whose success had provided a model for Henderson's band just four years earlier was following the lead of its protégé—as if Paul Whiteman had become the Fletcher Henderson of his race."[33]

The Second European Tour

The Whiteman Orchestra returned to New York in March 1926 for a flurry of recording, and then Whiteman and his 28 musicians and five vocalists were off to Europe in April. The British tour kicked off with a concert at the Royal Albert Hall, featuring the staple of Whiteman's programs, *Rhapsody in Blue*. But it was impossible to recapture the magic of his first visit. "The craze for jazz is dying in England," wrote *Variety*'s London correspondent. "Not even Paul's unusual gifts, personal popularity, charm of manner and bigboyishness have repeated the sensation of his last trip."[34] They left the country in June, four weeks early, for some quickly arranged book-

ings on the Continent, before returning to New York in late July.

Touring for Publix

Whiteman returned in the summer of 1926 to find that the market for live music had shifted again, as the demand for traditional dance orchestras declined, and once-popular bandleaders Ray Miller, Isham Jones, and Abe Lyman flopped in New York and elsewhere. "There are not five highlight engagements for a dance band left in the United States," *Variety* noted. "The hotels or vaudeville will not pay money, and it leaves picture houses and cabarets as the sole alternatives."[35] With his huge overhead, Whiteman sensed this shift right away. Earlier in the year, just before leaving on the European tour, Whiteman signed with the William Morris Agency to manage his road tours, starting that fall.[36] Morris already managed the Vincent Lopez and Ben Bernie bands. Whiteman took this opportunity to review his band's musical approach. They had already successfully pivoted from their initial dance-band phase with symphonic jazz to the concert pieces. For the next phase, he would jazz up the band.

Whiteman signed with Publix Theaters Corporation to perform in its theaters for $9,500 per week, starting in the autumn of 1926 for 18 weeks, with four performances daily and five on Saturday, Sundays, and holidays.[37] The tour started in September, with four weeks in Los Angeles, two weeks in San Francisco, three in Chicago, and a range of single-week engagements as far south as Atlanta.

Changing their musical program weekly, the Whiteman Orchestra gave 111 performances without a day off during their four-week run at the Million Dollar Theater in Los Angeles. Whiteman's manager Jimmy Gillespie checked out the other theaters in town, and at the Metropolitan Theater, another Publix house, a stage act billed as "Two Boys and a Piano: Singing Songs Their Own Way" caught his eye. A *Variety* stringer caught the same show a few weeks later, noting the boys "registered solidly and on the crowded Sunday shows [they]

practically stopped the show." Performing "blues of the feverish variety," he concluded, "Where ever the public goes for 'hot' numbers served hot, Crosby and Rinker ought to have an easy time."[38] The "two boys" were Bing Crosby, age 23, and Al Rinker, 18. They had been friends in Spokane, Washington, and were working in theaters on the West Coast. Following Gillespie's report, Whiteman sent some band members to catch the act, which led to an audition in Whiteman's dressing room. Although the band already had three vocalists, he offered the pair contracts on the spot, starting in December when they finished their current commitment with Publix.

In November Whiteman caught a performance of the highly regarded Jean Goldkette dance band at Detroit's Graystone Ballroom. During a New York engagement the previous month, Goldkette's Victor Recording Orchestra and the Fletcher Henderson Orchestra had both been booked into the Roseland Ballroom, and the all-white band had beaten Henderson in a heavily promoted "battle of the bands." Goldkette managed numerous bands; this one was led by saxophonist Frankie Trumbauer, featuring Leon "Bix" Beiderbecke on cornet

Above: Singers Al Rinker (left) and Bing Crosby (center) first performed with Whiteman's Orchestra in December 1926; but it was not until Harry Barris (right, seated) joined in March 1927 that the act found success as Paul Whiteman's Rhythm Boys. That June, the trio recorded the hit songs "Mississippi Mud" and "I Left My Sugar Standing in the Rain." In August 1928, Whiteman booked the act separately on the vaudeville circuit for six months. They rejoined Whiteman full-time from February 1929, and continued performing with the orchestra until the end of April 1930.

Left: Publicity photo from Whiteman's Paramount-Publix tour, probably for the stage show "U.S.S. Syncopation," ca. June 1927. Left to right: Max Farley (with clarinet), Paul Whiteman, Henry Busse, Teddy Bartell (with trumpet in arms), Jack Fulton, Jack Spertzel, Red Nicholls (with cornet).

and Bill Rank on trombone, playing arrangements by Bill Challis. Whiteman talked to the band members, dazzled by their hot sound, which he was determined to incorporate into his style. The following summer, the Goldkette group collapsed, and during the fall of 1927 Whiteman hired Challis and many of the group's best players, including Trumbauer and Beiderbecke.

When Whiteman returned to New York in early 1927, it was to play the recently opened Paramount Theatre. Supporting a weak feature, the demand for Whiteman was so strong that "by Monday the saying around was you couldn't get in the Paramount," *Variety* noted.[39] Whiteman exceeded the results from the previous week's *It* (1927) starring Clara Bow, supported by a John Murray Anderson unit show, "Venetian Glass." After the end of the engagement, the orchestra opened the Paul Whiteman Club, a nightclub at 48th Street and Broadway, across the street from where the Palais Royal had been located. In March they joined a Broadway show—*Lucky*, by Jerome Kern and Otto Harbach—which lasted only two months, at $8,200 weekly. Three days after the show closed, so did the nightclub. Paramount signed the orchestra for 44 weeks for the 1927–28 season, at $12,000 per week.[40]

In 1928, the band was at its peak musically. Whiteman's "Third Modern American Music Concert" took place on October 7, 1928, at Carnegie Hall. In contrast to the backward-looking "Livery Stable Blues" in the first concert, this one opened with a five-man jazz combo, comprising Bix Beiderbecke (trumpet), Bill Rank (trombone), Izzy Friedman (saxophone), and George Marsh (drums), with Lennie Hayton (piano), playing songs from the early 1920s associated with Whiteman. Then the full Whiteman orchestra came on stage, culminating with Whiteman's first performance (with a new Grofé arrangement) of George Gershwin's 1925 composition *Concerto in F*.

Whiteman had a good ear for talent, and a surviving payroll ledger from a week in January 1928 supports his claim that he was the best-paying bandleader in the business. Of the 33 performers, seven who had been with him for years were in the $300 to $350 category, while the remainder (including the Rhythm Boys, Jimmy Dorsey, Charles Strickfaden, Bix Beiderbecke, and Frankie Trumbauer) received from $150 to $200 apiece. Ferde Grofé topped the entire list at $375, with fellow arranger Bill Challis at $175, business manager Jimmy Gillespie at $350, and Whiteman's valet, William Black, at $50.[41] And these salaries do not reflect their additional income for recordings. "This is good pay," Whiteman agreed, "but then a well-trained, well-advertised jazz orchestra demands good money [for concerts] and gets it."[42]

Some of the musicians had come from symphony orchestras, while many had been recruited from other popular bands—all of which looked up to the Whiteman Orchestra as the most prestigious outfit in the business. Tours included vocalist Austin Young, along with several players who doubled on vocals, and the Rhythm Boys. Staff arrangers were Ferde Grofé, Bill Challis, and Lennie Hayton. Whiteman's business manager, Jimmy Gillespie, cited that in 1928 the orchestra grossed $380,000 for 37 working weeks.[43]

New Frontiers in Recordings, Radio, and Film

In May 1928, Whiteman left Victor for a two-year contract with the Columbia Phonograph Company, for a $50,000 annual guarantee. With the contract effective in mid-May, Columbia had planned publicity around Whiteman's first recording for the company on that day, with a Movietone News crew capturing the event. With Whiteman and the orchestra playing at Loew's Metropolitan in Brooklyn, the event was captured just after midnight on May 15th.[44]

Victor had discouraged the orchestra from radio work, and Whiteman's constant touring made a regular program nearly impossible. In September 1928, NBC premiered the Lucky Strike Dance Orchestra, hosted

---

Supplemented by twelve additional players, Whiteman's core ensemble on stage in 1928 was:

Violin:	Kurt Dieterle, Charles Gaylord, Matty Malneck, Mischa Russell
Trombone:	Boyce Cullen, Wilbur Hall, Bill Rank, Jack Fulton
Trumpet:	Charlie Margulis, Bix Beiderbecke, Eddie Pinder, Harry Goldfield
Saxophone:	Chester Hazlett, Frankie Trumbauer, Charles Strickfaden, Red Maier, Rube Crozier, Izzy Friedman
Banjo:	Mike Pingitore
Guitar:	Austin Young
Bass:	Mike Trafficante, Min Leibrook
Drums:	George Marsh
Piano:	Roy Bargy, Lennie Hayton

Right: Front-page advertisement in the entertainment industry trade paper *Variety*, January 4, 1928, promoting Whiteman's orchestra, including musicians, vocalists and arrangers.

22ND ANNIVERSARY NUMBER

VARIETY

PRICE
25
CENTS

Published Weekly at 154 West 46th St., New York, N. Y., by Variety, Inc. Annual subscription, $10. Single copies, 25 cents.
Entered as second class matter December 22, 1905, at the Post Office at New York, N. Y., under the act of March 3, 1879.

VOL. LXXXIX   NEW YORK CITY, WEDNESDAY, JANUARY 4, 1928   NO. 12

HAPPY NEW YEAR TO YOU   AND THIRTY-FOUR REASONS WHY IT SHOULD BE A HAPPY NEW YEAR FOR ME

AND HIS
GREATER ORCHESTRA

PERSONAL DIRECTION
JAMES F. GILLESPIE

TOUR DIRECTION
WILLIAM MORRIS

by bandleader B. A. Rolfe from the Palais D'Or restaurant at Broadway and 48th Street, formerly the home of the Palais Royal. Cigarette company Lorillard wanted to promote one of its brands on the radio, so Whiteman signed at $4,500 per program for *The Old Gold-Paul Whiteman Hour*, to start in February 1929 on CBS. While Rolfe was comfortable before the microphone, Whiteman was not, so CBS announcer Ted Husing introduced the program and the musical numbers.

At about the same time, the only medium not yet conquered by Whiteman called. The introduction of sound to moving pictures was transforming the industry, and the remarkable success of Al Jolson in *The Jazz Singer* (1927) and *The Singing Fool* (opening in New York in September 1928) showed that this was no fluke. The drawing power of the Whiteman Orchestra on the stage of a movie theater was undisputed—imagine the audiences waiting to see them on the screen!

After inquiries from several studios, including Fox and Universal, Whiteman's manager James Gillespie pursued a deal with Universal from a position of strength. The final arrangements were negotiated with Carl Laemmle and the studio's Nat Goldstone at the private German-Jewish Harmonie Club in Manhattan. The studio would pay the band's salaries during filming. Whiteman received director approval, would own publishing rights for any songs written for the film, and would receive 40% of the net profits, with a $200,000 guarantee. Whiteman signed the contract on October 18, 1928, with filming to start February 15, 1929, for as long as eight weeks. Universal received an option for a second picture with Whiteman, which would give him 45% of the net profits.[45]

A new chapter in Whiteman's career was about to begin, but neither he nor the Universal representatives could have predicted the 18-month adventure ahead of them.

In 1928 Whiteman shifted his recordings from Victor to Columbia, which supported his releases with a coast-to-coast publicity campaign of print and outdoor advertising, and a custom-designed label for his releases, but left Whiteman with less artistic control over his choice of music.

Whiteman whips his band into a frenzy in this expressionistic photograph taken
to promote the band's third annual cross-country concert tour in 1928.

Carl Laemmle Sr. and Jr., early 1930s.

Chapter 2

UNIVERSAL PICTURES
A FAMILY BUSINESS

The names of film pioneers Walt Disney, the Warner brothers, Louis B. Mayer, and William Fox endure today in the names of the companies they founded. The story of Universal Pictures is the story of Carl Laemmle and his commitment to the industry, but it is also the story of his family.

Laemmle was an unlikely captain of industry. He emigrated from Laupheim, Germany, at 17, and by the time he was nearing 40 in 1906 Laemmle was married with two children (Rosabelle and Julius), and managing an Oshkosh, Wisconsin, clothing store owned by his wife's uncle. That January he visited the owner's office in Chicago and argued himself out of his job. Unexpectedly unemployed, with encouragement from his wife, Recha, and advice from his friend, Chicago advertising executive Robert Cochrane, Laemmle decided to start his own business in Chicago. Initially drawn to the burgeoning five-and-ten-cent-store field, he was soon smitten by the new nickelodeons. "It was evident that the basic idea of motion pictures and Mr. Woolworth's innovation were identical—small price commodity in tremendous quantities," he recalled.[1] Laemmle's timing was excellent; a second nickelodeon followed the first, but as competing theaters opened he found it difficult to get good prints of new releases. The following year he founded Laemmle Film Service, applying merchandising principles to provide better service than competing exchanges.

Laemmle's distribution business expanded rapidly, and he later recalled that "during 1909 I had become known as the largest film renter in the world with some ten branches in this country and Canada, yielding ten thousand dollars weekly."[2] When the Motion Picture Patents Co. (MPPC), popularly known as "the Trust," was formed the previous year, it used control of the key camera and projector patents to attempt to create a monopoly where only licensed films would be produced, distributed, and shown. After a few months Laemmle withdrew his exchange from the Trust, and established his own production company, the Independent Moving Picture Company of America (IMP). Its first film, a one-reel adaptation of *Hiawatha*, was released in October 1909.

Laemmle was the most vocal of the Independents—the faction of the film industry that rejected the Patents Trust. A relentless press campaign of advertisements written by Cochrane, but signed by Laemmle, made sure that the issues of higher costs and limited selection for exhibitors couldn't be ignored by the industry. In May 1912, Laemmle and five other producers came together to form the Universal Film Manufacturing Company to strengthen their position in the market and fund ongoing litigation. There was an enormous amount of money at stake. Partner William H. Swanson later testified that before the formation of the Trust he was netting $100,000 per year from his film interests. When asked the primary reason why Universal was formed, his answer was concise—"to make money." What was the secondary reason? Again, "to make money."[3]

Gradually Laemmle gained full control of Universal. Partner David Horsley sold his interest in

In this advertisement, Carl Laemmle attacks the film trust for collecting a weekly license fee from each exhibitor. *Moving Picture World*, June 5, 1909, 738.

1913 for $280,000, predicting "Laemmle will eventually win out, because it will be recognized that he is the most capable man in the organization."[4] In October 1914, another faction sold a non-controlling interest for $750,000.[5] Finally, hold-out partner Pat Powers sold the rest of his holdings for several million dollars in 1920, leaving Laemmle and Cochrane as the sole owners of the company, running it from offices in New York City.[6]

Founding Universal City

As Universal consolidated the production companies it had absorbed, Laemmle's goal was to centralize production in Los Angeles. A ranch property leased by Horsley's Nestor Film Company in the San Fernando Valley was given up in favor of purchasing a better-positioned property to the west, bordering Lankershim Boulevard, at $250 per acre. Following groundbreaking in May 1914, the new 230-acre Universal City offered everything needed for a self-contained production complex—enclosed stages with artificial lighting,

outdoor sets, dressing rooms, restaurant, hospital, zoo, police department, ice plant, and even a bungalow for the animal trainer. The studio was already in operation when a train filled with Universal executives, salesmen, theater owners, and press arrived from Chicago after a week-long junket to witness the studio's official opening on March 15, 1915.[7]

By late summer, Laemmle was looking to hire ten more directors to supplement the 42 already busy filming features, shorts, comedies, and westerns.[8] This footage poured into the cutting rooms, where future cinematographer Hal Mohr was working as an editor. He recalled that Laemmle "used to come in the projection rooms when you would run the pictures—you would be cutting for seven or eight directors at one time." The president of Universal was accompanied by his seven-year-old son Julius, who, Mohr recalled, "was a bit of a pest … getting in everybody's hair. He'd come down to the cutting room, get tangled up in our film, we'd have to throw him out of the place."[9]

Of the thousands of entrepreneurs attracted to the motion picture business, Laemmle was one of the relative few who made his way to the top ranks. His ascension from salaried manager of a clothing store to industry magnate was as unlikely as it was rapid. Laemmle was able to anticipate changes in the industry, switch sides at opportune moments, and outwit competitors as well as his partners. His fight against the Patents Trust succeeded in October 1915 when a federal district court ruled that the Motion Picture Patents Co. was a conspiracy in restraint of trade, and thus illegal. Under his leadership Universal managed the transition from short films to features, and made money producing films that were no better, and sometimes worse, than those of its competitors. Laemmle stood a modest five feet one, had a receding hairline, and never lost his German accent. Observers also specifically remembered twinkling eyes that gleamed with determination. He attracted respect for his intelligence and business acumen, and as one writer noted, was "distinguished for his gentleness, charity and cleanness of life."[10] If he had weaknesses, they were also his strengths—a strong commitment to family that blinded his ability to judge capability, loyalty to those loyal to him, and a thriftiness which, while not conducive to quality filmmaking, did keep the company in business and Laemmle in charge for 30 years.

As the studio standardized the quality and consistency of the production companies brought together in the merger, releases expanded to include features. Most were programmers, with a few big releases each year. The first was the expedition documentary *Paul J. Rainey's African Hunt* (1912), but many of the highest-profile titles

The Laemmle family, ca. 1914. Seated, left to right: Recha Laemmle, Julius Laemmle, and Carl Laemmle. Standing, left to right: Carl's brother Louis Laemmle, Recha's sister Anna Stern Fleckles, and brother-in-law Maurice Fleckles.

had an exploitation angle—white-slavery-themed *Traffic in Souls* (1913), abortion drama *Where Are My Children?* (1916), adventure *20,000 Leagues Under the Sea* (1916), and anti-German propaganda films *The Kaiser, The Beast of Berlin* (1918) and *The Heart of Humanity* (1919).

Family Ties

Laemmle brought Recha's brothers Abe Stern and Julius Stern into the company early, appointing Julius as general manager of IMP and Abe as business manager of its comedies subsidiary L-KO. Later they became the managers of Century Comedies, releasing through Universal. Their approach to cinema was encapsulated in a possibly apocryphal story of Abe's response to a director who wanted to film on location: "A rock is a rock, a tree is a tree, shoot it in Griffith Park!"[11] Despite the inability of her brothers to see the film industry as anything but a business where the goal was to spend as little as possible, Recha Laemmle "was passionately devoted to them," screenwriter Leonore Coffee recalled. She "regarded

them as successors in the event of Laemmle Senior's death, and until such time as [Carl's son] Junior could take over."[12]

Recha Laemmle died in January 1919 from influenza, when daughter Rosabelle was 17 years old and son Julius was 11. Laemmle was a conscientious father, doting on his children, and after Recha's death he brought them on his trips, including what became annual three-month working vacations to Europe. Julius sat in on his father's meetings from the age of 5; by age 12 he knew the facts and figures of the company and the films it produced.[13] Rosabelle took over as head of the household in their large Manhattan apartment, at 465 West End Avenue, near Riverside Drive. Sometime that year, visiting her father at work, she met his new assistant. Irving Thalberg had prepared himself for an office career with evening classes, and after a chance meeting with Laemmle piqued his interest, applied for a job at Universal's New York office. Thalberg was working as a secretary in Laemmle's office when his memos recommending areas for improvement led to his appointment as Laemmle's assistant.

In early 1920, Laemmle brought Thalberg along

Top: Opening day at Universal City Studios, 1915. Carl Laemmle and his six-year-old son Julius Laemmle at right.

Bottom: Filming a western starring Harry Carey (wearing checkered shirt) on the front-lot stage at Universal City, with paying visitors watching from the bleachers, ca. 1915.

Child star Lawrence McKeen, Jr. (center) appeared as Snookums in Stern Brothers two-reel comedies based on the George McManus newspaper comic strip "The Newlyweds and Their Baby." McKeen, later known on screen as "Sunny Jim," appears here on the shoulders of Carl Laemmle's brothers-in-law Abe Stern (left) and Julius Stern (right), during a 1927 publicity tour.

on his annual Spring trip to the West Coast. Thalberg "would accompany the boss around the lot, sit in on conferences and such," remembered Robert Cochrane. "He was a keen observer and would make suggestions that were helpful and valuable. He had a good business mind as well as an artist's mind."[14] To reduce the infighting at the studio, Laemmle, possibly at Thalberg's suggestion, set up a management board consisting of his head of production, head of the studio (physical plant), and head of finance, with Thalberg staying in California to represent Laemmle. With no clear lines of authority, Thalberg recalled, "I took charge because there was no one left to take charge."[15]

When Thalberg returned to New York for meetings in May 1921, he had managed to double the pace of production so that he could lay off over 150 staff, cutting overhead by $11,500 weekly. The buzz on both coasts was that marriage to Rosabelle was imminent. She "is a very lovely young woman," Thalberg told the *Los Angeles Times*, "but I am only 22 years old, and have a bankroll to make before I could possibly think of asking any lady to marry me."[16] Thalberg was in a strong position with Laemmle, and "he was really fond of Rosabelle, who was

a bright and pretty girl," recalled Lenore Coffee, "but the family situation was not to his liking."[17]

Thalberg was the strongest production executive that Laemmle ever allowed, and he faced the challenge of upgrading the studio's output while controlling costs. The studio's biggest star of the period was dramatic actress Priscilla Dean, who frequently worked with director Tod Browning, in films such as *Outside the Law* (1920), which also featured character actor Lon Chaney. Universal's most renowned filmmaker was actor-turned-director Erich von Stroheim, whose *Blind Husbands* (1919) had been a surprise success. In 1920 Stroheim was given near-total authority by Laemmle to make *Foolish Wives* (1922), which spent 11 months before the cameras—"a nightmare without precedent in Hollywood," noted his biographer Richard Koszarski.[18] As Thalberg feared, even with all the notoriety raised by an outstanding publicity campaign, it was impossible to recover the film negative's cost of $1,123,259.

Thalberg championed a large-scale adaptation of Victor Hugo's novel *The Hunchback of Notre Dame* (1923) starring Lon Chaney. He ensured that Stroheim directed, but did not appear in his next production, *Merry-Go-*

Above: Universal City studio administrative building, 1925.

Right: Cover of the souvenir program for *The Hunchback of Notre Dame* (1923), the studio's big release for the 1923–24 season.

Round, and with Laemmle's support, in October 1922 when Stroheim ran far behind schedule, the director was summarily fired and replaced with Rupert Julian. Although his romance with Rosabelle had faded, Thalberg was shaken when Laemmle refused to give him a raise, and he left the studio the following January to work for independent producer Louis B. Mayer for a modest increase in salary. Released after Thalberg's departure, both *Hunchback* and *Merry-Go-Round* were successful. The Rosabelle and Irving relationship did not end with his departure from the studio. They were together again throughout early 1926, amid new rumors of an imminent marriage, but Thalberg married actress Norma Shearer the following year.

One Man's Family

Laemmle liked to think of Universal as his extended family. He appreciated the appellation of "Uncle Carl," and the company staged frequent anniversary tributes and birthday parties in his honor. The company had many aspects of a family business, with multiple family members (of varying abilities) on the payroll; general over-staffing; and long-term employees who liked the lack of accountability for failure. Laemmle quirks and aversion to clearly defined job roles drove the company. He liked fried chicken, but quality poultry was hard to get on the West Coast, so in June 1924 he invested $54,000 to develop the Universal Poultry Ranch, a five-acre chicken farm on unused land on the backlot; by 1929 the ranch was producing 200,000 eggs per year. This also served "to provide work for some relatives who showed little aptitude for the picture business," noted historian Robert S. Birchard.[19]

"At Universal you were very conscious of the network of relatives who belonged to Carl Laemmle so it was like a large family," Fay Wray remembered. "And

CARL LAEMMLE

↣ PRESENTS ↢

LON CHANEY

in "The
HUNCHBACK
of
NOTRE DAME"

VICTOR HUGO'S

*Mighty Epic
of a
Mighty Epoch*

Price
25¢

Above: View of Universal City, 1923. The arches of the *Hunchback of Notre Dame* cathedral set are visible on the backlot.

Right: Actors in Universal's features, shorts, and serials assemble to promote the big pictures of the 1925–26 season, prepared for shipment to New York. Spring 1925. Among the group are: Laura La Plante, Norman Kerry, Patsy Ruth Miller, Mary Philbin, Arthur Lake, Jack Hoxie, Hoot Gibson, Jean Hersholt, and Cesare Gravina.

if they were not relatives, they were related by coincidence of having been in the same town in Germany at some point."[20] One consequence was a breakdown of authority. The position of studio general manager was a revolving door, as any relative or person with a hardship story could appeal decisions to Laemmle. In late 1924, Laemmle hired away Thomas H. Ince's studio manager on a three-year contract. The new employee lasted three weeks before suffering a physical collapse and submitting his resignation.[21] This was such an obvious problem that a 1926 dinner paying tribute to Laemmle's 20 years in the industry presented a gag film that included what purported to be a parade of over 100 former Universal general managers.[22]

Not all of Laemmle's recruits were mediocre. One of Laemmle's cousins, Melanie Weiller, living in Mulhouse, Alsace, wrote Uncle Carl about her 19-year-old-son. Laemmle invited the young man to meet him

at his hotel when he visited Zurich. After an interview, future director William Wyler was offered a job in the New York office at $25 a week. He would work his way up through the ranks from low-budget westerns to features by the end of the decade. In the summer of 1920 Paul Kohner interviewed Laemmle in the Czech spa town Carlsbad (Karlovy Vary) for his father's Prague motion picture trade magazine. Spotting an opportunity, Kohner joined the company in New York in advertising and marketing focused on increasing the studio's sales overseas, and later as a production supervisor for directors imported from Germany.

Challenges to Growth

By the mid-1920s, with access to Wall Street capital for mergers and expansion, the major companies in the motion picture industry controlled the most profitable parts of the business. The strongest companies at the end of 1926 were Famous Players-Lasky (producer of Paramount pictures, with assets of $143 million), Loew's, Inc. (including production subsidiary M-G-M, $91 million), and Fox Film Corp. and its theater arm ($55 million). The next, much-lower, tier included First National Pictures, Inc., Universal Pictures Co., Inc., and Warner Bros. Pictures, Inc., with assets of about $16 million each, and distributor Pathe Exchange, Inc., at $10 million.[23] Profits followed accordingly, with the companies that included production, distribution, and exhibition being the most successful. Universal's $2 million profit for 1926 was a third of the net produced by Paramount or Loew's, and double the profit for First National or Pathe Exchange.

The largest companies in the industry owned theaters that dominated exhibition in different regions of the country and gave them leverage with competitors. Without a strong theater arm, Universal was getting squeezed in New York, Florida, parts of the Mid-West, and the Southwest. "I don't want to build theatres. I'm not an exhibitor and I don't want to compete with my customers," Laemmle told a convention of exhibitors following the establishment of the Universal Chain Theaters Corporation at the end of 1925.[24] A year later, Universal controlled 253 theatres, with showcase houses in 12 cities.

As it did not dominate any regions, Universal's exhibition strategy failed. The two companies were merged in the second half of 1927, at the same time that Universal rented the 1,980-seat Colony Theatre at 53rd and Broadway in Manhattan as a first-run house.[25] A year later, Universal was trying to get out of the lease. The Colony was ten blocks uptown from Times Square, and the box-office receipts did not even cover the $225,000 annual rent, let alone operating expenses.[26]

Laemmle retained close ties to Europe and became a patron to his hometown in Germany. Universal's distribution of F. W. Murnau's *The Last Laugh* (1924) in the U.S. market did not attract audiences, while the studio fared better with the heavily promoted, lavish French productions of *Les Miserables* (1925) and *Michael Strogoff* (1926).

In the mid-1920s Universal started recruiting European directors and actors, who were eager to work with Hollywood budgets, even at the price of laboring under Hollywood constraints. When Hollywood producers saw the German film *Variety* (1925), Paramount signed its producer Erich Pommer and stars Emil Jannings and Lya De Putti, while Universal recruited the director, E. A. Dupont. Laemmle also brought in Danish director Sven Gade and the Russian Dimitri Buchowetzki, but

Erich von Stroheim visits the set of *The Man Who Laughs* (1928), with actors Conrad Veidt and Mary Philbin in costume, and director Paul Leni on the right. Stroheim gave Philbin her first big role in *Merry-Go-Round* (1923).

the strategy really paid off with the studio's hiring of German star Conrad Veidt and director Paul Leni. On his arrival in New York in 1926, Leni told reporters he "has a great admiration for American dash and enterprise, and believes there is a place on the screen, as well, for a touch of Old World ideas and treatment."[27] Paul Kohner produced Leni's highly regarded adaptation of Victor Hugo's *The Man Who Laughs* (1928), starring Veidt and Mary Philbin. Not every import was successful. Ivan Mosjoukine, the great Russian star of French films, had impressed in *Michael Strogoff*, but not in his sole film at the studio, *Surrender* (1927). More important than the films they made was the influence of the imports, "completely transforming the visual style of Universal's heretofore lackluster product," Richard Koszarski noted. "The German mode of lighting, design, and camerawork quickly swept through the studio."[28]

Each spring or summer, studios would announce their product for the following season. Universal would have one or two "Super Jewels," such as *Foolish Wives*

(1922), a number of star vehicles (Jewels), then mid-range pictures (Bluebirds) or programmers (Red Feathers), along with westerns, shorts, serials, and a newsreel. In the mid-1920s the studio introduced the Universal Complete Service Plan, which allowed small exhibitors to pay a fixed weekly rental for any select features or shorts (excluding the newsreel and Super Jewels) from their local Universal exchange.[29] Universal had 43 regional exchanges in the United States and Canada, which promoted and sold its product to—and collected payments from— exhibitors. As Robert Cochrane stated, selling pictures individually "ran up sales cost to such an extent that we simply could not go on with it. We had to charge so much for the pictures in order to cover the sales cost on the repeated trips of the salesmen to every exhibitor, and we had to go into block booking to get anything at all."[30] Of course, block booking by Universal's competitors froze out booking opportunities for the studio's better films.

Box-office appeal was built around star personalities, and Universal was especially weak in this area. Universal

Carl Laemmle (center), flanked by Rosabelle Laemmle and Carl Laemmle Jr., on an ocean liner for one of the family's annual working vacations to Europe, ca. 1926.

paid at the low end of the scale, and the most successful stars, such as Mae Murray or Lon Chaney, moved on to better roles at other studios. *Variety*'s annual review of stars by box-office value at the start of 1926 provides a snapshot of Universal's position. Setting aside United Artists (whose founders Charlie Chaplin, Douglas Fairbanks, and Mary Pickford made a film a year at best), Paramount, M-G-M, and First National had a strong roster, led by Gloria Swanson, Lillian Gish, and Colleen Moore, respectively. Western stars top the list for Fox (Tom Mix) and F.B.O. (Fred Thompson), with Leatrice Joy at P.D.C., Monte Blue at Warners, and Harold Lloyd (about to leave for Paramount) at Pathe.

Universal's top draw that season was light comedian Reginald Denny, followed by Hoot Gibson, House Peters, Mary Philbin, Norman Kerry, Laura La Plante, and Virginia Valli. Universal's star line-up could not match the commercial appeal of even Paramount's second-string featured players, who that season included Wallace Beery, Ernest Torrence, Ricardo Cortez, Esther Ralston, Mary Brian, Warner Baxter, Lois Wilson, Jack Holt, Clara Bow, George Bancroft, and William Powell.[31]

Another challenge for Universal was the production quality of its films, as shown by their budgets. While there were savings from not paying top salaries, the studio's films did not have the selling value of pictures from other producers. For the 1926–27 season, Universal released 31

features and 30 westerns to M-G-M's 45 features. Most of the Universal titles cost below $200,000, with four specials with production costs from $200,000 to $400,000. M-G-M competed directly with an equal number of films in the sub-$200,000 range, but for theaters that could afford the rentals, M-G-M also had 26 pictures that cost more, including vehicles for Lillian Gish, Lon Chaney, John Gilbert, and Marion Davies.

Junior Laemmle

While still a minor, Carl Laemmle's son Julius had his name legally changed to Carl Laemmle, Jr. "Junior," as he was inevitably called, was being groomed by his father to eventually take over the company. Familial succession was common for family-controlled businesses owned by assimilated, secular German-Jewish families. Actor Joseph Schildkraut was at the studio during this period, and recalled wistfully, "I did not hold his age against him—Irving Thalberg or Mervyn LeRoy certainly proved that age in itself is not an essential prerequisite for a successful film producer." But he could not see what Junior brought to the job—he "had nothing to his credit."[32]

The plan for Junior's ascension was in sharp contrast to the path chosen by Famous Players-Lasky

Left: Dorothy Gulliver, George Lewis, and Churchill Ross in *The Collegians* series, based on stories by Carl Laemmle Jr.
Right: Lobby card for *Graduation Daze* (1929), from the third series of *The Collegians*.

founder Adolph Zukor for his son. When Eugene Zukor expressed interest in working in the family business rather than going to college, his father was strict. "You'll be paid according to your talents, if you have any," he told his son. "If you haven't, you'll be tolerated because you're my son, but if you want to get anywhere in this business, apply yourself to the maximum."[33] Adolph Zukor then put Eugene through a three-year apprenticeship starting in the shipping room, followed by a focus on sales and distribution, excluding production. At the end, Eugene's reward at age 22 was to be made Assistant to the President, his father.[34]

In Carl Laemmle's judgment, Junior was just what the industry needed; after all, he had correctly seen Thalberg's potential. His sense of urgency might have been colored by his brush with death. On board an ocean liner to Europe with Junior and Rosabelle in July 1926, the elder Laemmle was stricken with appendicitis. The ship's doctor managed to stabilize his condition for the rest of the voyage, until an operation could be performed in a London hospital. Following complications, Laemmle's personal doctor was summoned, and supervised a long convalescence.[35] When he returned, Laemmle focused on the succession issue. "One of its faults in the past [for the motion picture industry] has been amateurish leadership, too often, and mismanagement," he said. "To succeed [executives] must have a vast store of information and knowledge." Without any sense of irony, he concluded, "this knowledge can only come through training and experience."[36] Junior was going to get an accelerated course in the movie business.

Junior wrote some stories of life at prep school, and

those were adapted to the screen as a series of shorts, *The Collegians*, for the 1926–27 season, with scenarios by veteran writer Rob Wagner. But Junior was living in a different world. In the summer of 1926 on a European trip with his father, he spent $2,500 on telegraph charges to send a draft scenario from London to New York.[37] Heavily promoted by the studio, *The Collegians* starred George Lewis and Dorothy Gulliver. The first series, directed by Wesley Ruggles, was so well received, *Universal Weekly* breathlessly reported, that "it was necessary for him to cut short his college career in order to get into harness in the big Universal studio plant, but he was eager to get into the film game with both feet and without delay."[38]

In May 1926 Laemmle purchased the 32-acre Benedict Canyon estate of the late Thomas H. Ince for $650,000. Junior moved from New York to Los Angeles that fall, and in early 1927 his father and 25-year-old Rosabelle followed.[39] Actress Patsy Ruth Miller was good friends with Rosabelle. As she saw it, "She should have been the head, she should have been the one to take over, really, because she was the one with the brains." But that would never have happened, she acknowledged. Junior "was all right. I liked him, but he was kind of a nitwit."[40] Once Rosabelle teased her brother about his ambition to be a great producer. "It's indeed much bigger than that," Junior replied. He believed he could be a major producer, but his true goal was "to be an honorable man like my father."[41] With the stress of trying to achieve working alongside more experienced men, his father's expectations, and punishing long hours, Junior might well have appeared foolish to a young actress.

For the 1927–28 season, Junior was credited with being responsible for four features, along with the second series of *The Collegians*. The features were no better or worse than the rest of Universal's product, although Edward Sloman's *We Americans* (1928) was very well received. His education was happening very rapidly, but Junior wanted to make his mark. As it happens, so did director Paul Fejos.

Enter Paul Fejos

Every year or two an unknown talent emerged in Hollywood through an independent feature or short that received critical acclaim. In 1925 Josef von Sternberg made *The Salvation Hunters*, an artistic film, on a $4,500 budget, which attracted the attention of Charlie Chaplin and received a United Artists release. This led to a contract at Paramount, where he made the surprise

Universal advertisements to promote the upcoming 1927-28 season. *Motion Picture News*, May 13, 1927.

Paul Fejos filming *The Last Moment* (1927) at the Fine Arts Studio. Leon Shamroy (with mustache) is behind the camera.

hit *Underworld* (1927), and quickly became one of the studio's top directors.

Paul Fejos (originally Pál Fejös) had intelligence and erudition, with alternating careers in medicine, film, and anthropology. Fejos came to California from New York, but his experience directing films in his native Hungary meant nothing in Hollywood. He wanted to make a film so unique that it couldn't be ignored, even to signing Georgia Hale and Otto Matiesen, two of Sternberg's *Salvation Hunters* leads, for his $5,000 feature. Fejos used standing sets at a rental studio, negotiated discounts on film stock, and recruited cameraman Leon Shamroy.

For a plot, he chose to present the mind of a drowning man, whose entire life flashes before his eyes. Partly for effect and also because he had his leads for only a few days, he told much of the story in close-ups of hands and objects. Fejos previewed the completed film, receiving raves from Hollywood insiders. The film was viewed across the industry, although the unique style limited its appeal to the general public. Fejos met with executives at several studios, but wanted too much creative control. A meeting with Carl Laemmle was heading in the same direction when, Fejos recalled, "the door opened, in walked a young boy, he was then 17 years old. Carl Laemmle Jr. who was the apple of his father's eye and nothing that he wanted, his father would not do." Junior shared the industry's interest in the director of *The Last Moment* (1927). That Junior had not seen the picture did not keep the young producer from signing Fejos in December 1927.[42]

The first film that resulted from their collaboration, *Lonesome* (1928), is now considered one of the most artistically successful and visually expressive films of the late 1920s. "I wanted to put in a picture of New York with its terrible pulse-beat, that everybody rushes even when you have time," Fejos recalled, "this terrific pressure which is on people, the multitude in which you are still alone, you don't know who is your next-door neighbor."[43] The visual style would not have been out of place at Fox, and it shared elements of realism with King Vidor's *The Crowd* (1928) produced at M-G-M. Made at a negative cost of $156,735, mid-range for the studio, *Lonesome* returned a healthy profit of $63,534.

An exhibitor with a neighborhood theatre on Chicago's South Side liked the film, summing up the studio's predicament: "Here is a picture that is good, artistic, and worth while, but wasn't worth a dime at the box office. In Chicago, Universal pictures lack big first-run houses, and consequently these pictures when they are good, which is rare, never get the needed publicity." Then after a discussion of how the film could be improved, he concluded, "However, don't get me wrong. It was a rare picture, and this deserved criticism stands out in comparison of the reams that could be written about Universal's usual garbage."[44]

In the summer of 1927, Universal went to Wall Street for a $2.5 million loan to upgrade Universal City. Under the supervision of studio business manager Walter Stern and production manager Robert Welsh, this funded many improvements throughout 1928, including three additional stages designed for sound film production. The 1928–29 season would feature three big productions—two from director Harry Pollard: *Uncle Tom's Cabin* (completed in 1927, in general release in 1928) and

Filming the Coney Island sequence for *Lonesome* at Universal City. Director Paul Fejos oversees the action from next to the spotlight, while the camera is on the parallel platform to the right. Star Glenn Tryon is sitting in the center of the spinning disc.

Above: Universal's two most expensive films of the 1928-29 season, both directed by Harry Pollard, were hurriedly refitted for sound. *Uncle Tom's Cabin* had a six-month run at the Central Theatre, on Broadway at 47th Street in Manhattan in 1928. *Show Boat* (1929) was shot as a part-talking drama. After acquiring rights to the score, several songs were added, along with a prologue.

Left: Glenn Tryon and Merna Kennedy inspect a model of the elaborate Paradise Night Club set designed by Charles D. "Danny" Hall for Paul Fejos's *Broadway* (1929).

Show Boat (1929), and Paul Kohner's production of *The Man Who Laughs* (1928), directed by Paul Leni.

In mid-1928, the studio arranged with Fox to borrow a Movietone camera and sound truck to make tests for *Show Boat*. When the truck arrived in August, in nine days the studio shot a full all-talking feature, *Melody of Love* (1928), and talking sequences for three completed silents, including *Lonesome*; Fejos's second film at Universal, *The Last Performance* (1929); and some musical shorts.[45] *Melody of Love* opened in October 1928 as the first all-talking Movietone feature, beating Fox's *In Old Arizona* (1929) to the screen by three months.

Universal's Newest Associate Producer

In December 1928, Junior was officially named an associate producer at Universal. As soon as his father was out of town, in February 1929 he laid off over 100 staff, including many executives close to his father, some of them dating back to the Laemmle Film Service of the 1910s. "He is an aggressive young man," *Variety* noted, "and has determined to get rid of what he considers unnecessary overhead."[46] However, there was always room for new family members. In 1928 Rosabelle met Stanley Bergerman, an executive at the May Company, a Los Angeles department store chain. After their wedding in January 1929, Bergerman joined the family business, and in June he became Junior's associate assis-

The finale of *Broadway* was filmed in Technicolor. This frame from a Technicolor test shot shows the crew at work against the pillars and background of the set, which Universal publicity described as featuring "dazzling color combinations and cubistic shapes."

tant. Bergerman even moved into Laemmle's Benedict Canyon estate so Rosabelle could continue to look after her father.

Universal's productions were selected each year by Laemmle, Universal's general sales manager, and the company's treasurer. Junior was assigned one of the biggest productions of the season—a film adaptation of the 1926 stage hit "Broadway." Universal participated in an auction for the film rights a year later; when reached by radiophone in London, Laemmle made the successful bid of $225,000. Fejos recognized that the dialogue-driven drama about a song and dance man hoping to hit the big time possessed none of the scope or scale that Junior expected in a major Universal release. "'Broadway' is a very good play," Fejos recalled, "but the whole damn thing is happening in a tiny, little back room in a nightclub."[47] Fejos proposed to open up the film to include

sequences in the nightclub and cabaret musical numbers.

Fejos believed in the moving camera, writing, "even in a silent picture, the camera is the audience. What the camera records is the audience's point of view and a picture can be made in such a way that the camera, instead of merely witnessing the action, enters into it."[48] Placing the camera on a perambulator or hanging it from overhead tracks had worked before sound, but that mobility disappeared as the noisy camera was locked into soundproof cabinets. To achieve a continuously moving camera, Junior supported Fejos's proposal to work with cinematographer Hal Mohr and a Los Angeles engineering firm to design and build what became known as the "*Broadway* crane." The 28-ton crane (on a 12-ton trailer) was an engineering marvel, with a 25-foot boom supporting a camera platform that that could move smoothly and rapidly in any direction to capture shots

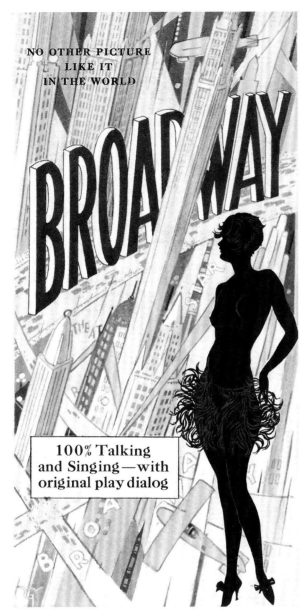

NO OTHER PICTURE
LIKE IT
IN THE WORLD

BROADWAY

100% Talking
and Singing—with
original play dialog

Promotional herald advertising *Broadway*. The stylized cityscape captures the abstract style, although not the specific design of the nightclub set. The well-known play was a bigger draw than Universal's contract players, Glenn Tryon and Merna Kennedy.

1925 *The Phantom of the Opera*. Fejos was a color skeptic, keeping the use of Technicolor to two minutes at the very end of the picture, believing that "as yet color films have only succeeded in transferring the prismatic hues which belong on the teacups to the screen, making of men and women not human beings but painted dolls."[49] The successful stage version benefited from the then-unusual backstage nightclub setting, while the film version of *Broadway* failed with audiences, partly as numerous stage and screen imitations had removed much of the novelty of the story.

Junior and Fejos missed the May 27, 1929 premiere of *Broadway* in New York; they were busy in Hollywood. That same week Carl Laemmle held a meeting of his executives and announced that he was appointing his son as general manager and head of the studio. Looking at Junior, he said "you have my complete confidence." To clear the way, the elder Laemmle fired general manager Robert Welsh and his production head. To demonstrate confidence in Junior in his new role, Laemmle left on a trip to Europe. Just two months past his 21st birthday, Junior was now in charge of all production at Universal City.[50]

from any height or perspective. The crane promised time savings by allowing sequences to be photographed in a single shot, justifying the $50,000 cost.

Broadway (1929) was filmed on the newly constructed Stage 12, Universal's largest. Art director Charles D. "Danny" Hall designed a colorful, geometric *moderne* set for the Paradise Night Club, and a large miniature of New York's Times Square. The final sequence of the film was photographed in two-color Technicolor, which had been used infrequently at the studio, most notably for the

Paul Fejos, Barbara Kent, and
Paul Whiteman. July 1929.

THE UNREALIZED
PAUL FEJOS VERSION

Paul Whiteman signed his contract with Universal Pictures on October 18, 1928, after several weeks of protracted negotiations. His fee of 40% of the net profits, guaranteed at a minimum of $200,000, was a new high for Universal, and demonstrated the studio's faith in Whiteman's celebrity.[1] Whiteman was to receive $50,000 upon signing the agreement, another $50,000 upon his arrival in Hollywood, $50,000 on completion of filming, and a final $50,000 when the film was released. Additionally, Universal would pay the salaries of the 25 band members then under Whiteman's employ, for a total of $7,800 per week for up to eight weeks of filming.

The contract not only gave Universal exclusive rights to Paul Whiteman's future screen appearances, but also the use of his life story. Whiteman was to provide "ideas and material" to the studio scenario writer, and would have final approval of the screen story. Similarly, although Universal was to select the director, the bandleader had power to veto this decision. These clauses were an unusual concession for Universal, but worth the risk, given the potential of the project. And for Whiteman, they were a necessary stipulation, considering the lengths he had gone to legitimize his music through lofty collaborations with George Gershwin, national concert-hall tours, and his 1926 autobiography, *Jazz*. Conversely, in the studio's favor, there was a standard morality clause stating that Whiteman's untarnished reputation must not be harmed before the film's release by any acts that would "degrade him in society or bring him into public hatred, contempt, scorn or ridicule." The title of this new picture

was to be *The Jazz King* or *King of Jazz*.[2]

The Whiteman deal came just ten days after the studio's first sound release, *Melody of Love*, which was shot rapidly for a thrifty $68,632 with borrowed sound equipment. Carl Laemmle rushed the musical into release while the novelty value of sound and song was still hot. Despite its largely unremarkable story and cast, *Melody of Love* struck a chord with audiences, and Laemmle's optimism regarding sound was rewarded with a healthy return of $274,049 in worldwide revenue—not bad for a film shot in less than nine days.[3]

Sound was sweeping the industry fast. Within two months of *Melody of Love*'s release, Universal had already constructed two sound stages, measuring 60 by 100 feet each, and had filmed dialogue sequences for over a dozen productions. The interiors of these stages were covered with an inch of cork-felt padding for soundproofing, while the ceiling was specially designed to prevent the penetration of overhead sounds from heavy winter rainstorms and passing airplanes. C. Roy Hunter was in charge of the construction and all technical aspects of sound recording, while A. B. "Archie" Heath—the writer and director of *Melody of Love*—became supervisor of sound production, overseeing dialogue, presentation, and other artistic matters.[4]

At the time of Whiteman's signing, the industry was still finding its feet with sound. The clunky crime drama *Lights of New York* was cheaply made and derivative, but as the first all-talking feature-length picture, it was a runaway success with audiences when it was released

Sound Captures Universal City

CARL LAEMMLE blazed the trail for motion pictures. He alone had the vision to see the industry as it is today. When in 1915 Laemmle established Universal City on the West Coast, he was the first motion picture producer Hollywood bound.

Laemmle was a pioneer of sound in films twenty years ago. The yellowed leaves of the Billboard of that date still bear testimony to the fact with the announcement of:

THE GREATEST IMPROVEMENT IN THE MOTION PICTURE BUSINESS

"If you believe I'm a good prophet, order a Synchroscope now, for I tell you that talking pictures are the coming craze in all America. Gentlemen, get it, first!"

Today Universal's sound stages are marvels of science and efficiency. 1929 sees the Universal Studio at Universal City, California, almost an entirely different studio from a year ago. Unprecedented building operations on the lot and the introduction of sound has transformed the appearance of the studio.

The biggest single enterprise was the construction of three sound-proof stages, one of which is the largest ever built for talking pictures, measuring 150 by 200 feet and is 50 feet to the eaves. This is being used in the production of "Broadway."

The hum of industry at Universal City is the dominant note in an arpeggio of sound being broadcast from Hollywood.

Construction on the huge sound stage for "Broadway" at Universal City.

One of the control room panels of Universal's new talkie stage. Ted Soderberg, sound engineer, is operating one of the multitudinous switches.

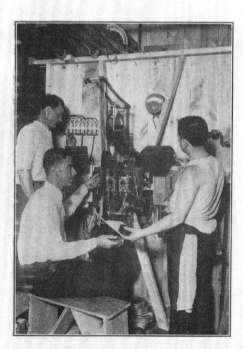

Recording room where sound is being recorded on the film of "Show Boat."

Universal's unique "camera crane," weighing 28 tons and 50 feet in height used for "Broadway." On the camera platform of the crane are Dr. Paul Fejos, the director, and Hal Mohr, chief cameraman.

Exterior of monitoring room on Universal's new sound-proof stage.

Above: Whiteman bought the front-cover advertisement for *Variety*'s annual New Year anniversary edition to celebrate his planned cross-country trip to Universal City. *Variety*, January 2, 1929.

Left: Universal promoted its new sound facilities in the souvenir program for *Show Boat* (1929).

by Warner Bros. in July 1928. The transition from silence to sound was gradual at most studios. In Universal's case, the gap between the studio's first all-talking release, *Melody of Love*, and its second, *Broadway*, was almost eight months. In between, the studio's more prestigious releases featured synchronized music and sound effects, as was the case with Paul Leni's *The Man Who Laughs* (1928) and *The Last Warning* (1929); or incorporated short dialogue sequences, as in William Wyler's *The Shakedown* (1929) or the first film version of *Show Boat* (1929). But the bread-and-butter releases—like the "Cohens and the Kellys" series—remained silent for the time being. When it was first announced in October 1928, *King of Jazz* would have been Universal's second all-talkie.

Show Boat's director Harry Pollard was apparently the first choice to helm the new picture, but the filming of his adaptation of Edna Ferber's novel dragged on into the new year. Universal's $100,000 acquisition of the rights to Florenz Ziegfeld's musical production of *Show Boat* in January 1929 further demonstrated the studio's

commitment to the new musical genre.[5] The "jazz king" baton was next passed to the confident young director Wesley Ruggles, who was at that time mostly known for his youth pictures and comedies, such as *The Plastic Age* (1925), with an up-and-coming Clara Bow, and the first series of *The Collegians* (1926), written by Junior Laemmle. Ruggles first had to finish up the Mary Philbin drama *Port of Dreams* (1929), which was completed as a silent picture in September, but re-entered production two months later to add talking scenes.

Seasoned screenwriter Paul Schofield came onboard to draft the story of Whiteman's life, but it was understood from the start that Whiteman wasn't "going to try to be a [John] Gilbert and carry the love interest," remarked a *Billboard* reporter.[6] The studio publicity announced that the film was to "trace the growth of jazz from tin-pan alley to the arty development of classical jazz," and was to be accompanied by the music Whiteman made famous.[7] Songwriters Mabel Wayne and L. Wolfe Gilbert were personally selected by Whiteman to provide new songs for the film. The pair had penned "Ramona," the "waltz hit supreme" that had proven so popular for Whiteman and Victor earlier in the year. Whiteman was set to "reap a rich harvest" from the numbers written for the picture, "since he has all music rights in sheet form, for records, radio recording, etc.," noted *Billboard*.[8]

Whiteman premiered his "Third Edition of Modern American Music" at Carnegie Hall on October 7, 1928, then the band departed on a three-month Transcontinental Concert Tour, stopping off in 23 different states. Schofield joined the bandleader on the road in Oklahoma City in November to consult on script ideas, then returned to meet with him in New York City in the new year. In December, Universal announced tentative plans to photograph concert scenes for the upcoming film during a benefit performance at the Carnegie Lyceum, capturing "the crowds going in, the audience, Whiteman's band on the stage, its music, and the audience departing," but this likely never materialized.[9] The original intention was for Whiteman and the band to convene at Universal City in February to film, but without a viable script in place the production had to be delayed. On January 10, 1929 an amendment was made to Whiteman's contract pushing back production to June 1.[10] A few days later Whiteman announced plans for The *Old Gold-Paul Whiteman Hour*, to be broadcast nationally across the 43 stations of the Columbia Broadcasting System. The 60-minute program of dance music was to begin on February 5, with weekly transmissions every Tuesday at 9 p.m. until April 2, neatly filling his newly freed-up schedule.[11] And beginning February 6, for 12 weeks the band also performed in Florenz Ziegfeld's *Midnight Frolic* on the roof of the New Amsterdam Theatre, with a top admission price of $7.70.

Finding a story

Paul Schofield's script, delivered in March 1929, drew heavily from Whiteman's career as outlined in his 1926 autobiography *Jazz*. It took a linear, straightforward approach in its narrative, beginning its story with Whiteman as a young man in the San Francisco Symphony, through to his introduction to jazz in a Barbary Coast café "syncopating the staid classics," then on to his early success playing at an "exclusive Los Angeles hotel." The script followed Whiteman and his band as they hit "the big time on Broadway," traveled to Europe on tour, and then returned for a triumphant concert at Carnegie Hall.

Whiteman and his band would play themselves, but as Whiteman expressed discomfort with playing a conventional romantic lead, Schofield added a (mostly)

fictional young couple to provide the mandatory love interest. Kurt was a "poor young violin player" whom Paul picks up on a street corner and nurtures, while Elsa—modeled on Ruth Etting—was a singer who joins the band and becomes an overnight success. Kurt and Elsa eventually fall in love, but Kurt feels he is a handicap to Elsa's career, so he retreats and takes off with a "flighty gold-digger." In the end the lovers are reunited through a music publisher friend, and Whiteman's orchestra makes a splash with Kurt's new composition.[12] Kurt, who rises from the gutter to become a celebrated jazz composer, was an obvious surrogate for George Gershwin, but his story was also inspired by a real-life event. While performing at the Paramount Theatre in 1928, Whiteman met a young newsboy, and decided to take him under his wing and pay for his musical education.[13]

Songwriters L. Wolfe Gilbert and Mabel Wayne were to provide several theme songs appropriate for this story, while Whiteman's primary arranger Ferde Grofé was to score and synchronize the film. Gilbert and Wayne consulted with Paul Schofield during his visit to New York in February 1929, and the result was two love songs

After churning out a host of program pictures in his first few years under contract to Universal, Wesley Ruggles soon graduated to larger middle-tier productions, like the riverboat crime drama *Port of Dreams* (1928) and the spooky *The Haunted Lady* with Laura La Plante and John Boles (released as *Scandal*, 1929). Both were written by Paul Schofield. *Exhibitors Daily Review*, December 29, 1928.

The Old Gold-Paul Whiteman Hour was promoted widely. This 11 x 21-inch advertisement was displayed in street cars.

written for the young composer Kurt. "Dream World" was a melancholy song about loss and longing after Kurt leaves Elsa: "You're always there in my dream world / Close in my arms til the dawn / Then I 'waken, find that I'm mistaken / And find my dream world gone." While "Forever and a Day" came after the lovers' reunion: "I won you, I lost you, and once again I found you / And I'll hold you, forever and a day."[14]

Whiteman felt the Kurt parallels to Gershwin in Schofield's script were too strong, and soon began a concerted effort to secure Gershwin in person, along with his *Rhapsody in Blue* composition. "Very anxious get Rhapsody to use for theme King Jazz," wired a New York-based company executive to Carl Laemmle. "Whiteman agrees to accompany Gershwin in his picture … only ask we send Ruggles East immediately if possible … spend four or five days with Whiteman going over script … start music preparations immediately."[15] In return for this demand Whiteman offered his orchestra to play at the Globe Theatre premiere of Universal's *Show Boat* in April. Laemmle was hesitant at first, unsure "what value [Gershwin's] personal appearance would have."[16] But Whiteman, who had final story approval, was adamant. "Would have to tell story Gershwin's life with love interest … Gershwin good looking … one greatest pianists country … had spectacular rise from gutter." To further support the case, Gershwin's name was internationally known, "his music tremendously popular throughout Europe as well as Australia," confirmed the

executive.[17] Laemmle ordered a screen test of Gershwin before discussions could continue.[18]

Sensing further delays and indecision, director Wesley Ruggles jumped ship after more than two years under contract to Universal. On March 23, 1929, he concluded negotiations with William Le Baron to direct Radio Pictures' first production, *Street Girl* (1929), starring Betty Compson as a violin-playing street urchin, with comic support from Jack Oakie. Released in July 1929, during the peak of the first musicals boom, the film was an enormous success for the fledgling RKO studio, earning over $1 million in worldwide revenues.[19] As it turned out, Ruggles's film at RKO was shot, cut, and released before any cameras would roll on *King of Jazz*.

Enter Paul Fejos

Ruggles's immediate replacement was Paul Fejos, the "Magyar Genius" whom Carl Laemmle Jr. had entrusted to bring "artistic advances" to the studio.[20] Fejos came onboard in early April, right after completing *Broadway*. And he was followed shortly thereafter by Junior as the film's production supervisor. The Hungarian director was reluctant at first to tackle the project, bemused by Whiteman's popularity and the story prospects. "But what on earth will you do with him?" quizzed Fejos. "He's a man inordinately fat. I don't think you can hang a love interest on him."[21] Fejos was soon ordered to New York

Some of the Whiteman boys lark around in their pajamas during a brief stopover on the way to Hollywood. May 1929.
Left to right: Charles Margulis, Rube Crozier, Andy Secrest, Roy Bargy, Kurt Dieterle, Min Leibrook (in wheelbarrow),
John Bouman, Mischa Russell, and Mel Lorenzon (stage hand).

for a series of urgent story conferences with Whiteman. He brought with him Edward T. Lowe Jr., his scenario writer from *Lonesome* and *Broadway*, who was assigned the task of doing a complete rewrite from scratch. The Gershwin negotiations were still in full swing, and Fejos was advised by Carl Laemmle to aggressively pursue the screen rights to *Rhapsody in Blue*, as well as a possible personal appearance of Gershwin in the film.[22]

"The script we are working on," Fejos announced to the New York press, "goes into Mr. Whiteman's life as if we were a total stranger. That is what we want. You people know all about him. So you take a great deal for granted. We want to fill in the background." He laid out some of his evocative ideas for an atmospheric Times Square backdrop, some possibly inspired by Whiteman's music: "screaming newsboys, shooting, taxicabs nicking corners off pedestrians, resounding music from dance hall windows, people panting at Nedick's [restaurant] … and subway jams down underneath."[23] After a month in New York, brimming with new story ideas, Fejos and Lowe returned to Hollywood in early May to further develop the script.

With a late-June production date in sight, the band prepared to depart for the West Coast. Whiteman's weekly Old Gold radio performances had been extended through the end of summer—now overlapping with his Universal commitment—so his radio sponsor dreamed up a grand exploitation stunt to send the band across the country in style. The boys were to travel aboard a deluxe eight-coach train decorated in red, green, and gold, that was christened the "Old Gold Special." Leaving May 24 with a grand send-off at New York's Pennsylvania Station, the twelve-day journey incorporated sixteen stops, including Philadelphia, Pittsburgh, Chicago, Kansas City, St. Louis, and Salt Lake City. At each city along the way, the band performed free public concerts, while regular Old Gold broadcasts were transmitted intermittently by local CBS affiliates. At one stop in Lincoln, Nebraska—typical of so many towns they stopped at—the band played a make-shift station concert in front of a crowd of 15,000, who had turned up in spite of a terrible storm.[24] Not missing any chance for a publicity gimmick, Old Gold "circused

Universal promoted its upcoming 1929–1930 season to exhibitors in trade journals like *Motion Picture News*. This advertisement, prominently featuring the recognizable Paul Whiteman "potato head" caricature, was designed before an appropriate story had been settled upon. The insert on the lower right is reminiscent of the promotional images used for *Broadway* (1929). *Motion Picture News*, June 24, 1929.

and ballyhooed Whiteman's advent in Barnumesque manner," remarked *Variety*. "Paul will have met more mayors of key cities by the time he reaches the coast than a trans-Atlantic flyer."[25]

The train held an entourage of 50 people, including Whiteman, his band, six music arrangers, Whiteman's staff of electricians, valets, Old Gold officials, reporters from *Variety* and the *New York Times*, as well as a Universal newsreel cameraman. "By the time Whiteman reaches the Coast," estimated *Variety*'s Abel Green, "not only will 100,000 people have personally viewed Whiteman and his orchestra for nothing, but every household of the country will have been reached by radio. That's ballyhoo exploitation on a grand scale."[26]

With much fanfare, the Old Gold Special concluded its journey at 3 p.m. on Thursday June 6, pulling into the Santa Fe depot in downtown Los Angeles a day after the band had given its final concert of the tour in Salt Lake City. The train had stopped at San Bernardino on the way to pick up director Paul Fejos for a last-minute consultation with the bandleader.[27] Upon arrival at the

final destination, Whiteman was greeted by both Carl Laemmle Senior and Junior in front of the press, before being whisked away to Universal City for more photo opportunities. Filming was not set to begin for another three weeks, so the band took a short one-week gig in San Francisco, followed by two weeks at the Pantages theater in L.A. The *Los Angeles Times* caught up with Whiteman mid-June. "I look ahead to the making of our production," confessed the bandleader. Whiteman had been making screen tests at Universal during this time, paying particular emphasis to the quality of the sound recording. "I have brought my own staff of engineers and electricians," he revealed, "the same who have attended to the details of my broadcasting en route as well as to the phonograph records I have made."[28]

When Whiteman and his band arrived at Universal City on June 21, Paul Fejos was ready to start. The first day of production was just ten days away. Edward T. Lowe's new script was ready, and Fejos had spent most of the month identifying a suitable female lead, reportedly viewing screen tests of 60 young ingenues.

Universal's trade magazine *Universal Weekly* announced that "Paul Whiteman Himself Is Publicity." To capitalize on this, a photographer from Wide World Photos (then a division of *The New York Times*) traveled cross-country on the Old Gold Special to snap Whiteman at every stop along the way. His arrival in Los Angeles and at Universal City was heralded with similar pomp and circumstance. Top: Carl Laemmle Jr., Paul Whiteman, Carl Laemmle Sr., and Paul Fejos. Bottom: Carl Laemmle Jr., Carl Laemmle Sr., and Paul Whiteman.

Among the most promising were Olga Steck, a rising star of both grand and light opera, and Evelyn Pierce, a 1925 WAMPAS Baby Star.[29] Additionally, an ambitious Expressionistic cabaret set—reportedly the largest indoor set ever, up to that time—had been built at a cost of $90,000. This "modernistic mansion of melody" was designed by Charles "Danny" Hall, the head of Universal's art department, while the overall construction was overseen by unit art director Thomas O'Neill.[30] The *Los Angeles Times* noted that one of the set's most sophisticated features "was a movable platform, manipulated by a series of hydraulic pillars at its base, concealed within a maze of lurid modernistic effects."[31] After eliciting "unstinted praise" for his camerawork on *Broadway*, freelance cinematographer Hal Mohr was again enlisted "to cavort with his kaleidoscopic lens"—utilizing the mobile "*Broadway* crane" to full effect in visualizing the rhythm of Whiteman's syncopated music.[32]

Lowe's first continuity synopsis was completed in April, and further revisions followed in June.[33] Lowe's take—later polished by husband-and-wife team Frank M. Dazey and Agnes Christine Johnson—was a strange cross between Fejos's *Broadway* and *The Last Moment*—only set in Hollywood. It was rumored the story itself was largely "negligible," reported *Billboard*, with Whiteman's music mostly "monopolizing the spotlight."[34] Whiteman and his band were again set to play themselves, but their appearance would remain outside of the main storyline. Lowe's loose plot was about an agent trying to convince a movie producer of the value of starring Whiteman and his band in pictures. The agent connives to demonstrate the excitement contained in a single day in the life of the "King of Jazz." Henceforth, we see "scenes in the rehearsal room with different kinds of 'cracked' musicians; the night club reviews; a fake hold up by crooks, etc. In the course of the club show many musical specialties are used to build up a great musical picture."

Self-referential and very much in line with the wave of backstage and behind-the-scenes musicals in vogue since the release of M-G-M's *The Broadway Melody* (1929), this new screen story mostly limited Whiteman and his boys to performing and clowning around—not too far removed from their onstage personas. Again, a tacked-on love interest was provided by a "romance between a song writer and the daughter of a strict, rich father."[35]

But Whiteman still wasn't happy, feeling that his act was being cheapened by a run-of-the-mill story and the need for him to act. "The music end of the matter is all right," Whiteman confessed. "But acting?" he hesitated. "I have seen myself in tests!"[36] The production was temporarily shut down while members of Universal's scenario department racked their collective brains. "The

powers who dealt with him," concluded *Film Weekly*, "attributed this odd request to modesty on the part of the portly impresario and interpreted it to mean that he should not be required to do any heavy emoting."[37] Again, more of the story elements were thrown out. Meanwhile, the Gershwin negotiations over the use of *Rhapsody in Blue* were reaching a roadblock too. "The trade papers have it that the iconoclastic composer … is asking a cool $100,000 to assuage his grief at parting with it," noted the *Los Angeles Times*.[38]

Spare time

With production stalled, Whiteman and his band were left with lots of spare time. For their off-hours, Universal built Paul and his boys a custom-designed bungalow situated next to Paul Fejos's office. Costing $26,000 and assembled over ten days, the "Whiteman Lodge" was a fully-equipped recreational quarters, with "every convenience" for Whiteman's musicians, including table tennis and pool tables, and refrigerated air. Measuring 110 ft. long by 40 ft. wide, the rustic log cabin was "charmingly furnished" with rugs, a great fireplace, mounted deer heads and birds, a profusion of comfortable sofas, and a $5,000 Steinway Imperial Grand piano.[39] Additionally, a soundproofed bungalow was erected on the lot for band rehearsals and fine tuning of the songs and score.

During this extended hiatus, the boys had little to do between their scheduled weekly radio broadcasts. The band had recently been expanded to 32 members, bolstered by the return in March 1929 of The Rhythm Boys (following a brief vaudeville tour) and Bix Beiderbecke (recovering from an alcohol-induced relapse), and the hiring in mid May of violin virtuoso Joe Venuti and jazz guitarist Eddie Lang. Contractually restricted from scheduling paid performances, as they might be called upon for shooting, the gang's activities instead mostly consisted of golf, drinking, and Hollywood parties. "We played golf in the morning, had lunch, and played another eighteen holes," remembered violinist Kurt Dieterle. "For three months, that's what we did." Their only commitment was to clock in at the studio each day, but that was soon circumvented. "We had a boy that used to sign in for us," recalled Dieterle. "[We] didn't even go over to sign in."[40] The studio paid the band members $200 each per week, while Whiteman—the real star of the film in Universal's eyes—got $5,000 in weekly installments, which went toward his next payment of $50,000.

The Old Gold broadcasts were made from the Universal lot every Tuesday at 5 p.m., then transmitted

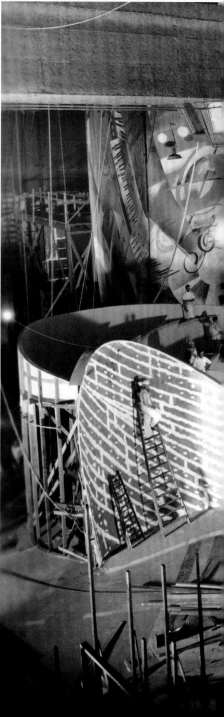

Universal Weekly noted: "The finished set features three towers such as the unfinished one lying in the foreground. The entire cafe sequence will be photographed in color." The impressive *King of Jazz* cabaret set (right) dwarfed the Paradise Night Club used in *Broadway* (left).

Paul Whiteman was photographed in a series of promotional shots to show off the new Whiteman Lodge.

eastward by relay from station KMTR in Los Angeles. CBS announcer Ted Husing had come out with the band in June, but due to commitments in New York he was replaced by native West Coaster Harry von Zell in July. Each week the band played its usual mix of hits from its repertoire and popular new songs, many of which were increasingly associated with the growing wave of Holly-wood musicals. Although the Universal lot was never identified on air as the location of the broadcasts—much to the studio's annoyance—several opportunities were taken to cross-promote Universal's product, including renditions of "Hittin' the Ceiling" from *Broadway* on July 2 and an instrumental of "Beautiful" from *Melody Lane* (1929) on August 27.[41] And on August 6, Universal contract player Mary Nolan appeared on the show as Whiteman's special guest. In honor of her visit the band played a trio of Mary-themed hits—"Mary Make-Believe," "Mary-Lou," and "Building a Nest for Mary"—as well as a selection of other "light summer dance tunes."[42]

Script problems

Since becoming general manager of the studio in June 1929, Carl Laemmle Jr. had tried to elevate the production output of his father's studio. Among his top priorities was the scenario department, in whose opera-tions he embedded himself. "I see all synopses prepared at the studio," he revealed in a rare 1929 interview, "sit in on several story conferences a day, watch all magazine material and all plays in New York."[43] And it was from Broadway that some of the 21-year-old's hot new writing talent was sourced. In late June, Junior hired the play-wrights of the fast-talking *The Front Page* (1928), Ben Hecht and Charles MacArthur, to pen the underworld drama *Homicide Squad*, a loose follow-up to *Broadway*; while in July, Maxwell Anderson, co-writer of the bawdy, profanity-laced World War I comedy *What Price Glory?* (1924), joined the payroll. Anderson's first assignment was to be another war-themed story, an adaptation of Erich Maria Remarque's devastating anti-war novel *All Quiet on the Western Front*, which Universal had

Per the original captions, top: Whiteman "seems to have a most comfortable way of reading script [*sic*] on the new music written for his forthcoming super production;" bottom: "Whiteman made his world-wide reputation, as the rajah of rhythm with a violin but the picture proves that he's quite at home with the ivories, too."

Paul Whiteman and Junior Laemmle.

resourcefully acquired the rights to soon after the publication of the English translation.

Junior had been thrown in at the deep end with *King of Jazz*. In addition to having to contend with 18-hour workdays and a $12-million annual production budget, the young mogul had the hard-to-please Whiteman to grapple with. But the small-framed executive and the rotund "rajah of rhythm" made unlikely companions, and according to reports they were close friends, despite the all-too-evident professional conflicts that kept arising. Junior certainly admired Whiteman, building him the luxurious Whiteman Lodge and catering to his every need; but even though Junior was technically in charge, Whiteman still had the last word on the story, per his contract.

Despite rounds of suggestions, revisions, and endless story conferences, no scripts met with Whiteman's approval. "Thirty writers tried to write a story," remembered Paul Fejos. "One was worse than the other. All of them falsified the figure, and all of them were terrible."[44] Whiteman repeatedly rejected being cast as the romantic lover in a sentimental story, instead favoring a vehicle which would showcase his performance and orchestra over a secondary love interest.[45]

In mid-July, Junior pulled Charles MacArthur from his writing duties on *Homicide Squad* to work on *King of Jazz* rewrites. MacArthur was stationed in Fejos's office. He "sat there day-in and day-out," recalled the director,

"and he told me day-in and day-out, 'You can't do anything on this.' And then finally … he gave it up and walked out."[46] Next up was *New York Daily News* columnist and short story writer Mark Hellinger, who built upon the work of the scenario department and Charles MacArthur to come up with a "semi-revue" which would largely take place in the huge nightclub set that had been sitting idle. Fanchon and Marco were to stage the dances, and Paul Whiteman and his orchestra would be the stars of the revue. And there would of course be a backstage story.[47] Ethnic comedian Harry Green was cast as a theatrical agent, and Australian character actor André Beranger was also signed for an undisclosed role. Ferde Grofé set to work writing a new number called "The Melting Pot," inspired by a stage show John Murray Anderson had first presented for the Publix movie theater chain.[48]

The original songs L. Wolfe Gilbert and Mabel Wayne had written for the film were no longer appropriate, so the songwriting duo were called upon again. But Gilbert had since signed a contract to work with DeSylva, Brown and Henderson on the Fox lot.[49] Mabel Wayne had no such conflicts, having remained with her long-term publisher Leo Feist. She was teamed this time with lyricist Billy Rose, who was already on the Coast, having accompanied his wife Fannie Brice to Hollywood for the production of her film *Be Yourself!* (1930) for United Artists. By the end of August the pair had penned the Mexican-themed "It Happened in Monterey."

A new direction

By the end of July, Paul Whiteman had reached the end of his tether. With his band, he was used to strict discipline, not the unstructured chaos he was encountering at Universal. With each day he became increasingly frustrated with the convoluted plot ideas Universal's scenario department was churning out. Universal even became so desperate at one point that they put out an outside call for story ideas, with a reward of $1,000.[50]

Junior Laemmle frantically searched for ways to curb the unwieldy expenses his studio was incurring. It was estimated that $350,000 had already been spent, without a single foot of film having passed through a camera.[51] In a telegram to business manager Lou Metzger on the East Coast, Junior carefully considered the studio's options. He informed Metzger that it would be "suicidal" to commence production with any of the existing scripts— either production had to be delayed to mitigate unnecessary expenditure, or the whole film had to be called off. Whiteman was "thoroughly disgusted" and "won't cooperate." But a delay would push the production of *King of*

Jazz into conflict with *All Quiet on the Western Front*—Junior's latest costly super-production, which was due to begin filming in November. "With two supers in production together," he warned, "withdrawals will be greatly increased." Another possibility was to cancel Whiteman's contract entirely and pay him off, "although I personally believe |we| can make picture money maker if based on suitable story."[52] On July 30, the production of *King of Jazz* was postponed by three months.

Whiteman and Junior had continued to clash throughout July, as the tension increased. Junior wanted Whiteman to make musical shorts for Universal while the script was being reworked, feeling "that 'The King of Jazz' must do something to earn his salary," suggested *Billboard*.[53] But Whiteman refused outright. In retaliation Junior barred Whiteman from performing at the Actors' Equity Carnival benefit on August 3 in Santa Monica. The free concert was part of a unionization effort by Hollywood actors, which the studios fought against firmly. Despite committing to the concert and featuring prominently in the event's publicity, Whiteman and his orchestra ultimately had to bow out at the last minute, or otherwise face a breach of contract.[54]

Sitting pretty with a weekly paycheck and just a one-hour radio commitment each week, the band members mostly wiled away their spare time. Some chose to accept occasional gigs. The Rhythm Boys, for example, had a week's run at the Orpheum in Los Angeles in late July, while banjoist Mike Pingitore and accordion player Mario Perry had made personal appearances at a local music store earlier in the month.[55] On July 31, a few days before the band was barred from the Actors' Equity Carnival, Whiteman arranged for his boys to perform a private concert in Santa Barbara, about 100 miles north of Los Angeles. Whiteman had generously bought the band members their own matching blue Fords—complete with hand-painted tire covers featuring Whiteman's trademark "potato head" caricature on the back—then had taken the liberty to deduct the expense from their weekly paychecks.[56] But *en route* Joe Venuti and Mario Perry were seriously injured in an auto collision on the Roosevelt Highway (now the Pacific Coast Highway). According to *Variety*: "A blow out of a front tire on their light Ford, in which both were riding, catapulted them into another oncoming car, capsizing them into a ditch."[57] Other reports indicated they might have run a stop sign. Venuti suffered a broken right arm and severe scalp lacerations, which laid him up for several weeks (in fact, his broken arm initially failed to knit properly, and necessitated Venuti temporarily changing his regular bowing position for many months to come).[58] Perry was not so fortunate; after sustaining heavy internal injuries,

Mabel Wayne's first published hit was "Don't Wake Me Up, Let Me Dream" (1925), written with lyricist L. Wolfe Gilbert. She was best known at the time for her romantic ballads of the Southwest, such as "In a Little Spanish Town" (1926), "Ramona" (1928), and "Chiquita" (1928).

he died four days later at the Queen of Angels hospital in Los Angeles. His remains were shipped to his family in New York for burial.[59] The 27-year-old Perry had been with the Whiteman band for almost seven years.

By the beginning of August, Whiteman and his boys still had a month's worth of Old Gold broadcasts remaining before they were free to return to New York, and despite the postponement of the production they remained on salary to Universal. Junior arranged an informal farewell party at the Whiteman Lodge on Sunday August 25, two days before they were to leave. Among the guests were Paul Fejos, *Lonesome* stars Barbara Kent and Glenn Tryon, George Lewis from *The Collegians*, screenwriter Mark Hellinger, and studio contract players Laura La Plante and Joseph Schildkraut, as well as Kathryn Crawford and her fiancé Wesley Ruggles. The evening was rounded out with an impromptu concert featuring Jack Fulton, Bing Crosby, Chester Hazlett, and Wilbur Hall.[60] The band's last radio transmission from the studio lot came on August 27; then everyone rushed to catch the night train for a quiet four-day journey back East. The gang arrived in New York on August 31, and headed straight to another engagement on Long Island.

"I realized we would be terribly criticized for delaying things," said Junior a week later. "I gave heed to all the remarks about wasting a fortune. But what's the difference if we finally get a good picture? We haven't spent a fortune. We have allowed Mr. Whiteman to return East and keep an engagement for the next two months, and when he comes back we will have a great deal better story than if we rushed into and made a mess of it."[61]

With production on hiatus, *King of Jazz* finally had the time to find its form. Settling on a story for the Whiteman film had been nigh on impossible. It had started as a straightforward biography of Whiteman's rise to fame, then mutated into a backstage musical after M-G-M's record-breaking success with *The Broadway Melody*. But the attempt to find a suitable story failed. And to make matters worse, Fejos's backstage drama-cum-musical, *Broadway*, was already showing signs of poor box office returns.[62] Now a new genre, the film revue, was beginning to find traction in Hollywood, with the opening of M-G-M's *The Hollywood Revue of 1929* in June, and the announcement of production on Warner's *The Show of Shows* in July. Universal was soon swept along in the prevailing trend. In everyone's minds, a revue was now clearly the answer.

As Universal had no musical talent of its own—other than perhaps John Boles—Junior Laemmle set his sights on Broadway, the same creative hotbed he had mined for writers earlier in the year. Theatrical impresario Florenz Ziegfeld was already committed to Paramount for the long-in-gestation *Glorifying the American Girl* (1929), so at Whiteman's suggestion the studio approached the next-best option—John Murray Anderson, who had made a name for himself on Broadway with a series of innovative and artistic revues, beginning with the first edition of the *Greenwich Village Follies* in 1919. Anderson signed with the studio on September 7, a week after Whiteman had returned East. He had two months to prepare.

In the interim Paul Fejos was reassigned. His new project was handed to him in early August, a week after *King of Jazz* was postponed.[63] Set during the French Revolution, *La Marseillaise* was an uninspired musical biography of Rouget de Lisle, composer of the French national anthem, set to star John Boles, with Laura La Plante as his muse. Fejos worked several weeks on the film in October, overseeing a series of impressive crowd scenes shot on the old *Hunchback of Notre Dame* exterior set. During filming on October 19 Fejos apparently fell from a 30-foot camera platform, and was found by the crew lying in considerable pain. He was immediately hospitalized, but his injuries turned out to be minor. He was released after a week, but took longer to recover fully. Cinematographer Hal Mohr hinted that Fejos's accident was highly suspicious. "You could never know if this was true or not," he recalled. There were no "scars or blood, no broken limbs."[64] In the meantime, Fejos was replaced by established director John S. Robertson, and the film was eventually released as *Captain of the Guard*, in March 1930.

The disgruntled Hungarian—who felt jilted by Junior after he chose Lewis Milestone to direct *All Quiet on the Western Front*—used his injury as an excuse to part with Universal, after a wasted summer of indecision and his latest lackluster assignment. "I had my belly full and finally went over to Junior," remembered Fejos. "I accused him that they broke the contract, that they made me make a picture I didn't want to make." "You can't quit," Junior screamed. "We'll put you on the blacklist." But following *Broadway's* failure and Fejos's evident dissatisfaction with being assigned *La Marseillaise*, Carl Laemmle Sr. shrewdly let the director leave. "It's no use to have an unhappy man," the elder Laemmle concluded.[65]

Paul Whiteman undergoes a medical examination by the insurance company's physicians. In June 1929, Universal issued a policy of $1 million, half of which was placed on Whiteman's life, and the other half against injury to the bandleader.

Chorines from John Murray Anderson's
1926 Publix unit show "Rhapsody in Jazz."

Chapter 4

JOHN MURRAY ANDERSON
AND THE BROADWAY REVUE

The American musical revue reached its zenith in the 1920s. These Broadway stage spectaculars dispensed with story in favor of theatrical pageantry and an entertaining mix of music, comedy, and dance. Although first appearing in the 1890s, the format did not begin to flourish in the United States until 1907, with the first of Florenz Ziegfeld's *Follies*, which ran in successive editions for twenty years, and featured some of America's greatest stage talent.

Ziegfeld's earliest *Follies* were inspired by the French revue vogue of the late 19th century, in particular the famous *Folies Bergère* in Paris, which presented the year in "review" through displays of feminine beauty and satire on life in the city. As the years progressed, the showman Ziegfeld became increasingly "overwhelmed with beauty and magnificence" as he tried to top the previous year's presentation. He hired the greatest artists to design elaborate costumes of fur, feathers, gems, and lace for his parade of girls, and brought in top entertainers like Eddie Cantor, Marilyn Miller, Bert Williams, Will Rogers, Fannie Brice, and countless others.[1]

A host of imitators all tried to outdo each other in size, lavishness, and color. *The Passing Show* (1912–24) at the Winter Garden mocked the previous year's theatrical offerings; *George White's Scandals* (1919–39) and *Earl Carroll's Vanities* (1923–40) teased with plenty of flesh and fancy; while the *Music Box Revue* (1920–24) showcased Irving Berlin's songwriting talents alongside Hassard Short's sophisticated mechanical stage effects. In Britain, producer Charles B. Cochran, director André Charlot,

and songwriter Noël Coward collaborated on a host of refined and sophisticated revues.

John Murray Anderson's annual *Greenwich Village Follies* joined this select group beginning in 1919. His slice of Bohemia utilized performers and situations from the Village colony as its foundation, but did not aim to match the spectacle or opulence of its big Broadway counterparts. Anderson's refreshing take on the revue brought culture and intelligence to the genre, transferring the simple stagings of the European art theatre movement to the popular musical theatre. But what the show lacked in scale it made up for in its fresh blend of artistry and technical innovation—"an agreeable potpourri of youth, style and distinction," as Anderson described it.[2] His approach of "simplicity with taste" set his work apart from Ziegfeld's extravagant and often titillating creations at the New Amsterdam Theatre.[3]

The ambitious director supervised every stage of the thrifty $38,000 production, questioning existing stage conventions in search of innovation, perfection, and beauty. This first edition opened in Sheridan Square in Greenwich Village, but was forced to move uptown to the Nora Bayes Theatre after six weeks, where it subsequently drew capacity crowds. The fortuitous timing of the show's release coincided with an actors' strike, crippling most other shows on Broadway but not affecting Anderson's non-equity *Follies*. The "Revusical Comedy of New York's Latin Quarter" ran for 32 weeks in New York before playing Boston, Philadelphia, and Chicago. It was a runaway hit, and reportedly made a staggering

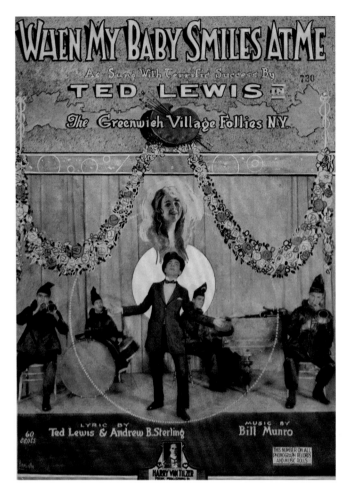

John Murray Anderson introduced Ted Lewis and his jazz band into the first edition of the *Greenwich Village Follies* with great success. *Billboard* noted Lewis brought "a lively riot into the performance, which caught the audience like wildfire." Anderson would continue to use jazz musicians in many of his subsequent shows.

$250,000 in profit for its investors, Bohemians, Inc.[4]

Further annual editions followed until 1928, most, but not all, overseen by Anderson. The series quickly gained a reputation for artistry and ingenuity, earning a place in the pantheon of the great American revues. Writing in 1924, cultural critic Gilbert Seldes rated Anderson's Greenwich Village Follies alongside the Shuberts' established *Passing Show*, Irving Berlin's *Music Box Revue*, and of course the *Ziegfeld Follies*—together, he argued, these magnificent revues defined "the four points of the compass in this truly magnetic field."[5]

As the son of a Newfoundland politician and businessman, John Murray Anderson (born in 1886) had a privileged upbringing, with an education in England, Scotland, and Switzerland. Although his father wanted him to study law or accounting, Anderson skipped out of his chartered-accountancy apprenticeship for a life in the theater. He studied in London for two years with the renowned actor Sir Herbert Beerbohm Tree, and travelled widely on the Continent, seeing hundreds of plays and performances. It was this liberal education, argued

theatre historian Thomas H. Gressler, that would place Anderson "far above the educational and cultural level of the average Broadway producer."[6] Later in New York, Anderson and his wife Genevieve Lyon found fame as a highly paid society dance team (second only to Vernon and Irene Castle, according to Anderson), before Genevieve succumbed to tuberculosis. While in Denver for his wife's treatment, Anderson "devised and staged" a pageant entitled *The Seven Ages* in celebration of the tercentenary of Shakespeare's death. It opened in May 1916 and featured a cast of 400.[7]

Back in New York, Anderson continued to develop his talents at the fashionable Palais Royal restaurant, one of many eateries owned by entrepreneur Paul Salvain (this is the same nightclub where Paul Whiteman's orchestra would later play for several years). Anderson performed as a dancer, but also subsequently produced several cabaret-style shows for Salvain's flagship restaurant. Among them were the "Fritzi Scheff Revue" (1917), headlined by the original star of Victor Herbert's operetta *Mlle. Modiste* (1906), and including Anderson himself

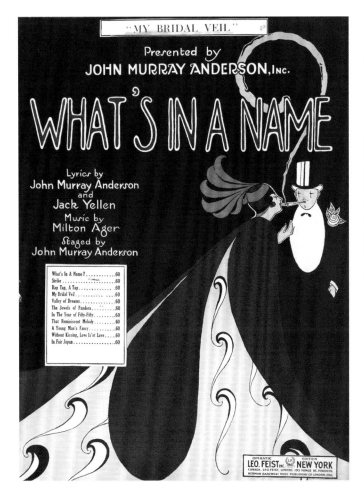

Left: "My Bridal Veil" was one of twelve songs written for Anderson's revue *What's In A Name?* (1920). The pageant was the show's grand finale and presented brides through the ages, with gowns designed by James Reynolds.

Right: John Murray Anderson, early 1920s.

as host and featured dancer; and "Venus on Broadway" (1917), containing original compositions by A. Baldwin Sloane with lyrics by Anderson (which were published by M. Witmark & Sons—a first for a cabaret revue).[8] Anderson's production of "Venus on Broadway" was hailed by the New York press as "a mode of entertainment familiar in Europe," but still "novel in America"—the show "uplifts the cabaret to the plane of big Broadway productions."[9]

Working practices

After the first *Greenwich Village Follies*, Anderson continued to challenge traditional stage conventions in *What's In A Name?* (1920). The revue was personally financed by banker Otto Kahn, and the director was given complete creative control. "Everything in the show has been done under my direct supervision," remarked Anderson soon after the show opened. "All the materials for gowns and designs for scenery were done under

my direct supervision and I handled all the staging and producing."[10] The revue was complicated to stage, with 22 changes of setting, but no physical scenery; instead the production utilized hangings, draperies, panels, and screens with projected scenery. Fifty grips were required to operate the sophisticated stagings, including a moving treadmill for subtle scene changes and numerous projectors.[11]

"We use as many changes of light in one song as would ordinarily be used for an entire production at the Hippodrome," boasted Anderson. "This elaborate and highly technical employment of light effects makes the electrician as much a part of the show as the principal actors. It is necessary, in view of this, to rehearse the electricians, so that they will handle the effects expertly. They cannot walk in, look at the typewritten directions and then take their places, as was always the custom. They must be trained to do their part."[12]

Anderson assembled his cast for *What's In A Name?* before he developed the show's assortment of numbers, relying on his players' specialties to inspire the content.

Additionally, unlike the tableaux style prevalent in the *Ziegfeld Follies*, each song in *What's In A Name?* (by Jack Yellen and Milton Ager) was based on a poetic idea that then influenced the costumes, settings, and choreography of the performers. The number must have a "plot or story which will give scope for ensemble and individual work by everyone," explained Anderson.[13] Many of the chorus girls were used to a particular kind of performance, but Anderson wanted to try something different. "The hardest task I had was to get them to walk naturally," he argued. "They all wanted to do the 'garbage' walk of the regular Broadway chorister, or to hop, skip and jump, in the traditional chorus way. But by careful and painstaking drill I broke each and every one of them of these habits."[14]

Upon opening, *What's In A Name?* was praised as "fifteen years ahead of its time," but Anderson's innovation came at a cost.[15] The budget ballooned to $85,000—over double that of the first *Greenwich Village Follies*. To break even the show had to return $16,000 per week, which was a tall order.[16] Everyone recognized Anderson's ambition and artistry, but his show lacked lightheartedness and didn't connect with its audience, although a few numbers, like the extravagant "Jewels of Pandora," Yellen and Ager's delightful "A Young Man's Fancy," and the grand finale "My Bridal Veil," stood out as exemplars of the genre. In the end, *What's In A Name?* was a financial failure and closed after 115 performances.

The following year Anderson packaged together some of his most celebrated stagings from the *Greenwich Village Follies* and *What's In A Name?* into a new revue called *The League of Notions* (1921). It was the first of several shows Anderson would devise for British theatrical impresario C. B. Cochran, who often imported the best of Broadway for London audiences. Anderson brought with him his regular costume designer James Reynolds, along with other trusted crew members, as well as "The Nine Most Beautiful Girls in New York," who had already passed his rigorous training.[17] *Notions* starred the Dolly Sisters—Rosie and Jenny—then at the peak of their international fame. The sister act would work for Anderson a second time in the 1924 *Follies* in New York, which proved to be his last in the series.

Also in 1924, Anderson was invited to stage the fourth edition of the *Music Box Revue* at Sam Harris's Music Box Theatre. (The previous editions had been directed by Hassard Short.) At a cost likely in excess of $200,000, the production was even more sumptuous than Anderson's earlier shows. And his cast was also more impressive: Fannie Brice, Grace Moore, Oscar Shaw, comedians Clark and McCullough, the Brox Sisters, and the first Broadway appearance of the dancer Claire Luce.

The Dolly Sisters were possibly the world's most famous sister act. They achieved fame on stage in the *Ziegfeld Follies* and subsequently played themselves in a series of movies. By 1921 they were living and working in Europe, demanding hefty salaries and socializing with aristocrats and royalty. *The League of Notions* (1921) included a special addendum to "The Bridal Veil" number in which the Dollies appeared as the bride and bridesmaid of the future in attire designed by Paul Poiret (as seen above).

Anderson worked closely with composer Irving Berlin, who wrote seventeen songs, of which only "All Alone" became a bona fide hit.[18] But the dominance of the stage revue was already beginning to fade in favor of operettas; opening in 1924, *Rose-Marie* ran for a record-breaking 557 performances before it was surpassed by *The Student Prince* at 608—the longest-running show of the 1920s.[19] Anderson's *Music Box Revue* still did well—it was the first in the series to enter profit before touring—but it was ultimately the last edition of the series.

Following a string of hits with his successive editions of the *Greenwich Village Follies* and the last *Music Box Revue*, Anderson began to settle into an extravagant lifestyle. He moved into an expensive penthouse apartment on Park Avenue, enjoyed annual vacations in Europe, and regularly entertained his friends and colleagues at excessive all-day binges. According to Anderson, his liquor bill regularly topped $150 per week.[20] Anderson's apartment also served as a location for meetings and creative gatherings throughout his career, his piano frequently hosting

The Brox Sisters were regular contributors to the *Music Box Revue* from 1921 to 1924. Their unique modulated style of singing was featured in multiple numbers in the 1924 edition, including "Tokio Blues," originally written as a showcase for the Duncan Sisters, and an "Alice in Wonderland" fantasy seen from both sides of the looking glass.

auditions of new talent or composers fine-tuning a song.

Publix

In October 1925, Famous Players-Lasky approached Anderson about producing stage presentations for its movie theaters across the country. The tradition of live prologues preceding a film was already popular, but these "unit shows" took a different approach. Rather than one-off local stagings inspired by the film playing that week, these centrally-produced stage shows would tour the Paramount theater circuit. The increased production investment in each presentation could then be spread over the longer booking.

Anderson's first production for Paramount opened the new Metropolitan Theatre in Boston on October 17, 1925, alongside Monta Bell's film *The King on Main Street* (1925). With 4,600 seats and costing $5,000,000, it was the largest and most exquisite theatre in New England. As Director-in-Chief of stage presentations, Anderson was charged with producing one unit show each week—"a complete five dollar revue in a nutshell"—which subsequently played at the Rivoli in New York, before heading to Shea's Buffalo, then moving on to Chicago.[21] For $1,200 per week "I had to provide the ideas, write, rehearse and light these artistic monsters," recalled Anderson. "Practically the only rest I got was on the weekly train journeys to and from Boston."[22]

His first presentation at the Metropolitan was "The Melting Pot"—"the most elaborate program that has ever appeared in Boston," heralded the local press.[23] It consisted of two historical tableaux about the founding of the nation, which then led into the grand finale. *Variety* described Anderson's impressive staging: "He used an ensemble of about 50 [actually 30], trotting them on in dancing and vocal teams in national costumes, running them into the melting pot and then putting on his closing ensemble in gold with American jazz as the outpouring of the pot."[24] Most of the talent was personally selected by Anderson from the vaudeville stage. Among the noted highlights were Johnny Dove, an acrobatic specialty dancer on roller skates, six accordion players, and soprano Lottice Howell singing an "Indian song." The show, and

After appearing in Boston in October, "The Melting Pot" played for a week-long run beginning Christmas Day at the newly renovated Rivoli Theatre in New York alongside the feature film *A Kiss For Cinderella* (1925). In addition to an ensemble of thirty on stage, the music for the unit show was provided by a 55-piece live orchestra in the pit.

The Allan K. Foster Girls performed in a number of John Murray Anderson's Publix revues, including "Cameos," which played at the Paramount Theatre in April 1928. The act was modeled after the famous Tiller Girls dancing troupe, who were matched in height and weight, and were known for performing high-kicking synchronized routines with their arms locked behind their backs.

those that followed in Boston, were hugely popular with audiences, matching the quality of the costly theatre and the highly polished Paramount films that played there. During its first month, the Metropolitan attracted an estimated 15,000 daily admissions.[25]

This runaway success spurred the newly rechristened Publix Theaters Corp. to expand its plans for unit shows across the former Famous Players and Balaban & Katz circuits, now incorporated as the nation's largest and most profitable theatrical chain, with over 500 theaters.[26] In December 1925, Publix president Sam Katz announced that acts and production crew for Anderson's presentations would be booked for twenty-week engagements, opening at the Metropolitan, Boston, then playing the chain's most prestigious theaters in New York, Rochester, Pittsburgh, Cleveland, Detroit, Milwaukee, Chicago, and Kansas City, with further locations to be added if this proved popular.[27] Sam Katz had pioneered the unit-show structure on the Balaban & Katz circuit in Chicago, and was now scaling it up to bring New York-caliber productions to the rest of the country.

As the chain built and acquired additional theaters over the following years, the unit tours also expanded, eventually reaching forty-week runs at its peak in 1927, playing to millions cumulatively. Publix boasted it was "the largest single employer of show people in the world, far surpassing many of the vaudeville circuits and producing companies combined." In 1927 alone the company presented 52 unit shows featuring 1,000 chorus girls, 250 dancers, 34 blues singers, 51 opera singers, 25 comedy singers, 50 comedians, and 1,200 musicians.[28]

Everything needed for Anderson's shows was designed and made in New York under his supervision before leaving the home base to tour. The sets were all scalable for different stages, and carpenters and electricians travelled with each unit to supervise the installation in each new city. James Dietrich used to play the piano during rehearsals. "We would take the milk train to New Haven Thursday morning, call in the MC and orchestra [and rehearse] that night," he remembered. "They'd break in the show in New Haven, then [go to] Boston, then play it in New York."[29]

Anderson enlisted the best designers in New York, including James Reynolds, Herman Rosse, and Clark Robinson, with all of whom he had successfully collaborated in the past. His regular choreographers included Albertina Rasch, Maria Gambarelli, Russell Markert, and Allan K. Foster, who all specialized in a style of synchronized precision dancing popularized by John Tiller's famous Tiller Girls troupe beginning in the 1890s.

Russell E. Markert and his "Sixteen American Rockets" first gained attention in 1925 in his native St. Louis, before Markert and his troupe moved East. Throughout the mid-to-late 1920s, Markert devised and staged dances for *Earl Carroll's Vanities*, the *Greenwich Village Follies*, and *George White's Scandals*, in the process developing six 16-girl dancing units to meet demand.[30] His dancers appeared in the musical comedy *Rain or Shine* (1927) with quirky comedian Joe Cook, the original stage production of *Animal Crackers* (1928) with the Marx Brothers, and numerous touring Publix shows, including two by Anderson. Markert partnered with Samuel

"Roxy" Rothafel from 1927 to present the 32 "Roxyettes" at the Roxy Theatre, and subsequently moved the girls to the new Radio City Music Hall in 1932 and renamed them "The Rockettes." Markert remained at Radio City for forty years, until his retirement, although his famous Rockettes have continued as an attraction there to this day.

Herman Rosse

The versatile and innovative Dutch artist Herman Rosse (1887–1965) was Anderson's closest collaborator during this time, teaming on more than thirty Publix shows between 1925 and 1928. Together they conceived the entirety of each presentation, Anderson in charge of the story and musical ideas, with Rosse responsible for realizing the creative design, encompassing everything on stage, from the sets and costumes to the backdrops, lighting, and curtains.

Rosse was a multi-talented stage designer, illustrator, decorative artist, and architect, who was at the forefront of his profession. His output was diverse and original, informed by study and travel, and not bound by one particular style. He gained early recognition for his interior decoration of the Peace Palace at The Hague (1911–13), before moving to the United States in 1915 to complete the designs for the Netherlands pavilion at the Panama-Pacific Exposition in San Francisco. In Chicago and later in New York, Rosse designed for books, theatre, ballet, and opera, working for the likes of author Ben Hecht, the Chicago Opera Company, and Florenz Ziegfeld.

Theatrical producer, critic, and publicist Kenneth Macgowan argued that Rosse's stage settings were an integral part of the overall performance, helping to form "an entertainment in which story, action, color, music, pantomime and voice would be fused to create a new type of continuous emotional spectacle."[31] Like Anderson, Rosse was a pioneer in "moving scenery," creating dynamic backgrounds through bold colors, lighting, and shadow effects, and animated projections using film. His early stage designs were informed by "currents flowing from the other arts," drawing elements of Post-Impressionism, Cubism, Expressionism, and even Dadaism.[32]

Rosse and Anderson first collaborated on the 1924 edition of the *Greenwich Village Follies*; Rosse designed the sets and costumes for the "Dream of Love" ballet and the Javanese pantomime, sharing the show's design credits with five others. Their partnership flourished for many subsequent years, ending with Rosse's cover designs for the dustjacket of Anderson's 1954 autobiog-

Herman Rosse, ca. 1916. Although born in The Netherlands, Herman Rosse studied architecture and design at the Royal College of Art in London and Stanford University in the United States. In 1913–14, he settled with his wife in Palo Alto, California, where his son and daughter were born. Rosse made his first set and costume designs for theater during this period, and taught courses at Stanford and the University of California, Berkeley.

raphy *Out Without My Rubbers*, published shortly after Anderson's death.

"Rhapsody in Jazz"

Anderson and Rosse's magnum opus for Publix was "Rhapsody in Jazz," staged in March 1926 and running 22 minutes. At a weekly operating cost of $10,000, the presentation was four times more expensive than any previous Publix show; the salaries alone for the 23 performers totaled $2,500.[33] It was inspired by George Gershwin's *Rhapsody in Blue*, although additional songs and music were added to expand the scope. Rosse's designs were fantastical and futuristic, and the pair incorporated a daring lighting gimmick in the finale that was a real knockout. The show featured five "startlingly effective scenes," described the *Boston Globe*, with "weird yet always pleasing color schemes."[34]

"The Bughouse Cabaret" (1926) was one of Anderson and Rosse's most praised Publix collaborations. The Dada-inspired settings suggested the padded cells of an insane asylum, where the inmates performed a series of eccentric routines.

1. **"Putting On The Dog"** — After a prologue the curtains parted to disclose a "a decidedly jazzy conception of Central Park," complete with a statue of Irving Berlin, the Stuart Sisters vocalizing, and a chorus teamed with four collie dogs.[35] Rosse's backdrop featured windows and office buildings reaching to the sky in a distorted false perspective.[36]

2. **"Banjoland" and The Syncopated Bootblacks** — This act was built around the talent, showcasing the popular vaudeville "Banjoland" routine. It was set amidst a syncopated shoeshine parlor and contained plenty of "fast stepping" and "a hot Charleston."[37]

3. **The Stock Exchange** — An ensemble of six girls paraded in fantastic costumes representing oil, copper, coal, real estate, steel, and gold against a dynamic backdrop of huge coins and figures trailing off into the distance. Neale Walters as a speculator and Cecile D'Andrea as the Spirit of the Ticker performed a specialty dance.

4. **Harmonica Rhapsody** — Gus Mulcahy wowed on the harmonica in a New York City street scene. *Variety* reported: "How that boy can pull blues and jazz from the mouth organ, and with it all he steps."

5. **"The Florida Low-Down"** — This closing scene featured an innovative color transformation that was "truly astounding in its novelty." Through the use of special costumes and red and blue lights, the interior of the cabaret scene was suddenly transformed into an "everglade wilderness," with the entire company now in blackface as "cannibals in the jungle doing an aboriginal dance."[38]

The "Stock Exchange" and "Florida Low-Down" numbers from "Rhapsody in Jazz."

Herman Rosse explained the preparation involved for each week's show in a 1926 article for *Theatre Arts Monthly*.[39]

On Tuesday at breakfast in J. M. A.'s apartment the real work starts. He is still in his bath, so I ring up the scene painter and the costumer, and quiet them down when they mumble something about impossibilities. In some mysterious way A. manages to get dressed and to decide upon the scenes between one thousand interruptions. Talking through various telephones at one time he hires [acrobatic] adagio teams, makes engagements, starts rehearsals. A score of sketches are made, discarded, ripped apart and combined.

An hour later we are in the rehearsal room. Special music is being tried out and arranged. The ballet master is already leading his ranks of girls through imaginary entrances on a rough floor plan. A few bare sketches set the carpenters going.

At 5 A. M. on Wednesday the working drawings for the carpenters are finished. On Wednesday, too, after a frantic effort the painters are provided with the first color sketches. The curtains are being sewn and everything is running smoothly in the shop.

By Thursday at 5 A. M. the bulk of the costume sketches are finished sufficiently to go into work. Hours are spent with bolts of cloth and pins and samples on the cutter's floor of the costumers. Miniature pieces of the selected materials are pinned to the sketches; fabrics are picked for color. Feather merchants and representatives of embroidery firms, property makers, shoe-makers, wig-makers are interviewed.

Friday. The costumes are cut and pinned. On large tables the painting on the costumes is started. The first costumes are sketched out ready to be gilded. Detail drawings have now to be made for the embroiderers. Not only have more costumes to be designed, but everything not started on Friday is out of the show.

So to Saturday. Properties are inspected and the rest of the morning is spent at the costumer's, where everyone brings his bit. Now comes the costume parade and an hour of political dickering with vaudeville "names" to induce them to wear clothes they never wore before.

Midnight Saturday and at the theatre the scene of last week's show is being struck as the final strains of the musical score of the picture die away. Between threats and swearing, the stage crew manages to direct dozens upon dozens of lamps on the right spots, to prepare the right color screens for these lamps, to hang the special draperies, and set the scenes. Notwithstanding these superhuman efforts and all the endless goodwill of the backstage crew it is 8 A. M. before everything is finally put together.

At nine rehearsals with full orchestra are in full swing. For the first time the actors have their musical accompaniment, but, as everything has been timed to the measure, no grave difficulties arise. For the first time, too, the lights are played on the scenery and costumes. Shouting voices, half drowned by the orchestra, howl messages to the electrician on the stage and the spotlight operators in the booth. In the midst of all this a light plot is worked out for the electrician, magician, one might say. Curtain plots are next. The properties are given out. Seamstresses make last minute alterations on costumes. A painter touches up scenes. A one o'clock conference between all the captains of everything follows. Rehearsals are held again in the rehearsal hall of the theatre, after which comes one more performance and more alterations and corrections. At last everything is right for the week. And the work for the next week begins!

These early designs for "Rhapsody in Jazz" demonstrate Herman Rosse's typically bold use of color.

Diversifying

Not all of Anderson's Publix productions were hits. During his first season, Anderson was expected to devise a new show each week—with taste and distinction, as well as wide appeal to audiences across the theater circuit. He mined ideas from his previous shows, working practically around the clock, often to near exhaustion. If a presentation didn't pass the test in its initial week run in Boston or New York, it was pulled from the circuit. Anderson's first failure was "The Garden of Kama," a "dance drama" with Dorothy Berke and Boris Petroff, set against passages from Laurence Hope's "Indian Love Lyrics." "It is a slow and dreary thing," reported *Variety*. "Scenically, it is adequate, but in entertainment value, low."[40]

"The Grecian Urn" from May 1926 was based on the John Keats poem and was another flop. Like "Kama" before it, the show's highbrow mix of recitations and ballet contrasted poorly with the more populist entertainment projected on screen afterwards. "That 'pas de deux' business is applesauce for the film palaces," offered *Variety*. "The thing that lays these pretentious presentations open to so much ridicule is that they set themselves up as pretty fancy in the first place, when they quote the Keats poetry, and then they follow it up with the old stuff—a series of specialties well dressed but loosely strung together."[41]

To reduce the pressure on Anderson and further diversify its output, Publix brought in additional producers for the 1926–27 season. Each created a different type of show; Frank Cambria was a Balaban & Katz veteran from Chicago who specialized in the classics, the Frenchman Paul Oscard infused a European flavor, while Boris Petroff staged ballet. In May 1927 the famed London revue director André Charlot joined this illustrious group. His first unit show consisted of highlights from his past hits. The unimaginatively titled "Bits from Charlot Revues" was a showcase for British performer Gertrude Lawrence, who was a hot property following her Broadway appearance in the Gershwins' musical *Oh, Kay!* (1926). Originally scheduled to run seven weeks on the Publix circuit, "Bits" was pulled after four weeks due to poor results. Charlot's second show, "Sailor's Lane," fared even worse: it played a single week at the new Paramount Theatre on Times Square. By August 1927 Charlot was out, and Publix began to reconsider its options.[42]

A year earlier Sam Katz had started to experiment with a different approach. Instead of the unit show being the main attraction, he brought in celebrities whose names had "box office power." Gilda Gray was contracted for sixteen weeks on the Publix circuit at $8,000 per week.

Situated at "The Crossroads of the World" in New York's Times Square, the Paramount Theatre opened in November 1926 as the flagship venue of the mighty Publix chain. For the opening week John Murray Anderson staged the "Pageant of Progress"—a history of the development of motion pictures, from the pre-history of the screen and Thomas Edison's first projected images, through to the latest in silent pictures.

Popular on Broadway and vaudeville as the originator of the "shimmy" dance, Gray was at this time under contract to Famous Players-Lasky and her personal appearances helped promote her new film *Aloma of the South Seas* (1926). During her five-week stay at the Rialto in New York, business soared to $25,000 weekly, far above the house average.[43]

Paul Whiteman and his orchestra were also engaged for a Publix tour in July 1926. The band played big cities around the country, stopping at San Francisco, Chicago, St. Louis, and Boston, among others, before ending the run in New York at the Paramount. The set at the Paramount

Top: Anderson reworked themes from many of his earlier revues for his Publix presentations. For example, "The Garden of Kama (1926)" was first staged for the 1923 *Greenwich Village Follies* with dancer Martha Graham.

Bottom: Cartoonist Anthony Muscio sketched Publix staff as they appeared at the Publix Theatre convention at the Hotel Ambassador, Atlantic City, January 1928. *Publix Opinion*, January 14, 1928, 3.

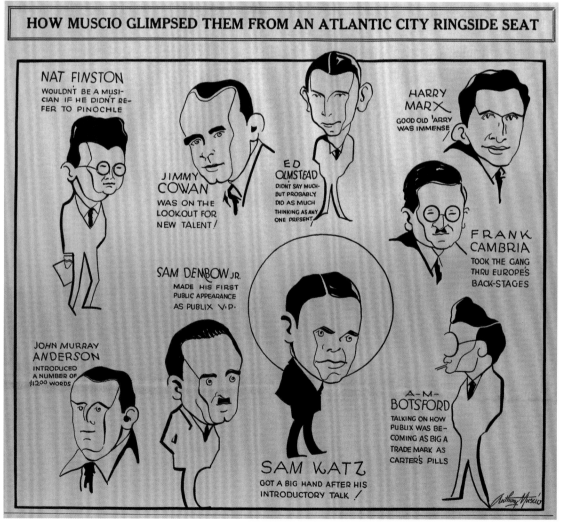

ran 42 minutes and was squeezed into a two-and-a-half-hour show, which included organ solos by Jesse Crawford, a recitation of Abraham Lincoln's Gettysburg Address, a newsreel, and the feature film *The Third Degree* (1926).[44]

Whiteman was such a hit that he was invited back for a second tour the following season, beginning with a six-week engagement at the Paramount in June 1927. Jack Partington was brought in from the Granada Theatre in San Francisco, where he had honed his skills producing shows for the playful bandleader Paul Ash each week. Based on the Ash model, Partington was to craft a new type of themed stage show for Whiteman each week, one that blended witty repartee, costumes, popular songs, and comedy. The idea was that "with little embellishment Whiteman's orchestra can serve as a road show in itself."[45] The band's second show was entitled "Rushia." Decked

out in Russian dress, Paul and the band performed a jazzed-up version of Tchaikovsky's "1812 Overture" as the centerpiece, and were accompanied in other routines by torch singer Ruth Etting (making her New York debut), "monologist" Charles Irwin, and a group of Russian dancers. The 50-minute live show also included a filmed trailer for the following week's Whiteman presentation, "U.S.S. Syncopation."[46]

The overwhelming success of these Whiteman shows inspired Sam Katz to shift direction. The unit shows by Anderson et al. were costly, with high production expenses each week and pricey salary lists for the extended performer contracts. Although profitable in the big metropolitan areas, they were too costly for smaller houses, where weekly grosses were limited. In the summer of 1927, Publix announced a big shake-up: the larger unit

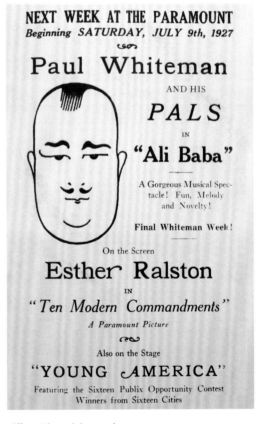

Paul Whiteman's six-week run at the Paramount Theatre in June and July 1927 presented a different themed show each week, with different song selections. The opening week was "Rhapsodyland," featuring George Gershwin's *Rhapsody in Blue* as the centerpiece. Subsequent themes were "Rushia," "U.S.S. Syncopation" (the Navy), "Jazz a la Carte," "Fireworks" (for the Fourth of July), and "Ali Baba," in which Whiteman and his band wore "tropical garb."

A band shares the stage with dancers and other talent in an unidentified "band unit" Publix production designed by Herman Rosse, ca. 1928.

shows were to be cut back, more secondary or Class B units were to be devised for smaller houses, and the new "band unit" productions under Jack Partington's supervision were to be expanded. Although Paul Whiteman and his band were receiving $12,000 per week for a 44-week engagement (for a record-breaking total of $528,000), the idea was that the average jazz band could be obtained from $1,000 to $1,500 per week—a small fraction of the cost of the high-end unit shows, which reportedly ran to as much as $25,000.[47]

What was once novel and hugely popular became a burden on Publix as production costs soared. Anderson's annual contract was renewed through the next season, but his commitment was decreased to ten shows annually. Performers were hired on indefinite contracts, extended only if the shows proved themselves profitable. And the ambition of the stage settings was scaled back to more simple backdrops. John Murray Anderson was once the star producer of live entertainment for Publix, with his name above the title; now, audiences wanted more. For just 99 cents—a fraction of the cost of a Broadway show—one could see "artists that it would have been impossible to

otherwise see," declared the Publix publicity. "Such stars as Gilda Gray, Paul Whiteman, Eddie Cantor, Borah [sic] Minevitch, the Duncan Sisters and others have appeared behind the footlights of Publix theaters."[48]

Anderson combatted the negative press of some of his more highbrow early efforts with faster pace and less story. "Highlights," for example, from December 1927, contained "ten distinct numbers, all of which are perfectly dove-tailed for one-half hour of super speed and crackerjack entertainment."[49] With the new band unit policy, the musicians were brought onstage to become an integral part of the show, an idea Anderson had first pioneered with Vincent Lopez and his Orchestra in the 1924 Greenwich Village Follies.

After three years and over fifty shows, Anderson left Publix at the end of 1928.[50] The trade papers blamed creative differences for his departure. Anderson "is a little dissatisfied with the manner in which production overhead has been cut and how artists are engaged by others and tossed at him," reported Billboard.[51] But Anderson's heavy drinking was undoubtedly also to blame. Anderson's alcoholism had worsened during

Unit show manuals helped local theatres promote the show, and typically included program information, profiles of the cast, publicity photos, catchlines, and ideas for tie-ins and lobby displays.

his three years with Publix, and frequently caused him to miss rehearsals; he was sometimes absent from work for weeks.[52] Anderson's last Publix unit show that year was "The Magic Rug"—"A Pilgrimage to the Mecca of Entertainment."[53]

Murray Anderson's Almanac

With his work for Publix behind him, Anderson's new revue, *Murray Anderson's Almanac* (1929), was practically a dry run for *King of Jazz*, with many of the same production personnel, structuring, and deficiencies. It allowed the director to set aside the constraints of the unit shows in favor of a production that better reflected his personal aesthetic. Like *What's In A Name?*, it was produced independently, partly financed by Anderson personally, with additional funding coming from banker and patron of the arts Otto Kahn, among others. Originally budgeted at $75,000, the production costs snowballed to $180,000 following delays caused by Anderson's perfectionism. "If something wasn't right," remarked

Anderson's frequent stage manager Carlton Winckler, "Murray would just stop, bang, right there and he'd work on it until we got it right—might take all night."[54]

The almanac theme provided a calendar structure for the revue—each new act would be introduced on a new page of the almanac—as well as a formula for subsequent editions, should the show prove a hit. And Anderson's penchant for history and progress was in full swing, as each successive routine would help demonstrate the development of the revue format from 1880 to 1930. The show's subtitle was "A Revusical Comedy of Yesterday—Today—Tomorrow."

Following criticisms that his previous shows lacked humor, Anderson brought in a host of comic writers and satirists to provide amusing inserts and "blackouts" between the larger musical comedy acts. Harry Ruskin wrote many of these original sketches, while other skits were adapted from existing comic material by Rube Goldberg, Ring Lardner, and *New Yorker* cartoonist Peter Arno. "There is about 70 per cent comedy in the revue," Anderson assured his audience. "The public wants to laugh today; when they pay for a theatre ticket

Herman Rosse's early design drafts for *Murray Anderson's Almanac* used the almanac book motif to introduce each act. Despite his initial involvement, Rosse's work was not used in the completed production when it eventually opened in July 1929.

Jack Yellen and Milton Ager wrote songs for three Broadway shows in the 1920s, *What's In A Name?* (1920), *Rain or Shine* (1928), and *Murray Anderson's Almanac* (1929). The songwriters entered the movies in 1929 with the theme song for First National's *Glad Rag Doll*, starring Dolores Costello.

MEET THE WRITERS
OF THE SONGS YOU SING

JACK YELLEN • *MILTON AGER*

Here's A Partial List Of Their Successes

AIN'T SHE SWEET?	MY PET	I WISH I HAD MY OLD GAL
CRAZY WORDS—CRAZY	MAMA GOES WHERE PAPA	BACK AGAIN
TUNE (Vo-do-de-o)	GOES	SHE KNOWS HER ONIONS
I WONDER WHAT'S BECOME	LOVIN' SAM	ARE YOU FROM DIXIE?
OF SALLY	LOUISVILLE LOU	A YOUNG MAN'S FANCY
FORGIVE ME	HARD-HEARTED HANNAH	EVERYTHING IS PEACHES
IF YOU DON'T LOVE ME	HULA LOU	DOWN IN GEORGIA
DREAM KISSES	BIG BAD BILL	FRECKLES
IS SHE MY GIRL-FRIEND?	HARD-TO-GET GERTIE	DOWN BY THE O-HI-O
COULD I? I CERTAINLY	SHE DON'T WANNA	I'M WAITING FOR SHIPS
COULD	CHEATIN' ON ME	THAT NEVER COME IN
I STILL LOVE YOU	ARE YOU SORRY?	JOHNNY'S IN TOWN

And The Hits From " RAIN OR SHINE "

" YELLEN & AGER HITS " ARE PUBLISHED BY
— AGER, YELLEN & BORNSTEIN INC. —
MUSIC PUBLISHERS
745 SEVENTH AVE   NEW YORK

they want more than mere beauty."[55] The show was headlined by popular vaudeville comedians Trixie Friganza and Jimmy Savo, while the rest of the cast was fleshed out with the kind of talent Anderson had drawn upon during his years with Publix: adagio dancers, a novelty drumming act, and the "suave impeccable magician" Fred Keating as master of ceremonies.[56]

For the score, Anderson re-teamed with songwriting duo of Jack Yellen and Milton Ager, whose knack for musical comedy was well-suited to the project. The pair had worked in collaboration for more than ten years, cementing their partnership in 1922 with the creation of the music publishing company Ager, Yellen & Bornstein Inc. Yellen and Ager are perhaps best remembered today for two Tin Pan Alley standards, "Ain't She Sweet" (1927) and "Happy Days Are Here Again" (1929), the latter of which was adopted as the presidential campaign song for Franklin D. Roosevelt in 1932. For Anderson's revue Yellen and Ager wrote seven new songs, the most enduring being "I May Be Wrong (But I Think You're Wonderful!)," sung by Friganza and Savo, which combined "a good satirical lyric" with "an ear-pleasing melody."[57]

Almanac opened for a two-week "try-out engagement" at the Colonial Theatre in Boston in July 1929, before moving on to Erlanger's in New York in August.

Variety was surprised by the show's lavish expenditure and big cast, which the reviewer had anticipated would be "merely another one of those summer 'things' along the lines of a glorified Publix unit."[58] *Billboard* thought the revue "a good piece of entertainment," although it was "seldom outstanding." Despite Anderson's efforts, many of the comic scenes failed to muster the desired laughs. "One wonders what happened when it came to selecting the sketches. With one exception … the blackouts are of the stereotyped, smoking room variety and without trace of intelligent humor."[59]

Murray Anderson's Almanac closed after a disappointing 69 performances. The show had opened during a heatwave, and according to Anderson was building up to capacity business when the money simply ran out. It became another one of the director's expensive flops, which ultimately lost him a lot of money. He had invested much of his own capital in *Almanac* and other draining ventures. "I fell behind in the rent of my [Fifth Avenue] apartment and owed a considerable amount to various tradesmen."[60]

Then, unexpectedly, in September 1930, when Anderson was almost at a dead loss, L. B. Metzger of Universal Pictures called. Would Anderson be willing to go to Hollywood to direct "The King of Jazz Revue" with Paul Whiteman? Florenz Ziegfeld was the studio's first choice to direct this reinvigorated project, but he turned the offer down. Whiteman then suggested Anderson. "Will you take the job?" enquired Metzger over the phone.[61] Despite Anderson's lack of experience with the movies, his terms were accepted, and he soon found himself on a train to California, about to begin his biggest production yet.

Concept art by Herman Rosse for
"The Melting Pot of Music."

Chapter 5

THE KING OF JAZZ REVUE

With the signing of John Murray Anderson on September 7, 1929, planning for *The King of Jazz Revue* moved into high gear. While the studio had lost months trying to convince Paul Whiteman he should be an actor as well as bandleader, Universal wanted Anderson to do what he did best—create a musical revue in the theatrical style, with top stage performers. After consultations with Whiteman, Universal signed Anderson for a ten-week minimum, to start in Universal City on September 28, 1929.

That year's *Murray Anderson's Almanac* had budgeted $500 per week for Anderson's services, and had the studio performed a little research, they would have learned that his significant personal investment in the show was a dead loss. Anderson's $2,500 weekly salary to direct *King of Jazz* was high even by Hollywood standards, as his name and reputation did not mean much outside New York theatrical circles. A year earlier John Ford had achieved the same salary, but only after 14 years in the business and a track record of successful films. But Whiteman had director approval, so the studio did not have much choice.[1]

Whiteman had arrived back in New York from the Coast on August 31, and had a light schedule, with a six-week engagement at a Long Island supper club, the weekly Old Gold radio broadcasts, and some recordings. Soon after returning, Bix Beiderbecke fell ill at a recording session, and on September 15 Whiteman and violinist Kurt Dieterle took the cornetist to Grand Central Station to take a train to his hometown of Davenport,

Iowa. Although Whiteman kept him on salary into 1930, Beiderbecke never fully recovered, and died the next year.

Between signing with Universal and his departure for Los Angeles, Anderson had two weeks of intense preparation, meeting daily with Whiteman and the studio's sales head, Lou B. Metzger.[2] Painfully aware of how much had been invested in the project already with nothing to show for it, Junior Laemmle joined the conversation with an 800-word telegram, stating the film "must be outstanding revue," but urging caution over "such unheard of expenditures."[3]

Junior suggested Anderson consider a long list of performers, including Ann Pennington, the Duncan Sisters, Fred and Adele Astaire, Winnie Lightner, Charlotte Greenwood, Ruby Keeler, Zelma O'Neal, Jack Buchanan, W. C. Fields, Bert Wheeler, and the team of Eddie Jackson and Jimmy Durante. These names were top artists in the Broadway and West End theater and vaudeville, and would have demanded much higher salaries than the performers Anderson had in mind.

Anderson's contract covered his direction of a "musical review, musical comedy or musical drama," but by the choice of director, the film was going to be a plotless revue. "Time and again on the stage, for example, we have started off with the thought in mind that we must have a plot for a revue," Anderson told the *Los Angeles Times*. "We feel the need of it, have always felt the need of it, and again and again we have had a sort of plot written out. But we have always thrown it away before we have gone very far with the actual production."[4]

On September 21, while still in New York, Anderson wrote a reassuring letter to Junior. "Although the whole production is still in its first chaotic state, I think already it is beginning to assume some definite form." While a movie might start by identifying stars and then shaping the material to their strengths, a revue took a different route, first choosing the musical numbers and comedy material. "To merely engage performers and specialties at random would only burden the production with an unnecessary overhead. It would be like casting a play before the play had been written."[5] The revue would center around Whiteman, with dancers, singers, and comedy sketches. But Anderson recognized what would be one of his biggest challenges—"the actual tying into the picture of Mr. Whiteman and his orchestra, the using of them in an effective way throughout the entire Revue."

Anderson used the lengthy letter to reinforce his support for his creative team. Herman Rosse's skills as a stage designer and architect ensured that his creations could be built, and "you will find that he will reduce the work of your technical staff to a minimum." Dance director Russell Markert had the advantage of many years of choreographing dancers for live shows before motion picture audiences and seeing the reactions; "the necessity of staging an entirely new show every week has taught him to work quickly."

Anderson was identifying revue sketches, "the majority of them new, several of them that have been successfully used, but which are unknown to the picture audiences." Six to eight short sketches would suffice, "and I shall have many more to choose from" to review with Junior. "Mr. Rosse and I, meantime, will endeavor to hit upon a unified and novel method of presenting them before the camera." Junior recognized the value of the comedy sketches, but planned to cast a skeptical eye on them; as he wrote in a telegram to Metzger, "[I] confidentially understand this [is] Andersons weakness."

Licensing the *Rhapsody*

Universal's executives were still ambivalent about the value of *Rhapsody in Blue* for the film, but Whiteman had no doubt. Robert H. Cochrane thought Gershwin might be just as valuable on the production as a songwriter. He wrote Junior from New York of his difficulty in getting Whiteman to sign a contract revision; Cochrane "promised [to] make every effort [to] get Rhapsody and Gershwin [to] do score" at his meeting with Gershwin on September 6.[6] Metzger thought that including *Rhapsody in Blue* would "absolutely assure pictures tremendous

success."[7]

Junior was concerned about the cost; after all, the original contract with Whiteman obligated the bandleader to acquire the music for the film.[8] And he did not agree that the success of the film would be based on this one number. Throughout this exchange, the studio's executives were sensitive about unnecessarily alienating Whiteman. Finally, Junior concluded, if "you really feel will get money back perhaps should go ahead … suggest you cable CL."[9] The studio was negotiating not with Gershwin, but Max Dreyfus, the head of his music publisher, Harms, Inc., who held firm on his fee of $50,000. No single piece of music had ever cost as much for a film, but Dreyfus reasoned that in other cases the increased profile from being in a film raised sheet music sales or royalties from record sales, which was unlikely with this piece.[10]

Once Gershwin turned down the opportunity to write songs for the film, Anderson supplemented songwriter Mabel Wayne with frequent Anderson collaborators Jack Yellen and Milton Ager, well known for "Ain't She Sweet" and "Glad Rag Doll."

Motion Picture Revues

Anderson used M-G-M's *The Hollywood Revue of 1929* as a point of comparison to describe what he hoped to achieve. The film offered a galaxy of M-G-M stars, specialties, dancers, and a ballet, with memorable songs and some sequences in two-color Technicolor. No one thought it was cinematic; *Variety* noted, "It's a revue from gong to gong with the audience proscenium arch conscious all the way... no semblance of story and considering cast nobody is going to care." Anderson preferred the second half; "they departed somewhat from the technique of the stage, and employed picture technique." For Universal he would build on the stage material "to try and make it in every sense of the word a picture and not a stage revue."[11]

The Hollywood Revue of 1929 was on its way to becoming M-G-M's most profitable release in the 1929–30 season. Counterparts from other studios did not take long to arrive, with Warner Bros.' all-star *The Show of Shows* (1929) starting production in July. It followed the same model, including a Master of Ceremonies and curtains to open and close acts; *Variety* wryly noted, "what it lacks in originality and sparkle it makes up in expense."[12] More revues entered production that fall for release in the spring of 1930. Fox Film's *Happy Days* (1930) used a thin framing story about putting on a benefit show to present music and comedy acts. *Paramount on Parade* (1930) had

PAUL **WHITEMAN'S**

KING OF **JAZZ**

ALL
QUIET
ON   THE
WESTERN
FRONT

PICTURES
NOT
PROMISES

With an unprecedented cast, featuring Louis Wolheim, with John Wray, Lewis Ayres, Owen Davis, Jr., William Bakewell, Ben Alexander, Walter Brown Rogers, Slim Summerville, and Joan Marsh.

ERICH M. REMARQUE'S astounding war novel . . . the greatest-selling best seller of all time . . . is now in production. . . . And when it comes out of the cutting room . . . after Maxwell Anderson and George Abbott have ceased their literary labors . . . after Lewis Milestone has given his last megaphone direction . . . it will be a picture that nobody will ever forget . . . a picture that will go down in history as a drawing card that nothing has ever equalled. . . . This sensational human interest story, translated into virtually every language, syndicated in newspapers everywhere . . . will get the BIGGEST MONEY any picture ever got for anybody, anywhere . . . That's one of of the things we mean by GREATER UNIVERSAL.

GET yourself set for the biggest news you've ever heard since the advent of the audible screen . . . for Paul Whiteman's King of Jazz Revue will be a startling new kind of entertainment . . a continuous innovation . . a luxury of song, dance, music and joy . . . Think of PAUL WHITEMAN, the King of Jazz himself, and his whole band, doing their stuff . . . including Whiteman's own interpretation of George Gershwin's Rhapsody in Blue · Songs composed by such famous songsmiths as Ager and Yellen . . . Mabel Wayne . . . Billy Kent, musical comedy star . . . Grace Hayes, radio, night club star . . . John Murray Anderson—producer of six Greenwich Village Follies and "Almanacs" . . . Herman Rosse doing the settings . . . Russell Markert Dancers . . . The Sisters G, European dancing and singing sensation . . . Tommy Atkins Sextette . . . more big names being added every day . . . and practically every Universal star and featured player . . . John Boles . . . Laura La Plante . . . Joseph Schildkraut . . . Mary Nolan . . . Barbara Kent . . . Kathryn Crawford . . . and about a million of the best-looking chorus girls you ever saw . . . The whole Universal studio force is burning up with enthusiasm over this one . . . Because it's another indication of the GREATER UNIVERSAL.

PICTURES
NOT
PROMISES

GREATER UNIVERSAL'S NEW SELLING SEASON STARTS NOW !

Universal heavily promoted the first season of features from Junior Laemmle, as in this advertisement in the December 28, 1929 issue of *Exhibitors-Herald World*. Expectations were set high for these two features; here the studio is asking to be evaluated on its results, not its advertising.

no plot and several MCs, and its segments played much like self-contained short films, with a variety of style and pace from the participation of 11 different directors. But Universal's *King of Jazz* would be a different type of revue.[13]

Universal was the only studio to make what was effectively a revue around a star with no established screen personality. With John Murray Anderson stage productions, the show was the star. But Anderson himself recognized that "I was confronted with the problem of making a hero out of a band of musicians. And there is probably nothing so dull as showing musicians sawing away on instruments, particularly in a picture."[14] The acts that Anderson recruited were excellent, and far more talented at dancing and singing than most of Universal's contract stars, who specialized in dramas and comedies. But these acts and performers meant nothing to film audiences; they would have been relegated to short subjects at other studios. Universal was going to turn the *Hollywood Revue* model upside-down by producing a big-budget revue that did not showcase its stars but instead sidelined them

to short comedy sketches. Of course, the other studios didn't have Paul Whiteman—but would that be enough?

Leaving New York

Anderson delayed his departure to California until Carl Laemmle returned from Europe on October 1, and they held a conference the following day. Anderson prepared a long list of potential acts and was considering whether they would "constitute good picture material." Each of the dancers "has some particular trick that has pictorial value or a trick that is particularly effective in sound." While some of the acts appeared in the film, Anderson's list of favorites primarily serves as a reminder of other directions the film could have taken, with prima donna Grace Moore, blues singer Marion Harris, dancers Bill Robinson and Florence O'Denishawn, and comedians Molly Picon, Charlotte Greenwood, and Will Fyffe.[15]

It had been a productive month, with signings of

The East Coast premiere of *The Hollywood Revue of 1929* on August 14, 1929 at the Astor Theatre in New York City's Times Square.

eccentric dancer Paul Howard (from the Broadway musical *Follow Thru*), William Kent, Charles Irwin, Grace Hayes (most recently headlining at the Palace Theatre), vaudeville dancers Nell O'Day and the Tommy Atkins Sextet, and an act that Carl Laemmle had seen in Germany, the Sisters G. The biggest recruitment was choreographer Russell Markert and his 16 precision dancers at a combined $2,750 per week, for a six-week minimum. Also hired were two Anderson revue veterans, writer Harry Ruskin and cartoonist Wynn Holcomb.

From Universal's contract players, Anderson was counting on John Boles, Joseph Schildkraut, and Mary Nolan, while keeping Laura La Plante, Hoot Gibson, Ken Maynard, and child actor "Sunny Jim" in mind.

Arriving at Universal City

A week after his meetings with Laemmle, Paul Whiteman saw Anderson and Herman Rosse off by train. Anderson arrived at Universal City as a complete outsider, with a month to prepare before his Whiteman revue was scheduled to start production. A luncheon welcomed him to Universal City, and he found his offices overflowing with flowers.

Junior Laemmle, who had been promoted from heir apparent to heir just months before, had an office to match his new status. Visitors walked through outer offices where people waited for their appointments, secretaries typed documents, and clerks filed them. Once inside, a visitor found "solid mahogany, Persian rugs, rich red velvet drapes, red leather chairs, tapestries against mahogany paneled walls. A portrait of Laemmle Senior, with his benedictory smile, facing the desk of his successor."[16] On an average day 2,000 people came to work at his studio. Junior initially showed more interest in Anderson's fashion sense in shoes and clothes, but the director himself soon gained respect for the producer, recalling "there were few more alive or astute executives than the young head of Universal Pictures."[17]

Junior introduced Anderson to Paul Fejos. Fejos had been injured on the set of *La Marseillaise* on October 19 and was released from the hospital after an X-ray identified no broken bones. As another director had taken over his picture, Fejos was available to be Anderson's co-director. Many years later, Fejos would state that he saw the revue film as beyond his abilities. "I didn't want to do the picture, but I didn't dare to say, 'I refuse to do it.'"[18] Anderson did not want him to do it either, recalling delicately that "his ideas did not completely coincide with mine." Anderson chose as his assistant Robert Ross, a long-time fixture at the studio, who had worked on many big pictures, including *The Phantom of the Opera* (1925) and *Show Boat* (1929). As assistant director for *King of Jazz*, Ross would become Anderson's sounding board for

what could be achieved at the studio, worked with all the departments to ensure that every resource was provided, and became the director's trusted ally.

Six stages at Universal City had been constructed or retrofitted with incandescent lights for panchromatic or Technicolor film, and outfitted with baffling for sound recording. Stages 10 and 11 were modest size, three others offered 70 by 150 feet of space apiece for sets, and Stage 12, the enormous *Broadway* stage, measured 150 by 200 feet, "occupied by the big Cafe Set originally constructed for the Whiteman Revue."[19] Junior asked Anderson to incorporate the "cabaret set completed for first story [that offers a] wonderful background."[20] At Junior's request Anderson and Rosse considered how the set could be adapted, and Rosse prepared some concepts, with the garish walls covered with draperies and new materials moved into place. While the set might have worked for a narrative story, it was not what Anderson aimed for, and the set was simply too inflexible.

Following a cross-country trip that received much less attention than the "Old Gold Special" earlier in

Carl Laemmle Jr. at his desk in Universal City, circa 1930.

"King of Jazz Revue" Celebrities
(Biographies reproduced from *Universal Weekly*, November 16, 1929, with minor errors corrected)

Grace Hayes (1895–1989)

Grace Hayes is known to millions of radio fans as well as to musical comedy and vaudeville devotees for her beautiful voice and her stage ability. She is admirably suited to talking pictures, and will prove a welcome addition to "The King of Jazz Revue" because of her ready-made audience.

Miss Hayes, a native of San Francisco, went on the stage at the age of fourteen. She made her first Broadway hit in *The Passing Show of 1926* and followed it up with *Rainbows*, *The Merry Whirl*, and several of the Charles Dillingham shows. During the past couple of years, Grace Hayes has been devoting the greater part of her time to radio work. Her role in the Whiteman revue is her first picture venture.

Twin Sisters G (Eleanore Knospe, 1909–1997 and Karla Knospe, 1910–?)

Recruited from the European stage, the twin Sisters G add sophistication and unique Continental flavor to the Paul Whiteman revue. Only eighteen years old, the exotic twins, Carla and Eleanor, have created a furore for the last two years in Paris, London, Berlin, Vienna, Biarritz and Barcelona. They danced in Mistinguett's revue at the famous Moulin Rouge in Paris, and have appeared in the smartest revues in London, such as the Café de Paris, the Kit Kat Club, the Bat Club, the Savoy and the Carleton. The Sisters G, whom critics compare to the Dolly Sisters, have danced before the crowned heads of Europe and always receive ovations wherever they appear.

"The King of Jazz Revue" is their introduction not only to motion pictures but to America as well. They were discovered three years ago by Lincoln Eyre, noted *New York Times* correspondent in Berlin, and were signed up by William Morris, Jr., under whose auspices they came six thousand miles to appear in "The King of Jazz Revue."

The mystery surrounding the reason for calling the lovely dancers the "Sisters G" still remains unsolved. The twins refuse to disclose the meaning and significance of the cryptic "G." and their agent, William Morris, is completely in the dark about the mystery.

[Despite Universal's claims, The Sisters "G" (Eleanore and Karla Knospe) were not twins. They were born to Dr. Horst Wilhem and Margarete Knospe in Germany. There was also a third sister, called Ines, born in 1908, who briefly appeared as part of the act. Their mother remarried in 1921, and the sisters used the "G" from their new stepfather, Georg Gutöhrlein, for their stage name. The Sisters G remained in Hollywood after *King of Jazz* completed production, appearing in *Recaptured Love* (1930), *Kiss Me Again* (1930), and *God's Gift to Women* (1931), all made for Warner Bros./First National. The part-Jewish sisters became U.S. citizens in 1933, after the Nazi Party came to power in Germany. In the late 1930s they married and settled in Sweden.]

One of Herman Rosse's first tasks was attempting to re-dress the cabaret set that had been constructed for Paul Fejos's unrealized version of *King of Jazz*.

the year, Whiteman reported at the studio on Friday, November 1. The rest of the band reported for rehearsals a week later. The band members retrieved their cars from storage, and the special Fords with the Whiteman caricature on the spare-tire cover were soon running around town. John Murray Anderson spent $9,000 on a custom-made Cord car from the Auburn Automobile Company. It served its purpose by attracting attention even in a city of conspicuous consumption; the chauffeur-driven car "stopped traffic wherever it went," Anderson recalled.[21]

"A Fable in Jazz"

Back in New York, Anderson had originated the idea of using an animated cartoon to show how Paul Whiteman became "The King of Jazz." An early list of ideas for the film includes a place for "Birth of the Jazz King" and the idea of "Jazz babies in nurses hands." Rosse sketched out five scenes in detail—the birth of Paul Whiteman, the infant Paul (complete with mustache) showing an early interest in music, young Paul kicked out of the house by his father, Paul receiving accolades as an orchestra leader, and the appreciation of his aging, proud parents. This narrative did not have much tension or character development, but might have worked well with narration and peppy accompaniment by the Whiteman orchestra.[22]

Also prepared, though not with the same amount of detail, was a second, much darker storyboard, beginning with the birth of baby Paul (again with mustache), a sad and smoky Tin Pan Alley before the advent of jazz, an adult Whiteman as the cook combining different ingredients into the melting pot, and a joyous Broadway transformed by Whiteman's music.

Anderson had engaged his close friend Wynn Holcomb to design the scrapbook and the cartoon.[23] Holcomb had gained fame as a caricaturist, and was featured in innumerable "how to become an artist" ads in popular magazines. Holcomb's primary work appeared in magazines and newspapers, but his theater work included a curtain of caricatures of stage critics for the annual Irving Berlin showcase, the *Music Box Revue*. Holcomb had worked on the most recent *Almanac* revue, designing the intermission curtain and some of the scenes. He wrote and provided the design for the witty cartoon, but the result is in the style of the other cartoons from Universal that season. Signing his work "Wynn," Holcomb also designed the film's scrapbook pages with caricatures of Whiteman.

Earlier in 1929, Universal stopped contracting out cartoon production and created an in-house animation unit. Walter Lantz was hired to set up the studio, and he brought in head animator Bill Nolan, who was renowned for his rubbery, non-realistic drawing. "We painted [the cels] red and green," Lantz recalled. Technicolor "gave us a color chart, but we couldn't get anything. We could get a brown out of red and green, but that was it." As there were no color paints manufactured for animation use, Lantz's artists used commercial paints. The paint did not adhere to the cels, chipping off even as the cels were being photographed.[24] Anderson and *Universal Weekly*, the studio's magazine for exhibitors, described the cartoon as Holcomb's creation, although screen credit went to Lantz and Nolan.

Blackouts

Comedy writer Harry Ruskin arrived in Universal City in November. At the start of production, all attention was on the musical numbers, so Ruskin was loaned to Pathe Studios for two weeks. Ruskin had worked for many years with Anderson, whom he considered "brilliant." During that time, Ruskin recalled, "I wrote the comedy and staged all comedy scenes of four Broadway shows for him."

Blackouts served an important purpose in revues—played before the curtain, they could cover a scene change, while providing a respite before the next musical number. They often ended with a punch line while the stage went dark. Ruskin's theory of comedy was minimalist:

- Never give a good line to an unfunny man—if he's not a comic you've wasted good material.
- No long speeches—two typewritten lines are my

absolute limit for any speech except a summing up speech at the end of a story.[25]
- Eliminate every single unnecessary word.[26]

Ruskin would be credited with all of the dialogue and comedy treatment for *King of Jazz*, and the skits fit this pattern. He spent the remainder of the year and January outlining potential blackout comedy sketches.

Designing the Whiteman Bandstand

Herman Rosse was working on ideas about how to present Whiteman's orchestra for the cameras. The most important set after *Rhapsody in Blue* would be the big bandstand for Whiteman's orchestra. Anderson was adamant that having curtains and prosceniums as in the theater was trite, and he wanted to have new ways to present scene changes. The unusable cabaret set was exactly what Rosse wanted to avoid—a rigid hierarchical stage set which relied on a moving camera, distracting the audience from the music. Rosse found the motion picture studio liberating, as he wrote to his family back in New York. "The work itself is much more interesting than theater work as far as designing is concerned. You don't have to sacrifice so much to practical considerations."[27]

Most orchestras simply provided musical accompaniment, but this orchestra was the star of the show. In the theater the orchestra was either on stage dominating the visuals, in the back of the stage, darkened, with performers upstage, or in the pit. None of these options would be effective for this film. Separating the orchestra on either half of the stage with the performers in the middle might work at times, but the orchestra must be together in the same shot for at least part of each number. And then came Rosse's breakthrough—a moving bandstand that separates in the middle.

Rosse prepared a unique design, incorporating motifs from classical architecture, and designed to dazzle the eye, lacking a vanishing point or other visual references to distract the viewer. *Variety*'s fashion reporter visited the set, noting the "silver bandstand backed with a white scrim over black velvet curtains."[28] In Rosse's designs for most sequences of this film, sets served as backgrounds—glistening to reflect the light, but largely lacking color, so they did not divert attention from the performers.

Start of Production

King of Jazz officially started filming on Friday,

Unused concept art for "Birth of the Jazz King"
by Herman Rosse.

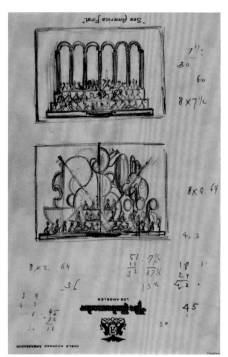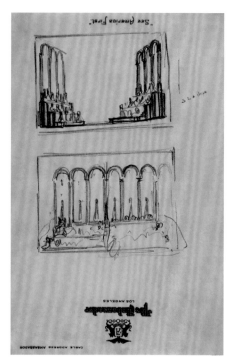

Herman Rosse's preliminary designs for the Whiteman Orchestra bandstand were sketched on stationery from the Ambassador Hotel, where Rosse and Anderson briefly stayed before finding more long-term accommodation in Los Angeles. The design in the lower part of the middle sketch emerged in the finale of "The Melting Pot of Music." November 1929.

November 15. Studios followed a six-day work week, and many long days would follow. Over half of the specialty acts were at the studio, with others either on call or on their way. The sixteen Markert dancers had been rehearsing for two weeks in the studio gymnasium with Anderson's associate James Dietrich on piano, working out the combination of music and precision dance routines with Russell Markert. While Anderson would rely on his back catalog of ideas for the film, Markert made a point of not reusing any of the choreography developed for the Paramount-Publix engagements. Additionally, Anderson selected eight showgirls from reportedly 2,000 applicants to appear as his "Hollywood Beauties."[29]

The production of *King of Jazz* would be spread over the lot, with sets under construction on several stages, and rehearsals underway on others. While a typical film required the principal players for nearly every scene, it was hoped that work on this film could occur in parallel, as each production number could be filmed as it was ready.

Many theater directors in Hollywood were ineffective, out of their element and manipulated by the agendas of the different departments at the studios, but Anderson avoided that trap. He earned the support of fellow creative staff by consulting them for their ideas, and exuded quiet confidence and decisiveness—a genius lacking arrogance.

"From the film point of view, he knew nothing about it," Technicolor cinematographer Ray Rennahan recalled, "but he could explain what he wanted definitely, not only to myself but to the art director, and to the costumers and everything."[30]

Ghosting

For Paul Whiteman, the music was his priority. The usual approach in 1930 was to photograph musical numbers live in performance, using multiple cameras in soundproof booths, microphones on the orchestra and stage, and an engineer mixing the sound during the performance. The loss of camera movement during the scene was offset by the ability of the editor to choose between different angles of the same performance. Occasionally production numbers were performed to playback, as when M-G-M restaged a musical number for *The Broadway Melody* (1929) and the performers mimed to the recording made during the first take.

With his extensive experience with Victor and then Columbia, Whiteman was dissatisfied with the prospect of live recording. Performing on a soundstage offered none of the acoustical control of a recording studio, but all of the added distractions of the film crew. For *King*

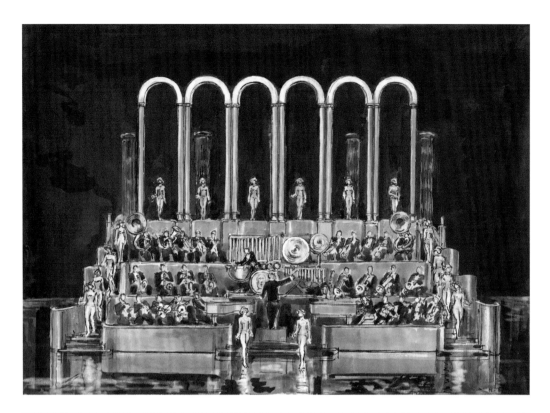

The bandstand—concept drawing (top), and as constructed on Universal's Stage 12 (below).

"King of Jazz Revue" Celebrities
(Biographies reproduced from *Universal Weekly*, November 16, 1929, with minor errors corrected)

Joan Marsh and George Chiles.

George Chiles (1903–1951)

With the signing of George Chiles for "The King of Jazz Revue" Universal secured one of the smartest ballroom dancers in New York. Chiles, who is a Harvard man (rare enough on Broadway), is well known among habitués of nightclubs like the Biltmore Cascades, Harry Richman's Montmartre, and the Casanova. Last year he danced with June in Hammerstein's *Polly*, a popular musical show.

George Chiles was born in Texas not so very long ago. He began his dancing career in Provincetown, Massachusetts. He appeared in John Murray Anderson's *Music Box Revue*, and since that time has been sought-after in the better night-clubs and roof theatres.

William Kent (1886–1945)

William Kent's name in the cast of "The King of Jazz Revue" assures plenty of comedy along with the brilliant array of singing, musical and dancing talent. Kent's famous comic interpretations have added pith to such musical comedies as *Battling Butler*, *Good Morning*, *Dearie*, *Rose-Marie*, *Lady, Be Good!*, *Ups-a-Daisy* and *Funny Face*. Kent will be the chief gag artist of the Paul Whiteman revue.

Born in St. Paul, Minnesota, William Kent deserted the family wholesale coffee house for a small repertoire company. A minstrel show, various roaming stock companies, parts in Henry Savage productions, and a comedy leap with Nora Bayes preceded Kent's regular appearance on the New York stage.

Jacques Cartier (1907–2001)

The acquisition of Jacques Cartier as a dancer in "The King of Jazz Revue" is particularly interesting in its relation to the birth of jazz, which many authorities trace to an African origin. No American dancer is more famous than Cartier for interpreting the throbbing tribal dances of the Congo. His Voodoo dance was first seen in a small theatre in Greenwich Village, later in the smart revue, *The Manhatters*, again in Hammerstein's *Golden Dawn*, and always when Cartier dances on the concert and vaude-ville stage.

Cartier was born in India, of British parents. Widely traveled, his knowledge of African dances is first-hand. When he came to America, he made an exhaustive study of Indian dances, particularly the Hopi tribal dances. Cartier has toured the Publix circuit and has been ballet master of the Cincinnati Civic Opera Company.

Russell Markert surrounded by his troupe, soon after arriving in Hollywood.

of Jazz, Whiteman said, "you can't get perfect sound conditions in a barn-like set while filming a scene."[31] Whiteman insisted that they pre-record all of the musical numbers, so he brought in E. T. White from Victor's recording studio in Camden, New Jersey, to supervise the sound recording during November and December.[32] Whiteman was pleased with the results of recording on 35mm film, considering it "many times more effective than disc recording," especially for the reproduction of the solo piano.[33]

The band would record in the mornings and then have the afternoons free. Anderson's arranger, James Dietrich, was impressed with Whiteman's skill: "Paul certainly had a lot of courage—it was a tough game. He had power over that orchestra—it was uncanny— with his baton. When Bargy or Hayton or Grofé would

conduct, it sounded like just any orchestra. Then Paul would get up there and they played like madmen."[34]

Prerecording offered the potential to free up the normally rigid camera, especially in shots with the *Broadway* crane, though this opportunity was seldom realized in the film. Instead, the recorded music from loudspeakers gave Anderson the freedom to direct the action in the musical numbers during photography, much like a silent film director. Anderson found he could "talk as much as I wanted to during shooting of the picture. Stage workers could make as much noise as they needed to; cameramen, technicians could all work undisturbed by the cramping necessity for silence. We were unhampered."[35]

Shooting any scene involved staging short segments photographed from specific angles to match a certain

The Paul Whiteman band on break from rehearsal at Universal City. Left to right: George Marsh (drums), Mike Pingitore (banjo), Andy Secrest (trumpet), Jack Fulton (standing), Bill Rank (trombone; with cigarette), and Harry Goldfield (trumpet).

number of bars of music. "With the sort of rhythm music in this picture, it was comparatively easy to get perfect synchronization," Anderson told *Photoplay*. "I defy anybody to detect, when *King of Jazz* is seen, that sound and sight were not shot simultaneously."[36]

The miming of the musicians to playback is generally excellent, especially for Whiteman's musicians, who had performed some of these pieces hundreds of times. However, sharp-eyed viewers have noticed that when Joe Venuti on violin and Eddie Lang on guitar play "Wild Cat" in the "Meet the Boys" number, Lang executes a 4-5 note descending run not matched by his fingers.[37]

Trick Photography

Anderson took advantage of the time before the start of production to meet with the technical experts at the studio. He and Universal's top cinematographer Hal Mohr hit it off, as did Anderson and cameraman Jerry Ash, a former magician. Ash was asked by Anderson "to make up a list of all the trick photography he had ever hoped to do in his life. [He] was filled with stunts he had

cherished for years. He came to us with a bag of tricks."[38] A typical way of staging a novelty number on film might be to have an MC pull out a prop, such as a shoebox and a pair of shoes, pretend that the band was inside, and then cut to a scene with the performers interacting with oversized props. That's exactly how the scene was staged in *Paramount on Parade* for the "Dancing to Save Your Sole" number featuring Nancy Carroll and Abe Lyman and his band.

For the introduction to the "Meet the Boys" sequence in *King of Jazz*, Ash staged a technical marvel. Whiteman enters the scene with a small bandstand and valise; then the band members climb out of the bag to a miniature bandstand that dissolves into the full-size set. Other sequences with multiple dissolves and mattes appeared in the "Monterey," *Rhapsody in Blue*, and "Melting Pot" sequences. Due to the limitations of Technicolor printing at this time, all of these effects had to be achieved in camera.

In the "Meet the Boys" number, Jerry Ash's trick photography creates the illusion that members of Paul Whiteman's band climb from a portmanteau bag and then assemble on a miniature bandstand.

All Quiet on the Western Front

Junior's other super-production began filming the week of November 24. *All Quiet on the Western Front* was a novel of the Great War by Erich Maria Remarque. An instant sensation when published in his native Germany in January 1929, the English-language edition was published in the United States on June 1, to equal acclaim. Universal exercised its option for film rights on July 5, and work started immediately on a screenplay. Junior considered director Herbert Brenon, whose *Beau Geste* (1926) had addressed some of the same themes of loss and sacrifice in war, and Lewis Milestone. Brenon wanted too much money, so Milestone was signed.

The cycle of war films had been revitalized by Paramount's *Wings* (1927), which both celebrated war and challenged its waste of lives, and now four major anti-war films were in production for release in the spring of 1930. Herbert Brenon had turned down *All Quiet* to direct *The Case of Sergeant Grischa* (1930) at RKO, based on the Arnold Zweig novel, with Chester Morris as a Russian soldier who is mistakenly executed as a spy. Howard Hughes' highly anticipated account of the war in the air, *Hell's Angels* (1930), had been in production since 1927, and was nearing completion. And the London stage hit *Journey's End*, about the despair of soldiers in trench warfare, was the first film by stage director James Whale.[39]

Production of *All Quiet* was planned for six weeks of filming, with a $891,000 budget. There would be many battle scenes, explosions, and sets, but no stars. It was to be the antithesis of the studio's experience with *King of Jazz*. Carl Laemmle gave full credit to Junior: "He decided that 'All Quiet on the Western Front' would make a great picture, purchased the rights, got his writers and director and went into production."[40] If Junior lacked any doubt, there was a lot of skepticism elsewhere, as *All Quiet* was called "Junior's End" by cynical observers.[41]

"King of Jazz Revue" Celebrities
(Biographies reproduced from *Universal Weekly*, November 16, 1929, with minor errors corrected)

Al Norman with two members of the Russell Markert Dancers.

Nell O'Day and the Tommy Atkins Sextet in "Laces and Graces" (1929), one of John Murray Anderson's unit shows for the Paramount-Publix circuit.

Al Norman (1906–1999)

Al Norman is well known to vaudeville followers for his clever eccentric dancing. He has toured over the Publix circuit, where his reputation has been steadily growing for the past two years.

His inclusion in the Paul Whiteman revue occurred through the enthusiasm of the Universal home office members who saw young Norman dance at their annual ball at the Astor Hotel in New York several weeks ago. The audience was so delighted with Norman's dancing and his unusually attractive appearance and personality that arrangements were made with the William Morris Agency for him to leave for Universal City at once to join John Murray Anderson's rapidly swelling ranks of talent. Al Norman comes from Chicago. He is one of the coming younger dancers whose ability will undoubtedly land him among the successful musical comedy and revue headliners before long.

[Al Norman appeared in several films while in Hollywood for *King of Jazz*: *New York Nights* (1929), *Paramount on Parade* (1930), *Good News* (1930), and the B-Western *Pardon My Gun* (1930).]

Tommy Atkins Sextet and Nell O'Day (1909–1989)

Among the vaudeville headliners who will add smartness to Paul Whiteman's talking, singing and dancing revue are the Tommy Atkins Sextet [Richard "Dick" Erskine, Toby Erb, Clayton Romler, Scott Jensen, Gilbert Herwood, and Robert Galer] and Nell O'Day. The act, which has played over the Publix circuit all through the country, derives its name from one of their favorite numbers, in which the sextet dress as typical Tommy Atkinses [slang term for a common soldier in the British army]. Nell O'Day is one of the most beautiful of vaudeville dancers, with a personality delightfully suited to the talking and singing screen. Miss O'Day and the Tommy Atkins Sextet are expert adagio dancers, and offer a versatile range of entertainment.

The Tommy Atkins Sextet and Nell O'Day have not yet appeared in pictures, and their debut in "The King of Jazz Revue" is eagerly awaited by their largest vaudeville following. The entertainment value of their act is well indicated by the fact that they contemplate going abroad next summer to dance at the Ambassadeurs nightclub in Paris, in the smartest revue intime in all of Europe.

Technicolor

By the time cameras rolled at Universal City in November, *King of Jazz* was the 13th all-color sound feature to enter production. Most earlier Technicolor features had production schedules of five or six weeks. No one expected that the Technicolor crew for *King of Jazz* would be engaged for nearly four months.

In black & white filmmaking, the wardrobe department and the art department could function independently, but with color photography it was necessary to carefully plan the colors in advance. Technicolor had devoted years to developing expertise in which colors reproduced well, and how a costume or set using particular colors would appear on screen. The two-color Technicolor process used red and green. Lacking a third component, there could be no true yellows, purples, or blues. Two-color photography was a precise art, and the company provided studios with an experienced crew and cameras. Natalie Kalmus, the ex-wife of Technicolor co-founder Herbert Kalmus, established the company's Color Control Department to consult with the studios over which colors would photograph properly. Technicolor's aesthetic was to "make a good picture of pleasant colors."[42] This was a pre-production role, as "color control people would come in and get the proper coloring on the sets, and they would be a go-between between the wardrobe department and the art department," cinematographer Ray Rennahan recalled.[43]

Technicolor had learned that any failed experiments would be blamed on them, so the company believed the advisor "should be given the privilege of choosing the colors of the walls, decorations, wall paper, etc. The same thing applies to the costumes." This was to support studio staff familiar with black & white photography, but new to color. "We must know and study the color

Assistant director Robert Ross, John Murray Anderson, Paul Whiteman (center), and cinematographer Ray Rennahan (facing the photographer), with two Technicolor cameras filming "My Bridal Veil."

relation between the sets, the furniture, the drapes and the costumes to obtain proper separation of values and harmony of color."[44]

Herman Rosse had been hired to design this film—in charge of both sets and costumes, roles that in film production were customarily assigned to two different department heads. Regardless of that responsibility, he was well-regarded and effective. Rosse was "a big gawky friendly guy, easy to get along with," James Dietrich recalled.[45] Rosse had not been impressed with the color films he had seen, saying that the standard Technicolor approach "created an over-rich and syrupy tendency" which tired the eyes by having to look at oversaturated colors. His plan was to emphasize color contrasts within the frame, using multiple variations of the same colors. Perhaps fortunately for her and Rosse, Natalie Kalmus was in Europe during the production, so it was left to one of her assistants to negotiate with Rosse.

The assistant Technicolor advisor's first meeting to discuss the colors for the "Bridal Veil" set was not propitious. "Very rough sledding with Rosse," he reported. "He is really an artist and doubtless will produce something out of the ordinary, but he is practically impossible at the present time to work with because of an unreasonable temperament." The next day he found Rosse "very affable," probably because of an intervention by Ray Rennahan, who ran some film for Rosse to explain different lighting effects.[46] There were still problems, however. Later that week he found that Rosse had commissioned pale yellow flowers for the bridesmaids' bouquets. "This, I discovered, quite by accident, with the aid of a suggestion from the wardrobe woman who seemed doubtful about Technicolor being able to produce a pale yellow."[47]

"My Bridal Veil"

Rosse's first set and costume designs were for the production number "My Bridal Veil." "I have gradually

Above: Herman Rosse and John Murray Anderson inspect costumes for the "Bridal Veil" production number. Behind them is a remaining section from the cabaret set constructed for the unrealized Paul Fejos version of the film.

Left: The principal set for "My Bridal Veil," with Jeanette Loff and Stanley Smith in the center.

completed quite a piece of work but no construction has begun on anything," Rosse wrote to his family. "Just a lot of activity with preparation of plans. So-called everything will begin at full speed on Monday." The staging for the film would be at a much greater scale than in the theater, Rosse remarked. "The brides will be first on the program with pages and bridesmaids this time!"[48]

Hoping Junior would still identify a role for him on the picture, Fejos was hanging around the production, amazed at the profligacy of Anderson's spending, imagining himself in Anderson's position. "Wherever we could spend money we tried desperately to do it. When the girl came over to me to okay some dresses, I would always say, 'It's too cheap. Back. Get some others.'" Yet Fejos had been an active participant in the over-produc-

tion of *Broadway* and then *La Marseillaise* for the studio. Recalling Anderson's film many years later, he recalled, "I remember we had a bridal number in it, in which Jeanette Loff walked up a long stairway to Whiteman's music and had a veil which was 110 feet long. It was Brussels lace. Just to spend the money somehow, because we didn't know what to do."[49]

Like many of the settings in *King of Jazz*, the environment that Rosse created is lavish, with painted wall curtains, a spectacular chandelier, and, as Anderson wished, largely empty. "Scenery properly should be merely a background, harmonizing with the theme of the number, or the situation, not obtruding or giving the audience more than a passing thought," Anderson told an interviewer in 1922. "You want your audience to concentrate their thoughts on what is being done on the stage, not on the setting, the lighting or even the costumes."[50] Rosse's monochromatic costumes are beautiful, in a restrained style and with detail of texture and pattern captured by the Technicolor camera.

The female lead announced for *King of Jazz* was Mary Eaton, who had appeared in several editions of the *Ziegfeld Follies* on Broadway in the early 1920s, and starred in two features produced at Paramount's New York Astoria studios, *Glorifying the American Girl* (1929) and *The Cocoanuts* (1929). Dropped by Paramount, she followed her new husband, director Millard Webb, to Hollywood. Anderson needed a female lead who had the talent and screen presence to support several of the big production numbers. Eaton was announced for the bridal number and a toe dance.[51] Before her contract was signed, however, there were increasing doubts that she could fill the role, and "an excess of temperament" sealed her fate.[52]

Young actress Jeanette Loff was recommended by Stanley Smith, who plays the groom. They had both been under contract at Pathe Studios, and together filmed a screen test for a proposed film musical of the Gershwins' *Treasure Girl*. Loff was not a trained singer, so Anderson taught her how to project to the microphone, "how to round her tones, how to warble from the throat and chest."[53] Whiteman took a liking to her voice and personality, and her youth, poise, and film experience, plus recording tests, got her the part.

Colored lighting for Technicolor photography

Technicolor used color filters for photography and color dyes for the prints, all subject to color shifts along the way from many sources, including the prisms in the camera and lighting on the set. To reduce variation, Technicolor applied an enormous amount of light, carefully chose colors for costumes and sets, and used lighting rather than color contrasts to distinguish actors from their background. If a wall needed to be a particular color, it would be painted that color rather than use colored light. Otherwise it was too likely that the color values of the projected light would shift between shots.

Rosse didn't like Technicolor's pastels, and tried to bring together combinations of costumes and sets that with color lighting would provide more intense colors on the screen. With his theatrical background, Anderson was familiar with using color gels on spotlights and floodlights. On November 7, Ray Rennahan ran some Technicolor footage for Rosse to explain different lighting techniques. The following day, Rosse met with Edward Estabrook, a former Technicolor cameraman who was now head of the company's camera department, to discuss using projected color on actors and sets. The Technicolor standard was to use white light. Rosse wanted the color to originate from the colored lights projected on a costume

Above: Installing the giant prop piano for the *Rhapsody in Blue* sequence. The huge piano was 40 feet long, 38 feet wide, and seven feet high, with a 30-foot keyboard—enough to seat five players. Each key was a foot wide and five feet long.

Left: Paul Whiteman bathed in red and green light as he stirs the giant melting pot of music.

or set. The Technicolor advisor for the production optimistically reported that "I think now that Mr. Rosse is convinced that color lighting is out."[54]

But Anderson and Rosse won out, and colored lighting was used throughout the film. Anderson confounded the electricians by continually referring to the various colored lights on the set by "pet" names. Instead of saying, for example, "can you bring up blue light 14 and lower red light 22," he'd say "can you bring up Ernest and lower Gertrude," Nell O'Day recounted to a friend. Every different colored light had a personal name assigned by Anderson, and it was up to the light operators to know them.[55]

Rhapsody in Blue in color

Anderson had met with George Gershwin several times in New York to learn if the composer had any visual references or ideas about how he wanted *Rhapsody in Blue*

staged. "Gershwin declared that the music was an abstraction: it had no narrative," Anderson told a reporter. The composer "had written it half-jestingly, employing a sort of 'melting pot' of modern themes in the classical form" with no concrete imagery.[56] Universal's contract with Gershwin licensed the work for recording "in synchronization with ballet performances (including—without being limited to—visual interpretation and pantomime)."[57] But an on-screen visualization of a Gershwin concert suite would have to wait until the 1951 motion picture *An American in Paris*, when Gene Kelly choreographed the title ballet to the music of Gershwin's 1928 tone poem.

To create visuals for the cinema screen, Anderson and Rosse discussed photographing the orchestra against a plain background to emphasize the musicians, instruments, and performance. After abandoning that approach, they focused on the audience response to the music, "illustrating the possible emotional reactions of a cross section of average and intellectual listeners to the

Herman Rosse's evocative concept drawing for the *Rhapsody in Blue* number was used to sell the staging to producer Carl Laemmle Jr. The end result realized in the film (overleaf) retained many of these original ideas.

Rhapsody."[58] After a cost analysis by the studio determined that the sequence would be too expensive, a more contained approach was chosen, focused on a giant piano.

During production Whiteman recognized the relationship between his work and the art direction, calling Rosse's design for the *Rhapsody* "music set to color."[59] The *Rhapsody in Blue* number uses green with silver highlights against a draped wall of a neutral gray/silver. A tree of glass and aluminum helps fill the space without distracting the eye. The suits worn by the musicians are dark green, with the costumes of the Sisters G and the Markert dancers a lighter green. This is the only number where the entire color scheme is shades of green, silver highlights, white, and gray. Red appears only as a natural color in the skin tones of the musicians and dancers.

The prologue for *Rhapsody in Blue* is one of the most striking visuals in the film. Years later Anderson recalled that "the result was so new and fantastic at the time that the sequence never failed to get applause whenever the picture was shown."[60] Jacques Cartier, glistening in black, dances on an enormous African drum, his shadow projected on a background screen, his muscles highlighted from red projected light from the right and green projected light from the left.

One of the challenges for the *Rhapsody in Blue* number was that audiences would naturally expect a blue color, while Technicolor's palette was orange-red and green. "The question continually comes up over this 'Rhapsody in Blue,'" Technicolor's advisor reported. "Had a talk with Mr. Anderson in which I advanced the opinion that the music was not intended to be interpreted as color but as emotion, something after the manner common to all blue songs. I explained that blue itself was in the category of happy color and suggested the effects obtained by drab—gray—shadows and general gloominess more in keeping with the 'blue' emotion. This was a new angle and has set Mr. Anderson to thinking about it."[61]

Anderson and Rosse thought about the meaning of blue, and decided to use an old trick to tease the eye. "Rosse and I made tests of various fabrics and pigments," Anderson wrote, and by using an all gray and silver background finally arrived at a shade of green which gave the illusion of peacock blue."[62]

There was some hope that Technicolor could simply adjust its printing to favor blue. A faulty print of a sequence in M-G-M's *Lord Byron of Broadway* (1930) should have been green, but turned out blue. The Technicolor engineers saw a positive side—"it holds out a hope for getting a good blue for our 'Rhapsody in Blue' for Universal's *Jazz King*," wrote George Cave, the technical director of the company's Hollywood plant. "As you

know, they have finally decided to shoot this sequence, and of course, when the picture is released, there will be a lot of criticism about the lack of blue in this sequence unless we can help it along some way on release prints."[63]

Socializing in Hollywood

Throughout their stay in Hollywood, the Whiteman musicians continued the weekly *Old Gold Hour* radio broadcasts every Tuesday. They went on the air at 6 p.m. so that the program would be heard at 9 p.m. on the East Coast. The band had only a few local performances, as Junior Laemmle wanted the players rested for their work at the studio, although that did not keep them from getting into trouble on their own time.

James Dietrich worked from a little office with a piano in the Whiteman Lodge. "Grofé would orchestrate the material and bring it to Whiteman Lodge," Dietrich recalled. "It was like a big living room [with] showers and dressing rooms in the back. They would all troop through drunk. They were even drunk on the air. They had to stop a recording session once!"[64]

November 14 was "Paul Whiteman Night" at the Blossom Room at the Roosevelt Hotel on Hollywood Boulevard, with Charles Irwin and bandleader George Olsen as masters of ceremonies. Whiteman's orchestra performed its hits, and then George Olsen's orchestra took over for the rest of the evening.[65] The following Monday was a private event at the Blossom Room, with Carl Laemmle Senior and Junior as hosts and Paul Whiteman and other artists to be featured in *King of Jazz* providing the entertainment. The attendees included Universal's star roster, and industry figures including Joseph Schenck, Tom Mix, and Sid Grauman.[66]

Introducing Jeanie Lang

Anderson's original requirements included a female ingenue, but it was January before Jeanie Lang was hired. She was a singer-dancer, working the vaudeville and motion picture theatre circuit. She had crossed paths with Nell O'Day and the Tommy Atkins Sextet during a ten-week engagement at the Oriental Theatre in Chicago. "Jeannie Lang [*sic*], peanut sized personality gal, gets a chance to frolic around with the m.c. in much the usual way," *Variety* reported. "Jeanie is the cute type that seldom tires, no matter how much seen."[67] In the film she introduced "My Bridal Veil," sang to Whiteman in the "I'd Like to Do Things for You" number, and sang with George Chiles in "My Ragamuffin Romeo."

Whiteman's musicians at play at Universal City, in costume for the "Bench in the Park" number.
Top: With their blue Ford cars. Bottom: On the *Show Boat* set.

Below: Ray Rennahan and crew photograph Jacques Cartier's Voodoo dance from above, with Paul Whiteman (center) observing. This angle was not used in the final film, as shown in the top image.

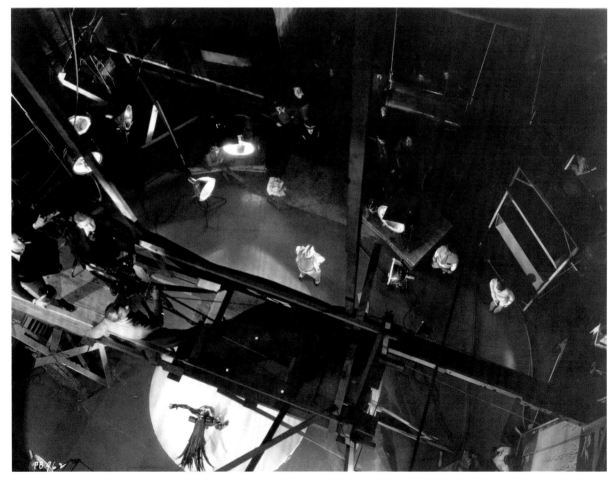

Whiteman's Players

The lost opportunities of *King of Jazz* include the participation of cornetist Bix Beiderbecke, who would have been in the film had it been made in early 1929, and the self-destructive activities of Bing Crosby, uneasy with the early stages of the fame he would soon achieve. Crosby and the Brox Sisters were at the studio on Saturday, November 2, for a rehearsal of "A Bench in the Park." Crosby had a drink or two before arriving and triggered a fight with Bobbe Brox, then walked to the Lodge to join a party celebrating the completion of the first week of production. "They had decorated the club building completely a la Halloween, with corn and pumpkins and straw and scarecrows with lights inside," Herman Rosse wrote. "Whiteman's orchestra played the music with solos by visitors, the 'Rhapsody in Blue' and so on. As far as parties go it was not a bad party but you know how much I care about parties."[68]

Driving a woman to her hotel after the party, Crosby crashed into another car, and was arrested. The next morning, James Dietrich found Paul Whiteman rushing through the hotel lobby—"Where can I get $500.00? One of our boys is in the can and needs bail."[69] After the trial the following week, Crosby arrived at the court in fashionable golfing attire, gave a snide response to the judge's question about his familiarity with the 18th Amendment, and was sentenced to sixty days for drinking. The studio managed to get Crosby transferred to a Hollywood jail, and after two weeks of negotiating, he was given a police escort from jail to the studio each day.

Whiteman was furious—his musicians put their professional responsibilities first—and he pulled Crosby's solo in the "Song of the Dawn" number. The beneficiary was more qualified for the part than Crosby. John Boles had been loaned to Warner Bros. for *The Desert Song* (1929), the first screen operetta, and then to Radio Pictures, where he starred opposite Bebe Daniels in the

Paul Whiteman and the members of his orchestra. This illustration accurately represented Whiteman's ensemble when this issue of *Motion Picture* magazine went to press in April, but by the time the June 1930 issue hit the stands, Whiteman had laid off ten band members, reducing the orchestra to 18 pieces. The layoffs included Bernie Daly, Roy "Red" Maier (reeds), Boyce Cullen (trombone), Ted Bacon, Otto Landau, Joe Venuti (violins), Eddie Lang (guitar), Min Leibrook (tuba), Bill Challis, Lennie Hayton (arrangers).

The Rhythm Boys perform at the Whiteman Lodge. Left to right: Harry Barris, Bing Crosby, and Al Rinker.

Ziegfeld musical *Rio Rita* (1929), which premiered in Hollywood on November 21. Eager to build up their contractee, the studio saw the change as an improvement. And as staged, the number is much more in Boles's range than Crosby's.

Studio finances

By November it was clear that the studio was going to run out of cash. In 1927, Carl Laemmle had borrowed $2.5 million to upgrade the studio. That loan would be due in full at the start of 1930. The previous year had been weak. In the quarter ending February 2, 1929, the company had written off $1,157,516 for losses from *Uncle Tom's Cabin* and *The Man Who Laughs*. *Broadway* was not meeting expectations. Universal was now producing two mammoth features simultaneously. Money was going out, but not enough money was coming in.

With *King of Jazz* and *All Quiet* in production at the same time, in mid-November Universal City laid off 70% of its regular employees, including everyone in the production area not working on those two pictures. This was estimated to save the studio about $250,000 per month. Untouched were the independent Hoot Gibson and Ken Maynard companies.[70] All was not lost, as studio casting directors hired about 100 laid-off assistant directors, electricians, grips, and actors as soldiers for *All Quiet*.[71]

Laemmle worked to close release deals for the studio's output for the upcoming year. Without a strong theatre affiliate, Laemmle's only leverage was the quality of his product. In October 1929 RKO booked Universal's product in the New York area and around the country.[72] In a complex deal not publicized at the time, RKO also agreed to advance $625,000 toward Universal's production costs on *All Quiet on the Western Front*, *Outside the Law*, and *East Is West*, with first claim on 60% of all revenue.[73] Laemmle was looking to unload all of Universal's theaters in a single transaction to Paramount's Publix subsidiary. In November the deal was "nearly set," with an expected closing by the end of the year.[74] Universal also took out a $1-million mortgage, maturing serially through 1935.[75]

On the day after Christmas, Laemmle signed to sell the company's Fort Lee film laboratory to Consolidated Film Enterprises, along with a contract to provide release printing for Universal for ten years.[76] In return Universal received a loan of $1 million, repayable at $100,000 per year.[77] The scrutiny of costs even reached the commissary. The studio restaurant was losing money, so it was sold to Maurice Fleckels, Laemmle's brother-in-law.[78]

Living in Hollywood

"I felt very much at home in Hollywood," Anderson recalled. "I took an apartment at the newly built and fashionable Colonial House. My rooms overlooked the patio of my old friend [costume designer] Howard Greer, on the floor below. We gave rival parties and I was even known to pour champagne from my darkened balcony upon Greer and Greta Garbo as they danced serenely by beneath me."[79]

Whiteman rented a house in the Hollywood Hills on Deronda Drive, at the edge of an 800-foot cliff, while his musicians rented rooms near the studio. On December 12, the orchestra performed at the 16th Annual Los Angeles Christmas Benefit at the Shrine Auditorium. Driving home after the Christmas Eve *Old Gold* broadcast, a car with three musicians was hit on Hollywood Boulevard and flipped three times. Saxophonist Bernie Daly was shaken up, but trombonist Boyce Cullen suffered a fractured nose and broken left arm, while violinist Mischa Russell had four broken vertebrae. Russell and Cullen missed two months of the filming while they recovered.[80]

The Melting Pot of Music

The finale of the film is "The Melting Pot of Music"—a production number that embodies scale and excess, representing both John Murray Anderson's strengths and weaknesses. "On its own terms, it's an exciting succession of sound and images," noted historian Richard Barrios, with the "song and dance of many (European) nations blended into a literal large pot."[81]

This view of jazz was common at the time: jazz was not the bringing together of African rhythms with European instrumentation and musical stylings, but unique to the modern day. "In speaking of jazz there is one superstition, and it is a superstition which must be destroyed," wrote George Gershwin in 1925. "This is the superstition that jazz is essentially Negro. The Negroes, of course,

take to jazz, but in its essence it is no more Negro than is syncopation, which exists in the music of all nations. Jazz is not Negro but American. It is the spontaneous expression of the nervous energy of modern American life."[82] And from this come the conflicting ideas in the production number that America is the melting pot of all nations and all cultures, and the role of African Americans in jazz music need not be recognized.

Anderson's use of the melting pot concept originated in his first show for Publix. In 1925 "The Melting Pot" featured a cast of 30 (including eight chorus girls and a six-member accordion band). Native Americans and then immigrants from eight countries presented folk dances and then Americanized jazz versions of the same dance. Each country was represented by a singer, two pages carrying standards, and a dancer. In the 1929 Paramount short based on his Publix show, the dancers perform a specialty number representing their nationality, and then for the finale emerge as Americans and join together for a hot jazz number.

Anderson "was the DeMille of the musical kind of thing," was the assessment of Ray Rennahan, who worked for both men.[83] And if DeMille was known for calculated excess, then with the 1930 staging, Anderson moved from offering the audience the best seat in the theater to giving the audience the opportunity to witness a pageant. For its 1930 incarnation, "The Melting Pot of Music" features one of the largest indoor sets ever constructed. Each country's sequence starts with 40 identically costumed performers on risers on either side of an enormous elevated melting pot. Behind the melting pot, noted a visitor, "are eight huge revolving pillars topped with eagles, also revolving. On either side of the stand are four additional pillars, also topped with eagles, also revolving. Parallel to them, but thirty feet to either side, are two more groups of four pillars. Directly in front of the set two immense cylinders belch varicolored smoke."[84] The final shots present at least 125 dancers on screen—most in gold-colored costumes—plus the 32-piece Whiteman orchestra emerging from behind the melting pot on a revolving stage.

Lighting this huge set were six rows of incandescent lights and sunlight arcs, requiring 20,000 amps. Although the lights were turned off between takes, the build-up of heat was tremendous. "We even warped the top of some of the pianos from the amount of heat coming out of those lights," cinematographer Hal Mohr recalled.[85] "The lights were so hot that no one could stand under them for more than a very few minutes or his/her hair would begin to smoke," Nell O'Day wrote. "We all gave ourselves many oil treatments during the shooting of the film because everyone's hair got completely dried out.

Herman Rosse's early designs for "The Melting Pot of Music."

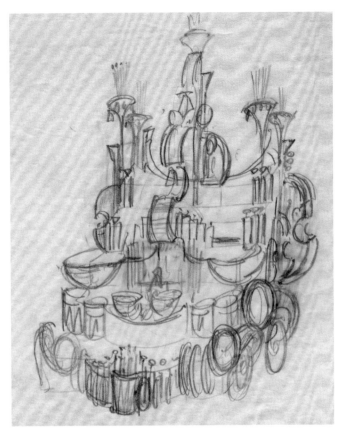

Finale of the "Melting Pot"—early concept
drawing and the final set with the *Broadway*
crane prominently in use.

The Sisters G said, 'Oh, Nellie we have such a hard time with our hairs!'"[86]

Filming the Blackouts

Finally, after the new year, with the major musical numbers either completed or underway, attention turned to Ruskin's work. During February, Anderson focused on editing, Herman Rosse returned to New York, and Ruskin and assistant director Bob Ross staged and filmed the sketches.

Many of Ruskin's sketches were based on the audience, though not necessarily the characters onscreen, knowing that the topic was illicit sex. Others took a simple idea—such as the World War I movie cliché of the promiscuous French farm girl—to its logical conclusion. One was credited to William Griffith, who had worked with Anderson on the 1929 *Almanac*, but the others were pure Ruskin. Although comedian and musical comedy star William Kent was a most unlikely film star, he managed to steal about every scene he appeared in.

Editing *King of Jazz*

Each segment of *King of Jazz* was edited under Anderson's oversight as filming progressed, so that Junior Laemmle could see the picture as it was coming together. Anderson and Robert Ross would be shooting one number, while another was in rehearsal as the sets were under construction, and still another was being planned while the song was being orchestrated and recorded.

Previous revues as well as narrative films tended to edit musical numbers in a similar fashion to the non-musical sections—cutting from long shots to medium shots with occasional close-ups. Anderson experimented; instead of cutting on action, he cut to the beat. "We tried to establish a new system whereby our photography danced to the rhythm of the music," he recalled. "Where a three-quarter bar of music was being sung we allowed it the full swing and at its conclusion jumped into another sequence with a similar beat."[87] As most of the sequences were photographed straight-on from the audience perspective, the film did not require sophisticated editing, but for Anderson, it was all about the pace. "I taught the cutters to work with a metronome, and only changed 'angles' at the beginning of a musical phrase," he recalled in his autobiography. "In this way, although an audience was not perhaps conscious of it, the film actually kept cadence with the music."[88]

Shooting *All Quiet*

As a realistic war drama in black & white with many location exteriors, *All Quiet on the Western Front* was the opposite of *King of Jazz* in most particulars, except for cost. The film quickly ran behind schedule, and Laemmle did not have the skills or possibly the will to rein in a strong-willed filmmaker. As with his approval of Whiteman's recommendation of John Murray Anderson, having selected his director, Laemmle felt his responsibility was to support his choice. Nonetheless, Junior persisted. "He is like a bulldog," Junior's father told a reporter. "Once he gets his teeth into a thing, he won't let go until the job is done. Once he makes up his mind to do a thing, he does it. Nothing will stop him."[89]

Milestone used the *Broadway* crane to capture the "over the top" battle sequence in *All Quiet*. A Belgian battlefield was recreated on a flat barley field at the Irvine Ranch in Orange County. "We went on location for about six or eight weeks down in the hills above Laguna Beach," recalled cinematographer Arthur Edeson. "They built roads and a concrete ramp for the big camera crane that Hal Mohr had built for them a few months before. It ran alongside the trenches they had dug for the battle stuff. It was really a big show."[90]

Milestone wanted to show wave after wave of

The *Broadway* crane on the battlefield location for *All Quiet on the Western Front*.

soldiers dropping from machine-gun fire as they headed for the enemy's trenches. Junior viewed the dailies at the studio, telling Milestone, "all I see is guys running to the left and guys running to the right. Where is the battle stuff?" The producer could not see the potential of the footage, while Milestone, a former editor, knew how he would cut it together. Fearing reshoots months later, Junior threatened to shut down production until he could see the sequence, so Milestone entered the cutting room.[91]

The first person to see the edited *All Quiet* battle scene at Universal was the inhabitant of an adjacent cutting room. "A cut was finished," Lewis Milestone remembered, "it was three o'clock in the morning and the only other guy alive around there in the cutting rooms was Paul Whiteman," working on *King of Jazz*. Milestone and Whiteman watched the attack sequence in the screening room, about 1,100 feet without sound. After the lights came up, Whiteman stayed in his chair, not speaking. Milestone asked, "Paul, are you still with us?" Whiteman replied, "If the rest of the picture is anything like this you've got the winner of all time."[92]

Routining *King of Jazz*

With Anderson entering the cutting room in February 1930, the Whiteman orchestra was not needed on the lot for two weeks. Starting February 13, the band was booked for seven days at the Loew's State Theatre in Los Angeles (supporting M-G-M's *The Mysterious Island*) and four days at the Fox Theatre in San Diego. They returned to the studio for two weeks of retakes (on half-pay plus actual overtime) starting March 6. The final day at Universal City was Thursday, March 20.

"I was now faced with the problem of putting the picture together, for nobody but myself knew precisely what it was all about," recalled Anderson.[93] Heading into the editing room, he had 31 different segments to select from for this jigsaw puzzle of a show, with Charles Irwin and Whiteman's scrapbook as the connecting threads. The goal was to have this assembly appear seamless, with one unit flowing into the next. "We have eliminated the curtain ... we try to bring in the orchestra in such a way as to surprise the eye and make it an integral part of the picture," Anderson told the *Los Angeles Times*. "We endeavor to change the scene without lapses and haltings in the picture's evolvement." Without a narrative to link the acts, "we can at least build up the picture with pictorial contrasts and the surprises that we afford in the entertainment."[94]

Anderson's philosophy of a revue focused on "routining," timing, and tempo. Lacking a plot or continuing characters, a revue is composed of units, and the show can lose its audience at any transition. There must be variety so that similar numbers do not follow each other. But this was much more than alternating comedy sketches and musical numbers. "The director must provide for a sense of progression, arranging the units so that there are several peaks throughout the revue as well as a build-up to the best, largest, most spectacular or most unique numbers at the finale," noted theater historian Thomas H. Gressler."[95] Many times the simple matter of placement of a number affected whether the segment was a hit or missed the mark.

This process had been more complex in Anderson's live theater shows. Sequences were written, planned, and rehearsed in isolation from each other. As the show was coming together, one associate recalled that Anderson wrote the name of each number on a slip of paper, keeping them in his pocket and rearranging the slips as rehearsals and then previews proceeded, to achieve a good flow.[96] In the theater, there were also practical considerations of the technical aspects of moving sets on and off stage and the speed of costume changes.

Working in live theater provided immediate feedback, and the director, writers, and cast could evolve their work based on audience reaction. Out-of-town previews would showcase all of the material ready for public view, with more units in reserve. A review of the Boston preview of *Murray Anderson's Almanac* noted, "it was goshawful in spots Tuesday night when it opened cold, but it had speed and novelty."[97] Audience reaction would immediately highlight what worked and did not. From the time when the curtain went down through the next morning, Anderson would work with the cast making changes. Each successive preview refined the running order, while the pace was adjusted, delays were eliminated, and length of numbers trimmed so that one number flowed naturally into the next. If you do that "day after day, and hour after hour," Anderson noted, "gradually the music and the color and the motion and the form are all melted into one brilliant, graceful outline."[98]

By the time of *King of Jazz*, Anderson had absorbed all of these elements and knew how to stage a musical number so it did not outstay its welcome, to alter the pace from segment to segment and build a show.

Production Wraps

King of Jazz had been in production from November 15 to March 20, equal to the combined production schedule of the three most recent Technicolor musicals at the nearby Warner Bros.-First National studio.[99] The

Paul Whiteman, Jeanette Loff, and John Murray Anderson clowning around on the set of *King of Jazz*.
The bandstand is to the left, while part of the "Bridal Veil" set is visible behind Anderson.

expense had been enormous, with all of the studio overhead allocated to just two productions. The fallout from this movie would affect Universal for years.

At the end of filming, Whiteman presented several gifts to key collaborators on the film. Anderson received a solid platinum cigarette case, with a pattern of diamonds on the front outlining Whiteman's face. Gold lettering on the front was cut from gold and attached with gold rivets.[100] Whiteman presented a star sapphire ring to the script girl, assistant director Bob Ross, and Ray

Rennahan. Whiteman bought a special gift for Junior Laemmle, whose drive had brought the film to completion. For his contributions along the way, Whiteman gave Paul Fejos a gold cigarette case, inscribed with the name of each member of the orchestra. Fejos treasured the gift and carried it with him for the rest of his life.[101]

Noted New York caricaturist Wynn Holcomb designed the pages and cover for Paul Whiteman's Scrap Book to introduce each act in the film.

Chapter 6

SCENE-BY-SCENE

King of Jazz is effectively a "greatest hits" of John Murray Anderson and Paul Whiteman, mixed with the best elements of Broadway and vaudeville. Many of the production numbers are adaptations of Anderson's most applauded accomplishments from his 1920s theatrical revues—even the idea of structuring the film around a scrapbook originated from his 1929 stage show *Murray Anderson's Almanac*.[1] Paul Whiteman and his orchestra are the stars of the film, but they share very little screen time as an ensemble; although the band's music can be heard throughout, in almost every sequence. Most of the song and dance talent in the film was signed from the stage, and had existing connections with either Whiteman or Anderson. Universal's own roster of stars is largely sidelined as support in the numerous comedy sketches dotted throughout.

The following scene-by-scene account documents the general release version of the film that played throughout the United States in 1930. The running order and content have been confirmed from close analysis of surviving picture elements, sound discs, a 1930 dialogue continuity, and fragments of a shot continuity. For comprehensive information about the music and a cast listing for each sequence, please consult the Appendix.

Paul Whiteman's Scrap Book

King of Jazz opens with a refrain from Gershwin's *Rhapsody in Blue* and an introductory title card that in scale and placement declares the stars of the film to be "Paul Whiteman and His Band." As the credits progress, the melody blends into Jack Yellen and Milton Ager's "Music Has Charms," with Bing Crosby on vocals, setting the scene for the film's eclectic mix of popular entertainment.

> Music hath charms
> That nothing else has,
> Music hath charms
> Tho' it's classic or jazz,
> A symphony grand by Schubert or Brahms,
> A popular band, or a uke 'neath the palms

After the credits conclude, we are introduced to "Paul Whiteman's Scrap Book" and our host Charles Irwin, in formal morning suit, with top hat and cane. "The pages are crowded with melodies and anecdotes," he announces, "which we are going to bring to life for you by the magic of the camera." The huge 20-ft.-tall book was designed by cartoonist and stage designer Wynn Holcomb, and is used throughout the film as a framework to tie together the otherwise disparate acts and musical numbers. The Irish humorist Charles Irwin had made a career on the American vaudeville stage as an agreeable master of ceremonies. Between 1927 and 1929 he crossed paths with both Whiteman and John Murray Anderson several times on the Publix theater circuit, most recently headlining Anderson's 1929 unit show "Say It With Music," which evidently landed him this job.[2]

SCENE No.

Whiteman gets mad – raises gun – shoots again –
using smae part of music as previous scene.

(X)

SCENE No.

Lion sticks out a row of huge teeth – bullets
hit them * zylophone effect – playing last
Two bars of A HUNTING WE WILL GO."

Lion jumps out of scene after Paul.

(2) *including exit –*

SCENE No.

Paul drops gun and runs – Lion comes in – runs
behind him – gaining and making menacing lunges.

Insert Closeup of Paul running .
"   "   "   Lion   "   .

Finish with
Stormy as lion lands
On Pauls Belly

SCENE No.

60

Lion catches Paul – slaps him down – ~~sits~~ *stands* on
top of him – ~~licks Paul's face like a big puppy
would~~ – Lion takes out his own teeth – pulls
out his tongue – sharpens teeth on tongue –
pulls out a hair from Paul's mustache – splits
it with his teeth – Paul gets idea – ~~stretches~~ *Pulls*
his mustache out ~~like~~ a violin ~~string~~ *and starts to play.*
~~up a stiff – plays on mustache like a violin~~ –
Lion is enchanted with music – gets off of Paul –
starts to dance.

Worm laughs –
becomes a bow –

Flattens Paul out + then comes back to normal

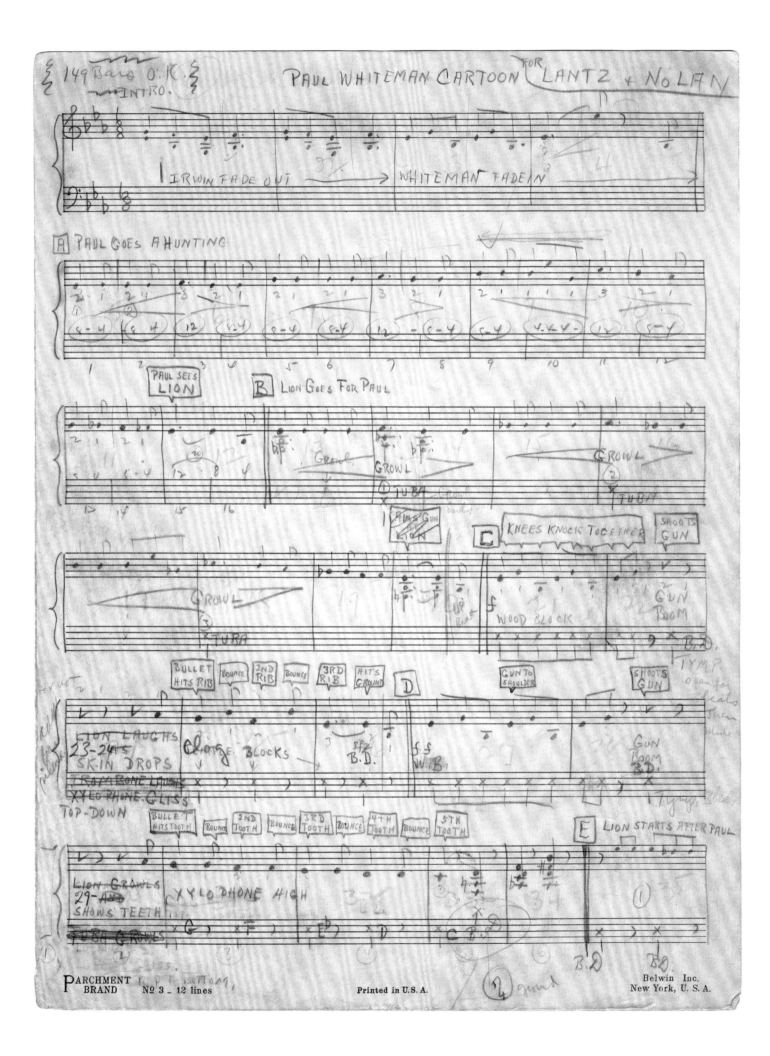

"A Fable in Jazz"

Written with "daring wit" by caricaturist Wynn Holcomb and animated by Walter Lantz and Bill Nolan, this introductory cartoon sends an animated Paul Whiteman big-game hunting in "Darkest Africa"—an origin story with some uneasy stereotypes that shows the bandleader neutralizing the savages with his infectious music.[3] Lantz had recently been made production supervisor of the new animation department at Universal, which was responsible for the popular "Oswald the Lucky Rabbit" series, featuring a character first developed by Walt Disney in 1927.

The early Lantz Oswald cartoons were crude, often with very basic stories fleshed out over two or three simple jokes. The animated prologue in *King of Jazz* shows much more polish, partly because of the larger budget and straightforward narrative, but also due to the impressive score. James Dietrich was responsible for this arrangement, seamlessly blending themes from ten different sources. This is aided by the performance of the Whiteman band, which creates a wall-to-wall score complete with musical gags and sound effects.

Lantz required the band to play at exact 2/12 tempo to keep sync with the animation, so he produced a metronome for Whiteman by punching holes into the reel of film every twelve frames. "We projected this film on a screen as Whiteman was conducting," recalled Lantz, "and this flash would come up all the time and Whiteman went nuts." The band leader refused to cooperate, insisting he didn't need any aids. "Let me tell ya, sonny, I can keep a rhythm on anything," he boasted. "Tell me how long the picture's going to be—three minutes, four minutes, whatever— and I'll give you the rhythm you want."[4] Lantz was impressed. "Darned if he didn't beat this thing out," he recalled. "It came to exactly four minutes at 2/12 tempo."[5]

The cartoon—the first photographed in Technicolor—finds Whiteman, dressed in two-color attire, hunting a lion in Africa.[6] Blasts from his blunderbuss do little harm to the ferocious beast, and Whiteman soon finds himself in a sticky spot. But "jazz" comes to the rescue when Whiteman pulls out his violin and begins to play (dubbed by Joe Venuti). The infectious melody of "Music Has Charms" sets the animals and plants dancing (including a cameo from Oswald the Rabbit), and brings out the natives, who scat with the voices of the Rhythm Boys. A monkey throws a coconut at Whiteman, which causes a crown-shaped bump to protrude. "And that's how Paul Whiteman was crowned the King of Jazz," Charles Irwin concludes.

Before his appearance in *King of Jazz*, Oswald the Lucky Rabbit had already traveled to Africa in *Africa Before Dark* (1928), made under Walt Disney, and would soon make another trip there in Walter Lantz's *Africa* (1930), which reused cel animation from the Paul Whiteman film.

Previous page, overleaf: Original styoryboard drawn by Walter Lantz, and music synchronization notes by James Dietrich.

Left: "And that's how Paul Whiteman was crowned the King of Jazz." The concluding shot of Walter Lantz and Bill Nolan's animation, "A Fable in Jazz."

Right: Animators Pinto Colvig (clarinet) and Walter Lantz (accordion) play alongside music arranger James Dietrich (piano), ca. 1930.

This photograph from the "Meet the Boys" number was taken in January or February 1930. During these months, trombonist Boyce Cullen and violinist Mischa Russell missed filming while they recovered from injuries caused in an automobile accident. Two unidentified musicians can be seen in their places.

Left, back row: Mike Trafficante, Harry Goldfield, Frank Siegrist, Andy Secrest, Charles Margulis

Left, middle row: Otto Landau, Ted Bacon, John Bouman, Chester Hazlett

Left, front row: Matt Malneck, Kurt Dieterle, Eddie Lang, Joe Venuti, Roy Bargy

Center: George Marsh, Paul Whiteman

Right, back row: Jack Fulton, [replacement for Boyce Cullen], Bill Rank, Wilbur Hall, Min Leibrook

Right, middle row: Charles Strickfaden, [replacement for Mischa Russell], "Red" Maier, Bernie Daly

Right, front row: Lennie Hayton, Frank Trumbauer, Harry Barris, Mike Pingitore, Irving Friedman

"Meet the Boys"

This introductory sequence was a regular and popular component of Whiteman's live concerts. The act was designed to showcase the virtuoso talents of his band members while also giving them due recognition. The stage would go dark and Whiteman himself would manipulate a baby spotlight to shine on each musician in succession as they performed solos.[7] The number was first introduced into the band's repertoire in September 1925, and was deemed so novel by Whiteman that he registered the stage idea and title with *Variety*'s "Protective Material Department" to avoid copycat acts.[8]

In the film version Charles Irwin welcomes Paul Whiteman, who places a model of a bandstand and a small Gladstone bag on the table in front of them. "Where's the band? Are you standing in front of them?" Irwin quips, while Whiteman ignores the "fat joke." Through the magic of Jerry Ash's trick photography, the band members proceed to climb out of the bag before the model dissolves into the full-scale bandstand and Whiteman sets up the act. "I'm really very proud of the boys collectively, and I'd like to have you meet them individually." The lights dim and Whiteman lights up each solo with a flashlight, which Ray Rennahan's camera follows by panning left or right. This serves to personalize the musicians (although only two are introduced by name), and demonstrate the high quality of musicianship that they brought to the ensemble.

Dressing in dapper orange and cream wide-striped jackets with green ties, the boys play snappy arrangements of several band favorites, including Henry Busse's "Hot Lips," performed by Harry "Goldie" Goldfield; Joe Venuti's "Wild Cat," with Venuti on violin and Eddie Lang on guitar; and "Nola," with clarinetist Chester Hazlett, pianist Roy Bargy, and Wilbur Hall on trombone, before the act reaches a crescendo with Mike Pingitore's banjo rendition of "Linger Awhile."[9] After this, Whiteman invites us to "Meet Our Girls"—dressed in silver sequins and pink feathers, the sixteen Russell Markert Dancers perform a precision routine seated in a line, in carefully choreographed syncopation, to instrumental versions of "Music Has Charms" and "I Like to Do Things for You."

Whiteman legal advertisement, *Variety*, September 16, 1925.

Below: The sixteen Russell Markert Dancers.

"My Bridal Veil"

Following the zippy introductory routines for the band and the Markert girls, the film slows down with the "Bridal Veil" number. The ceremonial spectacle had become one of John Murray Anderson's signature set pieces, honed over multiple iterations on the Broadway and West End stages, and on the Publix theater circuit. The sumptuously executed "Bridal Veil" number was originally devised as the finale to Anderson's 1920 musical revue *What's in a Name?* The music by Milton Ager, and lyrics by Jack Yellen and Anderson himself, remained the same through all versions.

As executed in the film, the sequence proves a little hard to follow, so Jeanie Lang was enlisted to provide a short explanatory passage (the sound for which exists, but the picture is missing from surviving copies of the film):

> We call our next divertissement "The Bridal Veil." It tells the story of a little girl who finds inside an old treasure chest a lace veil that has been worn by her ancestors. The ghost brides of all the ages pass before her, and in fancy, the boy who is to become her future husband joins her and they start on their honeymoon to the land of dreams.

John Murray Anderson's "My Bridal Veil" was staged three times before it appeared in *King of Jazz*. Herman Rosse's costumes and sets were already well developed when the number was presented at the Rivoli Theatre in 1926.

Above: Rosse's original design depicts Jeanette Loff's veil reaching down from the lovers' land of dreams. Although the honeymoon house in the clouds is not depicted in the film, the bridal couple does climb an endless staircase leading to the stars.

Right: Jeanette Loff and Stanley Smith prepare to film the concluding shot of the "Bridal Veil" sequence. The glassed-in booth at the top of the stage was the sound monitor room, and the playback loudspeakers can be seen just in front of the crane-tower.

Anderson and designer Herman Rosse were renowned on Broadway for their innovative scene transitions, and this is evident when Whiteman's bandstand splits down the middle to reveal a cavernous set behind it. But after Jeanette Loff enters, the remainder of the number becomes a facsimile of Anderson's theatrical hit from 1920. A few double-exposure camera effects are used for the appearance of the "ghost brides," but the number largely draws from its theatrical origins, with the sequence being filmed entirely from one viewpoint—effectively that of the theater audience.

In content typical of an early 1920s revue, the number pauses midway for a procession of pretty girls in elaborate costumes (played by the "Hollywood Beauties"), each modelling Rosse's meticulously designed wedding gowns, dating from the 1450s through to the 1890s. After the ghosts fade away, Stanley Smith appears for the romantic fantasy finale. The bride and groom walk arm-in-arm, accompanied by a coterie of bridesmaids, up an endless star-strewn staircase—trailed by a bridal veil made of 500 yards of gold and silver lace—on their way to "the land of dreams."[10] The enormous staircase set was only possible in the movies.

Herman Rosse designed wedding dresses for the film dating from 1450, 1575, 1750, 1800, 1850, 1880, and 1890, along with outfits for the bridesmaids, flower girls, and attendants.

"I'd Like to Do Things for You"

The introductory scenes continue with the musical comedy ensemble "I'd Like to Do Things for You." This time we're introduced to Jeanie Lang, Grace Hayes, William Kent, and the dance act Nell O'Day and the Tommy Atkins Sextet, who will all reappear throughout the film. The song is divided into three verses, each expanding upon the other in orchestration and tempo. Lang and Whiteman open the number in an intimate composition, although Lang appears to have some trouble with the lip sync. Comedians Hayes and Kent present the second verse as an amusing domestic argument, with Hayes pinching at Kent's face and tearing his clothes, and Kent trying to make up with her using a wincing child's voice. The final verse is sung by the Tommy Atkins troupe, with Nell O'Day, whose vocals are hard to make out in places. But O'Day is redeemed by her gravity-defying act with her male companions, who with grace and precision fling, toss, and spin O'Day, all at breakneck speed. According to O'Day this concluding section was originally 72 bars longer. Between her singing and the acrobatic dancing was a graceful waltz, which gradually escalated to the sensational ending we see in the film. A jarring cut is evident where this was removed, with some of the Sextet members clearly changing position between shots.[11]

William Kent and Grace Hayes.

"Ladies of the Press"

"The Daily Meows" reporters, Jeanie Lang, Kathryn Crawford, Grace Hayes, and Merna Kennedy, hand in their stories to the editor, Laura La Plante.

"Ladies of the Press" is the first of several "blackout" sketches in *King of Jazz*—a tradition carried over from the vaudeville and revue stage, in which the punchline of a brief comedy sketch is followed by a complete blackout of the lights to enhance the impact of the gag. The cinematic equivalent in this case is to cut suddenly to the next scene. This swift 45-second sketch is written by William Griffith (one of Anderson's writing cohorts from his recently closed *Almanac*) and its title is possibly a riff on Paramount's film *Gentlemen of the Press* from 1929.

Laura La Plante plays the editor of "The Daily Meows," who needs her news "hot off the griddle." A succession of reporters, played by Jeanie Lang, Merna Kennedy, and Kathryn Crawford each enter with stories fresher than the next. "When did it happen?" "Ten minutes ago!" — "When did it happen?" "Five minutes ago!" Grace Hayes bests the rest with the headline "Woman shoots husband!" — "When did it happen?" snaps La Plante. "Wait a minute. Listen!" A shot is heard off-screen. "That's great!"

"The Rhythm Boys"

This short musical interlude was among the last scenes filmed, in March 1930. It is a showcase for The Rhythm Boys, who were to remain only a peripheral part of the film until arranger James Dietrich convinced John Murray Anderson to feature them more prominently.[12] The sequence opens with Bing Crosby, Al Rinker, and Harry Barris singing "Mississippi Mud"—a song that had originally earned the young trio their contract with Whiteman, and soon became their signature tune.[13] They appear in silhouette, performing as *faux* negroes with some racially insensitive lyrics and some fast-moving banter, before Bing turns the lights on and they are revealed to be white. The boys then segue into "So the Bluebirds and the Blackbirds Got Together," which they first recorded in 1929. The song is a great demonstration of the Rhythm Boys' unique style of performance, mixing rhythmic scat, dialogue, harmonizing, and melody in a form heavily influenced by the great African American jazz performers of the time.

The "Rhythm Boys" set was originally designed by Herman Rosse for a different scene, but proved adaptable for this last-minute addition.

Opposite page, bottom: The Rhythm Boys: Bing Crosby, Al Rinker, and Harry Barris.

"The Piccolo Player"

This short comedy sketch by Harry Ruskin is missing from surviving prints, although the audio still exists. Paul Whiteman encounters William Kent on a window ledge on the thirteenth floor, ready to jump. Kent "always wanted to be a piccolo player," but after spending a fortune on lessons with "all the good teachers here and in Europe," he still can't land a job.[14] At Whiteman's invitation, Kent tries to play "Caprice Viennois" on the piccolo, but he is so bad the bandleader has to cover his ears. A description of the scene that was deposited for copyright purposes indicates that "Paul takes care of him nicely" by shoving Kent from the ledge, before brushing his hands with satisfaction.[15]

Overleaf: Excerpt from the 1930 dialogue continuity script.

Paul Whiteman	Hey, do you know you are on the thirteenth floor of this building? What are you trying to do, kill yourself?
Billy Kent	Yes.
Paul	Have you lost your mind?
Billy	You leave me alone, I know what I'm doing. It's my life. I can do what I want with it.
Paul	Why should you want to commit suicide? A nice, young-looking chap with everything in the world to live for.
Billy	Well, I -- I tell you Mister, I've had a very hard life. I had to quit school when I was sixteen and go to work, hard, unpleasant work -- days, nights, Sundays, for very small pay, at a job I didn't like.
Paul	That's too bad.
Billy	Then, when I was twenty-one, I got my big chance in life. My uncle died and left me twenty-five thousand dollars. I'd always wanted to be a piccolo player, so I immediately quit my job and studied a piccolo with all the good teachers here and in Europe. It cost a lot of money, but it was worth it.
Paul	I should say so.
Billy	And then, last year I graduated, but what good did it do me? I tried to get in to see all the big band leaders in the world, but they wouldn't even talk to me. In the meantime, I spent all my money and now I'm broke, without a chance of ever getting a job.
Billy (cont)	Oh, Mister, please -- please, let me jump out that window -- that's -- that's all I ask of you.
Paul	Oh, no, no, no, wait a minute. Do you know who I am?
Billy	No.
Paul	I'm Paul Whiteman.
Billy	Not -- not Paul Whiteman?
Paul	In the flesh, and, young man, this might be your opportunity of a lifetime. Have you got your piccolo with you?
Billy	I -- yes.
Paul	Play something for me -- maybe I'll be able to help you -- maybe I'll be able to give you a job.
Billy	Oh -- Oh Mister Whiteman -- I -- I don't know how to thank you. I -- I can't tell you how much I appreciate this.
Paul	Oh, that's all right - relax -- play something.
Billy	Play -- play as you've never played before.

"Monterey"

"It Happened in Monterey" is the first of two songs in the finished film by Mabel Wayne. The successful songwriter had originally been hired in November 1928 when *King of Jazz* was first announced, but the additional songs she wrote at that time didn't make it into the final production. Billy Rose's lyrics recount the story of an American tourist in Mexico falling in love with one of the locals. The number is bookended by John Boles's solemn piano player gazing upon a painting of his lost love, played by Jeanette Loff, the ethereal blonde featured in this and two other numbers in the film. The setting, costumes, and music may have been intended to capitalize on the success of John Boles's leading role in *Rio Rita* (1929), a film musical set in a Mexican border town, based on the 1927 Ziegfeld stage hit.

Concept drawings for "It Happened in Monterey" and the final set and costumes.

Technicolor cameraman Ray Rennahan photographs a dolly shot with Jeanette Loff, John Boles, and the Russell Markert Dancers.

After the painting dissolves into the real Jeanette Loff, we are swept off into an evocative recreation of "old Mexico." Herman Rosse's sets and costumes draw on cliché, but are nevertheless impressive in their intricacies. The set even includes a working canal running through it.

"Monterey" carefully balances many components without veering on excess. There are singing parts from Boles, Loff, and Nancy Torres, a simple story, colorful costumes, and subtle moonlight effects, as well as fan dancing from the Russell Markert girls, and high kicks from the Sisters G and George Chiles. Although a native New Yorker, Mabel Wayne specialized in Latin melodies; she also wrote "Ramona" and "In a Little Spanish Town." The Spanish rhythms of the wistful "Monterey" resulted in one of the film's most popular songs.

The atmospheric moonlight effect was created by a combination of subtle colored lighting, green foliage and sets, and glistening silver sequins on many of the native costumes.

"In Conference"

This short blackout skit features Merna Kennedy, Glenn Tryon, and Laura La Plante. It is typical of Harry Ruskin's succinct comedy style, which had been honed on the stage for more than a decade. Kennedy and Tryon are discovered necking by La Plante. "Now I've caught you," she declares. "So this is the way you act when I'm not around." Tryon begins to explain, but he is cut short by the distressed La Plante. "I'm through. You'll never see me again as long as you live. You brute! Goodbye!" The joke only reveals itself with Tryon's final line: "Well, wifey, there goes the best stenographer I ever had!"

Cabaret performer Jack White as "The Property Man."

"The Property Man"

Jack White, "a fellow of infinite jest, but just a little bit nutty," was a New York cabaret performer who specialized in brash irreverent humor.[16] His backstage skit in *King of Jazz* appears at first glance as absurdist stream of consciousness, darting from one topic to the next and back again, but it is actually carefully rehearsed with the Whiteman orchestra, with well-timed asides and musical cues. (It is the only time in the film the band plays live, as opposed to miming to playback.) The bulk of the scene is taken up by the comic song routine "Oh How I'd Like to Own a Fish Store," in which White flits between identities: boxing announcer, sleight-of-hand magician, street vendor, and storyteller. The number concludes with a gag from his regular nightclub routine, "And then the war broke out!," segueing into a World War I parody, before one final reprise of the chorus.[17]

"A Bench in the Park"

"A Bench in the Park" is a simple song designed to showcase the Whiteman band and the popular specialty singers the Brox Sisters. It starts intimately, with Jeanette Loff and Stanley Smith on a park bench, re-teamed again following the "Bridal Veil" number earlier in the picture. The camera then explores other lovers in the park before settling on the Brox Sisters, who spin around like the giant revolving set, wrapped together under one over-sized feathered evening cloak.[18] The harmonizing sisters are accompanied offscreen by Eddie Lang's exquisite jazz guitar, and are then joined by the Rhythm Boys, whose mellow vocals blend nicely with theirs.

The revolving set signals a change in pace as the Markert girls are given another chance to exercise their legs in tight synchronization in bright pink costumes. Ferde Grofé's characteristic orchestrations accompany their peppy dancing by cycling through sections of the band from brass to reeds to strings, before a reprise by the entire orchestra, when the Markert girls are joined by male partners dressed in green. The circular motif continues, as the set spins around again to reveal Whiteman's band dressed in white sailor suits, each musician partnered with a Hollywood Beauty. Rennahan's camera whip-pans from Charles Margulis (trumpet) to

Hal Mohr (in beret) consults with Russell Markert (wearing sweater) on the set of "A Bench in the Park;" Jerry Ash is behind the camera.

"Red" Maier (saxophone) to Joe Venuti (violin) to Harry Goldfield (trumpet), who perform short comic solos; then trombonist Jack Fulton sings a few lines, before Universal's child star "Sunny Jim" emerges from Min Leibrook's tuba. Whiteman is the last to appear; much to our surprise, he swivels around to reveal that the unexpected companion on his lap is a smiling little African American girl with braided hair, who pinches his cheek. In Whiteman's breast pocket is a packet of Old Gold cigarettes. The number ends with Paul Whiteman's face as a winking Man in the Moon.

Top: According to some reports the revolving stage for the "A Bench in a Park" number was so heavy it left large grooves in the studio floor when it was rotated.

Bottom: Herman Rosse's moonlit set design is largely devoid of color. The artificial grass and trees were rendered in reflective aluminum and silver-bronze, partly spattered light green to give the effect of shadows. Color was added mainly through the performers' costumes.

"Springtime"

Billed as "Another 'Quickie'," and running a mere 15 seconds, this is the shortest of all the film's blackout sketches. Slim Summerville and Yola D'Avril play an embarrassed couple who have been getting intimate in the woods—as hinted at by the suggestive title, "Spring-time." Still in possession of the back-seat cushions, or "springs," they hesitantly arrive at the police station to report their car stolen (the cop on desk duty is Walter Brennan). This "quickie" sketch, which flies by too fast for most people to get, was inspired by an illustration by the famed *New Yorker* cartoonist Peter Arno, which was purchased by Universal for $200.[19]

"We want to report a stolen car."

Between 1925 and 1968, Peter Arno's iconic cartoons and covers for *The New Yorker* typified the changing times and set the tone for the magazine's sophisticated humor. *The New Yorker*, December 7, 1929, 31.

"All Noisy on the Eastern Front"

Universal promoted *All Quiet on the Western Front* widely throughout 1930; some plugs included nods in other productions. Oswald the Lucky Rabbit was enlisted in the cartoon *Not So Quiet* (1930), which was playfully announced as "a travesty" on the World War I drama, while the studio attempted to recoup some of the production costs by reusing costumes and sets in comedy shorts, like *We! We! Marie!* (1930) with Slim Summerville.[20]

The playful "All Noisy on the Eastern Front" in *King of Jazz* was inserted not only to raise awareness of Universal's other great super-production of the year, but also to poke some lighthearted fun at its seriousness. The skit's premise is an old one. In quick succession, Walter

Brennan, Charles Irwin, and Paul Whiteman each enter to give gifts to their French lover Yola D'Avril (who did actually appear in *All Quiet on the Western Front*). "Marie, have you been true to me?" they all ask. Whiteman gives D'Avril a bar of Hershey's chocolate. In typical French farce fashion, they each end up hiding behind doors. William Kent, the General, is the last to arrive. "The enemy is shelling the town," he announces. "We must leave immediately. Come, my car is waiting." — "Have you got any room for me?" asks Brennan, whose query is echoed by Irwin and Whiteman, both poking out from their hiding places. The far wall collapses: "How about us?" shouts the whole battalion, who have all evidently been getting a piece of the action!

"Willie Hall, One of the Whiteman Boys"

Capitalizing upon popular entertainment trends of the time, Whiteman increasingly aimed to spice up his concerts in the mid-1920s with a variety of novelty acts, vocal interludes, and solo specialty spots. Wilbur Hall was brought in from Paul Ash's orchestra to add more "hokum" to the proceedings.[21] This sequence captures some of Hall's regular Whiteman stage routine, which was entitled "Free Air: Variations Based on Noises from a Garage."[22] In the best spirit of vaudeville, the deadpan Hall, wearing long flap-shoes in the style of British music-hall comedy star Little Tich, performs "Pop Goes the Weasel" on the fiddle while flinging his bow around at breakneck pace behind his head and between his knees. He concludes with an amusing rendition of "The Stars and Stripes Forever" on a bicycle pump.

The Rhapsody in Blue

George Gershwin's *Rhapsody in Blue* is a composition inextricably associated with Paul Whiteman and his orchestra, but it also has close connections with John Murray Anderson, who staged an ambitious Publix prologue in 1926 inspired by the same material. His "Rhapsody in Jazz" played at the Rivoli Theatre, and was described in the program as "A Syncopated Manhattan Cocktail … Based on George Gershwin's Rhapsody in Blue." Anderson used five scenes to illustrate New York's lifeblood and rhythms, from Central Park through to a shoeshine stand, the Stock Exchange, a street scene, and a nightclub—distilling the essence of the composition through performance, accompanied by Herman Rosse's

stylized settings.[23]

The *Rhapsody in Blue* sequence in *King of Jazz* takes a more straightforward approach. Its prologue, introduced by Whiteman himself, is a visually arresting Voodoo dance by Jacques Cartier that makes a stark contrast to Gershwin's sinewy music to follow. The white dancer—covered with black lacquer head-to-toe and glistening in partial silhouette—reprises his famous "Kongo Voodoo" witch-doctor dance routine from 1927. "He dances on a circular raised platform that suggests the top of a big bass drum," described *The Stage* in 1927; his "frenzied arms and feet casting a remarkable shadow on the curtain just behind him."[24] Cartier's exotic novelty dance first appeared on Broadway in *The Manhatters* by Alfred Nathan and George S. Oppenheimer, and six months

later was expanded for *Golden Dawn*, Oscar Hammerstein II and Otto Harbach's musical set in colonial Africa.

Ferde Grofé's orchestration of Gershwin's classic was originally written in 1924 for Whiteman's 23-piece orchestra and was revised for a small theater orchestra when Anderson's "Rhapsody in Jazz" toured the Publix circuit in 1926. The original emphasizes piano and clarinet, and sounds significantly different from Grofé's final version for orchestra, which became the standard from 1942 onwards. The film distills the *Rhapsody* down to its *andante* section (effectively the first half), which cut its running time to nine minutes, making the sequence more manageable for movie audiences. Roy Bargy performs the piano part on-screen, while Jacques Cartier returns in top hat, tails, and a swirling evening cloak to give character to the clarinet glissando, performed off-screen by Chester Hazlett.

Herman Rosse's designs attempt to capture the composition's mix of structure and formlessness, bringing together a potpourri of oversized horns and drums, and a massive piano at the center overflowing with musicians. The huge piano idea was inspired by Anderson's "The Giant Piano" Publix revue from 1926, which included a mock piano filling the stage, with the Rivoli orchestra seated in the instrument's body.[25]

Rosse's designs also bring a sense of sophistication—that of an evening performance—combining pianists and girls in formal evening attire and chandelier motifs, with the frenetic dancing of the Russell Markert girls, who appear in top hats and tails, and weave throughout the set, up and down ramps to the giant piano's keys, where they dance *en pointe*. Jacques Cartier is joined by the Sisters G for an obligatory fan dance that was a staple of all sister acts at the time, from the Dolly Sisters to the Dodge Twins. The performance concludes with further views of the orchestra playing its signature tune, before the principal performers return for the closing refrain. Paul Whiteman takes a bow and turns to acknowledge his musicians.

Top: Scene 2 of John Murray Anderson's "Rhapsody in Jazz" was set in a syncopated shoeshine parlor against a backdrop of New York City skyscrapers. *Theatre Arts Monthly*, November 1926, 763.

Middle/bottom: Herman Rosse's early design sketches drew from elements of John Murray Anderson's Publix shows "Rhapsody in Jazz" and "The Giant Piano." His designs paid close attention to the limitations of two-color Technicolor.

Opposite page, top: Herman Rosse's designs juxtaposed elements of a formal evening performance with more free-flowing dance and musical motifs.

Opposite page, bottom: The sixteen Russell Markert Dancers, joined by Beth Laemmle (back row center), dancing on the piano keys.

"Oh! Forevermore!"

"Oh! Forevermore!" was first performed by the comedian William Kent in *Smarty*, an early version of the Gershwins' popular musical *Funny Face* starring Fred and Adele Astaire, which was overhauled several times before it found success on Broadway in 1927.[26] One of Kent's specialties on the stage was the part of the drunken "souse," which he perfected in his 1921 vaudeville sketch "Shivers", and which he again draws upon here.[27] In "Forevermore," the inebriated Kent plays against comic foil Walter Brennan in a tale about the effects of Prohibition. Kent's comedy is often outward and illogical, and draws upon his increasingly drunken condition. He tells the story of his two goldfish, Ella and Emma, whom he watched "grow into womanhood — to manhood — to big fish." In the end the bootleg liquor gets to him, and he dives into the fish tank to join his friends.

William Kent calling out to his beloved goldfish, Ella and Emma.

"My Ragamuffin Romeo"

The "Ragamuffin Romeo" number was developed as a showcase for the eccentric dancing talents of Marion Stadler and Don Rose, whose rag-doll routine was already well established on the stage. The team had performed together since 1928, when Stadler was just 15, almost exclusively presenting their Raggedy Ann-inspired act, in which Stadler is bent and contorted by Rose in all manner of impossible positions. They hit the big time in 1929, when they were engaged to perform in *Ziegfeld's Midnight Frolic* in the New Amsterdam's famous rooftop theatre in New York. They appeared alongside Helen Morgan, Lillian Roth, the Duncan Sisters, and the show's main attraction, Paul Whiteman and his orchestra. Soon after, they toured the Publix circuit with John Murray Anderson's "Say It With Music" unit.

During the rehearsal period for the film, Stadler and Rose amazed audiences with a four-week run at the Cocoanut Grove in Los Angeles. A local reporter praised their popular routine, finding Marion Stadler "a marvel of boneless dexterity … she is pitched, tossed and catapulted into all kinds of awkward angles, graceful curves and tumble-bug huddles, until she loses all semblance of human shape, and yet withal, every move is achieved in rhythmic harmony with the orchestra. It is a wow of a turn and must be seen to be appreciated."[28]

Stadler and Rose performed their rag-doll adagio dance in John Murray Anderson's "Say It With Music" for seven months in 1929. It appeared on the Publix circuit in cities including Boston, New York City, Washington, DC, Rochester, Cleveland, Detroit, Indianapolis, and Chicago. *The Amateur Dancer*, November 1930, 19.

Radio personality Jeanie Lang and dancer George Chiles sing the introduction to Stadler and Rose's speciality dance.

The "Ragamuffin Romeo" song itself was a new composition written by Mabel Wayne, with lyrics by Henry De Costa. According to a story recounted by Universal's publicity department, the simple but catchy tune was written by Wayne in just 20 minutes. After hearing a description of the specialty number from John Murray Anderson, Wayne had a "flash of inspiration," and instantly knew she had a hit. She promptly called Anderson back, sung him the melody, and he accepted it on the spot.[29]

After the opening title card—which misspells "Stadler" as "Stattler"—the song begins with the entrance of Jeanie Lang and George Chiles on a junkman's cart pulled by a donkey. Wearing comically oversized hats, Lang piles on the cuteness with her childlike voice and exaggerated playfulness—a kewpie-doll style of singing popularized by Helen Kane and others—before Chiles joins her in a charming duet. Their lyrics set the scene for Stadler and Rose's rough-and-tumble dancing to follow—a type of talent rarely seen today.

Lovers William Kent and Kathryn Crawford are glimpsed through the keyhole.

"A Dash of Spice"

Jeanette Loff introduces this risqué comedy sketch about "the eternal triangle," which used to be missing from copies of *King of Jazz*, but has subsequently been found, except for Jeanette Loff's introduction.[30]

> A good show like a good sauce requires just a little dash of spice. So we ask you to peek through this keyhole at our next page, and if you see anything spicy, remember, you should never, never peek through a keyhole!

Kathryn Crawford rushes to hide her lover William Kent before her husband Glenn Tryon returns. But she is given away by her child "Sunny Jim," who reveals to his father that "There's a boogeyman in that closet." After catching the lover red-handed, Tryon scolds Kent unexpectedly. "Aren't you ashamed of yourself? A great big man like you running around scaring little children!"

"Happy Feet"

"Happy Feet" is the obligatory dancing scene—a good excuse to show off the nifty footwork of the Sisters G and the Markert Dancers, and the eccentric dancing talents of Al Norman (who got the gig after impressing executives at the annual Universal Club Ball).[31] Although the song was written for the film, the number's origins seem to stem partly from Paul Oscard's highly popular Publix stage presentation, "Dancing Feet," which toured nationwide in 1928, while the costumes are based on outfits the Sisters G wore on the Berlin cabaret scene.[32]

After a short stop-motion animation of a dancing pair of shoes by Jerry Ash, the Rhythm Boys get the ball rolling with a scat that's overflowing with bubbling energy. Then the Sisters G are introduced singing in a mix of English and their native German (although the words are heavily accented), before they dance hectically, with legs flailing. Al Norman's specialty rubber-legs dance is followed by the Markert Dancers, who shuffle

through the miniature model of Times Square built for the opening of Paul Fejos's *Broadway*. The dancers are dressed in black jackets and hats—and little else—their bodies blending into the background except for their line of stomping bare legs. In the song's instrumental reprise, a Whiteman double tricks us into believing the bandleader has a hidden talent for acrobatic dancing. But the substitute with the hot feet is soon revealed as the 300-pound Paul Small, who for a short while in the early 1930s made a living impersonating Whiteman "until the orchestra leader uncooperatively went on a diet."[33] This trick substitution is effective because Technicolor prints were notoriously indistinct in long shots, which helped to conceal the dancer's true identity.

Before coming to America in November 1929, the Sisters G were photographed by Manassé, a studio in Vienna that specialized in glamorous and Surrealist images for German-language magazines. Several of these images had a direct influence on how "Happy Feet" was designed and photographed.

Technicolor cameraman Ray Rennahan and assistants film the Sisters G.

Herman Rosse's bandstand parts and the Russell Markert Dancers perform bathed in colored light.

"Has Anybody Seen Our Nellie?"

Jack Yellen and Milton Ager's "Has Anybody Seen Our Nellie?"—a "song and slide" routine about a country girl gone astray in the big city—is a parody of 1890s variety and magic lantern shows. Anderson had already experimented with a "mock ballad" of this type in the 1922 edition of his *Greenwich Village Follies*, which featured John E. Hazzard and was singled out as "the funniest number in the show."[34] The old-time ballad singer in *King of Jazz* is performed by Frank Leslie, a veteran of such parts, who had already teamed with

Anderson and Yellen and Ager on the Publix unit show "The Bughouse Cabaret" at the Rivoli Theatre in 1926.[35] Leslie is joined in a barbershop-style quartet by Churchill Ross (from Universal's popular *Collegians* series, complete with familiar spectacles), Walter Brennan, and John Arledge (in his first film role). The song, accompanied by a host of amusing lantern slides—including one inserted upside-down and another in Yiddish—is missing part of its first verse in surviving copies of the film.

Frank Leslie in Anderson's "The Bughouse Cabaret" (1926), a daffy divertissement in which the inmates of an insane asylum put on a show.

John Boles sings "The Song of the Dawn."

"The Song of the Dawn"

Originally written as a vehicle for Bing Crosby, this rousing number was ultimately performed by John Boles, who stepped in due to Crosby's ongoing entanglement in court proceedings. Boles's operatic vocals serve the song much better than Crosby would have, and he also makes a considerably more convincing cowhand. With hindsight, Crosby agreed: "My crooning style wouldn't have been very good for such a number," Crosby wrote in 1953. "[Boles] had a bigger voice and better delivery for that kind of song than I had."[36]

The number itself is very simple, all shot from one viewpoint, mixing a variety of close-ups and long shots, and utilizing the *Broadway* crane to swoop in and out during the song's crescendos. Boles's booming voice adds scale to the effort, but his performance lacks character. By contrast, Crosby's recording for Columbia in March 1930 is more lilting and peppy—much better to dance to, but inappropriate for the dramatic staging required for the film.

"The Melting Pot of Music"

The "melting pot" concept had been around for a long time as a metaphor for the assimilation of immigrants and the resulting fusion of cultures. But the phrase only entered general usage in the United States around 1909, when Israel Zangwill's play *The Melting Pot* became a hit on Broadway. In *King of Jazz*, the melting pot acts as a framework to celebrate the influences on jazz, but it overlooks the recognized African American origins in favor of a more Eurocentric viewpoint.

Anderson's interpretation was probably less inspired by Zangwill's immigrant drama than by two showy numbers seen on Broadway in the 1910s. The first was the finale to the fourth edition of Ziegfeld's *Midnight Frolic*, staged in 1916 by Ned Wayburn. The *Variety* reviewer noted that "the finale is something of a red fire, both in the cauldron to the rear of the stage, into which the different nations disappear and through their national costumes."[37] The second featured in Sam and Lee Shubert's grand revue, *The Passing Show of 1919*, which ran at the Winter Garden for nine months. One of this show's highlights was "The Melting Pot of America's Popular Tunes," with Eddie Miller and the Winter Garden Highsteppers. Sigmund Romberg and Jean Schwartz's central composition—"America's Popular Song"—quoted from both classical and contemporary, mixing Mendelssohn, Chopin, and Verdi with smatterings from Tin Pan Alley.[38] Like Anderson's version, it attempted to show how the traditions of European music filtered through to American songwriters of the time.

Anderson's "Melting Pot" for the Publix circuit was visually more ambitious than the Ziegfeld and Shubert versions, despite the limitations of mounting the number on the stage of a different movie theater each week. It had an ensemble cast of 30, who appeared in a pageant of costumes and dances from Sweden, France, Italy, Ireland, Spain, Russia, Germany, and Holland, before emerging from the pot to perform "an Americanized jazz version" of the same dances, each "clad in glistening gold."[39]

Three months before Anderson was hired to direct *King of Jazz*, his Publix unit show was staged for the cameras at Paramount's East Coast Astoria studios. *All Americans* (1929) was among a series of short subjects based on content already staged by Publix. Joseph Santley directed the international cast of 23, who sang in the native languages of the six countries represented.[40] The 12-minute short was released in December 1929—midway through the production of *King of Jazz*—and Universal was obliged to secure permission for the number from Paramount, who had already paid Anderson for the privilege.[41]

Left: John Murray Anderson's stage production "The Melting Pot" toured Publix theatres around the country. The revue was presented at the Palace Theatre's inauguration as a Publix theatre in Dallas, Texas, ca. April 1926.

Right: Technicolor cameraman Ray Rennahan and crew film inserts for the "Melting Pot of Music" sequence.

Anderson's "Melting Pot of Music" is a spectacle worthy of the film's finale. The metaphor provides a good rationale for a series of specialty numbers and a reprise of the main cast. And the melting pot construction itself—and the huge columned arena surrounding it filled with a cast of hundreds—adds a sweep that eclipses everything before it. A parade of performers in national garb representing England, Italy, Scotland, Germany, Ireland, Spain, Russia, and France—each contribute to an extended nine-minute medley of traditional European folk songs and national anthems. Then, in succession, each nation is lowered into the melting pot, which Paul Whiteman stirs in a swirl of color. With the musical influences blended together, the doors at the cauldron's base open, and Jazz is born!

Echoing Anderson's earlier stagings, a stampede of dancing cowgirls appear in snazzy gold outfits accompanied by an orchestra of gilded saxophonists playing "Song of the Dawn." Then follows a reprise of many of the film's greatest hits—among them "A Bench in the Park," "It Happened in Monterey," and briefly, an original composition by Yellen and Ager called "Shadows," which is not heard elsewhere in the film.[42] With a frenetic pace we get blink-and-you'll-miss-them glimpses of Jeanette Loff and George Chiles, the Sisters G, Al Norman, Beth Laemmle, Paul Howard, and Nell O'Day and the Tommy Atkins Sextet. (Paul Howard, incidentally, was to have a specialty dance in "A Bench in the Park," but his routine didn't make the final cut. So his reprise here is no longer a reprise—he ends up on screen for less than ten seconds of the finished film!)[43]

Herman Rosse's melting pot spins around to reveal his most ambitious creation yet—a huge violin-shaped bandstand with giant horns and drum motifs spilling out from the sides. It's a visualization of Whiteman's music that is as sleek and well-finished as his refined form of symphonic jazz. "Song of the Dawn" is again reprised to signal the "new dawn" in American music. The grand concert concludes with one last refrain from Whiteman's signature *Rhapsody in Blue*, then the bandleader takes a final bow. Over a black screen we are treated to a further minute and a half of exit music, which includes alternate arrangements of "It Happened in Monterey" and "Song of the Dawn."

A cast of twenty-three, including an ensemble of six accordion players, performed folk songs and dances from Germany, Russia, Spain, Ireland, Italy, and France in the finale of Paramount's novelty short, *All Americans* (1929). Afterward, the performers emerged from the melting pot dressed in gold.

Top: Old World" nationalities are transformed into "New World Americans" in the gigantic melting pot, a striking design visualized by Herman Rosse.

Bottom: Saxophonists parade out of the crucible as the orchestra celebrates the birth of Jazz.

Conclusions

King of Jazz is a highly polished Broadway revue transposed to film. Director John Murray Anderson had no prior experience with the movies, so his film drew upon what he knew best from theater. But contrary to its reputation, the film is not a filmed stage production. With almost complete creative control and a practically unlimited budget, Anderson recreated some of his most celebrated production numbers from the stage and expanded them to meet the scale afforded by the cinematic canvas. As such, the film is often an odd mix of theatricality and film technique; deftly blending inventive camera angles, editing, music, and colored lighting in "Meet the Band," for example, before losing its momentum in the sumptuous but languorous pageant "My Bridal Veil."

Herman Rosse's sets are typically inventive but they too betray his theatrical origins. Despite the bandstand parting like a curtain or others rotating on an axis, his sets were all designed to be viewed from one angle, as in the theater. Hal Mohr and Ray Rennahan's photography makes use of the *Broadway* crane, dolly shots, whip pans, and creative angles, but the film viewer still feels like a theater spectator with the performers' choreography presented directly toward them. On the other hand, the stylized theatrical lighting that brings bold color to many of the sets ultimately works in the film's favor, exploring the visual aspects of Technicolor unlike any film before it.

Some of Anderson's earliest revues used a loose plot to connect each act; in the case of the first *Greenwich Village Follies*, the cast were searching for a good script to produce in the Greenwich Village Theatre. *King of Jazz*, on the other hand, is more typical of Anderson's revues from the mid-to-late 1920s, which used a master of ceremonies to set the scene and provide comedy. Charles Irwin's work on the Publix circuit was frequently praised for his ability to engage a large audience with his witticisms and monologues, but in front of the camera in *King of Jazz* his presence is largely unremarkable.

When viewed today, the very nature of the revue's fractured structure contributes to many of the film's failings. The film's lack of story, identifiable characters or recognizable Hollywood stars makes it hard for modern audiences to engage with. The few Universal contract players that are in the film—Laura La Plante, Glenn Tryon, and Slim Summerville, for example—are thankfully limited to the blackout comedy scenes, instead of being forced to sing and dance as other studios had opted to do. The real stars of the film (outside of Paul Whiteman and his band) are the talented performers that John Murray Anderson brought from New York. He chose the best in the business and developed musical numbers that showcased their unique speci-alities. Sadly, as few of these performers went on to further significant work in motion pictures, audiences today can have trouble identifying exactly who they are watching, given the lack of adequate introductions.

King of Jazz opens with a series of elaborate introductions to its chief performers; Paul Whiteman's "back story" is detailed in "A Fable in Jazz," then we are greeted by his orchestra in "Meet the Boys" and the Russell Markert Dancers in "Meet the Girls," before the ensemble number "I'd Like to Do Things for You" welcomes most of the remainder of the film's musical comedy talent. The diversity of the film's numbers and performers all help demonstrate the influences on American popular music and dance, from old-time lantern slide songs with Frank Leslie to cabaret performers like Jack White. Specialty numbers like "My Ragamuffin Romeo" and the short blackout sketches provide breathing space between lavish pageants like "My Bridal Veil" and "Monterey." "The Song of the Dawn" creates a rousing denouement to the film's string of acts before the majority of the cast returns for the grand "Melting Pot" finale.

Where the film ultimately comes unstuck is in its representation of the origins of jazz. The film's thesis—that jazz had its roots in African rhythms and European traditions—is problematic today, but it was a common discourse at the time. "Jazz came to America three hundred years ago in chains," declared the opening line of Paul Whiteman and Margaret McBride's 1926 book *Jazz*.[44] The origins of ragtime and jazz were in "primitive African swing," a sound that was "at once barbarous and sophisticated—the wilderness tamed to the ballroom."[45]

Walter Lantz and Bill Nolan's opening cartoon takes this popular interpretation literally, and the sentiment reappears later in the film in Jacques Cartier's "tom-tom" dance preceding *Rhapsody in Blue*—a visually arresting sequence that is unfortunately mired in racial stereotypes of the time. "For hundreds of years, savage tribes in far places rolled out rhythm on harsh drums of home-tanned hides," remarked Whiteman, several years before *King of Jazz* was made. "The vitality of the world's youngest nation has absorbed, added to, and carried on that rhythm, first in ragtime and blues, now in jazz."[46] The film accepts this origin concept, but avoids any interrogation, reaffirming its position that "Jazz was born in the African jungle, to the beating of a voodoo drum."

In direct contrast to this thesis is "The Melting Pot of Music" finale, which helps expand the film's viewpoint, albeit in a flawed manner. When Anderson applied this "melting pot" concept to jazz, he ended up distorting the original metaphor about the influences of European traditions on American life and culture. In taking this route, the visually spectacular but confused finale manages to whitewash any complexities in exploring the African-American roots of true jazz and remains in keeping with an industry that at the time largely marginalized black performers on screen.

Rhapsody in Blue provides the grand centerpiece to the film. Despite the enormous effort and cost of the number, Anderson's elaborate and inventive staging doesn't quite work. It comes across as off-tone and poorly contrasts with some of the composition's slower passages. Whiteman's orchestra is seen playing throughout the number, but the vivid colorings of Ferde Grofé's orchestration are mostly overlooked visually. In the program notes for Whiteman's 1928–29 concert series, critic Gilbert Seldes noted that *Rhapsody in Blue*'s "rhythms are the unmistakable beat and retard and syncopation of American popular song and dance music. But"—he concludes—"it is written to be heard, not to be danced."[47] This sentiment remains true. Anderson's spectacular stagings and the multitude of dance acts ultimately detract from the brilliance of Gershwin's music.

When viewed with an audience, *King of Jazz* is still a fantastic experience. Its infectious melodies, carefully choreographed ensembles and specialities, and grandiose sets all combine to create a well-balanced and enjoyable entertainment. Some scenes may not work as well as others—Harry Ruskin's regressive blackout skits come across as out of place to modern audiences amidst the sophistication of the production numbers—but *King of Jazz* is the sum of *all* of its parts. The spectacle and the quality of the staging are the star. Working with his most trusted collaborators from Broadway, John Murray Anderson created a unique type of screen entertainment that has not been attempted since.

One of a series of jumbo lobby cards produced to promote *King of Jazz* in 1930.

CARL LAEMMLE *presents*
PAUL
WHITEMAN
AND HIS **BAND**
in "**KING** *of*
JAZZ"

Chapter 7

CRITICS AND AUDIENCES RESPOND

With heavy promotion and stories of profligate expenses, the studio set high expectations for Junior Laemmle's first full year as head of the Universal studio. His personal productions for the 1930–31 season would be ready for big city engagements in the spring of 1930 and go into general release in the autumn. The first, *La Marseillaise*, had a troubled production history, initially under Paul Fejos, before being completed quickly by a different director under a much-reduced budget. Retitling the film *Captain of the Guard* and releasing co-star Laura La Plante from her contract did not show confidence in the picture. Similarly, the year-long period of indecision that followed the signing of Paul Whiteman revealed that the studio also did not know what to do with *King of Jazz*. There was optimism about *All Quiet on the Western Front* because of the remarkable success of the novel and the reputation of its director Lewis Milestone, but would American audiences welcome yet another war picture, especially one that presented German soldiers sympathetically?

Junior was growing into his new role, working long, long hours and possessing a great sense of responsibility to the studio and his father. "He was just a kid twenty years old, [so] it's not even fair to the kid to criticize him as a producer," Lewis Milestone recalled. "He was there, he was properly running the studio."[1] While Junior's transformation of Universal City was a work in progress, he was also seen as a risk-taker, attempting to shift its output to higher-class pictures that would succeed by their quality alone.

During the 16 weeks that *King of Jazz* was before the cameras, the studio invited friendly critics to the lot. Florabelle Muir, entertainment reporter for the *New York Daily News* and author of a syndicated column, was very enthusiastic about the box office chances of *All Quiet on the Western Front*. Her only characterization of *King of Jazz* was to praise Paul Whiteman's newly discovered comedy skills, and the studio managed to avoid showing her any of *La Marseillaise*.[2] Edwin Schallert of the *Los Angeles Times* was dazzled, but not moved, by "The Melting Pot of Music" number, commenting that an "amazing series of impressions of singers, musicians and dancers in appropriate costumes are flashed before the eye." He could see the potential on the screen for a novel production.[3] Other visitors included a critic from the *Hollywood Filmograph*, and bandleader Abe Lyman.

Coral Clyee of the *New York Morning Telegraph* had the full experience. "I sat beside Mr. Whiteman in the projection room at Universal City," with the white screen and an unseen projectionist, she wrote. "Suddenly the room vibrated with sound ... an amazing revelation of sound. I never heard anything like it." She saw "A Bench in the Park," "The Melting Pot of Music," and "My Bridal Veil" numbers and then visited the "Monterey" set. Clyee warmed to Jeanette Loff, "an utterly engaging person." She predicted "the release of the picture will put Jeanette at the top of the heap."[4] Welford Beaton of the *Film Spectator* praised the sound recording and predicted that the film would initiate a series of color revues.

Universal did not control publishing rights to the songs used in *King of Jazz*, so each composer's songs came from a different publisher, with different artwork.

Recordings for Columbia

Whiteman kept the orchestra out of the recording studio while they were on the studio payroll. After making no recordings during the leisurely summer of 1929, Columbia had brought Whiteman and the orchestra to Columbia's Okeh studio at 11 Union Square in New York for six recording sessions in September and October. The next spring, they recorded for one day during the two-week hiatus from filming in February, then entered the recording studio again for three days immediately following their last day at Universal.

Using the arrangements Ferde Grofé prepared for the film, the orchestra recorded six songs from *King of Jazz*, each with vocals, reflecting the current market preference. "Happy Feet" and "I Like to Do Things for You" featured the Rhythm Boys, "A Bench in the Park" included the Rhythm Boys and the Brox Sisters, while "Ragamuffin Romeo" showcased Jeanie Lang. "Monterey" offered the orchestra's Jack Fulton, and

"Song of the Dawn" presented Bing Crosby and male chorus. Recorded over four months after the singer's arrest, this performance of "Song of the Dawn" provides insight into how Crosby would have handled the song— less stentorian, without the held notes, and a faster, bouncier performance, more attuned to 1930s radio than 1920s operettas.

Press Screening

Although the film was not in its final form, the press screening for *King of Jazz* was held on March 24 to support magazine critics with early deadlines. The 1680-seat Belmont Theatre on South Vermont Street, just south of Beverly Boulevard in Los Angeles, was frequently used for press preview screenings. A studio would rent the theatre and invite the audience to stay for a free second feature. The biggest response from the friendly audience was for the "My Bridal Veil" and

Rhapsody in Blue numbers. After the film, the press and invited guests made their way to the Roosevelt Hotel on Hollywood Boulevard, where Whiteman hosted a farewell party on the mezzanine. The following evening, after their final *Old Gold* broadcast at KHJ radio studios with local friends and celebrities in the audience, Whiteman and his band would leave by train for a short tour of the Northwest.

The studio screenings, the previews, and the press screening provided audience feedback to Anderson, and resulted in a continual reshuffling of the sequences in the film. The major production numbers stayed, in varying order, the specialty and novelty numbers were moved around, and the comedy sketches came and went. Grace Hayes had been featured in two downbeat numbers: "They Call Dancing a Pleasure," as a dance hall hostess, sung ironically to the tune of "I Like to Do Things for You," and "My Lover," a song of unrequited love. Both of her numbers failed to connect with audiences, and were cut, leaving her presence in the film as nearer a series of cameos rather than the prominent participant that Anderson originally intended. And as with his stage revues, Anderson ruthlessly trimmed parts of numbers that dragged.

But the response of the preview audience was lukewarm. Instead, according to future director Edgar G. Ulmer, "the preview proved to the industry that they were on the wrong path and a dismal flop was to be expected."[5] Fortunately, while Junior had bet big on *King of Jazz*, the studio had another large production with better prospects opening around the same time.

Los Angeles Openings

Studios worked out release plans for each of their films tailored to the anticipated audience demand. *All Quiet* was a strong picture that satisfied preview audiences, would receive favorable word of mouth, and would build over time. It would be released as a "roadshow" to maximize its commercial value. The enormously successful release of *The Birth of a Nation* (1914) set the pattern. A film would be booked like a theatrical event, often in a rented legitimate theater, at higher admission prices, with reserved seats, limited to two shows a day. This maximized the value of the first-run exhibition while the promotion would increase the success of the film on its general release. *All Quiet* would go out as a roadshow around the country, with many of the engagements in Shubert-owned legitimate theaters, newly wired for sound. Universal also established a roadshow department to rent theaters in additional cities.

Based on the previews, it was apparent that audiences would not recommend *King of Jazz* to their friends. Without the benefit of positive word of mouth, the film needed to reach as many patrons as rapidly as possible by playing continuous performances at normal prices. *King of Jazz* received its world premiere engagement at the 1652-seat Fox Criterion Theatre, with admission prices at 35 cents and 65 cents for continuous performances from 11 a.m. to 11 p.m.

Part of the Los Angeles downtown theatre district, the Criterion had hosted the local first runs of *The Jazz Singer* (1927) and *In Old Arizona* (1928). *Montana Moon* (1930) with Joan Crawford closed on Friday at the Criterion, and *King of Jazz* opened on Saturday, including a midnight show. The KHJ radio station scheduled two programs that day featuring songs from the film. Paul Whiteman was not there—after shows in Portland and Seattle, he and the band were on a train back to New York. Two other musicals opened that same day in Los Angeles—Warner Bros.' Technicolor operetta of the Russian revolution, *Song of the Flame* (1930), at the Warner Hollywood, and the John McCormack dramatic musical *Song o' My Heart* (1930) at Grauman's Chinese Theatre. Paramount's all-Technicolor operetta *The Vagabond King* (1930) was playing nearby at Grauman's Egyptian.

Two days later, *All Quiet on the Western Front* premiered at the 1518-seat Carthay Circle theater in Westwood. Ticket prices were 75 cents and $1.60 for the matinee and evening performances. Afterwards, Junior hosted 300 guests at the members-only Embassy Club on Hollywood Boulevard.

Few motion pictures, and fewer still from Universal, had ever received such unanimously positive reviews. "So terrific, so dramatic and with a two and a half hour driving cry against modern warfare, *All Quiet on the Western Front* last night fairly shocked film fans at Carthay Circle when it was premiered." (*Los Angeles Daily News*) "On the scroll of great achievements of the screen let the name of this production be deeply and darkly engraved." (*Los Angeles Times*) "Thunders its message with a fidelity of purpose and a disregard of conventional entertainment values that has been equaled but once or twice in the history of motion pictures." (*Los Angeles Herald*) "A new plume for the young producer, Carl Laemmle, Jr." (*Los Angeles Express*).[6] The film program was supplemented by a prelude of martial music by Abe Lyman and his band, and a cartoon.[7]

The results from the first week were startling— *All Quiet* had sold almost every seat at every show and grossed $22,000. Soon evening shows were sold out ten days in advance. *King of Jazz* started off strong for the

FIRST DAY

THIRD DAY

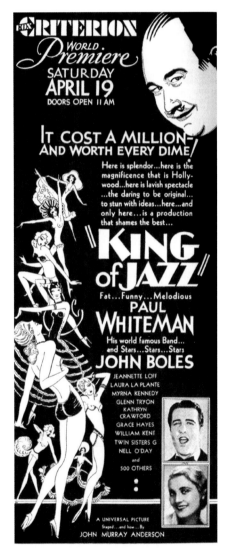

SIXTH DAY

Local print advertising for *King of Jazz* started the week before the Los Angeles premiere. *Exhibitors Herald-World*, May 31, 1930, 132-133.

SEVENTH DAY

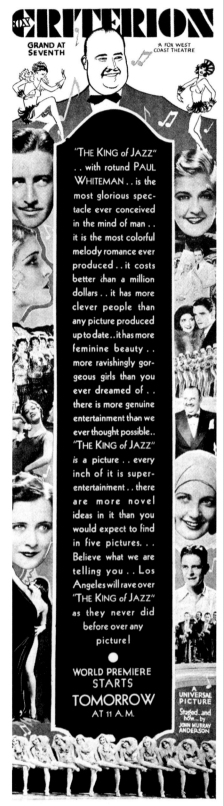

EIGHTH DAY

A handmade layout by Herman Rosse of a proposed souvenir program for the premiere of *King of Jazz*.

first few days, heading toward an $18,000 gross, but then attendance collapsed, ending the week at $13,000. *Paramount on Parade* opened a week after *King of Jazz* at the 3600-seat Paramount theatre (25 cents, 75 cents) downtown and followed the same pattern, with a "wildfire start" and then was pulled after a week.[8]

The press preview of *King of Jazz* showcased Jeanie Lang singing two songs—her speciality number with Paul Whiteman, "I'd Like to Do Things For You," in addition to the "Ragamuffin Romeo" duet with George Chiles, introducing Stadler and Rose's rag-doll number. By the time the film opened in Los Angeles, "I'd Like to Do Things For You" had been cut from the film, along with her screen credit. But the critical response to Jeanie Lang's contribution was so positive, possibly supported by her success in local radio, that the number went back in, even though it was too late to add Lang's name onscreen.[9] "I'd Like to Do Things For You" was added to the running order for the San Diego and New York engagements, which opened two weeks after the Los Angeles premiere.

The Trailer

Some films are easier to show than to describe, so Universal created separate nine-minute promotional shorts for *All Quiet on the Western Front* and *King of Jazz*. These were sent to the studio's exchanges in January to familiarize sales staff with their upcoming super-productions.[10] For the public Universal created a nearly four-minute trailer in Technicolor for *King of Jazz* that presents highlights from the biggest production numbers. Opening with half a minute of titles using the same style of kaleidoscopic backgrounds as the film, audiences were left with no doubt that the film was a revue—"loaded with song hits and hilarious comedy sketches." The trailer emphasized the film's scale, incorporating long shots of the more stately production numbers and a full minute of the *Rhapsody in Blue* on the soundtrack. The Rhythm Boys and the comic blackouts are absent, and there is only a brief appearance by Paul Whiteman. The emphasis is on John Boles, featured in a lengthy abridgement of the "Song of the Dawn" number.

Tent Shows

Carl Laemmle Sr. was concerned about getting playdates for *King of Jazz*, and during a layover in Kansas City on the way to New York, he speculated on Universal's options to get around monopoly exhibition markets. "The independent producer may be shut out if he will not accede to the [low] prices the combines are willing to pay." Laemmle suggested, "it is entirely feasible for a film production company of sufficient magnitude to play a succession of 'tent show' engagements throughout the agricultural sections" of the country.[11] It was subsequently reported that Universal bought 40 tents for showing *King of Jazz* in small towns in Southern and Western states.[12]

The East Coast Premiere

Universal was booking *King of Jazz* in major markets as rapidly as Technicolor could manufacture prints and the exchanges could line up theaters. Within a week of the Los Angeles opening, Baltimore hosted the East Coast premiere of the film at the Auditorium Theatre, with personal appearances by Paul Whiteman and John Boles. *King of Jazz* had a one-week first run before moving over to another theater for continuous performances from 9 a.m. to midnight. The Auditorium Theatre then opened a roadshow engagement of *All Quiet*, three shows daily, all seats reserved, advance prices of 50 cents to $1.50, that lasted four weeks. *King of Jazz* grossed $3,630 during its one week in Baltimore, while the following week *All Quiet* brought in $8,400 at the same theater.

A week after Baltimore, *King of Jazz* opened in San Diego, Washington, DC, Detroit—and in New York at the Roxy Theatre.

The New Universal

The first stage of Junior's strategy to produce higher-quality product was three films of roadshow caliber: *Captain of the Guard, King of Jazz,* and *All Quiet on the Western Front.* Much of the company's resources were tied up in these three films. But the ability to produce additional expensive pictures in the future depended on recovering as much of the studio's investment as soon as possible, rather than maximizing revenue from these pictures over the long run. To launch these films in the largest market of New York City, sales head Lou Metzger booked Universal's seven biggest features of the season into the Roxy Theatre. Six of the seven would have their

The San Diego engagement opened on May 2, 1930, two weeks after the Los Angeles premiere, and included the number "I'd Like to Do Things for You." *Motion Picture News*, June 14, 1930, 110.

The trailer for *King of Jazz* presented the film as a stately show with elaborate musical numbers of Broadway quality.

Carl Laemmle beams as his son's first two big productions open on Broadway. *Variety*, April 30, 1930, 22–23.

initial New York run at the Roxy, while *All Quiet* would screen as a roadshow, and then play at the Roxy two weeks after its New York roadshow run concluded.[13]

The 5,920-seat Roxy Theatre at 50th Street and 7th Avenue was the largest motion picture theatre in the world. Owned by the Fox Theatres Corporation, the Roxy showcased Fox's best productions. The theater had a weekly average gross of $100,000 during 1928, and 1929 was even better. Fox's military comedy, *The Cock-eyed World*, set the house record in August 1929, grossing $650,000 during its four-week run. The first of Universal's seven specials for 1930 was *Captain of the Guard*, playing two weeks with John Boles introducing the film in person in April 1930, doing adequate business with $100,000 the first week, and falling off to $70,300 the second.

To promote Junior's move to higher-class fare, Universal held its first international sales convention at the Savoy-Plaza hotel in New York, from Saturday April 26 through the following Thursday. Branch managers for each exchange across the U.S. and Canada, as well as international representatives, heard how in the next season the

studio was going to produce only 20 features, no series westerns, and its last four serials. For a follow-on session, Universal's general managers from Latin America, Europe, England, and Australia joined both Laemmles in Atlantic City, to discuss how to produce and sell sound films in "foreign language countries."[14]

The Universal convention was scheduled to give the sales heads the opportunity to see for themselves the results of Junior's initial program of big productions. On the Sunday evening there was a banquet at the Ritz-Carlton to celebrate Carl Laemmle's 24th year in the film industry. They attended a special midnight show of *King of Jazz* at the Roxy. Whiteman spoke to the convention, joking that the proper billing for the revue should be "Directed by John Murray Anderson and interfered with by Paul Whiteman."[15] For the final night of the conference they attended the premiere of *All Quiet on the Western Front*.

The New York City premiere engagement of *King of Jazz* was promoted with this electric sign at 48th Street and Broadway.

New York Openings

For the premiere and extended run of *All Quiet on the Western Front*, Universal booked the 922-seat Central Theatre, at Broadway and 47th Street, which a month before had concluded a 26-week run of Warner Bros.' *Disraeli* (1929) with George Arliss. *All Quiet* opened April 29 at the Central, with tickets priced $1 to $2.50. Actress Ginger Rogers was working at Paramount's Astoria studio, and attended the premiere. She recalled, "Mother and I put on our long evening gowns and joined the excited throng that gathered in the tiny foyer of the Central Theater. The V.I.P.s from the business world were joined by the Hollywood stars who happened to be in Manhattan." She wrote, "though it was April, ladies wore gorgeous long evening coats and capes trimmed with silver and white fox, ermine, mink, and sable. "[16]

The show started late and the film did not end until 12:30 a.m. Carl Laemmle Jr. threw an opening night party at the Embassy Club on East 57th Street.

The New York critics spoke with a single voice, lauding the film for having matched the power and impact of the book: "a memorable piece of work. A notable achievement sincere and earnest" (*New York Times*), "enormously compelling" (*New York Herald Tribune*), "audience stunned with its terrific power" (*New York American*), "marvelously artistic, supremely realistic. Far and away the most significant picture ever turned out by Universal" (*New York Evening World*).[17]

With only sixteen shows weekly in a small theatre, demand for tickets to *All Quiet* in Manhattan became intense. After complaints, police arrested over 30 barkers for blocking traffic in front of the theatre. They were calling out to pedestrians that otherwise unavailable

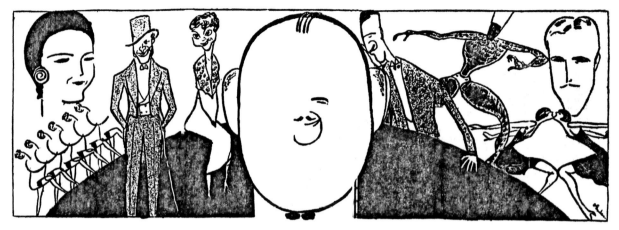

The *New York Telegram* used custom artwork by cartoonist A. Birnbaum to promote the Roxy screenings of *King of Jazz* in May 1930.

tickets could be bought upstairs. A speculator working from a Chinese restaurant on the second floor of the Central Theatre building was reselling the cheapest tickets for $2.75.[18]

King of Jazz opened three days later, on Friday May 2 at the Roxy, for a planned three-week run. There were five full performances daily including a stage show, plus an extra midnight show of just the film. The show was Whiteman on the screen and Whiteman and Gershwin on the huge Roxy stage. Whiteman and his orchestra performed for a reported $12,500 per week, folded into the Roxy Symphony Orchestra for a total of 135 players. George Gershwin was recruited at $5,000 per week to play the *Rhapsody in Blue* during the live performances.

Universal subsidized the show, contributing $1,000 per week toward Gershwin's salary. Universal also agreed to contribute up to half of the $6,000 cost to install and remove "additional machines necessary to run the sound track separate from the film."[19] First-run engagements of *Hell's Angels* (1930) used this approach, with a 35mm picture print and a separate 35mm soundtrack print running in synchronization, as did the Lawrence Tibbett operetta in Technicolor, *The Rogue Song* (1930), playing at the Astor Theatre.[20]

To make room for the stage show, *King of Jazz* was trimmed from 104 minutes to 98 minutes, with the entire program running 140 minutes. The performance began with a sound newsreel, followed by the orchestra performing Gershwin's "Strike Up the Band" and other show tunes (with vocals by Mildred Bailey and the Roxy Chorus). Then the familiar potato-head Whiteman caricature was projected on the screen, while a tuxe-doed Paul Whiteman, with a large red rose in his lapel, came to the podium before the combined Whiteman and Roxy symphony orchestras. George Gershwin came down the runway to the piano, greeted by loud applause,

and the live performance of *Rhapsody in Blue* began. The live program concluded with some Victor Herbert pieces, with vocals by John Fulton and the Roxy Chorus, followed by the film.

Presenting a show with the same piece of music twice, once live with no visual accompaniment and once in truncated form as a dramatization on screen with recorded music, was a curious choice. "After the full tone and beautiful playing of the *Rhapsody in Blue*

All Quiet on the Western Front was heavily promoted in *Universal Weekly*.

by the combined Roxy and Whiteman orchestras, with the composer as soloist, the screen rendition in the *King of Jazz* is thin and disappointing," penned a *Variety* staff writer. In the film, "the music is lost in a mass of glittering over-production." *Variety*'s editor complained that with the staging of *Rhapsody in Blue*, the film had sacrificed its centerpiece. "The millions who have never heard the great Whiteman band play this biggest of all jazz melodies won't hear it here, either. Mr. Anderson has seen fit to scramble it up with 'production.' It's all busted to pieces, and while it's all there, it's not the Whiteman number it would have been had it been played simply straight."[21]

Meanwhile, after the show, backstage at the Roxy, Gershwin had time to reflect on performing his most famous concert work five times a day in front of 20-30,000 people daily, and tried to put the music in perspective. "I feel the answer, the recognition, coming from the audience as the music goes," he told a reporter for the *New York Sun*. The *Rhapsody* had captured the popular imagination more successfully than his subsequent serious works. While John Murray Anderson associated the music with tuxedos, evening gowns, and dancers, Gershwin was more introspective. "It's growing on me, too, and I do not know why," he said. "But it is all New York, all America. It is a picnic party in Brooklyn, or a dark-skinned girl singing and shouting her blues in a Harlem cabaret. I try to depict a scene, a New York crowd. And it's vulgar. It's full of vulgarisms. That's what gives it weight. I never tried to prettify it as most composers do."[22]

The Roxy's first week's gross was an unimpressive $102,703. With Universal's $2 million revue on the screen and the Whiteman orchestra and Gershwin on the stage, the picture had grossed barely more than the $99,700 that *Captain of the Guard* had earned the month before during its first week at the Roxy. With the Roxy's running costs and nearly $20,000 added overhead for Whiteman's band and Gershwin for the first week, it was unlikely that anyone (other than Whiteman and Gershwin) was making money. *Variety*'s editor, Sime Silverman, was perplexed. "If Gershwin could have any box-office value at the Roxy at any time, which is doubtful beyond a few loge seats, it would be for the second week of this combo, if that happens, as an attraction for additional billing purposes. As is, the Roxy, with everything the first week, has nothing left to follow."[23]

Although Universal had positioned Jeanette Loff for stardom, a different star was born at the Roxy. "The 'discovery' of the picture is a little girl named Jeanie Lang, who stops the show when she croons to Paul Whiteman 'I'd Like to Do Something to You' [*sic*]," wrote Regina Crewe in the *New York American*."[24] Although Lang had not even been one of the nine players listed in the first

week's ads, she became so popular in the Roxy engagement that by the second week advertisements featured "Jeanie Lang, the new screen sensation," along with John Boles.[25]

For the second week Whiteman was gone from the stage, with Gershwin performing his *Concerto in F* with the Roxy Symphony Orchestra. Business collapsed to $62,700, the second-lowest gross since the theater opened. There was no third week. By comparison, *All Quiet* would play at the Central Theatre for 15 weeks.

Reviews

Neither the trade reviewers nor the popular press were kind to *King of Jazz*, seeing few of the film's virtues and all of its flaws. John Murray Anderson's static staging and lack of film sense drew criticism. He "knew nothing about picture direction and didn't seem to know any more, either, at the finish of the film," wrote *Variety* editor Sime Silverman. "He is apparently a stager who would rather have an audience know he knows more about colors and pretty backgrounds than anything else."[26]

This trade advertisement for *King of Jazz* featuring John Boles and Jeanie Lang appeared in *Variety*, as well as in *Motion Picture News*, May 24, 1930.

Promotional herald for *King of Jazz*.

The popular reviewers were equally harsh. With no connecting thread, *King of Jazz* "doesn't try to hold the interest of the audience," wrote the critic for the Brooklyn *Standard Union*. "It unfolds itself and defies the audience to lose interest."[27]

Some reviews were raves, though they usually devoted more space to describing the film than critiquing its virtues. "There is nothing imitative, all the various turns being blessed with originality," wrote Mordaunt Hall in the *New York Times*. Other critics felt that the film's flaw was not that it was a revue, but that it simply rehashed the weakest elements of the format, without bringing anything fresh. "One expects entertainment to be given on a broader scope and not in the same form seen for several years in the usual run of musical comedies," wrote trade reviewer P. S. Harrison. Los Angeles-based reviewers who had missed the Broadway revues of the 1920s acknowledged that the numbers might be "very conventional, but most superbly staged," but still criticized "an amazing lack of originality."[28] Others felt that the total was less than the sum of its parts, no matter how pleasant those parts might be. "What it lacks most is a little more skill in its construction, for it runs from the ultra artistic to the commonplace," wrote the editor of the *Film Daily*. "It is a magnificent patch work quilt clumsily sewn together."[29]

"When one leaves the theater after seeing the *King of Jazz* there is nothing that one carries away," remarked trade critic P. S. Harrison, "except a desire to see a picture that has continuity and that presents people with distinct personalities and not just fleeting glimpses of actors singing or dancing."[30] The other motion picture revues—from M-G-M (*The Hollywood Revue of 1929*), Warner Bros. (*The Show of Shows*), and Paramount (*Paramount on Parade*)—featured stars and built on audience familiarity with their established onscreen personalities. But with the exception of John Boles, *King of Jazz* incorporated familiar players only for blackout sketches (not even built around their personas). And the film was not staged in a way to introduce the performers or present their onscreen charisma. "In spite of its elaborateness, in spite of its good points," *New York Sun* critic John S. Cohen Jr. wrote, "there is such a lack of intimacy and outstanding personalities to hold it together—that it becomes a bit wearisome before it is over."[31] When the studio previewed the "Melting Pot of Music" number for *Los Angeles Times* critic Edwin Schallert back in January, he wasn't sure what he was seeing—"one gains the feeling there is an overwhelming massing of talent; yet perhaps the same people are used in the majority of the numbers."[32]

The greatest criticism was for the blackout sketches—"you can find most of the gags in any old minstrel book" (Brooklyn *Standard Union*); "in comedy the revue is almost barren" (*Variety*); and "just at the point where the audience gets warmed up to the point of thinking, 'this is something I shouldn't have missed,' there is inter-

This frame enlargement from an original release print of the film's trailer uses a green that is nearly turquoise for the *Rhapsody in Blue* number.

jected one of those dreary, time-worn blackouts to drop the building interest of the show a goodly measure." (*Harrison's Reports*)[33]

Technicolor

The color in *King of Jazz* was widely praised both for Rosse's production design and Technicolor's ability to accurately reproduce his intentions on the screen. "Color is used with a careful restraint that makes for a distinguished smartness of effects, wrote a critic who attended the Los Angeles premiere. "A rich burnt orange and a rather dark green predominate. Several scenes have a chic restraint as well as a spectacular charm from the contrast of white, silver, black and flesh tones."[34]

Six months before the premiere of *King of Jazz*, Technicolor had significant problems producing enough quality prints at a pace to meet the demand for films in color. "The public in general seems to be convinced that

Technicolor is essentially fuzzy," wrote Leonard Troland, the company's head of research, in an internal memo.[35] Technicolor introduced improved lenses during the filming of *King of Jazz*, and the company opened a new Hollywood laboratory in March 1930, which addressed many of the concerns. "Out here in this plant the first two subjects we have tackled—*The Jazz King* [*sic*] and *Song of the Flame*—have yielded prints in quantity as good as I have ever seen," Technicolor president Herbert T. Kalmus wrote in April.[36]

It is difficult to be certain how the color in *King of Jazz* appeared in 1930. Projection made much more difference for color than black & white films. "One producer source stated that he had made it a point to check on their color pictures in various houses and to his amazement found that they looked very good in one spot but terrible in another," *Variety* reported.[37] Technicolor would set aside the best prints for high-profile engagements. Yet a critic viewing the Roxy engagement of *King of Jazz* wrote, "while most of the scenes are emphatically effective, there are some stretches that are much too dark. Mr. Anderson, however, has worked marvels with salmon pinks, terracotta reds, sage greens and other pastel shades."[38] Another critic at the same screening agreed that "the general color effects are darker and denser than usual," but praised the use of color, saying "the pastel shades achieved in the girls' dresses in one number as they float together and fade apart are as lovely as reality and as true."[39]

On a visit to Manhattan, Technicolor's head of research Leonard Troland viewed Warner Bros.' *Song of the Flame* first. "I did not like the *King of Jazz* at the Roxy nearly as well, as this appeared to have green highlights and purple densities."[40] The *New York Herald Tribune* reviewer praised "the lovely coloring, especially the sea blue for background so frequently used," and other reviews—and even the British souvenir program—refer to the use of blue on the screen. There is no blue in surviving original prints, although in some cases Technicolor's green is much closer to turquoise, green mixed with a pale blue.

The Theatrical Environment

The release of *King of Jazz* faced headwinds, with repeated reminders that the film conceived during an unprecedented period of prosperity had missed its window of opportunity. The October 1929 stock market crash was slowing the economy, and cinema admissions were feeling the impact. Average releases were doing below average. "It is becoming increasingly apparent here that unemployment and adverse business conditions are taking a severe toll along the local rialto," wrote a *Variety* reporter from Minneapolis in March 1930. "Practically all the show houses are in a slump, from which they emerge only temporarily when they have outstanding attractions."[41]

In addition, the enormous audience excitement over musical films had faded, as the novelty had waned, and the average quality declined. Even when musicals were still acceptable to audiences, revues were not, and *Variety* documented the transition as audiences turned away from what they once adored. In January 1930, promotion

Caricatures of Paul Whiteman and advertising materials on display in the lobby of the 1800-seat Orpheum Theatre, Denver, Colorado, in 1930.

Children's band promoting the exhibition of *King of Jazz* at the Strand Theatre, Market Street, Wilkes-Barre, Pennsylvania.

for the Kansas City engagement of Ernst Lubitsch's *The Love Parade* (1929) included the announcement that the film was "not a revue." *Variety* concluded that this "shows that the exhibs have learned the public will go stronger for a musical with a plot."[42] In March, the State Theatre in Los Angeles advertised the M-G-M musical *Chasing Rainbows* (1930) as "not a revue" on the film's 24-sheet posters. The next month Fox's *High Society Blues* (1930), a comedy-drama with a few songs, was promoted by a Minneapolis theatre as "positively not a revue." A theatrical reporter investigated, determining that the local exhibitors believe "that the local public is fed up on the screen revue entertainment."[43] The newspaper advertisements for *Paramount on Parade*, which premiered in Los Angeles a week after *King of Jazz*, egregiously promoted the film as "not a revue, not a musical comedy."[44]

RKO's planned contribution to the revue cycle was to be *Radio Revels*, featuring NBC radio stars and five popular bands. Announced in June 1929, the property was delayed and reworked until it emerged as a standard Wheeler & Woolsey comedy, *The Cuckoos*, in spring 1930. Pathe developed two projects: *International Television Revue* was announced in October 1929 but never made it

past the script stage, and *Greenwich Village Follies*, based on John Murray Anderson's theatrical revue, ran into repeated delays until it was cancelled.

Then audiences turned against all musicals. For its San Francisco engagements in June 1930, Fox's *Movietone Follies of 1930* was retitled *Svensen's Wild Party*. Advertising emphasized the comedy with El Brendel and Marjorie White, and the picture did good business as a result.[45] Some theaters simply lied. In August, M-G-M's *Good News* (1930) was promoted in Los Angeles as "not a musical" when it definitely was. Planned productions were cancelled, while completed musicals were trimmed until there were virtually no songs remaining. Musical stars Jeanette MacDonald and Bernice Claire were assigned straight roles.

Into this environment, the long-delayed *King of Jazz* was released.

National Release

While Universal executives focused on the New York opening of *King of Jazz* at the Roxy, the film was also reaching the nation's capital. The Washington, DC, engagement beginning May 1 was heavily promoted, and the motion picture writer at the *Washington Post* loved the film, telling readers it was "one of the greatest pictures ever made." Critic Nelson Bell managed to mention *King of Jazz* in ten different articles, including a separate review for the second week of the engagement, and the Rialto Theatre returned the favor by purchasing ¾-page advertisements. The hoopla boosted attendance, attracting lines down the block for some evening shows. Bell's prophecy that "if other Technicolor revues have been able to run three and four weeks, this one should keep going all summer" was far too optimistic, as the film was pulled after two.[46] The film reached the audience for musical revues, but that audience was not as large as it had been six months before. *Variety* noted, "Just about as elsewhere—started two week stay, big after much exploitation and dwindled."[47]

Later Bell tried to identify why both *King of Jazz* and *Paramount on Parade* flopped in the Washington market. The two films were "as widely different as two plotless musical frolics might well be made. *King of Jazz* subordinated the human element to a perfected mechanical, technical and artistic quality that has never before been even remotely approached. *Paramount on Parade*, on the other hand, stressed its personnel and [unlike *King of Jazz*, minimized] its resort to massive investitures and bizarre trappings to gain its effects. To neither ... did the public respond in any downright heartening degree."[48]

The pattern continued for the rest of the first run of *King of Jazz* in the United States and Canada. The strength of audience response to the first run of a new release in a city's downtown theater would be a very accurate prediction of its strength as a box office attraction. After the first run, films would spread out to second-run and subsequently to third-run cinemas. *Variety*'s assessment proved prophetic; *King of Jazz* was "a box-office picture anywhere for one week."[49] But seldom more than one week.

Across the country *All Quiet on the Western Front* triumphed, while *King of Jazz* swept in and out of town. In Chicago both pictures were shown at regular prices. *All Quiet* ran four weeks to *King of Jazz*'s two, but still grossed as much in its last week as the Whiteman picture did for its entire run. In the cities where *All Quiet* was presented as a roadshow, the comparison was brutal. In Philadelphia, *All Quiet* ran for eight weeks, still grossing more in its final week than *King of Jazz* did during its first (and only) week first-run. In most cities *King of Jazz* lasted a week, never more than two, while *All Quiet* played eight weeks in Boston and Pittsburgh, four in San Francisco, and five in Toronto and Montreal.

My Pal Paul

Walter Lantz's animated "A Fable in Jazz" was universally praised, and Lantz's contract was renewed in March 1930. The "Oswald the Lucky Rabbit" series releases in the summer of 1930 included parodies of recent Universal features: *Hells Heels* (*Hell's Heroes*), *Not So Quiet* (*All Quiet on the Western Front*), *Spooks* (*The Phantom of the Opera*, reissued with sound in 1930).

One of the best is *My Pal Paul*, an affectionate tribute to the bandleader. The opening silhouette of

Newspaper advertisement for the Washington, DC, first-run engagement, in the May 1, 1930 issue of the *Washington Post*.

Whiteman conducting "Song of the Dawn" is revealed as Oswald. When the cartoon rabbit gets in trouble, the real (animated) Whiteman arrives in his roadster and comes to Oswald's rescue. Other songs reprised at length to animated accompaniment include "A Bench in the Park," "Monterey," "Ragamuffin Romeo," and "Happy Feet." While the animation and gags are not very sophis-

ticated, and the musicians are a studio orchestra and not Whiteman's band, the affection is real.

Some of the songs and animation from *My Pal Paul* were reused the next year in *The Bandmaster* (1931), which also offered animated rag dolls dancing to "Ragamuffin Romeo." And some of the animation from "A Fable in Jazz" reappeared in a different storyline in *Africa*

As was standard at the time, *King of Jazz* was promoted with a variety of different artwork available as lobby cards; jumbo lobby cards; one-sheet, three-sheet and 24-sheet posters; and newspaper ads. Above is one of eight artificially colored jumbo lobby cards from the 1930 release.

King of Jazz was photographed full frame (left), but the shots were composed for an optical soundtrack, with unneeded space on the left of the image. The image is instantly centered once cropped on the left part of the image (center). During projection the top and bottom were slightly cropped (right), properly framing the composition vertically.

(1930). After being brought out to Hollywood to work on *King of Jazz*, James Dietrich remained at Universal as Lantz's musical director. Dietrich regularly incorporated songs from *King of Jazz* in cartoons released as late as the autumn of 1933.

Aspect Ratio

King of Jazz was produced during a period of technological transition for sound films, and was released to theaters in two configurations: sound-on-film, or as mute prints with accompanying discs. In addition to different options for recording and reproducing soundtracks, each studio and theatre chain set its own specifications for photography or projection. During the silent era the image aspect ratio had been a pleasing 4x3 rectangle. Sound-on-disc projection did not affect the shape of the film on the screen, while the soundtrack required for sound-on-film processes blocked part of the image, creating the nearly square "Movietone" format.[50]

Almost as soon as the sound-on-film process was introduced, theaters arbitrarily enlarged and cropped the Movietone images to provide a wider and thus larger image on their screens. Projectionists seemed unconcerned. "Of course it is true that a wee bit will be cut off at both top and bottom of the photograph on the film," wrote one projectionist, while filmmakers and audiences complained that credits were truncated along with character's heads and feet.[51]

In August 1929, only Universal theaters were properly projecting the nearly square Movietone ratio, while Paramount Publix, Loew's, Fox West Coast, and Balaban and Katz were instructing their projectionists to crop all images top and bottom in projection.[52] Eventually an all-industry effort led by the Academy of Motion

Picture Arts and Sciences resulted in standards for prints and projection in 1932, with what became known as the Academy Ratio—an image masked to a 4x3 rectangle.

The Technicolor cameras that photographed *King of Jazz* exposed the entire height and width of the 35mm frame. The cameramen relied on a ground glass in the viewfinder that outlined the "safe action area" as a guide to compose the image. Although the film could be successfully projected in Movietone ratio, the images were composed to be cropped on the top, bottom, and left for projection at 4x3.

London

Whiteman's record sales and his two European tours made him a favorite in the United Kingdom, and there were high hopes that *King of Jazz* would be successful there. In February, Britain's contribution to the screen revue genre, *Elstree Calling* (1930), including ensemble numbers staged by André Charlot, had achieved a measure of success. For *King of Jazz*, Universal's managing director for Great Britain, J. V. Bryson, brought a print from the New York sales convention and the film received its London trade showing on June 8. John Murray Anderson was at the show, along with C. B. Cochran, who had produced Anderson's London theatrical revues in the 1920s. Cochran credited Anderson with raising the artistic level of popular entertainment in *King of Jazz*, and he and Anderson agreed that producers could be artistic without being dull and that "what is good entertainment need not necessarily be bad art."[53]

Additional trade shows were held in Manchester, Newcastle, and Glasgow. The reviews ranged from positive to ecstatic. "Interesting use of shadows in color is also to be discovered in *The King of Jazz*, particularly on

[Jacques] Cartier's voodoo dance, which is quite the best thing in this, or any similar film," wrote the *Manchester Guardian*'s critic after seeing the trade show. "There is an attempt to cut the dance in with the rhythm of the drums which it is exciting to find."[54] The blackout sketches were "among the most successful numbers," wrote the reviewer for industry trade paper *The Bioscope,* who mock-apologized that his ear must not be sufficiently sophisticated, so the efforts of the Rhythm Boys "in which half the words were inaudible, a goo-goo-girl whose archness approached the point of imbecility, three lovely ladies who sang out of tune under blue feather fans … were entirely beyond his comprehension."[55]

Universal's London office contributed to a summer fundraiser for the Queen Charlotte's Hospital Mother-Saving Campaign. The event was held on the Thames Riviera, a hotel and entertainment resort on Tagg's Island, on the River Thames near Hampton Court Palace, accessible by footbridge and ferry. The island had been purchased in 1912 by music-hall impresario Fred Karno, for his hotel the Karsino. After Karno went bankrupt, the island was purchased in 1930 by A. E. Bundy, who renamed the site the Thames Riviera, opening a cabaret, offering dancing in the hotel ballrooms and outdoor entertainment.

The "King of Jazz Carnival" was held on Thursday, July 17, 1930, featuring music, film, and outdoor events,

Pages from the British souvenir program for *King of Jazz*.

JOHN BOLES
The Screen's Greatest Singing Personality!

The Greatest Show on Earth!

KING OF JAZZ

JOHN BOLES JEANETTE LOFF
PAUL WHITEMAN & HIS BAND
ALL-COLOUR, MELODY & MIRTH

A Riot of Rhythm!
. . . impossible to overrate the excellence . . . more magnificent, tuneful, beautiful, and thoughtful than any of its musical predecessors . . . film one could see again and again.—
EVENING NEWS
UNIVERSAL'S SUPER EXTRAVAGANZA!

REGAL
MARBLE ARCH

ALHAMBRA
LEICESTER SQUARE

The London release of *King of Jazz* followed the pattern of *All Quiet on the Western Front* by presenting the film in two theatres simultaneously. *Daily Telegraph*, October 21, 1930, 8.

with three West End dance bands, including Hal Kemp and his orchestra, a "mannequin parade" (fashion show), and motor boat rally, plus the first public showing in London of *King of Jazz*, which received a great ovation. Many acts from London nightclubs and music halls appeared in person, including Marion Stadler and Don Rose (in London on a European tour), who performed their rag doll number from the film. The event began at 3 p.m., with the showing of *King of Jazz* at 6 p.m., followed by dancing and entertainment until 3 a.m.[56]

While Whiteman wasn't in London, his biggest British fan was. Lord Mountbatten was as knowledgeable and enthusiastic about films as dance music, and had silent film projectors in his London home. He contacted Universal's London office in July, asking if he could show

King of Jazz at an upcoming dinner party, and the studio sent a print and a portable sound projector.[57]

All Quiet on the Western Front had opened simultaneously at the 1,438-seat Alhambra Theatre in Leicester Square and the 2,400-seat Regal Cinema Marble Arch on June 14. Closing at the Regal after four weeks, it continued at the Alhambra Theatre for another ten weeks, and then moved to the Rialto Theatre for a total West End run of 26 weeks.[58]

Universal had challenges with exhibition in other parts of the country. Even after the success of *All Quiet* in the U.S., British exhibition chains saw the studio's product as weak and demanded excessive terms. In reaction, Universal leased legitimate theaters in major cities, dispatching one of seven three-ton trucks equipped with everything needed to outfit a theater with projection and sound, powered by an electrical generator on the truck.[59] *King of Jazz* played around the country during the summer, breaking a single show performance record at the Winter Gardens theatre in the seaside resort of Blackpool in Lancashire, and *All Quiet* did even better. Exhibitors that booked *All Quiet* for showings after the official release date of February 9, 1931 complained that the 24 "pre-release" engagements and the London showings had exhausted the commercial value of the picture.[60]

King of Jazz opened in London on October 4 with a split run at the Regal and the Alhambra. At the Regal, as at the Roxy, *Rhapsody in Blue* was performed before the feature, in this case by the Regal Symphony Orchestra. While the critic for the *Daily Telegraph* appreciated the "accompaniment of a gorgeous panorama of colour and movement" in the film, he preferred the "far greater vitality" of the live performance. While acknowledging the superiority of Whiteman's musicianship, "the interest of the reproduction was clearly less than that of the first-hand performance."[61]

The reviews ranged from positive to raves. "There is more art, wit, skill and understanding in this one film than in all the other Hollywood spectacles rolled together," wrote G. A. Atkinson in the *Sunday Express*. It "shows, I fear, that Elstree's alleged challenge to Hollywood is so much moonshine. When money and brains are combined on this scale we cannot possibly compete. Compare it with *Elstree Calling* and you will see what I mean."[62]

Again, the review in the *Times* was the inverse of critical opinion in America—audiences and critics loved the blackout skits—they "might have been done as well on the stage. It could not have been done better." The reviews were positive, as musicals were still popular in Britain. *King of Jazz* was "a little more intelligent than is customary in its kind." Less impressed by the big numbers, with "'The Melting Pot of the Nations,' [*sic*] a rather too extravagant extravaganza on the origin of jazz, which takes in everything from a Cossack dance to an Irish jig, but omits the negro influence which might reasonably be supposed to be the most important."[63]

Academy Awards

The third Academy Awards were presented on November 5, 1930, at a banquet of 600 industry members at the Ambassador Hotel Fiesta Room in Los Angeles. The qualifying films were released in the year ending July 31, 1930. The awards ceremony also served as the annual business meeting for the Academy, and was broadcast on a local radio station. Universal films received three of the "merit awards" for distinguished achievement. The award for Outstanding Production was presented by Louis B. Mayer to Carl Laemmle Sr., for *All Quiet on the Western Front*. The directing award was presented to Lewis Milestone. The award for Art Direction was presented by William Cameron Menzies to Herman Rosse for his work on *King of Jazz*. Rosse had remained in Hollywood to work on Universal's *The Boudoir Diplomat* (1930) for Junior Laemmle.

Herman Rosse with the Academy Award for his work on *King of Jazz*.

The Results From Junior's Strategy

The first three major productions under Junior's stewardship of the studio returned mixed results. *La Marseillaise/Captain of the Guard*—developed under Junior's protégé Paul Fejos, and completed by and credited to John S. Robertson— was not an artistic, critical, or commercial success. Both Fejos and star Laura La Plante left the studio, and only John Boles emerged unscathed. Even after heavy promotion, the film lost $271,296.

While *King of Jazz* looked like a million dollars on the screen, the negative cost was two million, partly due to the overhead accrued in the year before filming began, and expenses during four months in production. Foreign revenue of $1,198,172 was a creditable return, but domestic revenue was an anemic $548,683, leading to a loss of $1,272,629.

All Quiet on the Western Front also suffered from the poor cost controls endemic to Universal during the Laemmle regime, though the final result was worth it. From an original budget of $891,000, the final negative cost was $1,566,308. Lewis Milestone had followed the original script and shot less than the estimated footage. Partly due to the director's decision to shoot the film in sequence, however, the schedule more than doubled to 99 shooting days, driving up most other costs, especially with $241,000 of studio overhead charges. A world gross of $4,103,866 resulted in a final profit of $994,378.

The audiences for *King of Jazz* were very large for a Universal release, but not enough tickets were sold for the film to cover its costs. *King of Jazz* earned twice as much in foreign territories as in the United States and Canada, the reverse of most other releases during Universal's 1930–31 season.[64] Had *King of Jazz* been as proportionately strong in the domestic market as *All Quiet*, the musical would have netted an additional $350,000 from U.S. and Canadian theaters.

Overall, Junior's push to improve Universal's output was successful on an artistic basis. For the 1930–31 season, trade magazine editor P. S. Harrison concluded, "the Universal and Columbia products, in fact, from the point of view of quality as well as of box office pull were as good as the MGM."[65] The halo from the success of *All Quiet on the Western Front* meant a lot. In Harrison's assessment, "As a rule, sons of famous fathers are mediocrities. But in the case of Junior Laemmle, matters seem to have been reversed, for everyone who has come in contact with him seems to be of the opinion that he has a good head on his shoulders, is modest, and knows a great deal about pictures." Thanks to *All Quiet*, "his vision, in fact, has saved Universal, for it is doubtful it would have survived without the success of this picture."[66]

Above: Outside the big cities, exhibitors tailored their advertising for *King of Jazz* to the local markets.

Right: Jumbo window card advertising the first run of *King of Jazz* in San Francisco in June 1930.

Junior's vision was less successful commercially. Of Universal's 24 non-series western releases in the 1930–31 season, ten productions cost more than $300,000, and eight of the ten lost money. The exceptions were *Dracula* and *All Quiet on the Western Front*. A major production, Mal St. Clair's *The Boudoir Diplomat* with Betty Compson, and Jeanette Loff in a supporting role, was a significant misfire, losing $357,721.

But Universal was privately held by the Laemmle family and minority stockholder Robert H. Cochrane, and mistakes by family members were forgiven. A year after the first Universal international sales convention, the sales force was assembled again, in May 1931 in New York City. In a speech to the exchange managers, Carl Laemmle Sr. blamed the sales force, believing that *All Quiet* was sold too cheap, and should have grossed an additional $700,000 domestically. And for *King of Jazz*, "that was a great picture. If it had come out six months sooner we would have made one million dollars on that picture instead of losing a million."[67]

His entire tone changed when he talked about his studio's head of production. "I don't want to say much about my boy, but I can't help telling you he is a little wonder. He is the most enthusiastic chap of twenty-three years I ever saw in my life, working day and night at least five or six nights a week out at Universal City until twelve, one, two o'clock. I have been begging him on my knees not to do it. He loves work so much; he is so enthusiastic, I just can't stop him. That boy is coming along marvelously and he wants to help you. In a short period he has done a good job. I could talk from now until tomorrow morning about that boy. He is really all that I say. But he is my son and I would rather have others talk about him."[68]

KING OF JAZZ

WITH

PAUL WHITEMAN
AND HIS BAND
JOHN BOLES
LAURA LA PLANTE
and how!

LOEWS WARFIELD

Josef Fenneker's specially designed poster for the Berlin release of *Der Jazzkönig*, the German version of *King of Jazz*.

Chapter 8

FOREIGN VERSIONS

The introduction of sound to the film industry in the late 1920s shook up existing release practices and ushered in a period of experimentation for the Hollywood studios. No longer could a film be simply retitled for foreign release, as had been common during the silent era. At Universal, international distribution was significant throughout the 1920s, accounting for approximately 35% of the studio's total revenue.[1] It was initially feared that these markets might suffer if foreign audiences rejected American talking films. But as European sound production was at least a year or so behind, the U.S. studios were able to take advantage of the lead to explore options. The first American talking films were distributed in silent versions for audiences abroad, with dialogue scenes cut down and translated intertitles inserted. But some early sound films managed to break through the language barrier, particularly musicals, where song and dance could be enjoyed by all.

Sound—and talking in particular—proved an exciting novelty at first, and it drove unprecedented crowds to the cinema all over the world. Even Warner Bros' part-talking *The Singing Fool* (1928) went over well in Berlin in April 1929, despite being presented in its original English version without translation. Berlin audiences might not have entirely understood what Al Jolson was singing about, but they attended regardless because there was no domestic sound competition. This would change a few months later, in December 1929, when the first German-language production, *Melodie des Herzens* (*Melody of the Heart*, 1929) was released in Germany, to

huge success. The U.S. clearly led the way in the international transition to sound production, but as more markets began making films in their native tongues, pressure increased to find ways to maintain the U.S. domination of screens around the world.

Voice doubling or "dubbing" was one option considered to cater to foreign demand. Universal was among the first to experiment with this technique, on Broadway in the summer of 1929. "At night I took Joseph and Rudolph Schildkraut and I made them dub the English scenes with German dialogue," remembered production supervisor Paul Kohner. The next day he presented his "new invention" to Carl Laemmle, who exclaimed: "Why, that is marvelous, Kohner, wonderful. I want you to do all our pictures like that."[2]

The studio hoped to get the jump on other producers by cornering the business in newly wired theaters around the world. After the foreign soundtracks for *Broadway* were recorded, Spanish and German versions were prepared of *Show Boat* and *Shanghai Lady* (1929). On the latter, Mexican actress Lupita Tovar doubled for Mary Nolan. After rehearsing the lines with the Spanish and Latin American actors, the track was recorded in a projection room while the mute film was projected before them. "Our accents in Spanish were all different," recalled Tovar, "but no one seemed to mind. It took a little while to get it right, but I learned quickly."[3] The work took three days and the voice actors were paid $15 per day.[4] Unfortunately the quality of this dubbing was limited by the sound mixing capabilities of the time, and the poor

Paul Kohner, 1929. Among his production credits were Paul Leni's *The Man Who Laughs* (1928), William Wyler's *A House Divided* (1931), and the dual-language *S.O.S. Eisberg / S.O.S. Iceberg* (1933) starring Leni Riefenstahl.

Multiple language versions

After its failure with dubbing, Universal was among the first studios to set up its own foreign language department, complete with a regular roster of German- and Spanish-speaking players in stock. The unit was headed by Czech emigré Paul Kohner, a 27-year-old protégé of Carl Laemmle, who had worked his way up through the ranks at Universal from foreign publicist to casting director to production supervisor. After his experiments with dubbing, Kohner now convinced Laemmle of the potential of multiple-language versions. "They can be done at the same time the English versions are shot," he argued, "and at very little additional cost."[6] According to Lupita Tovar (whom Kohner would later marry), Kohner insisted that Universal "were wasting half the studio, because at six o'clock in the evening the lights were turned off until six the next morning. … They should hire an additional crew to come in at night."[7] The foreign-language versions could be produced cheaply and efficiently by using the same wardrobe, sets, and production equipment.

But before they embarked on any feature projects, this new department first cut its teeth on shorts and inserts. French, Italian, Spanish, and German shorts were announced beginning in October 1929; most were original productions, although some, such as a series with Slim Summerville, were economically made in dual English and Spanish versions.[8] Other Universal stars appeared in two-reel shorts destined for Latin America, including Laura La Plante, who introduced *Caprichos de Hollywood* (1930) in Spanish. *King of Jazz* was to be the first feature-length production the foreign department worked on.

Making multiple-language versions of a revue was not a new idea. These films—with distinct musical numbers, isolated sketches, and no plot—could be cheaply and quickly adapted into foreign versions with the addition of newly filmed introductions. M-G-M's *Hollywood Revue of 1929* had French, German, and Czech editions, each with different masters of ceremonies and additional scenes. The special inserts for the Czech version were filmed separately in London, and featured Jiří Sedláček and Slávka Tauberová, two respected stars of Prague's dramatic theater and grand opera, who had been personally selected by M-G-M's Director General for Central Europe.[9] Fox's *Happy Days* (1929) had only one documented foreign version; the studio hired Sôjin Kamiyama to introduce each musical number in Japanese.[10] *Paramount on Parade* (1930), made at the same time as *King of Jazz*, was the most ambitious of all the revues. In total, eleven foreign versions were made in addition

---

results were reportedly "laughed off the screen."[5] The synchronization was hard to maintain, and foreign audiences quickly tired of the attempt once domestic sound production in Europe began to gather momentum.

With the inadequacies of dubbing, many of Europe's first sound productions were simultaneously shot in multiple languages. Ufa's *Melodie des Herzens*, for example, was filmed in German, French, English, and Hungarian. Most of the American studios followed this lead. By the close of 1929, M-G-M was planning Spanish, French, and German versions of its Hal Roach Laurel and Hardy comedies, with the stars repeating each scene phonetically in a different language; and Ramon Novarro was made to work overtime in three versions of *Call of the Flesh* (1930), each with entirely different casts except for the multi-lingual lead. Paramount shot French versions of some of its films in its Hollywood and East Coast Astoria studios, but the company ultimately chose to open a new studio in Joinville, near Paris, to make its foreign-language versions. Some of these films were first made in the U.S. in English, before the scripts were translated and new sets were re-created in France for the production of up to five European facsimiles (at a lower cost and of noticeably inferior quality).

Sôjin Kamiyama, one of Hollywood's most prolific Japanese actors, introduced Fox's revue *Happy Days* for Japanese audiences. His introductions were filmed months after the completion of the film.

to the domestic release. The Spanish, Scandinavian, and Japanese editions were produced in Hollywood, while the French, Polish, German, Dutch, Hungarian, Romanian, Serbian, and Italian were prepared in France at Paramount's Joinville studio. For the Japanese version, the lead *benshi* from the studio's flagship theater in Tokyo was brought over to perform.[11]

Not to be outdone, Universal announced that *King of Jazz* would be produced in sixteen different languages! *Variety* reported that the "multi-versioned picture will be released in Spanish, German, French, Italian, Hungarian, Czecho-Slovakian, Danish, Swedish, Norwegian, Hindustan [*sic*], Russian, Swiss [*sic*], Portuguese, Dutch and Rumanian [*sic*];" but this would soon be cut down to nine.[12] Paul Kohner cast the foreign interlocutors from existing talent already in the Los Angeles area. Kohner's journalist brother, Frederick, recorded that "hundreds of alien actors who had made their way to Hollywood, but seldom landed a job, began to trudge out to Universal City. For hours and days on end they waited, trying to curry favor of an all-powerful secretary, who might open for them the door to Paul's office."[13] Established character actors like Nils Asther, Bela Lugosi, and Arnold Korff

were some of the more prominent names cast, while most of the smaller roles were fulfilled by relative unknowns. Paul Kohner led a small but dedicated production team, made up of young and determined emigrés like himself.

The group operated like a parallel studio on the lot, with its own directors and casting calls, and working mostly during the off-hours. The department's budget was small and the turnarounds short, so corners often had to be cut. Twenty-one-year old Kurt Neumann was already directing numerous multiple-language shorts for Universal's foreign department before he was assigned the international inserts for *King of Jazz*. For each short he was given just three days to complete filming, compared to the six days allocated for the domestic U.S. versions.[14] And on *King of Jazz*, there was further pressure to wrap up quickly due to the added expense of Technicolor. Kohner's personal assistant, John H. Auer (originally János Auer), was just two years older, at 23. The former child actor from Hungary had been working in the States since 1928, and possibly came to Universal via Paul Fejos. Auer supervised the Hungarian dubbing of *The Last Performance* for Fejos, and ended up appearing as the third-billed host in the Hungarian version of *King of Jazz*,

Frame enlargements from an original Technicolor nitrate release print of *La Féerie du Jazz*, featuring André Chéron.

The Japanese release, *Kingu Obu Jazu*, with Tetsu Komai and Iris Yamaoka, premiered on January 8, 1931 at the Taishokan Theater, Asakusa, Tokyo. *Kinema Junpo*, January 11, 1931.

entitled *Jazzkirály*.[15] Both Neumann and Auer would go on to lengthy careers as directors at other studios.

All nine of the foreign versions followed a similar structure. The comedy and dialogue sequences were removed entirely (as they would be incomprehensible to foreign audiences), and Charles Irwin's introductions were replaced.[16] In his place appeared a male emcee, accompanied by either one or two female assistants. In the Italian edition, *Il re del jazz*, Alessandro Giglio is joined solely by Nella Nelli, while in the Spanish-language release Martín Garralaga is assisted by both Lupita Tovar and Nancy Torres. Perhaps because of a lack of appropriate talent in the Los Angeles area, the Hungarian version differed from the rest by featuring a female host accompanied by two males; established star of Hungarian and Austrian cinema Lucy Doraine received top billing over the then relatively unknown Bela Lugosi and John H. Auer.

Footage of the new hosts was interspersed throughout the film. In *El Rey del Jazz*, made primarily for Latin American audiences, Catalan-born *maestro de ceremonias* Martín Garralaga is joined in the opening scene by Paul Whiteman, who greets the host as "Amigo." Later in the picture, Jeanette Loff is welcomed by Garralaga to introduce "A Bench in the Park." She tries her hand at Spanish—"Muchos saludos a mis amigos Hispano parlantes" / "Many greetings to my Spanish-speaking friends"—and is applauded for her efforts, then is kissed on the hand by Garralaga. In the French *La Féerie du Jazz*, compère André Chéron smokes a cigarette and hugs his Gallic partner Georgette Rhodes in the specially filmed introduction to "Happy Feet." After the main number, through cross-cutting, Chéron sets up Whiteman's dancing double, and acknowledges him mid-scene with a bow. The illusion of integration is somewhat ruined, however, when Charles Irwin—not Chéron—walks on stage in long-shot to greet the double after he completes a

Tetsu Komai was chosen as the lead host for the Japanese version of *King of Jazz*. In this revealing article from the Japanese film magazine *Kinema Junpo*, he provides a firsthand account of his involvement and the challenges he faced.[17]

After I was selected as the Japanese host, I had to wait a long time before I received the screenplay. It finally arrived, just two days before the shoot. I skimmed through it, and frankly, I was far from thrilled. Yes, it was written well, in a typically American way. It was light, witty, and sleek; it was, in short, a fine polished product. But these are features that shine when delivered in English. It's a different story altogether when it's delivered in Japanese.

Mr. Kohner, who was the supervisor for the project, looked around the room and asked how we were all doing. The translators were all quiet, as though they had been expecting a much higher bonus for their service.

As for me, I felt quite at home, having built my career as a second-tier actor, acting on a passing whim and for want of money. I had to tell them: "this is not so good." But Kohner is an exceptional character, who is, in short, a good sport. He listened to my following complaint without a hint of annoyance.

> Sure, the script flows well in English, but much of it won't make sense in Japanese. All the fine nuances would disappear if I were to translate it as it is. Perhaps a quarter of the nuances can be salvaged. The rest would be lost.

> I have no knowledge of other languages, but I refuse to do a word-for-word translation of the script into Japanese. I would happily accept the role if you can give me your word that I can freely adapt the script as I see fit, with the condition that I will try my best to keep as much of the original script as possible.

Now I was in real trouble. Sparing some parts that could be translated without much effort, I had to invent the rest by myself. All I had was a day and a half. I was at a loss.

Luckily, I procured help from Kisaku Ito, the stage designer at the Tsukiji Sho-gekijo theater, who happened to be in Los Angeles. Sipping cold coffee, and staring at a heap of cigarette butts mounted in front of us, we managed to complete the translation by the deadline, but there was hardly any time to rehearse it. What you see in the film is my performance based on the faint memory that I had of my own composition.

I pulled it off in a frenzy. Perhaps the supervisor had faith in me, or perhaps he meant to put me in my place. For whatever reason, I was made to go on first. The gag that I pulled in the opening turned out to be a hit, and other hosts were instructed to imitate it. Keep in mind that this was a group of actors, naturally endowed with big egos, who were further encouraged to be competitive in the international setting of a film shoot. I was competing with no time to rehearse, with instructions to repeat the same jokes, and with the Japanese lettering on the scrapbook attached upside down. On top of all that, the lighting was three times as strong as in a regular film shoot, since this was shot in Technicolor. Facing the blinding and scorching lights, I had to redo my make-up every two minutes.

After two days of hard work, I spent the third day in bed. All I could think of when I awoke was all the errors I made.

Georgette Rhodes introduces the "Happy Feet" number alongside André Chéron in the French version. Frame enlargement from an original Technicolor nitrate print.

cartwheel.

The huge scrapbook designed by Wynn Holcomb was adapted for each language with removable wooden lettering. "Paul Whiteman's Scrap Book" in the U.S. version was modified to "Carnet intime de Paul Whiteman" ("Paul Whiteman's intimate diary") for French audiences, or the "Raccolta artistica di Paul Whiteman" ("Paul Whiteman's art collection") in Italian. In some cases, such as with the "Bench in the Park" and "Melting Pot of Music" pages, the scrapbook dispensed with all text, and the illustrations were given more emphasis. Czech viewers were delighted to see that Universal spared little expense in preparing the Czech titles in color for *Král jazzu*, although one reviewer noted that the translations "suffer from carelessness."[18]

International release

Universal planned a wide release internationally, and of the 395 prints made in total, 215 were destined for overseas.[19] But because Technicolor only had laboratories in Boston and Hollywood, all of these prints had to be made in the United States. This was contrary to normal practice, whereby a negative would be shipped to foreign territories and the prints made there. This model saved considerably on shipping expenses and import duties. Faced with such exorbitant shipping costs, Universal opted to save at least some money by printing certain scenes in several of the foreign versions in black & white. The continuity script for *El Rey del Jazz* indicates that "My Bridal Veil," "It Happened in Monterey," and "A Bench in the Park" all appeared in monochrome for Spanish-speaking audiences.

In making up the prints for each of the foreign

Bela Lugosi, one of the hosts for the Hungarian version, shakes hands with Paul Whiteman. Before his work on *King of Jazz* (his first onscreen credit at Universal), Lugosi assisted Paul Fejos on the dubbing of the Hungarian release version of *The Last Performance* (1929).

The scrapbook was modified for each foreign version using replaceable lettering, as seen here in this promotional still for the Italian release. Some of the scrapbook pages designed by Wynn Holcomb, like the one with artwork for the "Bench in the Park" number (right), were not used in the U.S. version.

versions, Technicolor used "positive assembly"—the company printed the musical numbers from the domestic negative and the alternative introductions from each foreign negative, then these scenes were spliced together in the print.[20] In America, *King of Jazz* was distributed in sound-on-film Movietone prints, but abroad Universal chose a sound-on-disc release. These foreign prints featured extra image area along the left edge, which wasn't necessarily intended to be seen.[21]

Universal, like all the U.S. studios, relied heavily on international distribution. In the 1920s, Hollywood films accounted for as much as 70-90% of all screenings in Europe and South America. In 1926 Argentina was the second-largest international market after Australia, and Brazil was third.[22] Universal set up exchanges in key territories to import and distribute its product. Offices in Buenos Aires and Rio de Janeiro redistributed films to the rest of the continent, while exchanges in each European country catered for individual markets there. With the wiring of theaters for sound, U.S. films became even more dominant. In Japan, for example, where domestic

production filled most theaters during the silent era, Hollywood's market share leapt from just 11.2% for silent films in 1929 to 90.7% for sound films the following year.[23]

After the U.S. release in May 1930, Universal started rolling out the international versions of *King of Jazz* from September.[24] Argentina, Mexico, and other Latin American countries were among the first, as well as odd markets in Europe like Czechoslovakia and Sweden. The Portuguese-language version, *O Rei do Jazz*, opened in São Paulo, Brazil, in early October, but was forced to close abruptly after Getúlio Vargas's coup to gain political power shut down much of the country. But the film came back for a successful repeat performance in November once everything had calmed down.[25] Most European countries opened the film in October and November. The French release was possibly delayed to December due to problems with the film's title. Originally intended to be *Le Roi du Jazz*, Universal had to change the title in the opening credits to *La Féerie du Jazz* at the last minute, to avoid confusion with an earlier film released with the

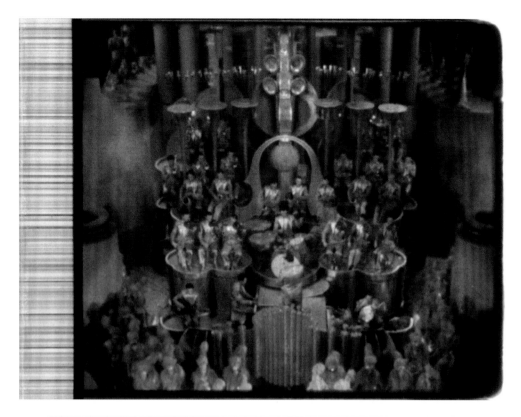

The musical numbers in the domestic and foreign release prints were made from the same negative but were printed differently. Shots in the U.S. prints were generally composed to allow for a soundtrack along the left edge. The foreign prints, however, did not have this soundtrack, so the careful compositions were compromised. Above: Domestic print (1.20:1). Below: French print (1.33:1).

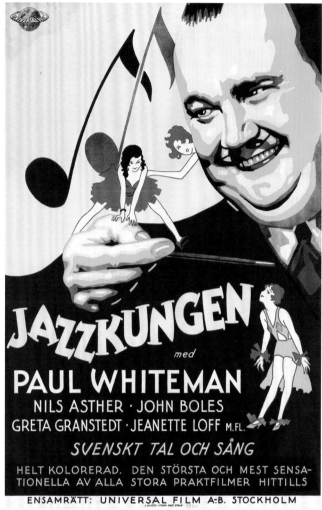

Announcements for the German and Swedish versions. Original promotional artwork for the film's foreign versions was not made in the U.S., but was instead produced in each territory and modified for each language. Left: *Kinematograph*, October 30, 1930.

same title.[26] Japan was the last territory to premiere the film, in January 1931.

Criticisms

Seduced by the high production values and catchy tunes, reviewers around the world generally received the film rapturously, although most were dissatisfied with the quality of the foreign inserts. Although the critics were impressed that Universal would go to the lengths of shooting new masters of ceremonies for each country, the delivery of these hosts was frequently singled out. One Swedish reviewer complained that it was "almost a pain to hear [Nils Asther] stumble over his native Swedish, reciting unsuccessful witticisms."[27] Meanwhile, in Brazil,

the press were even more critical of Olympio Guilherme and his partner. "There he is, describing in Portuguese what will happen in *O Rei do Jazz*. And by his side, at the same level of inept contribution, we see Lia Torá. One thing is true: if the factory that produced this film wanted to please the Brazilian audience, it would have pleased a lot more if it didn't give Olympio Guilherme and Lia Torá such a dreadful script."[28]

But perhaps the unfortunate Antonín Vaverka came off the worst. The once-celebrated Czech actor had been in the States for eight years, but had struggled to find even sporadic work in bit parts.[29] His English was practically non-existent, and apparently he had only mastered one sentence: "I am Antonín Vaverka, Czech actor of Prague National Theatre."[30] But Vaverka's fellow countryman Paul Kohner looked out for him and ensured he

The Czech hosts: Helena Bendová, Antonín Vaverka, and G. Kroutilová.

Opposite page: Asther and Greta Granstedt in a promotional shot for the Swedish version, *Jazzkungen*.

received occasional acting gigs, including presenting the Czech version of *King of Jazz* and translating its script. After completion, Kohner screened the print for Dr. Felix Janowsky of the Czech consulate in Los Angeles. "I hate to say this about one of our people," confided Dr. Janowsky, "but I did not understand what Mr. Vaverka was saying. It *sounded* like Czech, but believe me, Mr. Kohner, it was not my mother tongue."[31] The technical quality of the recording was reportedly muffled, but that did not disguise Vaverka's mannered delivery.[32] "It is laudable in principle that the Americans have tried to bring the film closer to non-English speaking nations by replacing the original presenter with one who speaks their native language," reported a member of the Czech press. "But if this task was to fall … on Mr. Vaverka, we would rather give up this pleasure. Because Mr. Vaver-

ka's performance was the most embarrassing thing in the whole film. You cannot accompany the simplest of presentations with such devilish grimaces and a voice twisted in mimic obsession."[33] Vaverka later blamed his performance as the reason that no other Hollywood films were made in Czech.[34]

Despite the shaky performances of some of the hosts, *King of Jazz* was a hit abroad. Its (otherwise) high production values, catchy songs, and the international drawing power of Paul Whiteman attracted foreign audiences who were still enamored of musicals. Europe's own musical films blossomed later due to the slower adoption of sound technology. Beginning in 1930—when American moviegoers were already rejecting the musical—a host of inventive operettas and musical comedies helped the genre hit its stride in Europe, leading to "a

JAZZKUNGEN

Universals glänsande, helt kolorerade Utstyrsel-Film

Med

PAUL WHITEMAN

och

hans världsberömda kapell

I SVENSK VERSION

med de svenska stjärnorna *Nils Asther, Jeanette Loff* och *Greta Granstedt*

I övriga roller en lång rad av världsberömda filmare och revyaktörer:

John Boles, Stanley Smith, Jeanie Lang, Sisters G., Paul Whitemans Rythm Boys, Brox Sisters m. fl.

Regi: *John Murray Anderson.* Uppsättning och dräkter: *Herman Rosse.* Musikbidrag av: *George Gershwin, Mabel Wayne, Milton Ager, Jack Yellen* m. fl. Produktionsledare: *Carl Laemmle* j:r

Kring Jazzkungen

Intrycket av en sådan film som "Jazzkungen" kan egentligen bara bli ett — *överväldigande.* "Jazzkungen" är kolossal. Den slår alla rekord. Vad sång, musik, dans och uppsättning beträffar torde den överträffa allt som förut bjudits i genren. Det är starka ord detta, kan lätt verka överord. Vi skulle ej heller använda dem om vi icke absolut visste med oss att de för en enda sällsynt gångs skull äro på sin plats. Något som också varje åskådare kommer att ge oss rätt i, när han

Detail from the Swedish program.

musical boom as forceful as that in the United States in 1929," in the words of historian Richard Barrios.[35] This was largely fueled by the success of Geza von Bolvary's operetta *Zwei Herzen im ¾ Takt* (*Two Hearts in Waltz Time*, 1930), and would be carried further by such inventive films as René Clair's playful *Le Million* (1931) and *À Nous la Liberté* (1932) in France, and Ufa's *Die Drei von der Tankstelle* (*Three from the Gasoline Station*, 1930) and *Der Kongreß tanzt* (*Congress Dances*, 1931) in Germany, both starring the popular team of Lilian Harvey and Willy Fritsch. Many of these films were resourcefully made in multiple-language versions to appeal to broader audiences across the Continent. It was into this energized market in Europe and other international territories that the foreign versions of *King of Jazz* landed in the fall of 1930.

Whiteman and his music were a key selling point as well; he had a big following internationally, spurred largely by successful sales of his Victor recordings. In Brazil, in fact, advertisements promoting the film's hit songs ran in newspapers several months before the film was even released.[36] In many countries the film was advertised as if it were a live performance. The film captured the spirit of the famous bandleader, and allowed audiences all around the world to see and hear the maestro and his orchestra at their best. The local Swedish press issued a regal proclamation: "His Majesty the King of Jazz, aka Paul Whiteman, arrives in Stockholm Monday evening, accompanied by his entire suite of world-famous jazz musicians. His Majesty's visit to Stockholm will take place at the Palladium, where he will receive the public every evening."[37]

Announcement for the release of the Portuguese-language version in Rio de Janeiro. *Cinearte*, September 24, 1930.

in revenues at home. That's impressive following a time of great uncertainty over the reaction of foreign audiences to U.S. talkies. For the 1930–31 season, Universal's total foreign revenues were just shy of 49% of its entire box-office takings, so the performance of *King of Jazz* abroad was an anomaly.[39]

Surprisingly, Paul Kohner's efficiently-produced inserts paid off. The Spanish-language version was so successful in Latin America that Universal chose to commit to more multiple-language versions for its 1931–32 season.[40] Lupita Tovar became a fully-fledged star in Mexico following her roles in *La voluntad del muerto* (1930), a version of *The Cat Creeps* co-starring Antonio Moreno, and *Drácula* (1931), starring Carlos Villarias, which many consider better than the U.S. original with Bela Lugosi. But this practice was ultimately short-lived, as dubbing and subtitling improved across the industry and audience preferences changed. Universal's foreign language department was dissolved accordingly by the close of 1931. In the end, the more cost-effective options for the studio won out. When *King of Jazz* was reissued around the world in 1933, it was in subtitled prints of the U.S. version. All of the scenes with the foreign hosts were discarded as they were no longer necessary.

Whiteman was clearly the star, although in most countries the names of the foreign hosts were also given prominence in the advertising. In reality there were few other established stars to promote, as most, like Laura La Plante, Glenn Tryon, and Slim Summerville had been cut out entirely. The names of George Gershwin and his famous *Rhapsody in Blue* were also surprisingly absent from promotion.

The Paul Kohner-produced inserts were made cheaply and quickly, with little time for polish. The press feedback on the quality of the scripts certainly testifies to this. All of the inserts for the nine different versions—featuring more than twenty hosts—were filmed in just two days. Kohner was unable to cast all the foreign emcees from native speakers, so he was forced to resort to several second-generation immigrants, whose Czech or Swedish or Italian was far from perfect.[38] Nonetheless, the experiment proved cost-effective for Universal, and it would ultimately reap dividends.

In spite of the lackluster domestic takings, the foreign release of *King of Jazz* helped to salvage some of the film's enormous production costs. The film brought in a staggering $1.2 million overseas, versus just $549,000

PROMOTION PACKAGE

The Songs · The Sentiment · The Stars
of the 1930's
live again in
MCA TV's

KING of JAZZ

The first and greatest of the
Technicolor musicals

More than 50 years after the film's original release, *King of Jazz* made its television debut. This MCA press kit, issued ca. 1983, contained a press release and stills to aid in promoting its screenings on cable TV.

Chapter 9

REDISCOVERY

In June 1930, Carl Laemmle announced his studio's production schedule for the 1930–31 season. *All Quiet on the Western Front* proved that Universal—and Junior Laemmle—could make a quality production to rival the other studios' best. For the new season ahead, Universal would concentrate its production on more specials, instead of the mix of lower-budget features with one or two specials that had become standard for the studio in previous years. John Boles, the closest thing Universal had to a musical star, was to headline *The Gypsy Love Song* and the operetta *The Love Cavalier*, as well as *Strictly Dishonorable*, based on the recent "New York smash hit" play by Preston Sturges. But possibly the studio's biggest production that year was to be a sequel to *All Quiet on the Western Front*—a new story being written by Erich Maria Remarque set in the aftermath of the war.[1]

The spectacular failure of *King of Jazz* at the domestic box office, and the general downturn in both the film industry and the U.S. economy, forced Universal to abandon these ambitious plans and retrench. The studio soon returned to its usual model of penny-pinching, buckling-down, and scraping through the early years of the Depression, losing $1,337,831 during the 1930–31 season, but rebounding a year later with $471,183 profit.[2]

Universal had brought a host of creative talent out to the Coast for *King of Jazz*, both in front of and behind the camera. But while the studio retained several of the film's production personnel, most of its onscreen talent—including Paul Whiteman—returned to live performance. Even Bing Crosby slipped through Univer-

sal's fingers. After leaving Whiteman's band in April 1930, Crosby stayed on in Hollywood, continuing his musical career as a solo artist and reaching new audiences nationwide through radio. He appeared in a series of film comedy shorts for Mack Sennett from 1931, before landing a contract with Paramount Pictures that saw his popularity rise to new heights.

Following his Academy Award win, Herman Rosse was put to work on other films at Universal, including Robert Florey's planned version of *Frankenstein*, which was to star Bela Lugosi as the monster, before James Whale took over the project and Boris Karloff was cast, and the creepy *Murders in the Rue Morgue* (1932), based on Edgar Allan Poe's short story. After more than a year working on a series of uninspired assignments, Rosse left Hollywood to return to his passions of musical theater and architecture, although his career did intersect with film again on Dudley Murphy's *The Emperor Jones* (1933), shot on the East Coast with Paul Robeson, and several Dutch productions a couple of years later.

John Murray Anderson was also retained by Universal on a term contract. Still hopeful of a strong audience response to the film, the studio signed Anderson for an additional year on May 2, 1930—the same day *King of Jazz* opened at the Roxy Theatre in New York. The terms were more than favorable to the director, who, for the sum of $3,000 per week, was to "personally produce and direct at least two filmusicals [*sic*] yearly."[3] But by August, when audience demand for musicals had completely dried up, rumors abounded that Universal might buy out its star director's contract if no suitable productions could be found. Evidently, by November, Anderson was downgraded to a dramatic project with the working title of *Fan Mail*, but that never materialized; and he came close to starting a drama called *Lilies of Broadway* the following April, which was firmly described by *Variety* as "non-musical" and "non-color."[4] He remained on the studio payroll—mostly idle—until June 1931, when his contract expired and was not renewed.[5] Of all the U.S. studios, Universal was the most wary of musicals. The widespread decline in audience demand for the genre and the failure of *King of Jazz* resulted in the studio not releasing another musical until *Moonlight and Pretzels* in 1933.[6]

After leaving Universal, Anderson went back to his "first love"—the theatre. In England he returned to form with the technically sophisticated revue *Bow Bells* (1932)

at the London Hippodrome, in which he continued his close collaboration with Herman Rosse. Over the following years, Anderson found inspiration and acclaim in partnership with impresario Billy Rose, beginning with the circus-themed *Jumbo* in 1935 (featuring Paul Whiteman and his orchestra), through crowd-pleasing aquacades at the 1937 Great Lakes Exposition in Cleveland, Ohio, and the New York World's Fair of 1939, and culminating in nightly revues at Rose's Diamond Horseshoe nightclub in New York. After starring Esther Williams in one of his extravagant aquacades, Anderson followed the swimmer to Hollywood to stage the spectacular finale of her first feature film, *Bathing Beauty*, in 1944. And he received another screen credit for his work on Cecil B. DeMille's *The Greatest Show on Earth* (1952), which recreated Anderson's astonishing presentations for the Ringling Brothers-Barnum & Bailey Circus, for

John Murray Anderson returned to the West Coast in 1941 to stage his homage to the movies, "The Silver Screen," at the Wilshire Bowl Theatre Restaurant in Los Angeles. It featured many stars of the 1920s on stage, including Betty Blythe, Clara Kimball Young, Betty Compson, Nick Lucas, and some of the original Keystone Kops: Hank Mann, Chester Conklin, Snub Pollard, and Clyde Cook.

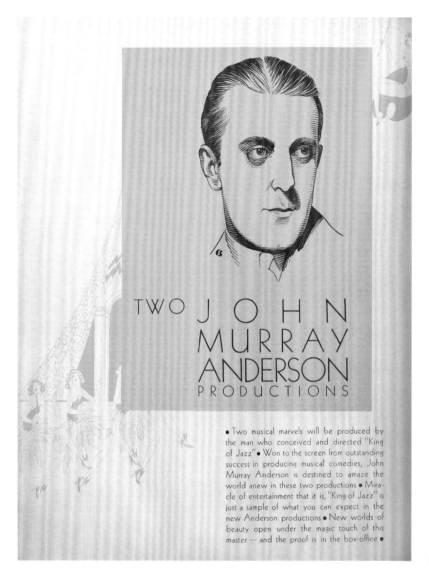

Film Daily, June 16, 1930, 16.

which he was director of shows for seven years. His final production was a return to the revue format on Broadway—a reimagining of *John Murray Anderson's Almanac* for 1953 audiences. He died—following a life full of creativity and excess—in January 1954, one month after *Almanac* opened.

During the 18 months from his initial contract with Universal to the premiere of *King of Jazz*, Paul Whiteman was active on radio and recordings, and making live performances around the country. In his peak year of 1929, he grossed $648,455 for 42 working weeks, minus $256,746 paid to the band. On his return to New York City, Whiteman found that audience tastes had changed—vocalists like Rudy Vallee were the headliners, while the bands became secondary. As his business manager put it, "a new generation voted the sex-appeal ticket straight, and Paul was fat and forty."[7] By 1932 the radio money was a fraction of what he had received from Old Gold, Columbia had bought out his recording contract, and the $10,000 a week he had been receiving for live engagements had become $3,000 a week.

Whiteman and his orchestra were active on radio and in live performances in the 1930s, and in 1943 Whiteman took on the additional role of music director for radio's Blue Network, which later became ABC. He continued to have an eye for talent, discovering singer and lyricist Johnny Mercer. He appeared as himself in a number of films, including Warner Bros.' George Gershwin biography *Rhapsody in Blue* (1945). Whiteman's fourth marriage, to actress Margaret Livingston, was successful, lasting from 1931 until his death in 1967, at the age of 77.

Reissue

After the popularity of musical films collapsed in 1930, the number of musicals produced in Hollywood fell off immediately. The market started to turn around in 1932 with the commercial success of *The Big Broadcast*, which expanded Bing Crosby's popularity from radio to films, and the critical response to Rouben Mamoulian's delightful *Love Me Tonight*, with Jeanette MacDonald and Maurice Chevalier singing songs by Richard Rodgers and Lorenz Hart. This recovery was confirmed by the enthusiastic response to Warner Bros.' backstage musical *42nd Street* in March 1933, and every studio put new musicals into production. Technicolor had been closely associated with the first musicals, but these new productions were in black & white. Instead, there were two reissues in Technicolor in 1933—Samuel Goldwyn's production of *Whoopee!* (1930), starring Eddie Cantor, and Universal's *King of Jazz*.

Whoopee! was reissued intact, while Universal trimmed *King of Jazz* by one-third, to a tight 65 minutes. The film was modernized—slow routines were cut, production numbers shortened, and there were fewer, and some different, blackouts. A revised credit sequence added close-ups of Paul Whiteman, Bing Crosby, John Boles, Slim Summerville, Jeanie Lang, Jeannette Loff, Harry Barris, and the Brox Sisters. After the cartoon and the "In the Bag" sequence, where the miniature band members get on stage, the reissue drops the entire "Meet the Boys" section. The "Happy Feet" number is brought forward, retaining the Rhythm Boys, but losing 3½ minutes, including the refrain sung by the Sisters G, and the segment where Whiteman's double dances to a reprise of "Happy Feet" to impress emcee Charles Irwin. Small cuts throughout pick up the pace. The Rhythm Boys singing their hit "Mississippi Mud" in silhouette is gone, along with Jeanette Loff's vocal reprise in the "Monterey" number, two sections totalling 2½ minutes from the *Rhapsody in Blue* segment, and half a minute towards the end of "Ragamuffin Romeo." Among the numbers missing entirely from the reissue was "I'd Like to Do Things For You."

The only blackout sketch retained from 1930 was "Ladies of the Press," supplemented by three very short routines filmed in 1930 but not used. Known by their punchlines—"Pretty Lucky So Far," "Look What It Makes Me," and "Horse's Neck" (detailed in Appendix V: Unused Scenes)— they were racy for the time, and can still startle modern audiences. The manager of the Delmar Theatre in Morrill, Nebraska, warned fellow exhibitors, "You may be wise in screening this before you run. Some of the comedy sketches are pretty rank—you

When Paul Whiteman proposed to the actress Margaret Livingston, she famously said: "I'll marry you on the day that I'm able to put my arms round you." She wrote about their romance and his diet in a 1933 book, *Whiteman's Burden*.

may want to cut them. They get the laughs, though." The operator of the H&S Theatre in Chandler, Oklahoma, felt they added nothing to the film, which he saw as "Just some old worn out songs connected with dirty jokes. (These smutty jokes are what the public want to hear, so be sure and stress them in all your advertising)."[8]

The five big production numbers remained, though in a different order, with John Murray Anderson's considerations of pace completely ignored. "My Bridal Veil" was moved from early in the film to the middle, and the film now concluded with three big numbers in a row: the order of "Song of the Dawn" and the *Rhapsody in Blue* was switched, while the grand finale remained "The Melting Pot of Music."

Reissuing *King of Jazz* was a thrifty exercise, appropriate for the Depression, just as the original production had reflected the excesses of the late 1920s. The re-editing by the studio came to a total internal charge of $3,319.26. Technicolor recut the original two-color picture negative, and disposed of the trims. As usual with a film released in Technicolor, the prints were a big cost—$47,650.29 for 127 prints for domestic distribution and 28 for foreign exhibitors. Completely new advertising materials were also prepared.

Universal's small-town exhibitor customers

uniformly praised the color—"color is so wonderful it could hardly be described"—and several praised the sound recording. For most, the new version was an improvement because of the faster pace, more in line with the new peppy musicals such as *42nd Street* or Universal's own *Moonlight and Pretzels* (1933). "Don't be afraid of this because it's a reissue," reported the Clyde Theatre in Clyde, Kansas. "It grossed more in two days than *Cavalcade* did in three."[9]

Universal's advertising emphasized Paul Whiteman less than in 1930, but all official billing was still subject to the original contracts, which focused on Whiteman. Exhibitors had more flexibility. San Francisco newspaper ads read "*King of Jazz*, starring Bing Crosby."[10] Other theaters promoted John Boles, who had recently scored in the Universal melodrama *Back Street* (1932). The audience response to the new edition of *King of Jazz* matched that of its original release. The film did outstanding business in some venues, and sank without a trace in others. Whatever draw Paul Whiteman was for audiences in 1930 had nearly vanished by 1933.

For other theaters, the second time was not the charm. "This picture did for us exactly the same as it did when first shown three years ago. Nothing. Can't understand why." A feature which played like a succession of

Jeanie Lang was still popular three years after the original release of *King of Jazz*. *Universal Weekly*, April 22, 1933.

unrelated music and comedy shorts was still confusing to audiences. An exhibitor in Menard, Texas, thought the "absence of any plot or story seemed to be the trouble, just as it ruined the musical show picture several years ago."[11]

The film did well in some rural markets. It was the highest-grossing picture of the year at the 800-seat Victoria Theater in Oklahoma City. The film finally arrived in New York City in August, at the tiny Cameo Theater, for the theater's lowest-grossing week of the year.[12] At the end of the day, the reissue of *King of Jazz* worked for Universal in a way that the original never had, delivering domestic rentals of $156,724.66 and foreign of $79,880.92, for a profit of $102,824.08.[13]

Losing Control

In November 1935, Carl Laemmle borrowed $750,000 to complete films then in preparation, including the million-dollar cost of John Stahl's melodrama *Magnificent Obsession*. But the loan also gave the lenders a three-month option to purchase the studio for $5.5 million and the acceptance of nearly $2 million in debt. In March 1936 this option was exercised and the Laemmles lost control of the studio, just before the release of Junior Laemmle's *Show Boat* (1936) and the costly Edmund Grainger production *Sutter's Gold* (1936). Laemmle's final personal production, *My Man Godfrey* (1936), started shooting during his last week at the studio.[14] After an unproductive six months at M-G-M trying to launch a remake of *The Hunchback of Notre Dame*, Junior Laemmle left the industry, and never produced another film. Carl Laemmle Sr. devoted the remaining four years of his life to supporting the immigration of persecuted Jews from Europe.[15]

At this distance, it is hard to judge Junior's abilities. He had no shortage of enthusiasm. Playwright and screenwriter Samson Raphaelson called him "very sweet, harmless—without a spark of aptitude."[16] Yet he championed *All Quiet on the Western Front* and the work of director James Whale, and he was responsible for Universal's remarkable string of horror films, starting with *Dracula* (1931), *Frankenstein* (1931), and *The Mummy* (1932). The prestige films often cost too much, and were aimed at sophisticated audiences that Universal was not positioned to reach. "He was a very strange producer," Edgar G. Ulmer told Peter Bogdanovich. Junior "didn't have much education, but had great respect for intelligence, and for creative spirit."[17] He got better with experience, stepping down as head of production in December 1934 to run his own production unit at the studio, a model that M-G-M had implemented the previous year.

Universal produced entirely new advertising materials to promote the 1933 reissue of *King of Jazz*. To capitalize on Bing Crosby's new fame, the crooner received more prominent billing than in 1930, as evidenced on this lobby card.

To be fully successful would have required the story skills and character insight of Irving Thalberg, the organizational skills of Louis B. Mayer, the drive for recognition of David O. Selznick, the energy of Darryl F. Zanuck, the talent-spotting skills of Jack Warner, the interpersonal skills of Fox's Winfield Sheehan, and the ruthlessness of Adolph Zukor. That is a requirement that few could meet, and certainly no one, other than perhaps Thalberg, at the age of 21.

In a different time and place, Carl Laemmle might have applied the model followed 80 years later by Rupert Murdoch. After placing his two sons in competition to be his successor, in 2015 Rupert Murdoch appointed 42-year-old James Murdoch as CEO of 21st Century Fox. During the previous 20 years the younger Murdoch progressed through many positions of increasing responsibility at the company. He ascended to the position because of his family, but no one can argue that he did not work very hard for it.[18]

Bits and pieces

After the international reissue finished its run in 1934, *King of Jazz* effectively disappeared from public view. The film was never issued on 16mm for the non-theatrical market, nor was it reissued theatrically or included in the package of films Universal licensed to Screen Gems for television broadcast in 1957.[19] Although Universal could access the original camera negative (edited down for the shorter 1933 reissue), it was unable to print from it, as Technicolor's two-color process had long been obsolete. This was confirmed when Whiteman's widow Margaret Livingston inquired about Universal's holdings in 1971, and was told that the studio was "unable to locate a print" and didn't have "a printable negative."[20] When *King of Jazz* did start to resurface, it was in bits and pieces, and in severely compromised forms. The first discoveries were all made in Europe, independently of each other and spread over many years. The eventual rediscovery of the film in the 1960s and 70s was due to the dedication of archives and individuals, not the studio itself.

When the British Film Institute hosted a three-month "Song and Dance" season at the National Film Theatre in London in 1954, all that was thought to survive of *King of Jazz* was the trailer. The beginning of the series was limited to a "very sketchy survey of the early years of the American musical," because, as the program notes explained, "the distribution companies have in the great majority of cases not bothered to preserve copies of the films."[21] The trailer was presented as a "taste of one of the great successes" of early musicals. "The few feet of film are sufficient to give an indication of the extraordinary size of the film and the boldness of its showmanship," although the BFI warned hopeful attendees in advance that the four-minute trailer did not include any of Bing Crosby's first screen appearance.[22]

Eleven years later, more footage turned up—at least for British audiences. A total of 27 minutes of excerpts were located at the Danske Filmmuseum in Copenhagen, and played in 1965 as an extra alongside a complete print of *Lonesome*, again at the BFI's National Film Theatre in London. The print was in English with explanatory intertitles in Danish, and consisted of eight incomplete scenes, including "Ragamuffin Romeo," "Ladies of the Press," and "I'd Like to Do Things for You."[23]

This archival screening was made possible because both the British Film Institute and the Danske Filmmuseum were members of the International Federation of Film Archives (FIAF)—an organization, which by 1965 had grown to 33 members all over the world, working together to collaborate on the best archival practice, sharing of collective knowledge, and exchanges and loans.[24]

At FIAF's 21st annual Congress in Oslo in 1965, a new version of *King of Jazz* was unveiled for the first time. The Československá filmotéka (now the Národní filmový archiv) presented a major reconstruction of the film, made possible by the discovery of a mute print of the French version and Czechoslovakian soundtrack discs. The private screening created a "real sensation" among the attending archivists.[25]

The effort was an impressive undertaking for the Czech archive, and was largely without precedent at the time. Czech film collector Bohumil Veselý owned a complete set of discs for the Czechoslovakian release of *King of Jazz* for many years, but despite the archive's best efforts, no complete film elements could be located. However, in 1964 Czech film archive delegates visiting the Staatliches Filmarchiv in East Berlin located a mute nitrate print of the French version, *La Féerie du Jazz*.[26] It featured André Chéron and Georgette Rhodes as hosts.

The format of the French release matched that of the Czech one, except that the hosts were speaking different languages. Despite the challenges, the Czech archive boldly decided to embark on the complicated task of synchronizing the Czech audio to the French picture. The sound for the musical numbers matched with little difficulty, but some creative sound editing was required to overlay Antonín Vaverka's dialogue onto Chéron's lip movements. The celebrated film editor Miroslav Hájek, who had made a name for himself working with Czech New Wave directors Milos Forman and Jan Němec, supervised this sound editing, and was effectively able to re-dub the voices after several weeks' work.[27]

The resulting prints were made at the Barrandov film laboratory in Prague on Orwocolor film stock, an East German successor to Agfa. But this stock, like all color film available at the time, was not well-suited to copying directly from older prints, and by today's standards the colors appear pale and the contrast weak when compared to the two-color Technicolor original.[28]

Such a project would likely be deemed controversial today for mixing such wildly different sources, but at the time this was the only known way of making the film viewable again. Ultimately, despite the strong feedback from the screening at the 1965 FIAF Congress, this hybrid reconstruction does not appear to have circulated widely, as it was soon to become obsolete.[29]

Label for the sound disc for the Czech release, pressed in Bridgeport, Connecticut.

35mm frame enlargements from the 1965 reconstruction by the Československá filmotéka.

Philip Jenkinson was a host for the BBC's *Late Night Line-Up* from 1967 to 1972. During this time he interviewed many Hollywood stars and filmmakers, including John Ford, Ramon Novarro, Joan Crawford, and Gloria Swanson.

The Jenkinson print

A few years later, another near-complete print resurfaced, but its existence was largely kept quiet, and its exact origins remain cloudy and wrapped in rumors. Some say this print was liberated from Benito Mussolini's personal film collection after his death in 1945, and then made its way into the hands of the British Bing Club, later the International Crosby Circle, who threaded it up for private screenings every year to celebrate Crosby's birthday.[30] Other sources indicate the print might have been owned by an executive of MCA (the parent company of Universal at the time), who obtained it from an old exchange that handled Universal film prints.[31] Perhaps we will never know the full details. Nonetheless, the print has become known to some as the "Mussolini print."

In 1968, the British film collector, historian, and broadcaster Philip Jenkinson gained access to this mysterious "Mussolini print." Jenkinson, who died in 2012, is today best remembered by British film fans as a host of the BBC's *Late Night Line-Up* from 1967 and *Film Night* in the 1970s. Jenkinson was an enthusiastic expert on early sound cinema and musicals, and as a result became a

credited advisor on Ken Russell's 1920s-nostalgia musical *The Boy Friend* (1971) and the director's biopic of silent film star *Valentino* (1977). On the side Jenkinson was an avid film collector, often subsidizing his acquisition of 16mm prints through his work for the BBC, and gaining access to rare titles through contacts at the British Film Institute. Jenkinson made his own negatives of the harder-to-find titles, so he could order up new prints to trade with other collectors around the world. This was a time before the advent of home video, when many older films still remained out of circulation and buying a print was the only way to see a rare, desirable film.

"As far as I know I have the only surviving three reels [of *King of Jazz*] outside of the soviet union [*sic*]," Jenkinson wrote to American collector David Bradley in 1969.[32] Jenkinson's 16mm copies of *King of Jazz* were extremely rare, and were sought out by some of the most dedicated film collectors, who operated as part of the "black market," under the radar of the film studios and copyright holders. "This for your ears only. The biggest find of my whole career. V. good quality. Can't afford to trade on this one, I'll need cash."[33]

Film historian and professor William K. Everson was among the first to obtain a copy in the United States.

He programmed a special screening at the Theodore Huff Memorial Film Society in New York on September 22, 1969. "Tonight's print is a good new reversal made from an original 35mm print found in Europe," Everson's program notes announced, while still keeping the true source concealed. "Apart from the brief dance wrap-up to 'Ragamuffin Romeo', it's apparently fully complete, much more so than the Czech print which is down to 6 reels [sic]."[34]

The first high-profile screening of this Jenkinson print was at the New York Film Festival on September 27, 1970. The film was eagerly anticipated as a major rediscovery, although audiences were unsure what to expect from the advance promotion. The program notes downgraded the film as "an omnibus of vaudeville" with some "enchanting if naive production numbers." Bing Crosby, Walter Lantz, and George Gershwin were given most prominence, while Paul Whiteman was largely sidelined.[35] In his report about the festival screening for *Film Comment*, Richard Koszarski admitted that the film was "an arduous experience" for some, and not for all tastes. "Those among the audience who came expecting to see a Ruby Keeler extravaganza in Technicolor were immediately turned off when they found the sets moving around the cameras, instead of the other way around," but "if you can appreciate the studio 'revues' of 1929–30, or are a student of John Murray Anderson and the American musical theatre of the twenties, then THE KING OF JAZZ [sic] is a fabulous find."[36]

Jenkinson was warily protective of the prints he traded, only dealing with trusted collectors he knew well. This was a time mired in paranoia over film piracy and copyright infringement, overseen by Jack Valenti's Motion Picture Association of America. The homes of actor Roddy McDowall and many others were raided by the FBI during this period and 16mm collections were frequently seized. Everson's Huff Society screenings were obscure enough to remain under the radar, and the New York Film Festival showing had been cleared through Universal. But a planned event in October 1970 at the Los Angeles County Museum of Art did not seek the necessary permissions, and Universal was tipped off by an advance article in the *Los Angeles Times*, which was less-than-favorable. Jazz critic and historian Leonard Feather's negative review called the film a "musical travesty," with "the grand total of actual jazz content … less than two minutes out of close to two hours. ... The Afro-American role in creating jazz [was] downgraded in every area of potential exposure."[37]

The museum was forced to pull out of the screening and issue a hasty announcement: "The Los Angeles County Museum of Art and its entire staff devoted to

At its New York Film Festival screening in 1970, *King of Jazz* was presented alongside "Cinema and Color," a special program of films personally selected by Henri Langlois of the Cinémathèque française.

the presentation of little-seen films are dismayed by those last-moment 'circumstances beyond our control' which make it impossible to show THE KING OF JAZZ [sic] as announced. ... We promise to labor without rest until the matter is resolved and hope some day to present the film with proper protection and support. ... we offer our most contrite apologies for the eleventh-hour crisis which has prevented our showing the film."[38]

LACMA's Head of Educational Programs Philip Chamberlin had borrowed a collector's 16mm print of the Jenkinson version, but failed to secure permission for public performance. As a result Universal demanded the surrender of the print under legal action. The situation was diffused when Chamberlin offered to turn over the print to the Library of Congress, although the original owner was not consulted and received no compensation for his loss.[39]

Jenkinson was understandably concerned about getting embroiled in the fiasco. "I am just finishing up my small heart failure over your reported bust up over K of J," he wrote David Bradley. "How in hell's teeth did the LA Museum get a copy—who let them have it, and why wasn't it cleared with Universal? I also hear the

Frame enlargements from a 16mm Philip Jenkinson print made in 1986.

announcer, when he made his apology for non-projection of advertised program, used my name several times in connection with the print. ... Luckily the original source of the master is from a parent company of MCA so I doubt if they'd sue one of their own executives so to speak. But it does show how unreliable people are. I know exactly who has material, and I can't believe any of them would be so stupid to inaugurate a public showing at which the cameraman [Hal Mohr] is present, advertise it all over LA, without first getting clearance. It's a positive death-wish."[40]

TV and video

Following interest from the BBC in 1973, Universal made new 35mm preservation elements from what was left of the original camera negative, which had been cut down to 65 minutes in 1933, with the trimmings discarded. The preservation entailed making black & white separations from the negative (one for the red record and one for the green), then these were each printed through color filters and superimposed onto modern color film stock. The BBC were sent a new 35mm color print of this shortened version and this was subsequently broadcast on BBC Two. In 1975, Philip Jenkinson made 16mm copies of sections of this BBC print to supplement his existing version. With access to this new source of footage, Jenkinson was able to fill in the dance routine from "Ragamuffin Romeo," the second chorus of "Song of the Dawn," and several blackout scenes, although almost ten minutes was still absent.[41] This extended version was later shown on BBC One in 1976.[42]

In the United States, MCA began offering the film to cable networks in March 1983, and later that year released the film on home video, reaching the widest audience yet. But this video transfer left a lot to be desired. In addition to being marred by the poor condition of much of the source material, the VHS release suffered from the manipulation of an over-zealous colorist intent on enhancing the limitations of the original color process. With little awareness of the original look of original two-color Technicolor prints, the video grading re-balanced the spectrum to appear more "natural" to modern audiences. This is most evident in the *Rhapsody in Blue* sequence, which cranks up the blue—a color incapable of being reproduced in early Technicolor.

The VHS release was largely compiled from the 35mm camera negative, with the remainder of the footage filled in from Jenkinson's 16mm print. Although re-edited to a shorter running time, the negative contained some additional sequences, and evidently caused some confusion to the home-video department at MCA. The end result was a bastardized version of *King of Jazz*—a mishmash of the 1930 and 1933 releases compiled to create the longest possible cut. The scene order of the VHS version largely corresponds to the 1930 general release, except the number "I'd Like To Do Things For You" was shifted to a position after "Happy Feet," almost an hour later into the film. And three "blackout" sequences—used in

The color manipulation seen in the *King of Jazz* VHS version was not a unique occurrence. Home-video releases of *Whoopee!* (1930) and *Mystery of the Wax Museum* (1933) display a similarly distorted two-color Technicolor palette.

Neither the 1983 (left) or 1995 (right) VHS covers featured Paul Whiteman prominently, deciding instead to highlight other performers like the Sisters G and Bing Crosby.

the 1933 reissue but not in the 1930 release—found their way into this new version. They include Slim Summerville and Walter Brennan in the "Horse's Neck" skit; the "Look What It Makes Me" gag with Merna Kennedy, Glenn Tryon, and William Kent; and Summerville and Otis Harlan in the risqué "Pretty Lucky So Far." Missing entirely from the VHS is the "Piccolo Player" sketch with Paul Whiteman and William Kent, Jeanie Lang's introduction to "My Bridal Veil," the blackout "A Dash of Spice," which preceded "Happy Feet," and the exit music.

In the 1980s and 1990s, *King of Jazz* finally became available to a larger audience. The film could be purchased on VHS or caught on regular television screenings. Perhaps less known is the long history of getting the film

back on our screens, and the complicated task of piecing it together from multiple sources. For close to forty years—from 1934 to 1970—*King of Jazz* was effectively impossible to see, but due to several unsung champions of the film and a host of rediscoveries, a version of *King of Jazz* came back into circulation and has been reappraised. Ironically though, the VHS format that made the film widely accessible is now largely obsolete, and *King of Jazz* has again faded from view (except for the poor-quality bootleg copies floating around). But thanks to the dedication of NBCUniversal, which is investing in restoring its back catalog, *King of Jazz* has been made available again in a restored version as faithful as possible to the aesthetic, length, and order of the original 1930 release.

A close-up of Bing Crosby from "The Rhythm Boys" scene, scanned at 4K resolution from the original two-color Technicolor camera negative.

Chapter 10

UNIVERSAL'S 2016 RESTORATION

NBCUniversal's digital restoration of *King of Jazz* premiered at The Museum of Modern Art in New York City on May 13, 2016, as the cornerstone of an ambitious series celebrating Universal's output of the 1930s and the studio's ongoing restoration program. For many fans of the film, this moment had been a long time coming. For Universal, the restoration further demonstrates its commitment to its heritage. The restoration itself was not an easy task, requiring a groundswell of support to get started, and a host of digital fixes to reconstruct the film as closely to its original version as possible. The restoration is the first time a two-color Technicolor negative has been scanned and recombined digitally, and the results are remarkable. But it is also remarkable that any of this negative survives at all, as so many early Technicolor negatives were destroyed.

After years of the film only being available legally as a poor-quality VHS release, the restoration has come as a revelation. The film can now be fully appreciated for its incredible design and use of color. John Murray Anderson's vision and careful "routining" also becomes more meaningful, with previously missing footage restored or recreated, and the director's intended running order reconstituted. And Paul Whiteman's music is clearer than ever, sourced from the original soundtrack negative. But this complicated and costly restoration only became possible in recent years due to the (re)discovery of a nitrate print acquired by Raymond Rohauer and the strategic lobbying of a dedicated few to get the film recognized on America's National Film Registry.

Despite the fact that *King of Jazz* has been available in an assortment of different versions and formats since the late 1960s, a high-quality upgrade has not been possible until recently, due to only incomplete elements surviving. Universal has long counted the original two-color Technicolor camera negative among its assets, but this negative was considerably shortened in 1933 for reissue, with approximately 40 minutes removed. In Britain, film collector Philip Jenkinson made a limited number of 16mm prints for fellow enthusiasts well into the 1980s, but as lab prices rose and VHS copies became more prevalent, demand for his prints declined.[1] Despite investigations by archivist Scott MacQueen and others, the original 83-minute 35mm nitrate print that Jenkinson had used as the source for much of his 16mm reconstruction could not be located.

Only recently has it come to light that the infamous film entrepreneur and collector Raymond Rohauer acquired this nitrate print of *King of Jazz*.[2] According to Rohauer's former assistant Ed Watz, this print, along with a copy of the silent release of *All Quiet on the Western Front* and the sound discs for the 1930 reissue of *The Phantom of the Opera*, were being discarded from warehouse storage, likely from an old distribution depot in the UK. "There were other titles, features and shorts, but these were three that Raymond was interested in," remembered Watz. "The man [selling the films] told Raymond that Universal had instructed him to destroy the picture & sound elements. Instead, he gave them to Rohauer and signed an affidavit that all material had been destroyed."[3] Rohauer was a film collector with the resources to indulge his hobby—by the early 1970s he had amassed a personal collection of 12,000 titles. Over time he turned his collection into a business, fueled by a shrewd knowledge of international copyright law. Among many other libraries, he acquired the rights to much of the silent output of Buster Keaton, Douglas Fairbanks, and parts of D. W. Griffith's oeuvre. This led to repeated conflicts with other rights-holders and archives.[4]

When Rohauer died in 1987, a significant portion of his film collection was still in storage, spread across France, Spain, Germany, and England, stashed in "garages and barns and châteaus," noted film historian Kevin Brownlow.[5] In 1996, the Douris Corporation took over the ownership of Rohauer's physical collection, as well as the distribution rights to the 700 titles Rohauer had controlled. For the next twenty years, Douris archivist Tim Lanza worked diligently to consolidate Rohauer's many disparate holdings, with the nitrate copies ultimately finding a home at the Library of Congress—recognized as the national library of the United States, and the repository of one of the world's largest moving image collections. Rohauer's *King of Jazz* print arrived at the Library in 2002 as part of a shipment of eight large wooden crates of film sent from the Centre National de la Cinématographie (CNC), the French archive that had assumed responsibility for much of Rohauer's nitrate collection in France after its storage fees had gone unpaid.

Although stored safely in specialist nitrate vaults, this "Rohauer print" did not undergo a detailed inspection at the Library of Congress until December 2010, when outside interest was expressed in possibly projecting the print at Turner Classic Movies' TCM Classic Film Festival, at either the Egyptian Theatre or UCLA's Billy Wilder Theater, the only two venues still capable of projecting nitrate film in the Los Angeles area. The inspection by nitrate film vault manager George Willeman revealed that the print measured 7,440 ft. (close to 83 minutes)—the longest known surviving element—but was precariously fragile, with numerous weak splices and shrinkage at 1.8% (too high to be projected, but not unusual for a print of this age). The Eastman Kodak edge code on the film confirmed the print was made in 1930. "The beauty of the film images and the richness of the 2-color really took me by surprise," recalled Willeman. "I had gotten used to the washed-out look of the MCA VHS, so it was like I had never seen the film!" Willeman took many pictures of the print and shared these with the interested parties. "The more I inspected, the more exciting it got [to] know that quite possibly a top-drawer restoration would be possible."[6]

Although it would ultimately take close to five

Raymond Rohauer (1924–1987) traveled to Europe frequently for business. In the late 1960s and early 1970s he was a consultant on two BBC television compilation programs, *Golden Silents* (1969) and *The Sound of Laughter* (1971), both of which used film clips from Rohauer's collection. It was possibly around this time that he acquired the nitrate print of *King of Jazz*.

years, Willeman's inspection of the Rohauer print in 2010 set the wheels in motion for the NBCUniversal digital restoration that we can see today. Vitaphone Project co-founder Ron Hutchinson saw some of Willeman's photos and began exploring how to get the film restored.[7] He shared the images with writer and film preservation patron David Stenn, who contacted preservation staff at Universal Pictures. Stenn pitched the idea of a new restoration to Bob O'Neil, then Vice President of Image Assets and Preservation at Universal. O'Neil was a staunch supporter of the film, and had already undertaken analog printing tests using some of Universal's existing elements, prior to learning of the existence of the 83-minute Rohauer print. In July 2011, with permission granted by Douris, the Rohauer print was sent to YCM Laboratories in Burbank, California, to be incorporated into the printing tests.

The specialist preservation laboratory YCM was founded in 1982 by the late Pete Comandini. With partners Richard Dayton and Don Hagans, and later with

The Raymond Rohauer print — A timeline of ownership

Although not enough evidence exists to be 100% certain, this timeline attempts to unravel some of the mysteries surrounding the changing ownership of what has been dubbed the "Rohauer print."

1930
The print was made in the United States and shipped to Britain for exhibition. At some point during its release, or later in its history, some footage was lost to damage or was removed. After 1930, the print likely remained in storage.

1960s
The print was still held in storage (probably at an old distribution warehouse for Universal prints). The International Crosby Circle gained access to this print for private member screenings.

1968
British collector Philip Jenkinson borrows the print from storage (with the help of an "MCA executive") and copies it to make a 16mm reversal master (from which he subsequently makes other 16mm prints for sale), after which the nitrate print is returned to storage. To cover his tracks Jenkinson possibly fabricates the Benito Mussolini origin story, which is told to fellow collector William K. Everson.

Late 1960s/early 1970s
Raymond Rohauer travels to England many times for business. He learns of the existence of the *King of Jazz* print and acquires it from storage before it is destroyed.

1970s or 1980s
Rohauer moves the print into storage in France.

1990s
Following Rohauer's death, many of his storage fees go unpaid. The Centre National de la Cinématographie (CNC) pays these back charges for storage in France and acquires parts of Rohauer's former nitrate collection.

2002
Eight crates of nitrate film once owned by Raymond Rohauer are shipped from the CNC in France to the Library of Congress vaults in Dayton, Ohio, and are then subsequently moved into new storage in Culpeper, Virginia, in 2007. This shipment from France includes the *King of Jazz* print.

Raymond Rohauer's Technicolor dye-transfer print at the Library of Congress was discovered to be well worn, with tears, edgewave, spoking, bad perforation damage, fractures throughout, and many splices, but the colors remained good and there were no signs of decomposition. Photographs by George Willeman.

Eric Aijala, the lab pioneered new techniques to restore color films, especially those made using the obsolete Technicolor process. In collaboration with preservationist Robert Gitt from the UCLA Film & Television Archive, YCM completed groundbreaking analog restorations of *Toll of the Sea* (1922), recombined from the original two-color Technicolor camera negatives, and *Becky Sharp* (1935), the first three-color Technicolor feature. Subsequently, YCM has become the premier laboratory for the photochemical restoration of Technicolor films, both for the Hollywood studios, like Disney and Warner Bros., and for film archives across the United States.

Working closely with Dayton and Aijala of YCM, O'Neil oversaw analog printing tests of the "Happy Feet" production number from Reel 9, switching between the camera negative and the Rohauer print. The full sequence runs for almost 5 minutes; however, the re-edited negative contains just over 2 minutes of this number. Using proprietary techniques, YCM printed footage from the negative, with the remaining 3 minutes sourced from the print. The number was a good test case, as in several instances the source of the footage had to change from the negative to the print and back again, sometimes midway through a shot. The results of YCM's tests were impressive, but a restoration using these techniques would have been particularly labor-intensive, and very expensive given the complicated printing techniques required. It was estimated at the time that the potential cost could have exceeded $250,000. With limitations on its annual restoration budget, Universal was unable to proceed with such a costly project at that time.[8]

The National Film Registry

David Stenn and Ron Hutchinson believed that one way to encourage Universal to commit to such a costly restoration was to have the film's importance officially recognized. Together, they planned a campaign to have the film inducted into the National Film Registry, a list of "culturally, historically, or aesthetically significant films," which was established following the National Film Preservation Act of 1988. The Registry began a year later and continues to grow, with 25 new titles added each year. Stenn and Hutchinson teamed with film historians Robert S. Birchard and Richard Koszarski to prepare a letter addressed to each member of the National Film Preservation Board, a supervising committee of established practitioners in the field who debate and pre-select each year's nominations for the Registry before the final decisions are made by the Librarian of Congress. The committee consists of more than 50 members, drawn from archives, studios, and bodies representing academics, filmmakers, and trade organizations.

King of Jazz had been proposed to the Registry once before, in 2008, as part of an unsuccessful effort spearheaded by jazz historian David Sager, but this time around the approach was more systematic. "David [Stenn] and I reviewed the composition of the Registry's board of judges and between us we knew just about everyone," recalled Ron Hutchinson. "So we split the list between us and spoke to each judge. Little convincing was needed with any of them, as they all knew the film, its importance, and agreed it was a worthy candidate."[9]

Stephen C. Leggett, the program coordinator for the National Film Preservation Board, recognized that the lobbying was very successful. "More individual Board members voted for [*King of Jazz*] than any other film that year," he revealed.[10]

In December 2013, with the Board's recommendation, Librarian of Congress James Billington selected *King of Jazz* to be inducted into the National Film Registry. Other new additions that year included celebrated favorites like *Mary Poppins* (1964) and *Pulp Fiction* (1994), and more diverse fare like the silent Native American drama *Daughter of Dawn* (1920) and the experimental film *Decasia* (2002), made from decomposing fragments of nitrate film. "The National Film Registry stands among the finest summations of more than a century of extraordinary American cinema," remarked Billington in the accompanying press release. "This key component of American cultural history, however, is endangered, so we must protect the nation's matchless film heritage and cinematic creativity."[11] Some titles added that year, like *King of Jazz* and the 1926 Colleen Moore comedy *Ella Cinders*, only survived in abridged or incomplete versions. Naming the original release versions of these films to the Registry was an important step in raising awareness of the plight of certain titles and ensuring their further preservation. One stipulation of the Registry is that the Library subsequently has to acquire a print of each title for its permanent collection.

Restoration begins

The naming of *King of Jazz* to the National Film Registry provided further rationale for Universal executives to justify the high cost of such a complicated restoration. "There is a committee [at the studio] that consists of executives, experts in the field, [and] historians," explained Peter Schade, Universal's vice president of technical services. Part of the committee's selection criteria for new projects includes such questions as "Is the film nominated for awards? Are there key anniversaries or milestones that come up in the history of that film? And, does it appear on the Registry, or other lists? All of that factors in."[12]

The digital restoration of *King of Jazz* was approved by this committee in early 2015. The time was right. In the three years since Bob O'Neil's first analog printing tests, Universal had expanded its digital restoration activities, driven by the success of the studio's 100th anniversary in 2012, when thirteen studio classics were restored and issued on Blu-ray disc. These ongoing efforts are overseen by the studio's Content Management depart-

ment, which works in collaboration with its in-house StudioPost facilities. The Content Management team, headed by Peter Schade and his colleagues, Emily Wensel, Cassandra Wiltshire, Seanine Bird, and Ken Tom, manages the restorations, whereas "StudioPost is the internal post facility," clarified Wensel, Director of Content Mastering. "StudioPost is a full service post-production facility with all the equipment necessary to conduct high-quality restorations. The facility has film scanners, editorial, and a variety of cutting edge digital restoration capabilities. The majority of our restoration work is conducted internally with workflows designed to provide greater control and cost efficiencies. From time to time, outside post facilities are used to supplement our restorations."[13]

Some of the burgeoning department's most notable projects to date have included high-profile digital restorations of *All Quiet on the Western Front* (1930), *The Birds* (1963), and *Jaws* (1975), for the studio's centennial in 2012; 6K scans of *Spartacus* (1960) and *One-Eyed Jacks* (1961) from the Technirama camera negatives; fourteen classic monster movies; the Marx Bros. Paramount comedies from the early 1930s; and an ongoing effort to digitally restore fifteen silent feature films over a four-year period. These digital restoration activities operate in parallel with the studio's long-running analog film preservation program, which has preserved thousands of titles in the studio's library on 35mm film.

The first step in any restoration project is to determine what elements survive. "Our policy when we restore all of our films," Schade revealed, is to "use the original elements. If the original element no longer exists, we look at the intermediate and follow on from there."[14] For the team's recent restoration of Stanley Kubrick's *Spartacus*, for example, this meant scanning the original large-format camera negative, which it hadn't been possible to use for the film's previous analog restoration in 1991 due to extreme color fading. With the new tools that digital scanning and color correction can offer, the color can be regained and remarkable sharpness and clarity can be retained.

The original two-color Technicolor camera negative for *King of Jazz* had been in Universal's possession for many years. Although the studio donated much of its nitrate pre-print elements to the Library of Congress in the late 1960s (as part of an American Film Institute initiative), a significant quantity of additional nitrate materials remained in commercial storage vaults in Kearny, New Jersey. This is where the *King of Jazz* negative was housed until Universal deposited this collection at the UCLA Film & Television Archive in 2010.[15] As the earliest generation element for *King of Jazz*, this negative was called in as the primary source material for the new restoration.

The fact that this negative exists at all is remarkable. Of the 34 all-color features produced in two-color Technicolor, only five survive as original camera negatives—a dismal survival rate of 15%.[16] This is partly because many early Technicolor negatives were purposely destroyed. By the 1950s, Technicolor's two-color process was considered thoroughly obsolete, having been replaced by its "glorious" three-strip process, memorably used for such multi-hued classics as *The Adventures of Robin Hood* (1938), *The Wizard of Oz* (1939), and Busby Berkeley's over-the-top *The Gang's All Here* (1943) with Carmen Miranda, among many other titles. Technicolor had continued to store all of the studios' two-color negatives into the late 1930s. When Technicolor offered to return these negatives when two-color printing was discontinued, most of the studios—seeing minimal commercial prospects for these old films— declined, and instead approved their destruction. As a result, approximately two-thirds of all two-color Technicolor films made between 1922 and 1936 are now lost, or survive only in black & white or significantly incomplete copies.[17] Universal was among the few studios and independent producers that accepted Technicolor's offer. For Universal this included the return of negatives for several Walter Lantz "Cartune Classics," *King of Jazz*, and one of the Technicolor scenes from the 1925 silent version of *The Phantom of the Opera* starring Lon Chaney.[18]

In the 1970s, Universal made two black & white fine grain masters on safety film as positive protection elements of the *King of Jazz* nitrate camera negative (one was a copy of the red record, and the other of the green record). A recombined duplicate color negative was then made from these fine grains by printing them in two passes with red and green colored light.[19] This duplicate negative, which had poor contrast and muted colors, was later used as the source for much of Universal's 1983 VHS release and broadcast video master.

As mastering supervisor at NBCUniversal, Ken Tom is responsible for assessing the studio's existing film elements. "I will look at film reports and will gather up all the film elements," Tom explained. "The usual procedure is to do a one-light element evaluation. And then I'll take a look at those and I'll bring in the desirable elements. We evaluate all [these] elements, and then we start sending them to the scanner."[20] For the *King of Jazz* restoration, sixteen different picture elements were evaluated—not unusual for a project of this complexity—although only four were ultimately used to reconstruct the picture. This included reviewing Universal's preservation elements from the 1970s, but they were ultimately not required

for the restoration due to the exceptional condition of the camera negative.

1. **35mm nitrate camera negative** (Universal, 65 minutes)
2. **35mm nitrate soundtrack negative** (Universal, 104 minutes)
3. **35mm nitrate soundtrack negative** (Universal, 65 minutes)
4. **35mm safety fine grain protection master, green record** (Universal, 65 minutes)
5. **35mm safety fine grain protection master, red record** (Universal, 65 minutes)
6. **35mm safety color duplicate negative** (Universal, 65 minutes)
7. **35mm nitrate Technicolor dye-transfer print** (Rohauer print, Library of Congress, 83 minutes)
8. **35mm safety b&w print** (Czech-French reconstruction, Library of Congress, 78 minutes)
9. **16mm safety color print** (Jenkinson print, Library of Congress, 83 minutes)
10. **35mm nitrate Technicolor dye-transfer print** (Danish Film Institute, 2 reels)
11. **35mm nitrate Technicolor dye-transfer print** (UCLA, 1 reel)
12. **16mm safety color print** (UCLA, 1 reel)
13. **35mm safety color print** (BBC, 65 minutes)
14. **Scan of 35mm nitrate Technicolor dye-transfer print** (George Eastman Museum, 2 reels)
15. **Scan of 35mm nitrate Technicolor dye-transfer print** (British Film Institute, 2 reels)
16. **DVD copy of 35mm nitrate Technicolor dye-transfer print** (French version, Gosfilmofond, 78 minutes)

Scanning

In the summer of 2015, the camera negative and the Rohauer print were sent to Cineric in New York City for scanning (as Universal's in-house film scanner was not yet certified for nitrate film). After assessing the elements, the specialist film laboratory determined that the print was too fragile and shrunken to be scanned on the lab's existing equipment, so it was returned to Universal. The negative, on the other hand, remained in excellent condition, due to minimal handling over the years. Cineric's staff scanned this negative at 4K resolution (4,096 x 3,112 pixels) on an Oxberry Cinescan. The pin-registered film scanner captures rock-steady frame scans at a rate of one frame every six seconds. That equates to approximately 48 hours continuous scanning time for each 2,000-ft. film

The original camera negative for *King of Jazz* survives in remarkably good condition.

reel of Technicolor negative.[21] Cineric supplied Universal with raw black & white DPX files of each color record, plus additional files of the green and red separations recombined into a color image.

Meanwhile, the returned film print was scanned in Burbank, California, by Prasad Corp., a digital post-production service provider with operations worldwide. Under the supervision of Colleen Simpson, Vice President of Operations, Prasad scanned the delicate nitrate print using a Scanity, a continuous motion film scanner featuring a sprocketless capstan drive that can run up to 15 frames per second at 4K resolution. This machine is able to handle severely warped, damaged, and shrunken film without issues because it does not use sprocket teeth to advance each frame.

Once Universal received these scans, Ken Tom did further evaluation "to make sure all the information we can get out of the film is not crushed or clipped out"—meaning that as much detail as possible in the highlights and shadows is retained from the original source elements.[22] The team then began the task of piecing the film back together, laying out both scans on a timeline using Autodesk's Inferno software, which was primarily developed for visual effects and image manipulation. Using notes on the contents of the soundtrack as a guide, the negative scans were used as the primary source in

filling out the timeline, then the scans from the print fleshed out large parts not present in the negative. This procedure allowed the restorers to identify portions of the image that were still missing.

Researching the original version

Early on in the project the restorers at Universal had to decide exactly what edition of the film they were restoring. *King of Jazz* had been released in multiple different cuts in the early 1930s, and its first reconstruction by Philip Jenkinson in the 1970s was hampered by his access to incomplete elements. Just what exactly was the original cut? In order to further understand the film's exhibition history and how best to piece the film back together, Universal enlisted the support of the authors of this book, as well as other specialist help from Robert S. Birchard, an expert on the history of Universal Pictures. Birchard had looked into contemporary reviews and film programs to study how the film was originally presented to audiences in 1930. With his help, the team at Universal settled on restoring the 104-minute general release version, which appeared to match the longest soundtrack negative in the studio's holdings. Ideally, a cutting continuity script, outlining the content and length of each shot, would have revealed exactly what was in the film's original release, but no such script could be located. In the end, cross-checking a number of sources helped to confirm that the soundtrack negative in Universal's possession was indeed for the U.S. general release version. But additional research was required to help fill in the remaining missing picture elements.

By September 2015, the restoration assembly was comparable in content to Universal's video master from the 1980s. The same footage was present, although the running order was now more in line with the film's original release. Matching the picture to the sound, it became evident exactly which parts were missing, and conversely, which parts were superfluous. For example, three brief sketches present in the negative—"Pretty Lucky So Far," "Look What It Makes Me," and "Horse's Neck"—were eliminated from the restoration because they were not present in the film as it was released in 1930.[23]

No complete print of the U.S. general release exists at any archive in the world, but odd reels and excerpts for the film did survive scattered across different collections. The UCLA Film & Television Archive has a highlights reel of short excerpts, individual reels are housed at the Academy Film Archive and the British Film Institute, two reels are at George Eastman Museum, and approximately 27 minutes of excerpts are at the Danish Film

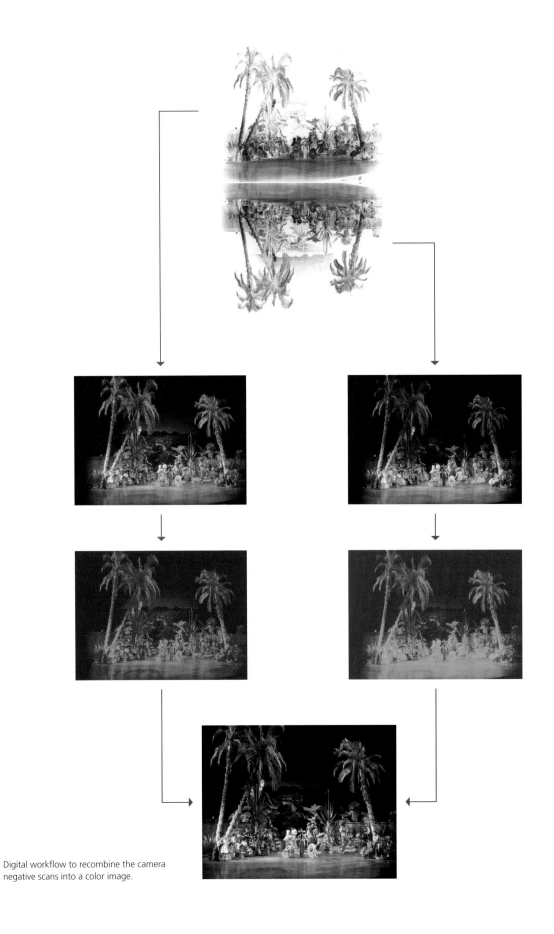

Digital workflow to recombine the camera
negative scans into a color image.

The nitrate print from the Danish Film Institute contained one sequence not present in any other surviving prints. At 59 seconds long, the "Dash of Spice" sketch is a mix of visual gags and brief dialogue. As Danish audiences wouldn't necessarily understand the English dialogue, Danish language intertitles were added while the audio continued. There were three such intertitles in this sequence. To maintain continuity, the restorers removed these intertitles and used freeze-frames to cover their absence.

Institute. Additionally, a mute nitrate print of the French version of *King of Jazz* is in the collections of Gosfilmofond of Russia. As the exact content of these reels was not always readily apparent, Universal called in several of these prints for inspection.

The Danish reels contained approximately one minute of previously missing footage from the sketch "A Dash of Spice," featuring Kathryn Crawford, William Kent, Glenn Tryon, and child actor "Sunny Jim" McKeen. The audio was in English, but the print contained Danish intertitles cut into the action of the scene when dialogue was spoken. Most of the sketch was present, but Jeanette Loff's introduction was missing. Despite being choppy, the UCLA highlights reels had extra footage that could be used to fill out short gaps in the "Ladies of the Press" sketch and "The Property Man" scene, including the previously missing ending to the latter with Jack White's nonsensical punchline.

Both of these prints were scanned by Universal onsite using the department's ARRISCAN. Universal has used this scanner on many restoration projects before, but only for safety film elements. In mid-2015 the scanning room was certified for nitrate film; too late for the *King of Jazz* negative and the Rohauer print to be scanned, but it was up and running in time for these shorter reels. The scanner has a wet-gate attachment, which helps minimize the appearance of dirt and scratches in the scan. But even with the addition of the Danish Film Institute and UCLA material, several holes in the restoration still remained.

Missing footage

As Universal's goal was to restore the film to its 1930 general release version, the restoration team had to find a way to cover missing footage. With the picture synchronized to the complete audio track, it was immediately apparent where parts were missing. The Rohauer print was worn and damaged, with many short pieces missing, but in most cases these one- or two-frame gaps could be repaired with digital tools. Using visual effects software like Inferno, the restoration staff could "interpolate [the footage] and create those missing frames from what's before and after," explained Peter Schade. "We've used [this process] in the past on some of the older monster movies. It works really well."[24]

For larger gaps the team had to get creative. In the *Rhapsody in Blue* sequence, there was a gap of 63 frames of picture near the start during the clarinet *glissando* that would have caused a notable jump in the music if the audio had to be excised. "Obviously filling it in [in] the middle of a musical number is difficult," recalled restoration project manager Seanine Bird. In this case "we actually stole [a shot of Jacques Cartier] from later on in the sequence. [We had to] reframe the image a little bit, to make it work with the timing of the music."[25] "In that case," added Peter Schade, "it's because the music was all pre-recorded and you're basically instrument syncing the track. We were able to put footage in to bridge the gap that wasn't necessarily shot for that same sequence and time."[26] As a final confirmation, Bird brought in two experienced musicians to view the rough cut to make sure that the reused footage of Cartier matched the music being played. It did, and the trick will be imperceptible to most viewers.

Bird admitted that tackling the missing footage has required "quite a hodgepodge of solutions."[27] For the longer gaps, the team chose to use stills—an established practice in film reconstruction, but interestingly, a technique that had never been used at Universal before. This approach has been notably adopted in restorations of the original cut of Frank Capra's *Lost Horizon* (1937) and the original release version of *A Star Is Born* (1954) with Judy Garland.[28] In both cases the audio survived for the missing scenes and a selection of stills helped fill the void for viewers.[29]

The restorers drew upon the original keybook stills for *King of Jazz*, now conserved in the studio archive, but once housed in the New York Public Library for the Performing Arts. Keybooks are the studio's master set of reference photographs that document every aspect of a film's production. The stills are usually linen-backed with punched holes along the edge so they can be grouped in ring binders. For *King of Jazz*, Universal had 220 stills covering most scenes in the movie, but the set was incomplete. Most conspicuously missing were stills for the majority of the film's comedy sketches.

Keybook stills of Jeanette Loff were used to fill in her missing introduction to the sketch "A Dash of Spice," while Jeanie Lang's introduction to "My Bridal Veil" and some of Charles Irwin's and Paul Whiteman's introductions were covered with a mix of stills and freeze-frames. In cases like these, the color freeze-frames were converted to black & white images to indicate that they had been inserted as part of the restoration.

But for one lengthy scene—"The Piccolo Player," with William Kent and Paul Whiteman—which runs

A three-second gap of missing footage in the *Rhapsody in Blue* sequence was filled with a duplicated shot of Jacques Cartier from later in the sequence. This approach avoided having to cut or alter Gershwin's music to conceal the missing picture.

In addition to cleaning signs of significant damage and repairs, there were also "thousands of little specks, and little bits of dirt" that had to be cleaned throughout, according to Peter Schade, Vice President of Technical Services at NBCUniversal. Some blemishes "were obviously from the red record or the green record, because the little dots and specks were different colors."

approximately 2½ minutes, no related stills could be found. Without any visuals to cover the audio, the decision was made to remove the scene entirely from the restoration, as it would have made little sense without the accompanying image.

Picture clean-up and color correction

Universal's restoration staff typically work on many projects simultaneously. For example, in early 2016, the team had nine ongoing restorations. To efficiently accomplish each project, many tasks happen concurrently. Once the picture and sound components are locked in a timeline, different teams tackle image clean-up, color correction, and audio restoration.

"We have ten dedicated digital restoration operators that go through and clean frame-by-frame," revealed Seanine Bird. "The clean-up was done mostly with the MTI software, called Nova. We [used] Phoenix for some pre-processing; also for deflicker. And we used Diamant for deflicker. We've got quite a bag of tricks! We have to figure out what fits the best element. The idea overall for all of our work is that we try to use something that results in a more natural-looking fix. If the fix results in drawing more attention to itself, we'd rather just leave it the way it is."[30]

In recent years, "we've really changed the way that

The difference in image quality between the scanned print sources (top) and negative scans (bottom) is very evident when compared side by side, as is demonstrated by these two shots of Jeanette Loff from the "Monterey" number. When two image sources were used in the same scene, the effect can be jarring, but it also provides a clear picture of what shots were eliminated for the shorter 1933 reissue.

we apply these digital tools," Peter Schade continued. "We apply them only if they help and if they contribute in a way that doesn't detract from the original intent. I think we've become a lot smarter, and a lot more conservative as far as how we apply those tools. And that's OK. If it's a 90-year-old film element, it's not going to look like it was shot yesterday." The team notes audience feedback, and adapts accordingly. Online reviews have helped the department gauge what consumers are looking for, and the result is a toned-down approach. "Certainly over the years the tools have gotten better, and we always have to

ride that balance. You want to employ some automation, so you're not incurring lots of man-hours of work, but only to the point where it doesn't create anything artificial. I feel we've come a very long way, and I think the reviews of some of the [titles] we've been putting out, like *Jaws* and *Spartacus*, reflect that."

One of the biggest challenges was having to combine different film elements that look very different when played back-to-back. The scans from the negative are sharp and contain a wide range of detail in the highlights and shadows, whereas the scans from dye-transfer film

The subtle colorings of Herman Rosse's sets and costumes are now revealed in stunning detail in the 4K scans from the original camera negative. After close study of the film's careful compositions, the Academy aspect ratio of 1.37:1 was selected as the most authentic form to present the restored images.

Members of the NBCUniversal picture restoration team: colorist Mike Holgate, digital restoration artist Paul Martinez, restoration project manager Seanine Bird, digital restoration lead Mike Wonser, technical supervisor Ken Tom, Flame artist Rob Williams, engineer Henry Ball.

prints lack resolution or subtle contrast. Additionally, the Rohauer print is "very grainy," explained Schade. "We can mainly tell the difference as we cut between the print and the negative because the grain structure of the negative is so much tighter. The grain in the print is huge."[31] Mastering supervisor Ken Tom had to make sure the different elements played as smoothly as possible. "The difference in resolution was oftentimes considerable," he remarked. "The most difficult part of this is trying to get everything to cut and flow as best as possible. You try to dig as much detail out of the print as you can, but at the peril of having milky blacks, which no one wants. And then the grain structure on the print is completely different than what's on the negative. Seanine has been herding the footage through various grain processes, then she kicks it over to myself and Mike Holgate, the colorist, and we put our eyes on it, and either it's good or we send it back for another round of processing."[32]

"There are many places in this movie where it's very obvious [that] you're going from the print to the neg," added Bird, "like in the 'Monterey' sequence and in the Rhythm Boys sequence. There was nothing we could do

about it. You want to have the neg as much as you can. You don't want to dumb it down and go [to the] print for the entire sequence, so there is going to be the 'pop'" between sources.[33]

King of Jazz is the first two-color Technicolor film that Universal's digital restoration staff have worked on. To ensure that the outcome was going to be faithful to the original aesthetic of the process, the restorers worked closely with the authors of this book, and also brought on board experienced preservationists Richard Dayton and Eric Aijala from YCM Laboratories to consult on the color correction. "When we went into this project I was very concerned about achieving the right look," revealed Peter Schade. "The color continues to be a challenge in color correction because it isn't natural." Universal had access to several original film prints of *King of Jazz*, but each looked different, which is not uncommon for Technicolor prints of the era. "That's always the toughest question, if talent is no longer around to give us a ruling, you really have to rely on other sources and references, and try to triangulate in on what we feel is the right look."[34]

The end result is a clean vibrant aesthetic that

Members of the NBCUniversal sound restoration team: audio supervisor Andrea Riehle and re-recording mixer John Blum.

respects the original color palette of two-color Technicolor. The scans from the camera negative are stunning—considerably sharper and more vivid than anyone has seen this film look before—but the footage from the print sources is variable, ranging from dark and contrasty (the "Monterey" number) to pleasantly acceptable ("Has Anybody Seen Our Nellie"). The switch between sources remains noticeable, but is necessary given the condition of the surviving copies. For the most part, considerable damage, dirt, and scratches have been digitally repaired, and shakiness in the image has been stabilized. Universal's policy of removing blemishes that are distracting or detrimental to the viewing experience, while maintaining the inherent flaws or limitations from the original source material, results in an organic and very watchable end product.

The sound

In a typical restoration project, the sound work is normally undertaken after all the picture elements are locked. For *King of Jazz*, the audio restorers came on

board from the start because of the complexity of the reconstruction. The original soundtrack negative on 35mm nitrate film was identified as the longest and best surviving element for the film. This sound negative, as well as the sound negative for the 1933 reissue, were transferred in Burbank at Deluxe Media Audio Services, an established audio restoration facility. A Sondor sound reader was able to capture optimal audio quality directly from the negative.

Universal's audio supervisor Andrea Riehle documented the content of the audio files provided by Deluxe, and made detailed notes on each scene for the restoration staff working on the picture elements. After thoroughly consulting the sound files, as well as transfers made from a set of original Vitaphone sound discs, Riehle compiled her master sound files for the full 104-minute running time of the film. In the end 98% of the audio was sourced from the 1930 soundtrack negative, with the remaining 2% filled in from the 1933 negative element. This was necessary as the audio for Jacques Cartier's Voodoo drum dance contained significant distortion in the 1930 optical track. Here, StudioPost re-recording mixer John Blum had to seamlessly blend the two sources.

The same restoration methodology was used on the sound as the picture. The goal is to create a seamless presentation that is not distracting for audiences, but also respects the filmmaker's original intentions and the limitations of the technology of the time. As such, the restored audio is presented in its original mono form, although inherent background noise and distortion have been minimized, and distracting pops, ticks, and hums have been eliminated using iZotope software.

Public presentations

The digital restoration of *King of Jazz* took a little over a year from start to finish. This duration is "not atypical," explained Seanine Bird. It "includes the research aspects as well; when we start to go out to look for elements, talk to people, and figure out where everything is. [Most of Universal's restoration projects] can be about a year, soup to nuts."[35]

"Once you've put all the labor and effort into something, you want to show it off, you want to share it," revealed Peter Schade. "We want to make sure [Universal's legacy] is accessible to people who are fans and to people who may not have seen these titles. I'm very proud of the work we do and what the team does, my team as well as our own internal facilities, the partner facilities, and the collaboration between the different film archives, and other preservation-centric institutions all over the world. We're really making an effort to publicize what we're doing, to build those relationships and to further the library."[36]

Presentation is the final, and perhaps most important, stage of a film's restoration. *The King of Jazz* restoration premiered in a 4K DCP at The Museum of Modern Art in May 2016 as the opening film in a month-long celebration of Universal's early 1930s output under producer Carl Laemmle Jr. The 30-film series—entitled "Universal Pictures: Restorations and Rediscoveries, 1928–1937" and programmed by MoMA adjunct curator Dave Kehr—bypassed the well-known monster movies like *Frankenstein* and *Dracula* in favor of the overlooked and underseen gems produced mostly under Junior's tenure. This ambitious series, which was also presented a month later in a condensed form at the preservation and restoration film festival Il Cinema Ritrovato in Bologna, Italy, is part of a larger initiative for making the work of Universal's digital restoration department more accessible. In addition to Blu-ray and DVD releases, many of the department's other recent restorations have received high-profile screenings at the TCM Classic Film Festival in Hollywood, the San Francisco Silent Film Festival, and the Cannes Film Festival, for example, as well as popular repertory houses like Film Forum in New York City.

"A lot of [other studios] are going in opposite directions and are not investing in restoring their libraries," commented Seanine Bird, but "our company has shown a commitment to this effort and we're proud to be part of the team."[37]

The completion of this meticulous restoration draws to a close another chapter in the history of *King of Jazz*. After being practically impossible to see for close to forty years, the film has gradually won back audiences since the 1970s in revival screenings, on TV, and through home video; but few have realized the versions they have been watching were so compromised. NBCUniversal's new restoration finally reveals the film's remarkable vision, but it also remains a stark reminder of what is still missing. Approximately 60% of the restoration's 100-minute running time is sourced from the camera negative and looks pristine. The remainder, with the help of new digital tools, is a considerable improvement over the old VHS releases. The end result highlights the important role of film preservation, and just what can be achieved when a studio commits to its heritage. The story of this restoration is a long one, and involves many parties. Fortunately, despite several impediments, everything eventually aligned to make this project possible. And now the next chapter of the film's rediscovery begins.

The majority of the "Meet the Boys" sequence was cut from the 1933 re-issue of *King of Jazz*. As a result the best picture source available for NBCUniversal's restoration was a nitrate print. After dust and scratch removal, stabilizaton, and color correction, the results are impressive.

APPENDIX

By Crystal Kui and James Layton

King of Jazz had a complicated production history, and an exhibition history that was even more complex. The content shown at the preview screening was recut before the premiere version, which was itself modified before the general release. Additionally, nine alternate international versions were prepared—each with a different host—and the film was cut down and reordered for its reissue in 1933, from the 104-minute version seen widely in 1930. To further confound audiences today, the versions that have been available in recent years do not represent what audiences originally saw during the film's various theatrical runs.

This appendix attempts to provide a comprehensive guide to every version of *King of Jazz* over the years. Numerous sources have been used to inform this survey, from viewings of multiple prints; assessment of scripts, studio production files, and music cue sheets; and careful study of contemporary reviews, promotional material, and stills. The breadth of this appendix would not have been possible without the groundwork laid by historians Diane and Richard Koszarski in the 1970s. Between them, they consulted—and made notes on—hundreds of pages of studio production files, correspondence, contracts, and scripts. Much of this primary source material is no longer available to us in 2016.

There have been endless misconceptions about *King of Jazz* due to incomplete viewing copies, inaccurate assumptions, and poor documentation. This appendix aims to clear up some of these errors and to reveal new discoveries—although many mysteries still remain.

The following nine sections list every known member of the cast and production crew, all music heard in the film, what film elements survive and where, and how each successive version of the film—from the 1930 general release to the 2016 digital restoration—differs. Included is an almost day-by-day account of the production, from the day Paul Whiteman signed his contract with Universal to the day the film was released. A compilation of deleted scenes offers a glimpse of what was planned, shot, and abandoned, before and after *King of Jazz* reached movie screens. Also, the film's production costs and weekly box office returns are itemized in detail.

The ultimate goal of this appendix is to be a useful reference resource that can be consulted throughout the reading of this book. The further context it provides should only help enrich future viewings of the film.

Appendix I:

FILMOGRAPHIC INFORMATION

KING OF JAZZ
(Universal Pictures Corp., 1930)

Director: John Murray Anderson; **producer**: Carl Laemmle, Jr.; **assistant directors**: Robert Ross, Sergei Petschnikoff (uncredited); **comedy sketches**: Harry Ruskin, William Griffith (uncredited); **supervising film editor**: Maurice Pivar; **film editor**: Robert Carlisle; **cinematographers**: Hal Mohr, Ray Rennahan, Jerry [Jerome] Ash (trick photography); **assistant cameraman**: Wilfred M. Cline (uncredited); **make-up**: Jack Pierce (uncredited); **settings and costumes**: Herman Rosse; **assistant art director**: Thomas O'Neill; **recording supervision**: C. Roy Hunter; **music**: Milton Ager; lyrics: Jack Yellen; **additional musical numbers**: George Gershwin, Mabel Wayne, Billy Rose; **orchestrations**: Ferde Grofé; **musical arrangements**: James Dietrich (credited for "additional music numbers"); **dance director**: Russell E. Markert; **animated cartoon**: Walter Lantz, Bill Nolan, Wynn Holcomb (uncredited); **scrapbook design**: Wynn Holcomb (uncredited)

Cast: Paul Whiteman and his band [**Violins**: Kurt Dieterle, Matt "Matty" Malneck, John Bouman, Giuseppe "Joe" Venuti, Otto Landau, Ted Bacon, Mischa Russell; **Trumpets**: Harry "Goldie" Goldfield, Charles A. Margulis, Frank Siegrist, Andy Secrest; **Reeds**: Chester Hazlett, Charles Strickfaden, Irving "Izzy" Friedman, (Orie) Frank "Frankie/Tram" Trumbauer, Roy J. "Red" Maier, Bernie Daly; **Trombones**: John C. "Jack" Fulton, William "Bill" Rank, Boyce H. Cullen, Wilbur Hall; **Piano**: Roy Bargy, Leonard George "Lennie" Hayton; **Banjo**: Michael "Mike" Pingitore; **Guitar**: Eddie Lang (Salvatore Massaro); **Bass**: Michael "Mike" Trafficante; **Tuba**: Wilford F. "Min" Leibrook; **Drums**: George Marsh], The Rhythm Boys [Harry Barris, Harry Lillis "Bing" Crosby, Alton "Al" Rinker]

Charles Irwin, the Russell Markert Dancers (credited as The Russell Markert Girls), Jeanette Loff, Stanley Smith, the Hollywood Beauties (Betty Caldwell, Marion Dabney, Geraldine [Jeraldine] Dvorak, Helen Hargrave, Bessie Lee, Lucile Powers, Elaine St. Maur, Renee Torres, and Evelyn Vaughan, all uncredited), Jeanie Lang, Grace Hayes, William Kent, Nell O'Day and the Tommy Atkins Sextet (credited as The Tommy Atkins Sextette) [Richard "Dick" Erskine, Toby Erb, Clayton Romler, Scott Jensen, Gilbert Herwood, and Robert Galer], Laura La Plante, Merna Kennedy, Kathryn Crawford, John Boles, Nancy Torres, The Sisters G [Karla and Eleanore Knospe], George Chiles, Glenn Tryon, Jack White, Joan Marsh, the Brox Sisters [Josephine/Dagmar/Bobbe Brox, Eunice/Lorayne Brox, Kathleen/Patricia Brox], Lawrence "Sunny Jim" McKeen, "Snowdrop," [George] Slim Summerville, Yola D'Avril, Walter Brennan, Jacques Cartier, Marion Stadler (credited as Marion Stattler), Don Rose, Al Norman, Paul Small, Frank Leslie, Churchill Ross, Johnson [John] Arledge, John Peel Quartet, Beth Laemmle, Cathleen [Cathlyn] Bessette, Felipe Delgado, Manuel and Vida, Michael [Mikhail] Vavitch, Bob Gilbert, Paul Howard

Additionally the Internet Movie Database (IMDb) lists these unconfirmed cast members:
Joan Barclay (chorine, uncredited), Richard Cromwell (chorus boy, uncredited), Arthur Gardner (chorus boy, uncredited), Charlie Greco (pianist, uncredited), Cecilia Parker (chorine, uncredited), Pauline Wagner (page-turner hands, uncredited)

Production dates: November 15, 1929–March 12, 1930 (per studio files)

Los Angeles preview: March 24, 1930 (Belmont Theater)
Los Angeles opening: April 19, 1930 (Fox Criterion Theatre)
Baltimore opening: April 24, 1930 (Auditorium Theatre)
Washington, DC, opening: May 1, 1930 (Rialto Theatre)
New York opening: May 2, 1930 (Roxy Theatre)
U.S. general release: August 17, 1930
British charity premiere: July 17, 1930 (Thames Riviera Hampton Court, London)
British opening: October 9, 1930 (Alhambra and Regal theatres, London)

Length of U.S. general release:
>   9,320 ft. (104 min.), according to Technicolor release shipments, May 14, 1930;
>   9,398 ft. (13 reels, 104 min.), according to New York State censorship certificate, May 1, 1930;
>   8,721 ft. (97 min.), according to *Motion Picture News*, May 10, 1930;
>   105 min. (approx. 9,450 ft.), according to *Film Daily*, March 30, 1930;
>   98 min (approx. 8,820 ft.), according to *Variety*, May 7, 1930;
>   13 reels (105 min.), according to surviving soundtrack negative held by Universal

Length of British release: 9,388 ft. (104 min.), according to *The Bioscope*, June 18, 1930
Domestic prints: 184
Foreign prints: 215
Total prints: 399

Appendix II:

PRODUCTION CHRONOLOGY

The following chronology has been adapted and expanded from Diane Koszarski's paper submitted to Jay Leyda's New York University class "The Authorship and Manufacture of Films" in the Department of Cinema Studies in 1977. It draws upon a number of sources:

Universal Weekly (UW), Universal studio files and contracts transcribed by Diane and Richard Koszarski (SFC), original contracts (OC), George Gershwin Collection at the Library of Congress (GG), Universal library properties (LP), and United States Immigration passenger lists (PL).

1928

Oct. 18	Paul Whiteman signs with Universal to make "The King of Jazz," a synchronized sound film based on "dramatic incidents in Paul Whiteman's life." Ferde Grofé will do the scoring. Whiteman and his band will interrupt their concert tour in mid-February to make the production at Universal for eight weeks. (UW)
	Whiteman will be paid $5,000 a week plus $200,000 as a guarantee of 40% of net profits. 25 band members and 5 arrangers will be paid $7,800 per week. (OC)
Nov. 3	Songs written by L. Wolfe Gilbert and Mabel Wayne. (UW)
Nov. 15	Original story by Paul Schofield, 12 pages. (LP)
Nov. 17	Schofield to join Whiteman on his cross-country concert tour. "The film will depict Whiteman's eventual triumph as the creator of symphonic jazz. It will include his most popular compositions played by his band." Wesley Ruggles is mentioned as the director. (UW)

1929

Jan. 10	Shooting is postponed to June 1. Whiteman's contract modified and notice extended. (SFC)
March 16	Continuity by Paul Schofield, 440 scenes. (LP)
April 13	Director Paul Fejos travels to New York this week to confer with Whiteman. (UW)
	Edward T. Lowe Jr., who will prepare the script and arrange the dialogue, is in New York until mid-April. (UW)
April 18	Continuity synopsis by E. T. Lowe Jr., 48 pages. (LP)
April 27	Carl Laemmle Jr. takes charge of the production. "The film will bring to the public the insistent dissonances of modern music of which the famous 'Rhapsody in Blue' by George Gershwin is typical." (UW)
May 21	Anderson sells his interest in "Melting Pot" to Paramount-Publix for $1,000. (SFC)
May 24	Whiteman and band leave for California on "Old Gold Special" concert tour. (UW)
May 27	Ferde Grofé, Whiteman's official arranger, arrives at Universal City. (UW)
	Mabel Wayne will go to the Coast early in June. (UW)
	Actual production probably will start about June 14. (UW)
June 1	L. Wolfe Gilbert, lyricist, is at Universal City for a week or more, conferring with Universal script writers. (UW)

June 10	Original story by E. T. Lowe Jr. and Ilona Fulop, 11 pages. (LP)
June 11	Treatment by E. T. Lowe Jr. and Ilona Fulop, 6 pages. (LP)
June 13	Treatment by E. T. Lowe Jr. and Ilona Fulop, 17 pages.
June 21	Treatment by E. T. Lowe Jr. and C. Gardner Sullivan, 9 pages. (LP)
June 25	Original story by Frank M. Dazey and Agnes Christine Johnson, 17 pages. (LP)
June 29	Carl Laemmle welcomes Whiteman at Universal City. (UW)
	Fejos is casting; screen tests being made in New York City and California. (UW)
July 4-18	Five continuity revisions by E. T. Lowe Jr. (LP)
July 9	A soundproof bungalow has been constructed for Whiteman on the Universal lot; it is known as the Whiteman Lodge. (*Variety*)
July 17	Harry Green has been signed for a prominent role as a theatrical agent. (*Variety*)
July 20	Frank T. Dazey will assist Edward T. Lowe Jr. in writing the continuity and dialogue. (UW)
July 27	The first player cast, aside from Whiteman, is André Beranger, who last appeared in *The Small Batchelor*. (UW)
July 31	Whiteman signs three-month extension with Universal; contract modified. Due at Universal City on Nov. 1. (SFC)
Aug. 7	Paul Fejos, director previously assigned to the Paul Whiteman film, will direct *La Marseillaise*. (*Variety*)
Aug. 10	Ferde Grofé announced working on "Melting Pot" number. (UW)
	Mabel Wayne and Billy Rose are working on the music. (UW)
	Arthur Franklin will act as musical advisor. (UW)
Aug. 15	Paramount-Publix clears use to Universal of "Melting Pot." (SFC)
Aug. 24	Postponement announced of "famous Paul Whiteman film without a story" until Nov. 1. Carl Laemmle Jr. says "it has been postponed until a more suitable story has been found to fit Whiteman's unusual ability." (UW)
	Whiteman and his orchestra begin a concert tour of the Pacific Coast. (UW)
Sept. 5	Herman Rosse signs; notice to report to Universal City by Sept. 16. Compensation: $300/week for services in New York City, $500/week at Universal for first four weeks, $650/week for next six weeks, $750 thereafter. (SFC)
Sept. 7	John Murray Anderson signs for a minimum of 10 weeks at $2500/week beginning Sept. 28. If services extend beyond 14 weeks, Anderson will receive $2500/week for the first 12 weeks and $2500/week for all work commencing with the 15th week. (OC)
	Anderson and Rosse to begin planning by Sept. 23. (SFC)
Sept. 13	Russell Markert and his Dancers sign. Due at Universal City by Nov. 1 and Nov. 10 respectively.
	Markert will work for no less than 6 weeks at $1500/week. Dancers will be paid $1250/week. (SFC)
	William Kent, comedian, signed for 4 weeks minimum at $1000/week plus options; due at Universal City by Nov. 15, then Dec. 15. (SFC)
Sept. 21	Paul Whiteman travels East from his Pacific Coast tour to confer with Metzger and Anderson. (UW)
	Announcement that Paul Whiteman revue film to be directed by Anderson, designed by Rosse. (UW)
Sept. 25	Paul Howard, eccentric dancer, signs for 4 weeks minimum at $300/week; due at Universal City by Dec. 1. (SFC)
	Grace Hayes signs for 4 weeks minimum at $1000/week ($500 penciled in) plus options; due at Universal City by Nov. 25. (SFC)
Sept. 28	Milton Ager and Jack Yellen, Broadway songwriters, announced signed; due at Universal City by Oct. 7. (SFC)
	Universal contract players suggested for skits: John Boles, Laura La Plante,

	Joseph Schildkraut, Mary Nolan, Hoot Gibson, Ken Maynard. (UW)
Sept. 30	Sisters G sign for 3 weeks minimum at $500/week plus options; due at Universal City by Dec. 1. (SFC)
Oct. 1	Paul Whiteman welcomes Carl Laemmle in New York City, returning from Europe. Laemmle announces signing Sisters G in Germany. (PL, UW)
Oct. 3	*Rhapsody in Blue* licensed to Universal for $50,000. (GG)
Oct. 8	Nell O'Day and the Tommy Atkins Sextet, vaudeville dancers, signed for 4 weeks minimum at $1000/week; due at Universal City by Dec. 15. (SFC)
Oct. 9	Anderson and Rosse leave for Universal City. They have been in New York for several weeks making preliminary designs and plans in conference with Whiteman and Universal officials. Anderson has signed with stage and vaudeville performers to take part in the revue. (UW)
Oct. 12	Harry Ruskin, comedy sketch writer, signed: $300/week for the first 4 weeks, $500/week afterwards plus options; due at Universal City by Nov. 15. (SFC)
Oct. 14	Wynn Holcomb, caricaturist, signs: $1000 for scrapbook and cartoon plus cost of transportation to California. (SFC)
Oct. 15	Al Norman, eccentric dancer, signs for 3 weeks minimum at $400/week plus options; due at Universal City by Dec. 15. (SFC)
	Jacques Cartier, dancer, signs for 4 weeks minimum at $350/week plus options; due at Universal City by Dec. 15. (SFC)
Oct. 25	Sisters G arrive in New York City from Europe. (PL)
Oct. 26	William Kent *en route* from New York City; will work as chief gag artist. (UW)
	Charles Irwin, vaudeville headliner and MC, signed. (UW)
	Harry Ruskin arrives at Universal City. (UW)
	John Boles, Mary Nolan, Laura La Plante, Joseph Schildkraut, Glenn Tryon, Ken Maynard, and Hoot Gibson announced to participate in skits. (UW)
	Paul Fejos is "injured" on the set of *La Marseillaise*. (UW)
Nov. 1	Paul Whiteman arrives at Universal City. (UW)
Nov. 2	Wynn Holcomb will leave this week for Universal City. (UW)
Nov. 5	Harry Ruskin loaned to Pathe Studios for 2 weeks. (SFC)
Nov. 15	Shooting starts on *King of Jazz*. (SFC)
Nov. 16	George Chiles, Broadway ballroom dancer, *en route* from New York City. (UW)
	Chiles signs for 4 weeks' work at $200/week, plus $200/week for additional services; due at Universal City by Dec. 15. (SFC)
	Russell Markert, Nell O'Day and Tommy Atkins Sextet announced *en route* from New York City. (UW)
Nov. 20	Nancy Torres announced for the revue. (*Variety*)
Nov. 21	*All Quiet on the Western Front* begins production. (SFC)
Nov. 30	Grace Hayes "left Monday" for Universal City. (UW)
	Jeanette Loff, contract player, assigned to the revue; due Dec. 1. (UW)
	Stanley Smith, contract player, assigned. (UW)
	Sisters G "left today" from New York City. (UW)
	William Kent, Charles Irwin, Paul Howard, George Chiles, Nell O'Day and the Tommy Atkins Sextet, and Al Norman have arrived at Universal City. (UW)
	The Russell Markert Dancers have been on the lot for two weeks rehearsing special numbers. (UW)
	Carl Laemmle Jr. and Anderson have selected members of the Hollywood Beauties: Betty Caldwell, Marion Dabney, Helen Hargrave, Bessie Lee, Lucile Powers, Renee Torres, Elaine St. Maur, and Evelyn Vaughan. (UW)
	Ferde Grofé is writing several original compositions. (UW)
Dec. 19	*King of Jazz* rushes previewed by Florabelle Muir, *Daily News*: "Whiteman's newly discovered clowning genius seems to rest on solid premises." (UW)

Dec. 21	Frank Leslie, Broadway comedian, signed for a skit; he will "leave for Coast this week." (UW)
Dec. 28	John Boles to have two singing numbers in the revue. (UW)

1930

Jan. 8	"I'd Like to Do Things For You" treatment by Isabelle Campbell. (SFC)
Jan. 24	Frank Leslie arrives at Universal City. (UW)
Jan. 25	Jeanie Lang, radio singer, announced for the revue. (UW)
	Revue is announced "approximately half-completed." (UW)
Feb. 1	Beth Laemmle will perform a dance solo in "Melting Pot" sequence. She adopts the stage name Carla Laemmle as a compliment to her uncle. (UW)
	"Wait for the Happy Ending," a number from John Murray Anderson's "Almanac," which played this season on Broadway, will probably be introduced in *The King of Jazz*. Another unique song by Ager and Yellen is entitled "Shadows." (UW)
Feb. 4	Jack White signed to do a speciality number with Whiteman's orchestra for $1000. (SFC)
Feb. 8	Herman Rosse has returned to New York City; all sets in working order. (UW)
	King of Jazz rushes are previewed by Welford Beaton, who writes in *The Film Spectator* that the film "will open the world's eyes." (UW)
	Coral Clyee, *New York Morning Telegraph*, views rushes from "Bench in the Park," "Bridal Veil," "Melting Pot," and "Monterey." (UW)
	"Aase's Death" scene from Ibsen's *Peer Gynt* being planned, to feature Joseph Schildkraut. (UW)
Feb. 22	Robert Ross is helping Harry Ruskin to film comedy sketches he is writing. (UW)
March	Treatment for sketch based on Anton Chekhov's one-act play *The Boor*. (SFC)
March 11	George Sidney and Charlie Murray signed for 2 days' work at $2000. (SFC)
March 12	Production finished on *King of Jazz*. (SFC)
March 15	Laura La Plante announced released from her contract—"before her departure she will be pictured in *The King of Jazz* sequences for which she is scheduled." Scenes planned for Glenn Tryon, Kathryn Crawford, and Merna Kennedy. (UW)
March 24	*All Quiet on the Western Front* finishes production.
	King of Jazz preview at the Belmont Theatre, Los Angeles. (UW)
March 29	All-color cartoon announced completed; in progress since the beginning of production in mid-November 1929.
	Blackout sketches featuring Laura La Plante, George Sidney, Charlie Murray, Glenn Tryon, and Merna Kennedy are announced completed. (UW)
	"Paul Whiteman has shot all necessary retakes." Editing and running order now to be determined. (UW)
March 31	Peter Arno *New Yorker* cartoon (from Dec. 27, 1929) is purchased for $200 as the basis of the sketch "Springtime," which has already completed shooting.
April 5	Both of Grace Hayes' numbers are removed from the Los Angeles premiere print. (SFC)
April 12	Seven Universal super- and special productions are booked at the Roxy Theatre: *Captain of the Guard*, *King of Jazz*, *All Quiet on the Western Front*, *The Storm*, *What Men Want*, *Czar of Broadway*, and *White Hell of Pitz Palu*. (UW)
April 16	Whiteman and his band and Jeanette Loff leave for New York. (UW)
April 19	Los Angeles premiere, Criterion Theatre. An African drum dance serves as a prologue to the film. (*Los Angeles Times*)
April 24	Baltimore opening, Auditorium Theatre. (*Baltimore Sun*)
April 26	John Murray Anderson "will arrive in New York Wednesday to consult with Roxy (Rothafel) for the premiere of his production." (UW)

April 27	Paul Whiteman and his band arrive in New York City. (UW)
	Print approved for screening in New York by State of New York Education Department Motion Picture Division. (LP)
May 2	New York premiere at the Roxy Theatre, including live performances on stage by Whiteman and his band and composer George Gershwin, who plays *Rhapsody in Blue*. (*New York Times*; *Roxy Theatre Weekly Review*).
May 9	Gershwin plays his *Concerto in F* (first movement) for the second week of the film's premiere engagement at the Roxy. Whiteman no longer appears. (*Roxy Theatre Weekly Review*)

Appendix III:

U.S. RELEASE VERSION

Following its Los Angeles premiere, King of Jazz received a gradual release beginning in late-April 1930. It is this widely distributed U.S. release version that is described here.

This detailed listing of the U.S. release version includes a comprehensive running order broken down by reel, as well as the full cast and performers, and music cues for each scene. As this general release version no longer survives complete, this list has been compiled and confirmed from multiple sources, including but not limited to: ERPI and ASCAP music cue sheets, 1930 dialogue continuity, original sound discs, and viewings of the film.

The majority of the music pieces listed here are performed only in part, while others are reduced to just a few bars. Those performed in their entirety are preceded by an asterisk (*).

REEL 1

Opening Titles

"Rhapsody in Blue" (Andante movement) by George Gershwin
*"Music Has Charms," music by Milton Ager, lyrics by Jack Yellen; sung by Bing Crosby

Paul Whiteman's Scrap Book
Cast: Charles Irwin

A Fable in Jazz (Color Cartoon)
Animators: Walter Lantz, Bill Nolan

"Hunting Song," by James Dietrich (incorporating variations on "A-Hunting We Will Go") (instrumental)
"Rhapsody in Blue" (instrumental)
"The Mosquitoes' Parade," by Howard Whitney (instrumental)
"Didn't My Lord Deliver Daniel?" traditional spiritual; sung by Bing Crosby
"Mess Call" (improvised) (trumpet)
"Andante Cantabile" from String Quartet No.1, Opus 11, by Pyotr Ilyich Tchaikovsky (instrumental)
"Music Has Charms"; instrumental, then scat singing by the Rhythm Boys
"Hootchie Kootchie" ["The Snake Charmer Song,"

from "The Streets of Cairo"], by Sol Bloom and James Thornton, arranged by M. L. [Mayhew Lester] Lake (instrumental)
"Music Has Charms" (instrumental)
"Aba Daba Honeymoon," music by Walter Donovan (instrumental)
"Music Has Charms" (instrumental)

Meet the Boys
Cast: Charles Irwin, Paul Whiteman and his band

"It Happened in Monterey," music by Mabel Wayne; whistled by Paul Whiteman
"When Good Fellows Get Together: A Convivial Song," by Frederic Field Bullard and Richard Hovey (instrumental)
"Ragamuffin Romeo," music by Mabel Wayne (instrumental)
"Hot Lips," by Henry Busse, Henry Lange, and Lou Davis; played by Harry "Goldie" Goldfield (trumpet)
*"Wild Cat" by Joe Venuti; played by Joe Venuti (violin) and Eddie Lang (guitar)
"Piccolo Pete" by Phil Baxter, played by Bernie Daly (piccolo)
"Caprice Viennois," Opus 2, by Fritz Kreisler; played by Otto Landau, Ted Bacon, John Bouman, Matt Malneck, Kurt Dieterle, and Joe Venuti (violins)
"Tambourin Chinois," by Fritz Kreisler; played by Otto Landau, Ted Bacon, John Bouman, Matt Malneck, Kurt

Dieterle, and Joe Venuti (violins)
"Nola," by Felix Arndt; played by Chester Hazlett (clarinet),
Roy Bargy (piano), and Wilbur Hall (trombone)
"Linger Awhile," music by Vincent Rose (instrumental);
played by Mike Pingitore (banjo)

REEL 2

Meet the Girls
Cast: The Russell Markert Dancers

"Music Has Charms" (instrumental)
"I Like to Do Things for You," music by Milton Ager
(instrumental)
"Music Has Charms" (instrumental)

My Bridal Veil
Introduced by Jeanie Lang
Cast: Jeanette Loff, Stanley Smith, Marion Dabney (bride),
2 unidentified bridesmaids, Helen
Hargrave (bride), Gloria Fisher (flower girl), R. Smith
(page), Robin Smith (page), Betty Caldwell (bride),
Marcia Mae Jones (shepherd boy), Page ? [last name
unknown] (shepherdess), Crane Twins (bridesmaids),
Geraldine [Jeraldine] Dvorak, 4 unidentified pages, Lucile
Powers (bride), Arline Aber (bridesmaid), Charline Aber
(bridesmaid), Renee Torres (bride), Thelma Woodruff
(bridesmaid), Levern Chase (bridesmaid), Elaine St.
Maur (bride), P. Celsan (bridesmaid), Betty Jane Graham
(bridesmaid), Bessie Lee (bride), [Maracchet?] Hurrell
(cupid), the Russell Markert Dancers

"My Bridal Veil," music by Milton Ager (instrumental)
Bells (improvised)
"My Bridal Veil," music by Milton Ager, lyrics by John
Murray Anderson and Jack Yellen; sung by Jeanette Loff
*"Oh Happy Bride," by Milton Ager and Jack Yellen; sung
by female chorus
*"Passepied" by James Dietrich (instrumental)
"Orpheus" (Ballet Suite) by Christoph Willibald Gluck
(instrumental)
"Minuet in G" by Ludwig Van Beethoven (instrumental)
"Amaryllis" (old French air, attributed to Louis XIII) by Henri
Ghys (instrumental)
"Long, Long Ago" by Thomas Haynes Bayly; sung by
female chorus
"My Bridal Veil"; sung by Stanley Smith, Jeanette Loff, and
female chorus
Improvisations by James Dietrich

REEL 2A

I'd Like to Do Things for You
Cast: Jeanie Lang, Paul Whiteman, Grace Hayes, William
Kent, Nell O'Day and the Tommy Atkins Sextet [credited as
Tommy Atkins Sextette]

*"I Like to Do Things for You," music by Milton Ager,
lyrics by Jack Yellen; sung by Jeanie Lang, Grace Hayes and
William Kent, and Nell O'Day and the Tommy Atkins Sextet
"A Bench in the Park," music by Milton Ager
(instrumental); danced by Nell O'Day and the Tommy
Atkins Sextet
*"I Like to Do Things for You"; sung by Jeanie Lang, Grace
Hayes, and William Kent; sung and danced by Nell O'Day
and the Tommy Atkins Sextet

REEL 3

Ladies of the Press (Sketch)
Written by William Griffith
Introduced by Charles Irwin
Cast: Laura La Plante, Jeanie Lang, Merna Kennedy,
Kathryn Crawford, Grace Hayes

The Rhythm Boys
Cast: Harry Barris, Bing Crosby, Al Rinker

"Mississippi Mud," music by Harry Barris, lyrics by James
Cavanaugh
*"So the Bluebirds and the Blackbirds Got Together,"
music by Harry Barris, lyrics by Billy Moll
Vocals: Harry Barris, Bing Crosby, Al Rinker; piano: Harry
Barris

The Piccolo Player (Sketch)
Cast: Paul Whiteman and William Kent

"Caprice Viennois," Opus 2, by Fritz Kreisler; played by
William Kent

REEL 4

Monterey
Cast: John Boles, Jeanette Loff, Nancy Torres (Mexican
soloist), the Sisters G, George Chiles, the Russell Markert
Dancers [credited as Russell Markert Girls]

Bells (improvised)
"La Paloma," by Sebastián Yradier (instrumental)
*"It Happened in Monterey," music by Mabel Wayne, lyrics
by Billy Rose; sung by John Boles, Jeanette Loff, and female

chorus

"La Paloma"; sung in Spanish by Nancy Torres; danced by the Sisters G, George Chiles, and the Russell Markert Dancers

"It Happened in Monterey" (instrumental); danced by the Russell Markert Dancers

"La Paloma"; sung in Spanish by Jeanette Loff

"It Happened in Monterey"; sung by John Boles and Jeanette Loff

In Conference (Sketch)

Cast: Laura La Plante, Glenn Tryon, and Merna Kennedy

REEL 5

The Property Man

Introduced by Charles Irwin

Cast: Jack White, the Rhythm Boys, members of the Whiteman band

"Old Black Joe" by Stephen Foster; sung by the Whiteman band

"Oh, How I'd Love to Own a Fish Store," music by Billy Stone, lyrics by Al Koppell; featuring Jack White and members of the Whiteman band

Piano (improvised); featuring Jack White, the Rhythm Boys, and the Whiteman band

"Asleep in the Deep," music by H. W. Petrie; featuring Jack White and Frankie Trumbauer

"The Stars and Stripes Forever" by John Philip Sousa (instrumental); featuring Jack White

"Semper Fidelis" by John Philip Sousa (instrumental); featuring Jack White

"There's a Long, Long Trail," music by Alonzo "Zo" Elliot; featuring Jack White and Harry "Goldie" Goldfield

"On the Road to Mandalay," music by Oley Speaks; featuring Jack White

"Oh, How I'd Love to Own a Fish Store"; featuring Jack White

"On the Road to Mandalay"; featuring Jack White and the Whiteman band

A Bench in the Park

Cast: William Kent, Stanley Smith, Jeanette Loff, George Chiles, Joan Marsh, the Brox Sisters, the Rhythm Boys, the Russell Markert Dancers, the Hollywood Beauties, Paul Whiteman and his band, "Sunny Jim" McKeen, "Snowdrop"

*"A Bench in the Park," music by Milton Ager, lyrics by Jack Yellen; sung by Stanley Smith and Jeanette Loff

"When Day Is Done," music by Robert Katscher

(instrumental); featuring George Chiles and Joan Marsh

*"A Bench in the Park"; sung by the Brox Sisters, the Rhythm Boys (guitar by Eddie Lang), Stanley Smith and Jeanette Loff; danced by the Russell Markert Dancers; featuring the Hollywood Beauties and members of the Whiteman band: Charles A. Margulis (trumpet), Roy J. "Red" Maier (saxophone), Joe Venuti (violin), Harry "Goldie" Goldfield (trumpet), John C. "Jack" Fulton, Wilford F. "Min" Leibrook (tuba); "Sunny Jim" McKeen; Paul Whiteman, "Snowdrop"

REEL 6

Springtime (Sketch)

Cast: Slim Summerville, Yola D'Avril, and Walter Brennan

All Noisy on the Eastern Front (Sketch)

Introduced by Charles Irwin

Cast: Yola D'Avril, Walter Brennan, Charles Irwin, Paul Whiteman, William Kent

Willie Hall, One of the Whiteman Boys

Cast: Wilbur Hall

"Liebesfreud," by Fritz Kreisler; played by Wilbur Hall (violin)

*Original Violin Speciality by Wilbur Hall; played by Wilbur Hall (violin)

*"Stille Nacht" ("Silent Night"), by Franz Xaver Gruber; played by Wilbur Hall (violin)

*"Pop Goes the Weasel," English nursery rhyme song; played by Wilbur Hall (violin)

"The Stars and Stripes Forever," by John Philip Sousa; played by Wilbur Hall (air pump), with offscreen piano accompaniment

The Rhapsody in Blue (Voodoo drum dance)

Introduced by Paul Whiteman

Cast: Jacques Cartier

Drum Roll (improvised), danced by Jacques Cartier

REEL 7

The Rhapsody in Blue

Cast: Jacques Cartier, Paul Whiteman and his band, Roy Bargy (solo pianist), the Sisters G, the Hollywood Beauties, the Russell Markert Dancers, 5 unidentified piano players [the first, closest to the camera, is Johnson Arledge]

*"Rhapsody in Blue" (condensed version); featuring Roy Bargy (piano solo), Paul Whiteman and his band; danced

by Jacques Cartier, the Sisters G, the Russell Markert Dancers, Beth Laemmle

REEL 8

Oh! Forevermore! (Sketch)
Cast: William Kent, Walter Brennan

My Ragamuffin Romeo
Cast: Jeanie Lang, George Chiles, Marion Stadler, and Don Rose

*"Ragamuffin Romeo," music by Mabel Wayne, lyrics by Harry De Costa; sung by Jeanie Lang and George Chiles; instrumental, danced by Marion Stadler and Don Rose

REEL 9

A Dash of Spice (Sketch)
Introduced by Jeanette Loff
Cast: Kathryn Crawford, Glenn Tryon, William Kent, "Sunny Jim" McKeen

Happy Feet
Cast: The Rhythm Boys, the Sisters G, Paul Whiteman and his band, Al Norman ("rubber-legs" dance), the Russell Markert Dancers, Charles Irwin, Paul Small (Whiteman dance double)

*"Happy Feet," music by Milton Ager, lyrics by Jack Yellen; sung by the Rhythm Boys and (in German and English) by the Sisters G; danced by Al Norman and the Russell Markert Dancers
"Happy Feet" (instrumental); featuring Charles Irwin and Paul Whiteman; danced by Paul Smalll

REEL 10

Has Anybody Seen Our Nellie?
Introduced by Charles Irwin
Cast: Frank Leslie, Churchill Ross, Walter Brennan, Johnson Arledge

*"Has Anybody Seen Our Nellie?," music by Milton Ager, lyrics by Jack Yellen; sung by Frank Leslie, Churchill Ross, Walter Brennan, Johnson Arledge

The Song of the Dawn
Cast: John Boles, male chorus

*"Song of the Dawn," music by Milton Ager, lyrics by Jack Yellen; sung by John Boles and male chorus

REELS 11 & 12

The Melting Pot of Music
Introduced by Charles Irwin
Cast: Paul Whiteman and his band, John Peel Quartet, the Russell Markert Dancers, Beth Laemmle, Cathleen [Cathlyn] Bessette (Scotch dancer), George Chiles, Jeanette Loff, Felipe Delgado (Spanish singer), the Sisters G, Manuel and Vida (Spanish dancers), Michael [Mikhail] Vavitch (Russian singer), Bob Gilbert (Russian dancer), Nell O'Day and the Tommy Atkins Sextet, Al Norman, Paul Howard

"Rhapsody in Blue" (instrumental)

England
"Rule, Britannia!," by Thomas Arne (instrumental)
"A Hunt in the Black Forest," by George Voelker Jr. (instrumental); played on French horns by massed huntsmen
"D'ye ken John Peel," music: old English air; sung by John Peel Quartet, danced by the Russell Markert Dancers
"A Hunt in the Black Forest" (instrumental)
"D'ye ken John Peel"; sung by John Peel Quartet, danced by the Russell Markert Dancers with 16 unidentified male dancers
"A Hunt in the Black Forest" (instrumental)

Italy
"Garibaldi's Hymn" ["Giovinezza"], music by Giuseppe Blanc (instrumental)
"Santa Lucia," traditional Neapolitan song; performed by massed accordion players; sung by two unidentified female singers
*"Tarantelle" [sic; "Tarantella"] by James Dietrich (incorporating strains of "Funiculì, Funiculà") (instrumental); danced by Beth Laemmle and the Russell Markert Dancers

Scotland
"Scots Wha Hae," traditional Scottish air (instrumental)
"Comin' thro' the Rye," music: traditional Scottish country dance ["The Miller's Wedding"], lyrics by Robert Burns; sung by unidentified female singer
*"Money Musk," old Highland fling (instrumental); played by massed bagpipers; danced by Cathleen Bessette and the Russell Markert Dancers

Germany
"Die Wacht am Rhein," by Carl Wilhelm, arranged by T. M. [Theodore Moses] Tobani
"Die Lorelei," German art song, music by Friedrich Silcher, lyrics by Heinrich Heine; sung by female chorus; featuring

the Hollywood Beauties

"Spring, Beautiful Spring" [also known as "Chimes of Spring"], waltz by Paul Lincke (instrumental); played by massed violinists; danced by George Chiles and Jeanette Loff

Ireland

"Wearin' of the Green," old Irish air (instrumental); played by massed harpists

"Killarney," music by Michael William Balfe, lyrics by Edmund Falconer; sung by unidentified tenor

"Garryowen," Irish quickstep tune, arranged by T. M. Tobani (instrumental); danced by Russell Markert Dancers with 16 unidentified male dancers

Spain

"Royal March of Spain" ["Marcha Real"], instrumental, arranged by M. L. Lake

"Ay, ay, ay!" by Osmán Pérez Freire; performed by massed guitar players; sung in Spanish by Felipe Delgado; danced by the Sisters G, the Russell Markert Dancers, and Manuel and Vida

Russia

"The Hymn of Free Russia" ["Gimn svobódnoi Rossii"], by Alexandre Tikhoovich Gretchaninoff, arranged by Otto Langey (instrumental)

"Song of the Volga Boatmen," Russian folk song (instrumental); played by balalaika ensemble

"Dark Eyes: Black Eyes" ["Ochi chornye"], Russian folk song, arranged by Harry Horlick and Gregory Stone; played by balalaika ensemble; sung in Russian by Michael Vavitch and Russian choir

*"Roosters" ["Petukhi"], traditional Ukrainian balalaika tune, adapted/arranged by Michael Vavitch (instrumental); played by balalaika ensemble; Ukrainian folk dance, the gopak, danced by Bob Gilbert

France

"La Marseillaise," by Claude Joseph Rouget de Lisle

"The Three Captains" ["En passant par la Lorraine"], French folk song, arranged by Julien Tiersot; played by massed drummers; sung in French by unidentified male singer

"Le Régiment de Sambre et Meuse," by Robert Planquette, arranged by André Turlet (instrumental); danced by Nell O'Day and the Tommy Atkins Sextet

"The Three Captains"; sung in French by unidentified male singer

Whiteman Stirs the Pot

"Cauldron Music," by Ferde Grofé

Finale

"Song of the Dawn" (instrumental); danced by the Russell Markert Dancers

"A Bench in the Park" (instrumental); danced by George Chiles, Jeanette Loff, and the Sisters G

"I Like to Do Things for You" (instrumental); danced by Al Norman

"It Happened in Monterey" (instrumental); danced by Beth Laemmle and Paul Howard

"Shadows," by Milton Ager (instrumental); danced by Nell O'Day and the Tommy Atkins Sextet

"Song of the Dawn" (instrumental); played by Paul Whiteman and his band

"The Stars and Stripes Forever" (instrumental); played by Paul Whiteman and his band

"Happy Feet" (instrumental); danced by the Russell Markert Dancers

"Song of the Dawn"; played by Paul Whiteman and his band; sung by ensemble

"Rhapsody in Blue" (instrumental); played by Paul Whiteman and his band

Exit Music

"It Happened in Monterey" (instrumental)

"Song of the Dawn" (instrumental)

Appendix IV:

FOREIGN VERSIONS

King of Jazz was presented in nine foreign-language versions for international release. Each followed the same structure: the comedy and dialogue-based sketches were removed entirely, and the film was distilled down to its most impressive musical numbers. The use of music in these versions remained largely the same as the U.S. domestic version, except for the opening titles over each release. These differences and the known production credits are outlined below.

Sources consulted include Diane and Richard Koszarski's notes on the Spanish dialogue and cutting continuities; analysis of the surviving French print; promotional stills; and foreign trade publications.

"El Rey del Jazz"
(Spanish-language version)
Directed by Kurt Neumann
Supervised by Paul Kohner
Hosts: Martín Garralaga, Lupita Tovar, Nancy Torres
U.S. screening of Spanish version: week of August 22, 1930 (Palace Theatre, San Antonio, Texas)
Argentinian release: September 5, 1930 (Cine París, Buenos Aires)
Spanish private preview: September 21, 1930 (Palacio de la Musica, Madrid)
Mexican release: September 18, 1930 (Cine Regis, Mexico City)
Uruguayan release: October 5, 1930 (Rex Theatre, Montevideo)
Spanish release: November 28, 1930 (Callao Theatre, Madrid)
Notes:
- Music cues over opening titles: "Introduction" by Andor Pinter; "Los Toreadores" [Toreador Song] by Georges Bizet; "Modulation" by Andor Pinter; "It Happened in Monterey" by Mabel Wayne and Billy Rose; "Coda" by Andor Pinter.

REEL 1

Opening Titles

Paul Whiteman's Scrap Book
Martin Garralaga and Paul Whiteman talk in front of the scrapbook. Whiteman jokes with his "amigo."

A Fable in Jazz (Color Cartoon)
Introduced by Whiteman.

Paul Whiteman introduces his boys—and the girls
Garralaga offers a few words of explanation, then looks off-screen to Whiteman, who introduces the band. As Whiteman's musicians emerge from the bag, we see Garralaga's facial reactions.

REEL 2

Band Medley
Garralaga introduces the Russell Markert Dancers.

Meet the Girls

REEL 3

My Bridal Veil
Lupita Tovar, Martín Garralaga, and Nancy Torres stand before the pages of a "Bridal Veil" scrapbook. After the number, Garralaga returns to the stage and speaks.

REEL 4

Monterey
Garralaga approaches the scrapbook on stage and introduces the scene. Afterwards, an embarrassed Garralaga brings Jeanette Loff on stage and kisses her hand. Loff says: "Muchos saludos a mis amigos Hispano-

parlante."

REEL 5

A Bench in the Park

REEL 6

Willie Hall
A specially designed scrapbook page in Spanish introduces this act.

The Rhapsody in Blue (Voodoo drum dance)
Garralaga comes forward onto the stage and bows. Behind him on the scrapbook is an illustration of a giant piano. He introduces George Gershwin's *Rhapsody in Blue*, and mentions its premiere at Aeolian Hall.

REEL 7

The Rhapsody in Blue

REEL 8

"El Romeo Truhanesco" (My Ragamuffin Romeo)
The scrapbook highlights the Spanish title for this number.

REEL 9

Garralaga stands in front of the scrapbook and smokes, then some girls in costume walk past him. Lupita Tovar comes up to him, and they converse. Tovar is consulted in Spanish about "una idea feliz" (a happy thought), to which she replies "los pies...unos pies felizes" (feet...some happy feet).

Happy Feet
Garralaga bows after the number and gestures offstage to the next part, which features Paul Whiteman's dancing double.

"Canción del Alba" (Song of the Dawn)
The scrapbook highlights the Spanish title for this number.

REEL 10

The Melting Pot
The scrapbook page is a replica of the giant melting pot. Garralaga makes an announcement, gestures, and bows.

REEL 11

The Melting Pot (continued)

End Titles
"Fin" is superimposed on the screen, over a whirling mass of color.

"Král jazzu"
(Czech-language version)
Hosts: Antonín Vaverka, Helena Bendová, G. Kroutilová
Release: September 5, 1930 (Bio Adria, Prague)
Notes:
- The script was translated into Czech by Antonín Vaverka.
- Music cues over opening titles: "Die Verkaufte Braut" [The Bartered Bride] by Bedřich Smetana; "Modulation" by Andor Pinter; "Slovan Jsem" (Czech folk song); "Coda" by Andor Pinter.

"Jazzkirály"
(Hungarian-language version)
Hosts: Doraine Luci [Lucy Doraine], Béla Lugosi, János [John H.] Auer
Premiere: September 18, 1930 (Budapest)
Notes:
- Music cues over opening titles: "Hungarian Rhapsody" by Franz Liszt; "Cadenza" by Andor Pinter; "Marche Hongroise" by Hector Berlioz; "Coda" by Andor Pinter.

"Jazzkungen"
(Swedish-language version)
Hosts: Nils Asther, Greta Granstedt, Jeanette Loff
Premiere: September 29, 1930 (Palladium Theatre, Stockholm)
Notes:
- The Swedish name for Paul Whiteman's Scrap Book was "Minnen Av Paul Whiteman."
- Swedish titles were given to the following numbers: "Så var det för länge se'n och så är det nu" (It Happened in Monterey), "Morgongryning" (The Song of the Dawn), and "Nationernes Parade" (The Melting Pot of Music).
- Music cues over opening titles: "Call of the Vikings" by Christiaan Kriens; "Modulation" by Andor Pinter; "Moder Svea" by O. E. Swanson (arr. Gaston Borch); "In Norway" by John Itzel; "Coda" by Andor Pinter.

"O Rei do Jazz"
(Portuguese-language version)
Hosts: Olimpio Guilherme, Lia Torá
Brazilian premiere: October 2, 1930 (Pathé Palace, Rio de Janeiro)
Notes:

- The Portuguese name for Paul Whiteman's Scrap Book was "Diario de Paul Whiteman."
- Music cues over opening titles: "Introduction" by Andor Pinter; "Canção do Figueiral" (Portuguese folk song); "Modulation" by Andor Pinter; "A Moda Gallega" (Portuguese folk song); "Coda" by Andor Pinter.

"Der Jazzkönig"

(German-language version)
Directed by Kurt Neumann
Supervised by Paul Kohner
Host: Arnold Korff
Austrian release: October 2, 1930
German premiere: October 15, 1930 (Ufa-Palast am Zoo, Berlin)
Notes:

- Paula Wedekind, Joseph Schildkraut, Lya Mara, and Lucy Doraine were mentioned as hosts in pre-release announcements, but do not appear to have been in the final released version.
- German titles were given to the following numbers: "Mein Brautschleier" (My Bridal Veil), "So war es in Sanssouci" (It Happened in Monterey), "Eine Bank im Park" (A Bench in the Park), "Lumpengesindel" (My Ragamuffin Romeo), "Tanzende Füßchen" (Happy Feet), "Der gesanganden Morgen" or "Zigeunertraum" (The Song of the Dawn), "Der Schmelztiegel" (The Melting Pot of Music).
- Music cues over opening titles: "Walhall-Motive" by Richard Wagner; "Die Meistersinger von Nürnberg" by Richard Wagner; "Siegfried-Motive" by Richard Wagner; "Freut euch des Lebens" by Hans Georg Nägeli; "Coda" by Andor Pinter.

"Il re del jazz"

(Italian-language version)
Hosts: Alessandro Giglio, Nella Nelli
Premiere: October/November 1930
Notes:

- The Italian name for Paul Whiteman's Scrap Book was "Raccolta artistica di Paul Whiteman."
- Music cues over opening titles: "Capriccio Italien" by Pyotr Ilyich Tchaikovsky; "Funiculì, Funiculà" by Luigi Denza; "Coda" by Andor Pinter.

"La Féerie du Jazz"

(French-language version)
Hosts: André Chéron, Georgette Rhodes
Premiere: December 20, 1930 (Olympia Theatre, Paris)
Notes:

- The French opening credits read: Carl Laemmle présente / PAUL WHITEMAN ET SON ORCHESTRE / dans / La Revue de Jazz / "LA FEERIE DU JAZZ" / Une Production de Carl Laemmle, Jr.
- Further credits listed onscreen: Le Compère: André Chéron / La Commère: Georgette Rhodes / Adaptation Française de Paul Kohner / Photographié par le Procédé "Technicolor"
- The French name for Paul Whiteman's Scrap Book was "Carnet intime de Paul Whiteman," while "The Song of the Dawn" was billed as "La Chanson de L'Aurore, interprèté [*sic*; interprétée] par John Boles".
- Music cues over opening titles: "French Introduction" by Andor Pinter; "Cadet Rousselle" (French folk song); "Fanfan la Tulipe" (French folk song); "Coda" by Andor Pinter.
- It is believed that the original title of the French release was intended to be the more literal translation "Le Roi du jazz." However, this was changed to La Féerie du Jazz shortly before release.

"Kingu Obu Jazu"

(Japanese-language version)
Hosts: Tetsu Komai, Iris Yamaoka
Premiere: January 8, 1931 (Taishokan Theater, Asakusa, Tokyo)
Notes:

- The script was translated into Japanese by Tetsu Komai.
- Music cues over opening titles: "Introduction" by Andor Pinter; "Suite Japonaise" by Kosaku [Kôsçak] Yamada; "Coda" by Andor Pinter.

Appendix V:

UNUSED SCENES

The Hollywood Parade

This unused number, orchestrated by Ferde Grofé, may have been intended as the original introduction to the Russell Markert Dancers. The following lyrics by Jack Yellen, set to music by Milton Ager, were discovered in the Ferde Grofé Collection at the Library of Congress.

Lyrics (excerpt):

For your delight
Tonight,
We now present, the Hollywood Parade.
A pretty sight,
And quite
A smart event, the Hollywood Parade.
Presently,
Pleasantly
Nodding, you'll see the stars,
Strolling by,
Rolling by
In their big motor cars.
We offer you
A view
Of an assembly of the film elite,
Brought at immense
Expense
By Mister Laemmle here for you to meet.
Their success
By their dress
So proudly displayed;
In bright array,
This way —
It's coming now — it's Hollywood on Parade.

Here come Doug and Mary;
Lupe and her Gary;
John and Missus Gilbert — here they are!
Fans are fighting for a
Glance at lovely Laura,
Miss La Plante, the Universal star.

Listen to a thrilled crowd
Cheering Joseph Schildkraut;
Kathryn Crawford, gorgeously arrayed.
All the movie bright lights,
Rowing in the white lights,
Hollywood is on Parade.

Paul Howard Specialty Dance

Paul Howard was an eccentric dancer known for his ability to twist himself into and out of knots. He was to have a specialty dance in the "Bench in the Park" number, supported by a dog and a drunken policeman played by William Kent. Ferde Grofé's orchestrations at the Library of Congress note that Howard performs a "pendulum kick" and "spin into split." The number ends with a crash as Howard steps on a bug. Despite the specialty dance being cut, Howard appears briefly in what was intended to be a reprise in the "Melting Pot" finale.

Whiteman Origin Story

Plans for a story based on Whiteman's life were developed in these early production sketches by Herman Rosse, which most likely would have been visualized in an opening animation. The sequence fills us in on Whiteman's childhood, his early aptitude for music, and his rise to fame.

They Call Dancing a Pleasure

This tragicomic song was designed as a showcase for Grace Hayes, with support by William Kent. Although the lyrics were different, the music was a variation on "I Like To Do Things For You." The number was originally seen by audiences in an early preview (along with "My Lover"), but it was cut before the Los Angeles premiere.

A plot synopsis in the Herman Rosse Collection at Williams College describes the following set and action:

> Opens with shot of typical 14th street [*sic*] dance hall, old and young sheiks and shebas dancing around. Close-ups of comedy couples.

> Close-up of setee [*sic*], adjoining ticket booth. Half a dozen hostesses awaiting customers who buy tickets at booth, hand tickets to hostesses and dance off with them.

Miss Hayes limps on scene, accompanied by apologetic escort. She is a hostess and he is a guest who has just danced with her and nearly crushed her toes. She limps on, holding one foot in her hand. Her escort, a foreigner, Greek or Frenchman is gesticulating and making excuses. She finally sits down on the settee and the song which follows is assumedly [*sic*; presumably] what she is telling the girl sitting next to her.

The excerpt below is drawn from lyrics in the Ferde Grofé Collection at the Library of Congress:

> And they call dancing a pleasure —
> But it's darn little pleasure for me —
> I'm soon headin' for the five and ten store
> And no hostess business for me any more
> Oh boy how they push and shove me —
> They're making a nervous wreck of me —
> We have moonlight waltzes and I have a time
> We dance in the dark I tell you it's a crime
> What some guys expect of a girl for a dime!
> And they call dancing a pleasure —

William Kent and Grace Hayes.

Nell O'Day and Tommy Atkins Sextet Specialty

In a letter to Robert McKay dated June 21, 1977, Nell O'Day recalled that an additional 72 bars of dancing were shot for the "I'd Like to Do Things for You" number, but were removed before the film's release. After singing the third verse, O'Day originally danced a graceful waltz with two members of the Tommy Atkins Sextet, then with two others in a different style, before the pace suddenly quickened and she was thrown around acrobatically by the troupe. An abrupt jump cut is evident where this footage was removed. Several members of the Tommy Atkins Sextet clearly change position between shots.

Revolving Room Sketch

In a 1972 American Film Institute interview with historian Charles Higham, Technicolor cameraman Ray Rennahan described a scene not present in any of the film's original release versions. The scene was likely not included in the finished film due to its similarity to parts of the "Oh! Forevermore!" sketch, which featured William Kent and Walter Brennan.

Rennahan: "…Walter Brennan and this little comic who was with him…[had] been drinking and they walked into a scene and they walked up the walls, and up the ceiling and down, well that was live, that was on the stage. They built a revolving room on the stage. The camera stayed still and the room revolved."

"My Lover" (working title: "I Want a Man Who Loves Me")

Like "They Call Dancing A Pleasure," this Grace Hayes torch song was shown at the Los Angeles preview screening but was cut for the subsequent release. The sequence featured a girl in a room with a telephone, and the music was composed by James Dietrich, with lyrics by Jack Yellen. According to Dietrich, Whiteman refused to lead the orchestra for the song, and demanded that the scene be cut. Grace Hayes recorded her solo on March 21, 1930, for release on 78 by Victor.

Lyrics (excerpt):

He may be poor,
Of lonely station
But if his heart is true he'll ever be mine
In rain or shine,
I want a man who loves me.
I've had affairs,
I've spent a fortune,
But all the money in this world couldn't buy
My kind of guy.
I want a man who loves me.
My heart is sad,
My life is empty,
My tears keep falling like showers.
What would I give
If I could find him
To cheer these unhappy hou-rs.
Where can he be?
The man I long for.
I'd give my very soul if he would appear
And call me dear.
I want a man who loves me.

The following three scenes were shot in 1930, but were not used in the film's original general release version. They finally surfaced in the 1933 reissue version.

"Pretty Lucky So Far" (Sketch)

Written by Harry Ruskin, this blackout skit originated in *Murray Anderson's Almanac* (1929) on stage. In the film, Charles (Slim Summerville) asks for the hand of Otis Harlan's daughter (Kathryn Crawford). Charles is questioned regarding his financial ability to support a wife and family. He confesses that they do not intend to have children, concluding with the punchline: "We've been pretty lucky so far."

"Look What It Makes Me" (Sketch)

A married couple (Glenn Tryon and Merna Kennedy) discover that their minister was an impostor. As they wonder aloud about their status as a bachelor and a spinster, their baby (William Kent) gurgles and winks: "What are you two squawking for? Look what it makes me!"

"Horse's Neck" (Sketch)

Walter Brennan sticks his head out from the front of a horse costume and says: "This moving picture business is the bunk, and this skin certainly gets my nanny. I feel like a horse's neck." Slim Summerville sticks his head out from the rear and replies: "Horse's neck? How do you suppose I feel?"

Unidentified Comedy Scenes

Scene with Slim Summerville and Kathryn Crawford.

George Sidney and Charlie Murray, playing their popular characters from the "Cohens and Kellys" series, here in a "dilemma with firing squad." The set was reused from the "Monterey" number.

Scene in a barbershop with Walter Brennan, William Kent, Otis Harlan, and Johnson Arledge.

A painting falls off the wall during a party. Guests include: Walter Brennan, Laura La Plante, Kathryn Crawford, Churchill Ross, Johnson Arledge, Glenn Tryon, Grace Hayes, Jeanette Loff, the Sisters G, Charles Irwin, Jeanie Lang, William Kent, and Merna Kennedy.

Appendix VI:

FINANCIALS

World Revenue Report from Universal Financial Summary Ledgers, courtesy of David Pierce and Dr. Jan-Christopher Horak. Domestic exhibition statistics courtesy of Karl Thiede, compiled from *Variety* and *Motion Picture News*. Domestic returns from Universal studio files and contracts transcribed by Diane and Richard Koszarski.

World Revenue Report By Picture 1930/31 Products			
	King of Jazz	*Captain of the Guard*	*All Quiet on the Western Front*
Domestic Revenue	$548,682.57	$292,694.77	$1,757,554.04
Foreign Revenue	$1,198,172.00	$491,263.03	$2,336,921.22
Total World Revenue	$1,746,854.57	$783,957.80	$4,094,475.26
Negative Cost	$2,012,348.79	$729,170.02	$1,566,307.64
Domestic Print Cost	$129,865.41	$22,328.29	$56,513.83
Foreign Print Cost	$265,871.10	$30,000.00	$50,312.97
Total World Cost	$3,019,484.40	$1,055,883.54	$3,106,200.78
Profit / (Loss)	($1,272,629.83)	($271,925.74)	$988,274.48

For his first year as head of production at Universal, Carl Laemmle Jr. produced three large-budget features for the 1930–31 season. Each performed well in foreign markets, while *All Quiet on the Western Front* was very successful in the U.S./Canada domestic market as well. Universal calculated Total World Cost by adding the film's negative cost and print costs to a distribution fee (calculated as 35% of the world revenue). Total World Cost would be subtracted from Total World Revenue to determine profit or loss.

Domestic Exhibition

City	Week beginning	No. weeks	Theatre	High week gross	Low week gross	Total gross
Los Angeles, California	April 19, 1930	4	Fox Criterion 1,652 seats $0.35, $0.65	$13,000	$4,000	$37,300
Baltimore, Maryland	April 24, 1930	1	Auditorium 1,572 seats $0.35, $1.00	$3,630		$3,630
Washington, DC	May 1, 1930	2	Rialto 1,978 seats $0.35, $0.50, $0.60	$7,500	$7,000	$14,500
New York City	May 2, 1930	2	Roxy 5,920 seats $0.50, $0.75, $1.00, $1.50	$102,700	$62,700	$165,400

City	Week beginning	No. weeks	Theatre	High week gross	Low week gross	Total gross
Detroit, Michigan	May 2, 1930	1	State 3,000 seats $0.35 to $0.65			light
Portland, Oregon	May 24, 1930	1	Music Box 2,000 seats $0.25, $0.50	$6,900		$6,900
Seattle, Washington	May 24, 1930	2	Blue Mouse 950 seats $0.25, $0.50, $0.75	$7,000	$5,600	$12,600
Boston, Massachusetts	May 31, 1930	1	Keith-Memorial 4,000 seats $0.35, $0.50, $0.60	$21,000		$21,000
Denver, Colorado	May 31, 1930	1	Orpheum 1,650 seats $0.25, $0.35, $0.50	$8,000		$8,000
Tacoma, Washington	May 31, 1930	1	Blue Mouse 650 seats $0.25, $0.50	$5,100		$5,100
Minneapolis, Minnesota	June 7, 1930	1	Century 1,600 seats $0.75	$9,200		$9,200
San Francisco, California	June 14, 1930	2	Warwick 2,672 seats $0.50, $0.65, $0.90	$19,000	$17,500	$36,500
Chicago, Illinois	June 21, 1930	2	Roosevelt 1,500 seats	$16,000	$5,400	$21,400
Pittsburgh, Pennsylvania	June 28, 1930	1	Stanley 3,600 seats $0.25, $0.35, $0.60	$20,000		$20,000
Philadelphia, Pennsylvania	July 5, 1930	1	Karlton 2,000 seats $0.50	$6,000		$6,000
St. Louis, Missouri	July 12, 1930	1	Ambassador 3,000 seats $0.35, $0.50, $0.65, $0.75	$25,000		$25,000
Providence, Rhode Island	July 19, 1930	1	RKO Victory 1,619 seats $0.15, $0.50	$10,500		$10,500
Omaha, Nebraska	July 25, 1930	1 1	State 1,200 seats $0.25, $0.40	$4,350		$4,350
Louisville, Kentucky	August 9, 1930		Strand $0.35, $0.50			
Topeka, Kansas	August 16, 1930	1	Grand 1,485 seats $0.50	$3,000		$3,000
Cleveland, Ohio	August 23, 1930	1	RKO Palace 3,150 seats $0.35, $0.75	$17,000		$17,000
Cincinnati, Ohio	August 30, 1930	1	Albee 3,300 seats $0.35, $0.75	$20,000		$20,000

City	Week beginning	No. weeks	Theatre	High week gross	Low week gross	Total gross
Oklahoma City, Oklahoma	September 6, 1930	2	Liberty 1,600 seats $0.10, $0.50	$10,000	$6,500	$16,500
Des Moines, Iowa	September 13, 1930	1	Strand 1,100 seats $0.20, $0.30	$5,500		$5,500
Kansas City, Missouri	September 27, 1930	1	Uptown 2,000 seats $0.25, $0.35, $0.50	$11,400		$11,400

Canada

City	Week beginning	No. weeks	Theatre	High week gross	Low week gross	Total gross
Toronto, Ontario	July 5, 1930	1	Uptown 3,000 seats $0.35, $0.80	$16,000		$16,000
Montreal, Quebec	July 19, 1930	1	Palace 2,700 seats $0.40, $0.75	$15,500		$15,500
Ottawa, Ontario	November 22, 1930	1	Avalon 900 seats $0.15, $0.25, $0.35	$1,350		$1,350

Domestic Returns (net to studio)

The following figures offer a month-by-month account of the total domestic revenue returned to the studio for the original release of *King of Jazz*. These figures do not include income generated by the 1933 reissue.

Total To	Amount
May 31, 1930	$34,147.81
June 28, 1930	$92,091.26
July 12, 1930	$165,000.00
Aug. 2, 1930	$173,788.04
Sept. 27, 1930	$340,688.25
Nov. 1, 1930	$432,643.78
Nov. 29, 1930	$463,066.32
Dec. 27, 1930	$481,328.30
Jan. 31, 1931	$500,355.29
Feb. 28, 1931	$515,073.50
March 28, 1931	$517,927.66
April 2, 1931	$524,266.60

Total To	Amount
May 30, 1931	$528,242.32
June 27, 1931	$531,185.37
Aug. 1, 1931	$533,423.03
Aug. 29, 1931	$536,116.92
Sept. 26, 1931	$536,622.79
Oct. 31, 1931	$538,695.72
Nov. 28, 1931	$539,902.21
Dec. 26, 1931	$540,905.57
Jan. 30, 1932	$541,963.01
Feb. 27, 1932	$542,818.72
March 26, 1932	$542,188.97
April 30, 1932	$543,906.58

Total To	Amount
May 28, 1932	544,343.89
June 25, 1932	$545,310.59
July 30, 1932	$546,894.20
Aug. 27, 1932	$546,331.50
Oct. 29, 1932	$546,631.18
Nov. 26, 1932	$546,745.91
April 4, 1933	$548.592.57
May 27, 1933	$548.612.57
June 24, 1933	$548.682.57
July 29, 1933	$548.682.57
Aug. 26, 1933	$548,682.57
Sept. 23, 1933	$548,682.57 (final)

Appendix VII:

ALTERNATE VERSIONS

1933 Reissue

When *King of Jazz* was reissued in 1933 it was in a significantly truncated form, with over 30 minutes removed. The running order was changed, and some numbers were re-edited to make Bing Crosby's role more prominent.

Sources include: 1933 continuity and dialogue script; 1933 reissue license from the State of New York Motion Picture Division; Universal restoration staff analysis of original camera negative (re-edited for 1933 reissue).

First screening: May 20, 1933 (Rialto Theatre, Washington, DC)
Release date: June 1, 1933 (reset from May 18), according to *Film Daily, Harrison's Reports,* and *Motion Picture Herald*
Length of 1933 reissue:

> 5,828 ft. (65 min.), according to Technicolor release shipments, May 9, 1933;
> 6,077 ft. (8 reels, 68 min.), according to New York State censorship certificate, August 19, 1933;
> 6 reels, according to *Motion Picture Heral*d, May 20, 1933;
> 61 ½ min., according to *Harrison's Reports*, August 19, 1933

Domestic prints: 127
Foreign prints: 28
Total prints: 155

Removed scenes: Charles Irwin's Introduction to Paul Whiteman's Scrap Book, "I'd Like to Do Things for You," "The Piccolo Player," "In Conference," "The Property Man," "Springtime," "All Noisy on the Eastern Front," "Willie Hall," "Oh! Forevermore!," "A Dash of Spice," "Has Anybody Seen Our Nellie?," Whiteman's dancing double in "Happy Feet"

REEL 1

Opening Titles
These titles were rephotographed to include opening headshots of Paul Whiteman, Bing Crosby, John Boles, Slim Summerville, Jeanie Lang, Jeanette Loff, Harry Barris, and the Brox Sisters; and a new text foreword was added signed by Carl Laemmle:

Countless thousands throughout the world have requested the revival of "The KING of JAZZ." It is my great pleasure to present it again and I hope that you, too, will thrill to its rhythm and beauty.
*Charles Irwin's introduction was removed

A Fable in Jazz
Includes Charles Irwin's closing remark, "And that's how Paul Whiteman was crowned the King of Jazz!"

Meet the Boys
Scene ends after members of the band descend ladder and take their places on the stage.

Happy Feet
*Whiteman dancing double removed from end of sequence

REEL 2

Pretty Lucky So Far
This sketch was shot in 1930 but was not used at the time. It was revived for the reissue. For more information see Appendix V.

Monterey

Look What It Makes Me
This sketch was shot in 1930 but was not used at the time. It was revived for the reissue. For more information see Appendix V.

REEL 3

A Bench in the Park
The end of this number was revised to incorporate the "Springtime" sketch at the end. After Stanley Smith sings the line "You and I in the dark," the scenes cuts to Slim Summerville and Yola D'Avril arriving at the police station while the music continues.

Springtime

After the sketch concludes, Whiteman's face in the moon returns and winks.
Missing opening title card

My Ragamuffin Romeo

Horse's Neck

This sketch was shot in 1930 but was not used at the time. It was revived for the reissue. For more information see Appendix V.

REEL 4

My Bridal Veil

Linger Awhile

After "My Bridal Veil" the scene cuts to the end of the band medley from the "Meet the Boys" sequence. On a darkened stage, a spotlight settles on Mike Pingitore, who plays "Linger Awhile" on the banjo.

REEL 5

The Rhythm Boys

Meet the Girls
Missing Paul Whiteman's introductory remarks

Ladies of the Press

The Song of the Dawn

REEL 6

The Rhapsody in Blue

REEL 7

The Melting Pot of Music

REEL 8

The Melting Pot of Music (continued)

Comparison of 1930 U.S. general release and 1933 reissue versions

The following chart presents a complete listing of each scene from both the 1930 and 1933 releases. This side-by-side comparison enables direct study of each version by reel, thereby demonstrating in which places the reissue was shortened and reordered.

1930	Reel	1933
Opening credits Paul Whiteman's Scrap Book A Fable in Jazz Meet the Boys	1	Opening credits A Fable in Jazz Meet the Boys Happy Feet
Meet the Girls My Bridal Veil	2	Pretty Lucky So Far Monterey Look What It Makes Me
I'd Like to Do Things For You	2A	
Ladies of the Press The Rhythm Boys The Piccolo Player	3	A Bench in the Park Springtime My Ragamuffin Romeo
Monterey In Conference	4	Horse's Neck My Bridal Veil
The Property Man A Bench in the Park	5	Linger Awhile The Rhythm Boys Meet the Girls Ladies of the Press The Song of the Dawn
Springtime All Noisy on the Eastern Front Willie Hall The Rhapsody in Blue (Voodoo drum dance)	6	The Rhapsody in Blue
The Rhapsody in Blue	7	The Melting Pot of Music
Oh! Forevermore! My Ragamuffin Romeo	8	The Melting Pot of Music (continued)
A Dash of Spice Happy Feet	9	
Has Anybody Seen Our Nellie? The Song of the Dawn	10	
The Melting Pot of Music	11	
The Melting Pot of Music (continued) Exit Music	12	

Philip Jenkinson 16mm print (1968/1975)

Philip Jenkinson's reconstruction started as a straight copy from an incomplete 35mm print in 1968, but was extended in 1975 as additional material became available. The running order differs from earlier released versions and some sequences are missing entirely (namely the "Piccolo Player" sketch and "A Dash of Spice"). Three blackout sketches first seen in the 1933 reissue were arbitrarily inserted. "I'd Like To Do Things For You" was included later than its original placement between "In Conference" and "The Property Man." The running time after the 1975 additions was approximately 93 minutes.

Sources include: analysis of William K. Everson's 16mm Jenkinson print by Diane and Richard Koszarski conducted in 1975, study of 16mm Jenkinson print transferred to DVD, additional feedback from film collector Robert McKay and historian/archivist Scott MacQueen.

Length (1968): 3,151 ft. (88 min.)
Length (1975): Approx. 3,429 ft. (95 min.), based on inspection of William K. Everson's "Jenkinson print"
Missing scenes: "Meet the Girls," Jeanie Lang's introduction to "My Bridal Veil," "The Piccolo Player," "A Dash of Spice"

Opening Titles
Paul Whiteman's Scrap Book
A Fable in Jazz
Meet the Boys (missing "Meet the Girls" dance)
My Bridal Veil (missing introduction by Jeanie Lang)
Ladies of the Press
The Rhythm Boys
Monterey
In Conference
I'd Like To Do Things For You
The Property Man
A Bench in the Park
Springtime
All Noisy on the Eastern Front
Willie Hall, One of the Whiteman Boys
Pretty Lucky So Far (added in 1975)
The Rhapsody in Blue
Oh! Forevermore!
My Ragamuffin Romeo (Stadler & Rose dance added in 1975)
Horse's Neck (added in 1975)
Happy Feet (expanded with additional footage added in 1975)
Look What It Makes Me (added in 1975)
Has Anybody Seen Our Nellie? (missing introduction by Charles Irwin)
The Song of the Dawn (second chorus added in

1975)
The Melting Pot of Music

VHS release (MCA, 1983/1995)

Like the Philip Jenkinson reconstruction, MCA's VHS release created a new version of *King of Jazz* that merged content from the 1930 and 1933 releases. "I'd Like To Do Things For You" was inserted toward the end of the film rather than near the start. Several brief sequences from the 1930 release were also not present. This running order matches the version shown on Channel 4 in the UK in 1987.

Running time: 92 min.
Missing scenes: "The Piccolo Player," "A Dash of Spice"

Opening Titles
Paul Whiteman's Scrap Book
A Fable in Jazz
Meet the Boys
Meet the Girls
My Bridal Veil
Ladies of the Press
The Rhythm Boys
Monterey
In Conference
The Property Man
A Bench in the Park
Springtime
All Noisy on the Eastern Front
Willie Hall, One of the Whiteman Boys
The Rhapsody in Blue
Oh! Forevermore
My Ragamuffin Romeo
Horse's Neck
Look What It Makes Me
Happy Feet
Pretty Lucky So Far
I'd Like to Do Things for You
Has Anybody Seen Our Nellie?
The Song of the Dawn
The Melting Pot of Music

Universal restoration (2016)

Universal's digital restoration offers the most complete version of the film since 1930. Using the original soundtrack of the 1930 general release as its framework, the scenes are presented in order, and for the most part, in their entirety. The restoration is sourced from four different film elements, but is still missing picture for one scene, while several of the missing introductions have been recreated with stills and freeze-frames.

Running time: 99 min. 32 sec.

First public screening: May 13, 2016 (The Museum of Modern Art)

Missing scenes: "The Piccolo Player"

Sources: original camera negative (Universal, 57:38), Rohauer print (Library of Congress, 37:14), Danish print (Danish Film Institute, 00:59), UCLA print (UCLA Film & Television Archive, 00:42), stills and freeze-frames (01:32)

REEL 1

Opening Titles

Sourced from Rohauer print (01:14)

Introduction to Paul Whiteman's Scrap Book

Sourced from Rohauer print (0:50)

missing one second of picture: "bring to life for you" line not present

missing one second of picture as book opens

A Fable in Jazz

Sourced from original camera negative (02:31)

Meet the Boys

Sourced from original camera negative (02:04, two sections) and Rohauer print (03:18)

missing eight seconds of picture at end: "now that you know the boys, I want you to meet our girls" — recreated with stills of Paul Whiteman (00:05)

REEL 2

Meet the Girls

Sourced from original camera negative (01:55)

My Bridal Veil

Sourced from original camera negative (07:44)

missing picture for Jeanie Lang introduction — recreated with a freeze-frame and still of Jeanie Lang (00:27)

REEL 2A

I'd Like To Do Things For You

Sourced from Rohauer print (04:41)

29 intermittent frames missing — frames digitally recreated using "time-warp" software tools

REEL 3

Ladies of the Press

Sourced from UCLA print (00:12, book opening and title card) and original camera negative (00:30)

missing ten seconds of picture for Charles Irwin's introduction — recreated with a freeze-frame (00:06)

The Rhythm Boys

Sourced from Rohauer print (00:30, Mississippi Mud and banter) and original camera negative (02:15)

missing intermittent frames — frames digitally recreated using "time-warp" software tools

["The Piccolo Player" sketch removed entirely due to no picture elements surviving]

REEL 4

Monterey

Sourced from original camera negative (05:47, two sections) and Rohauer print (00:21, Jeanette Loff singing)

In Conference

Sourced from Rohauer print (00:43)

missing picture at end of last sentence "ever had"

REEL 5

The Property Man

Sourced from UCLA print (00:30, four sections, one as short as 3 frames) and Rohauer print (03:31, four sections)

A Bench in the Park

Sourced from original camera negative (04:44, two sections) and Rohauer print (01:45, two sections)

REEL 6

Springtime

Sourced from original camera negative (00:18, opening title card looped to cover missing frames) and Rohauer print (00:01, fade out at end)

All Noisy on the Eastern Front

Sourced from Rohauer print (01:43)

missing intermittent frames — frames digitally recreated using "time-warp" software tools

Willie Hall, One of the Whiteman Boys

Sourced from Rohauer print (03:04)

missing a few frames of picture at end

The Rhapsody in Blue (Intro and Voodoo drum dance)

Sourced from original camera negative (01:56)

REEL 7

The Rhapsody in Blue
Sourced from <u>original camera negative</u> (04:28, three sections) and <u>Rohauer print</u> (02:25, three sections)
missing 63-frame section filled with reused and resized footage of Jacques Cartier playing clarinet

REEL 8

Oh! Forevermore!
Sourced from <u>Rohauer print</u> (03:42)
missing intermittent frames

My Ragamuffin Romeo
Sourced from <u>original camera negative</u> (03:37, two sections) and <u>Rohauer print</u> (00:34, part of Stadler and Rose dance)
missing intermittent frames — frames digitally recreated using "time-warp" software tools

REEL 9

A Dash of Spice
Sourced from <u>Danish print</u> (00:59)
missing picture for Jeanette Loff introduction — recreated with stills of Jeanette Loff (00:21)
intertitles from Danish print covered with freeze-frames

Happy Feet
Sourced from <u>original camera negative</u> (02:17, four sections) and <u>Rohauer print</u> (04:02, five sections, including Sisters G mirror shot, Al Norman dance, and Paul Whiteman dancing double)
missing 2 seconds of picture at end, "What for, Paul?" — covered with freeze-frame and fade out

REEL 10

Has Anybody Seen Our Nellie?
Sourced from <u>Rohauer print</u> (02:54)
missing picture for Charles Irwin introduction and first verse of song — covered with behind-the-scenes stills and a still of Frank Leslie (00:33)

The Song of the Dawn
Sourced from <u>original camera negative</u> (03:36)

REEL 11

The Melting Pot of Music
Sourced from <u>original camera negative</u> (05:42, four sections) and <u>Rohauer print</u> (00:54, three sections)
45 frames missing from Charles Irwin introduction — covered by slowing down book opening

REEL 12

The Melting Pot of Music (continued)
Sourced from <u>original camera negative</u> (06:08, three sections) and <u>Rohauer print</u> (01:05, four sections)

Exit Music (01:26)

Appendix VIII:

ARCHIVAL HOLDINGS

Academy Film Archive, Los Angeles: (a) 35mm nitrate Technicolor print (incomplete, 1 reel, "Rhapsody in Blue" sequence); (b) 16mm acetate color duplicate picture negative (trailer); (c) 16mm acetate duplicate soundtrack negative (trailer); (d) 16mm acetate color print (trailer)

BFI National Archive, London: (a) 35mm nitrate Technicolor print (incomplete, 531 ft.); (b) 35mm nitrate Technicolor print (288 ft., trailer); (c) 16mm acetate color print (incomplete, 3,152 ft., 1968 "Jenkinson reconstruction"); (d) 16mm acetate duplicate soundtrack negative (3,152 ft., 1968 "Jenkinson reconstruction"); (e) 16mm acetate duplicate soundtrack negative (incomplete, 467 ft., 1975 additions to "Jenkinson reconstruction"); (f) 16mm acetate color duplicate negative (116 ft., trailer); (g) 16mm safety print (incomplete, 467 ft., 1975 additions to "Jenkinson reconstruction"); (h) 16mm safety composite color print (trailer)

Danish Film Institute / Archive and Cinematheque, Copenhagen: 35mm nitrate Technicolor print (incomplete, 2,461 ft., includes excerpts from "My Ragamuffin Romeo," "Meet the Boys," "A Dash of Spice," "I'd Like To Do Things For You," "My Bridal Veil," "Ladies of the Press," and "The Melting Pot of Music")

Deutsche Kinemathek, Berlin: 1 sound disc, double-sided, Reels 5A and 7A (German version)

George Eastman Museum, Rochester: (a) 35mm nitrate Technicolor print (incomplete, ca. 800 ft.); (b) 35mm nitrate Technicolor print (ca. 800 ft., trailer); (c) 16mm acetate color print (3,562 ft., William K. Everson's print / "Jenkinson print," includes trailer)

Gosfilmofond of Russia, Moscow: 35mm nitrate Technicolor print (11 reels, French release version, mute)

Kungliga biblioteket, Forskarservice för audiovisuella medier (The National Library of Sweden, Division of Audiovisual Media), Stockholm: 6 sound discs, double-sided (Swedish version)

Library of Congress, Washington, DC: (a) 35mm nitrate Technicolor print (incomplete, 7,440 ft., "Rohauer print"); (b) 35mm nitrate Technicolor print (trailer, 1 reel); (c) 35mm acetate b&w print (6,885 ft., 10 reels, Czech/French reconstruction, acquired in 1970 from Staatliches Filmarchiv); (d) 16mm acetate color print (3,151 ft., "Jenkinson print")

Národní filmový archiv, Prague: (a) 35mm acetate Orwocolor duplicate picture negative (French release, made in 1965); (b) 35mm acetate duplicate sound negative (Czech release, made in 1965, edited to match French picture); (c) two 35mm acetate Orwocolor prints (7,035 ft., Czech archive reconstruction, made in 1965); (d) 35mm acetate Orwocolor print (7,035 ft., Czech archive reconstruction, made in 1983)

UCLA Film & Television Archive, Los Angeles: (a) 35mm nitrate Technicolor print (incomplete, 1 reel, highlights, including "A Fable in Jazz" cartoon, "Ladies of the Press," and "Rhapsody in Blue"); (b) 16mm acetate b&w print (incomplete, ca. 3,200 ft.); (c) 16mm acetate b&w print (incomplete, ca. 1,600 ft.); (d) 16mm acetate color print (trailer, 200 ft.)

NBCUniversal: (a) 35mm nitrate camera negative (ca. 5,828 ft., 1933 reissue version); (b) 35mm nitrate soundtrack negative (ca. 9,320 ft., 1930 general release version); (c) 35mm nitrate soundtrack negative (1933 reissue)

Private Collections: (a) Milan Wolf, 11 sound discs, double-sided (Czech version); (b) Ron Hutchinson, 3 sound discs, Reels 1, 3, and trailer (U.S. version); (c) John Newton, 13 sound discs (U.S. version), 1 sound disc, double-sided, Reels 1 and 3 (French version)

Appendix IX:

SELECTIVE DISCOGRAPHY

The following is a list of all commercial recordings of songs featured in *King of Jazz*, recorded by the performers while they were in Hollywood for filming, and subsequently released on 78 rpm records. Additionally, it contains entries for *Rhapsody in Blue*, prominently featured in the film and first recorded by the Whiteman band in 1924. This list is ordered by recording date.

Sources: Paul Whiteman discography compiled by Whiteman scholar Don Rayno (2003) and Discography of American Historical Recordings (University of California Santa Barbara Library).

Rhapsody in Blue, Part 1 (Composed by George Gershwin, arranged by Ferde Grofé)
George Gershwin; Paul Whiteman and His Concert Orchestra
Recorded at Victor Talking Machine Co., New York
Takes 1-3 on June 10, 1924; 1st take selected as master (matrix #C-30174-1)
Released on September 5, 1924; Victor phonograph release, Vic 55225-A [also Gramophone 4-0588, HMV C-1171, Gramophone (France) L-563]
Instrumentation: 4 violins, 4 saxophones, 2 French horns, 2 cornets, 2 trombones, tuba, piano, traps
Soloists: Ross Gorman (clarinet), Arturo "Arthur" Cerino (French horn), Al Corrado (French horn), Frank Siegrist (trumpet), George Gershwin (piano), Ross Gorman (bass clarinet), Ross Gorman (oboe), Henry Busse (trumpet), Frank Siegrist (trumpet), Charles Strickfaden (baritone saxophone), Edward Stannard (B-flat soprano saxophone), Roy Maxon (trombone)

Rhapsody in Blue, Part 2 (Composed by George Gershwin, arranged by Ferde Grofé)
George Gershwin; Paul Whiteman and His Concert Orchestra
Recorded at Victor Talking Machine Co., New York
Takes 1-4 on June 10, 1924; 2nd take selected as master (matrix #C-30173-2)
Released on September 5, 1924; Victor phonograph release, Vic 55225-B [also Gramophone 4-0589, HMV C-1171, and Gramophone (France) L-563]
Instrumentation: 4 violins, 4 saxophones, 2 French horns, 2 cornets, 2 trombones, tuba, piano, traps
Soloists: George Gershwin (piano), Charles Strickfaden (baritone saxophone), Kurt Dieterle (violin), Nat Shilkret (celeste), Wilbur Hall (trombone)

Rhapsody in Blue, Part 1 (Composed by George Gershwin, arranged by Ferde Grofé)
George Gershwin; Paul Whiteman and His Concert Orchestra
Recorded in Liederkranz Hall, New York
Takes 4-6 on April 21, 1927; 6th take selected as master (matrix #CVE-30174-6)
Released on July 1, 1927; Victor phonograph release Vic 35822-A [also Vic 35891, Vic 01501, Vic 42-0149, Vic 420-0145, Vic L-24001, Gramophone (Spain) AF-382, Gramophone (Czechoslovakia) AN-576, Gramophone (Austria) BB-217, HMV C-1395, RCA Victor 27-0111, RCA Victor LPT-29, RCA Victor LPV-555, RCA Victor 27-0149]
Instrumentation: 5 violins, cello, 2 violas, bass, 4 saxophones, 2 French horns, 3 cornets, 3 trombones, tuba, banjo, piano, celeste, traps
Soloists: Chester Hazlett (clarinet), Arturo "Arthur" Cerino (French horn), Al Corrado (French horn), Frank Siegrist (trumpet), George Gershwin (piano), Chester Hazlett (bass clarinet), Charles Strickfaden (oboe), Henry Busse (trumpet), Frank Siegrist (trumpet), Charles Strickfaden (baritone saxophone), Harold McLean (B-flat soprano saxophone), Boyce Cullen (trombone)

Rhapsody in Blue, Part 2 (Composed by George Gershwin, arranged by Ferde Grofé)
George Gershwin; Paul Whiteman and His Concert Orchestra
Recorded in Liederkranz Hall, New York
Takes 5-9 on April 21, 1927; 8th take selected as master (matrix #CVE-30173-8)
Released on July 1, 1927; Victor phonograph release, Vic 35822-B [also Vic 35892, Vic 01502, Vic 42-0149, Vic 420-0145, Vic L-24001, Gramophone (Spain) AF-382, Gramophone (Czechoslovakia) AN-576, Gramophone (Austria) BB-217, HMV C-1395, RCA Victor 27-0112, RCA Victor 27-0149, RCA Victor LPT-29, RCA Victor LPV-555]
Instrumentation: 5 violins, cello, 2 violas, bass, 4 saxophones, 2 French horns, 3 cornets, 3 trombones, tuba, banjo, piano, celeste, traps

Soloists: George Gershwin (piano), Charles Strickfaden (baritone saxophone), Kurt Dieterle (violin), Harry Perrella (celeste), Wilbur Hall (trombone)

Happy Feet (Music by Milton Ager, lyrics by Jack Yellen)
Paul Whiteman and His Orchestra
Recorded at Columbia Phonograph Co., Los Angeles
3 takes on February 10, 1930; 1st take selected as master (matrix #149810-1)
Released on April 30, 1930; Columbia phonograph release, Col 2164-D
Soloists: Eddie Lang (guitar), Frank Trumbauer (alto saxophone), Andy Secrest (cornet), Joe Venuti (violin)
Vocals: The Rhythm Boys

It Happened in Monterey (Music by Mabel Wayne, lyrics by Billy Rose)
Paul Whiteman and His Orchestra
Recorded at Columbia Phonograph Co., Los Angeles
Takes 1-5 on February 10, 1930, takes 6-10 on March 21, 1930; 7th and 10th takes selected as masters (matrix #149811)
Released on April 30, 1930; Columbia phonograph release, Col 2163-D [also CB-88]
Soloists: Eddie Lang (guitar), unidentified musician (steel guitar), Boyce Cullen (megaphone muted trombone), Bernie Daly (flute), Chester Hazlett (subtone clarinet), Kurt Dieterle (violin)
Vocal: Jack Fulton

It Happened in Monterey (Music by Mabel Wayne, lyrics by Billy Rose)
John Boles
Recorded at Hal Roach Studios, Culver City, California
4 takes on March 17, 1930; 2nd take selected as master (matrix #PBVE-54713)
Released in June 1930; Victor phonograph release, Vic 22372-A [also Gramophone B-3456 and RCA Victor LPV-538]
Instrumentation: 4 violins, viola, cello, bass, flute, 2 clarinets, 2 French horns, trumpet, trombone, steel guitar, harp, traps
Vocal: John Boles (tenor)

Song of the Dawn (Music by Milton Ager, lyrics by Jack Yellen)
John Boles; The Rounders
Recorded at Hal Roach Studios, Culver City, California
4 takes on March 17, 1930; 4th take selected as master (matrix #PBVE-54715)
Released in June 1930; Victor phonograph release, Vic 22372-B [also Gramophone B-3456]
Instrumentation: 4 violins, viola, cello, bass, flute, 2 clarinets, 2 French horns, trumpet, trombone, harp, traps
Vocals: John Boles (tenor) and The Rounders (male chorus)

Song of the Dawn (Music by Milton Ager, lyrics by Jack Yellen)
Paul Whiteman and His Orchestra
Recorded at Columbia Phonograph Co., Los Angeles
3 takes on March 21, 1930; 1st and 2nd takes selected as masters (matrix #149822)
Released on April 30, 1930; Columbia phonograph release, Col 2163-D [also CB-87]
Soloists: Eddie Lang (guitar), Charles Strickfaden (baritone saxophone), Joe Venuti (violin)
Vocals: Bing Crosby, "King of Jazz" Chorus

My Lover (Music by James Dietrich, lyrics by Jack Yellen)
Grace Hayes
Recorded at Hal Roach Studios, Culver City, California
3 takes on March 21, 1930; 2nd take selected as master (matrix #PBVE-54738)
Released in May 1930; Victor phonograph release, Vic 22388-A
Instrumentation: 2 violins, cello, bass, clarinet, 2 trumpets, piano
Vocal: Grace Hayes

I Like to Do Things For You (Music by Milton Ager, lyrics by Jack Yellen)
Grace Hayes
Recorded at Hal Roach Studios, Culver City, California
3 takes on March 21, 1930; 1st take selected as master (matrix #PBVE-54739)
Released in May 1930; Victor phonograph release, Vic 22388-B
Instrumentation: 2 violins, cello, bass, clarinet, 2 trumpets, piano
Vocal: Grace Hayes

Ragamuffin Romeo (Music by Mabel Wayne, lyrics by Harry De Costa)
Paul Whiteman and His Orchestra
Recorded at Columbia Phonograph Co., Los Angeles
4 takes on March 22, 1930; 1st and 2nd takes selected as masters (matrix #149823)
Released on May 15, 1930; Columbia phonograph release, Col 2170-D [also CB-88]
Soloists: Frank Siegrist (trumpet), Lennie Hayton (celeste), Kurt Dieterle (violin), Roy "Red" Maier (bassoon), Charles Strickfaden (baritone saxophone), Chester Hazlett (subtone clarinet)
Vocal: Jeanie Lang

A Bench in the Park (Music by Milton Ager, lyrics by Jack Yellen)
Brox Sisters; Paul Whiteman and His Orchestra
Recorded at Columbia Phonograph Co., Los Angeles
3 takes on March 22, 1930; 1st and 2nd takes selected as masters (matrix #149825)
Released on April 30, 1930; Columbia phonograph release, Col 2164-D [also CB-86]
Soloists: Chester Hazlett (subtone clarinet), Eddie Lang (guitar),

Bill Rank (trombone), Andy Secrest (cornet)
Vocals: The Brox Sisters, The Rhythm Boys

I Like to Do Things For You (Music by Milton Ager, lyrics by
Jack Yellen)
Paul Whiteman and His Orchestra
Recorded at Columbia Phonograph Co., Los Angeles
4 takes on March 23, 1930; 1st and 2nd takes selected as
masters (matrix #149826)
Released on May 15, 1930; Columbia phonograph release, Col
2170-D [also CB-87]
Soloists: Eddie Lang (guitar), Andy Secrest (cornet), Roy Bargy
(piano), Lennie Hayton (piano), Frank Trumbauer (C-melody
saxophone)
Vocals: The Rhythm Boys

A Bench in the Park (Music by Milton Ager, lyrics by Jack Yellen)
Paul Whiteman's Rhythm Boys
Recorded at Columbia Phonograph Co., Los Angeles
4 takes on May 23, 1930; 3rd and 4th takes selected as masters
(matrix #149840)
Released on July 15, 1930; Columbia phonograph release, Col
2223-D
Vocals: Harry Barris, Bing Crosby, Al Rinker; piano: Harry Barris

NOTES

Chapter 1

1. Thomas A. DeLong, *Pops: Paul Whiteman, King of Jazz* (Piscataway, NJ: New Century Publishers, 1983), 27.
2. The 1921 copyright registration credits Grofé and Whiteman with the arrangement, so that the bandleader also received royalties.
3. Paul Whiteman and Mary Margaret McBride, *Jazz* (New York: J. H. Sears & Co., 1926), 65.
4. Whiteman and McBride, *Jazz*, 225-26.
5. Sime Silverman, "Paul Whiteman Orchestra (11), 32 mins.; Full Stage (curtains). Palace," *Variety*, October 7, 1921, 21.
6. Alexander Woollcott, "A Dancer's Revue: 'George White's Scandals of 1922'," *New York Times*, August 30, 1922, 18. "I'll Build a Stairway to Paradise" was the highlight of a show that otherwise had a mixed reception. Opening night included a 25-minute opera set in Harlem titled *Blue Monday*. Although pulled from the show after that one performance, it reappeared, reorchestrated by Ferde Grofé, in Whiteman's 1925 Carnegie Hall concert as *135th Street*.
7. George Gershwin, in "Music by Gershwin," NBC radio program, broadcast March 9, 1934, quoted in Deena Rosenberg, *Fascinating Rhythm: The Collaboration of George and Ira Gershwin* (New York: Dutton, 1991), 55.
8. Whiteman and McBride, *Jazz*, 248.
9. Although Whiteman introduced "Whispering" in live performance, four other recordings of the song were released ahead of his in October 1920, and his own label Victor released a version with vocal from a different orchestra. See Tim Gracyk, with Frank Hoffmann, *Popular American Recording Pioneers*, 1895-1925 (New York: The Haworth Press, 2000), 359. For details, see the Discography of American Historical Recordings, http://adp.library.ucsb.edu/
10. "Music Men," *Variety*, March 15, 1923, 42.
11. Whiteman and McBride, *Jazz*, 69-70.
12. "Whiteman Biggest London Hit Ever Made by Importation," *Variety*, April 5, 1923, 2.
13. Mary Margaret McBride, in her own autobiography, *A Long Way from Missouri* (New York: G. P. Putnam's Sons, 1959), 170.
14. "Paul Whiteman and His Orchestra Receive Unprecedented Welcome on Return from Europe," *Talking Machine World*, September 15, 1923, 72-73; The *New York Times* coverage stated that Whiteman was "crowned King of Syncopation." "Fans Greet Jazz King," *New York Times*, August 14, 1923, 16.
15. "Éva Gauthier—New York and Celebrity," *The Virtual Gramophone*, Library and Archives Canada. Accessed March 5, 2016. http://www.collectionscanada.gc.ca/gramophone/028011-1009.3-e.html
16. Carl Van Vechten, "George Gershwin, An American Composer Who Is Writing Notable Music in the Jazz Idiom," *Vanity Fair*, March 1925, 40, 78, 84. Reprinted in Robert Wyatt and John Andrew Johnson, eds., *The George Gershwin Reader* (Oxford University Press, 2004), 77-82.
17. "Éva Gauthier—New York and Celebrity," *The Virtual Gramophone*, Library and Archives Canada. Accessed March 5, 2016. http://www.collectionscanada.gc.ca/gramophone/028011-1009.3-e.html
18. Paul Whiteman, "Paul Whiteman Denies 'Jazz'; Plays 'Syncopated Rhythm'," *Variety*, January 3, 1924, 4.
19. Gilbert Seldes, "Toujours Jazz," *Dial*, August 1923, 75, 151-66. Reprinted in Gilbert Seldes, *The 7 Lively Arts* (New York and London: Harper & Brothers, 1924), 103.
20. "'Round the Rialto," *Billboard*, December 22, 1923, 25.
21. Whiteman and McBride, *Jazz*, 95.
22. Olin Downes, "A Concert of Jazz," *New York Times*, February 13, 1924, 16.
23. Izetta May McHenry, "An Experiment in Modern Music," *Billboard*, February 23, 1924, 30.
24. Downes, "A Concert of Jazz," 16; Karl Koenig, ed., *Jazz in Print (1856-1929): An Anthology of Selected Early Readings in Jazz History* (Hillsdale, NY: Pendragon Press, 2002), 297.
25. Gilbert Gabriel, *New York Evening Sun*, quoted in Whiteman and McBride, *Jazz*, 110.
26. "$800,000 F.P. Contract Refused by Whiteman—Prefers Concert," *Variety*, September 23, 1925, 1.
27. Paul Whiteman, "George and the Rhapsody," essay in Merle Armitage, ed., *George Gershwin* (New York: Longmans, Green & Co., 1938), 25.
28. Whiteman and McBride, *Jazz*, 218.
29. Gunther Schuller, *Early Jazz: Its Roots and Musical Development* (New York: Oxford University Press, 1968), 192, fn. 21.
30. Whiteman, "George and the Rhapsody," in Armitage, ed., *George Gershwin*, 1938, 25
31. Seldes, "Toujours Jazz," *Dial*, August 1923, reprinted in Seldes, *The 7 Lively Arts*, 1924, 104.
32. Duke Ellington, *Music Is My Mistress* (Garden City, NY: Doubleday, 1973), 103.
33. Joshua Berrett, *Louis Armstrong & Paul Whiteman: Two Kings of Jazz* (New Haven: Yale University Press, 2004), 49. Jeffrey Magee, *The Uncrowned King of Swing: Fletcher Henderson and Big Band Jazz* (Oxford, New York: Oxford University Press, 2005), 119.
34. Hannen Swaffer, "What London Looks Like," *Variety*, May 12, 1926, 2.
35. Abel, "Straight Dance Bands Without Chance With Only Straight Music," *Variety*, June 9, 1926, 41.
36. "Paul Whiteman With Morris," *Variety*, January 6, 1926, 4.
37. Agreement, Publix Theatres Corporation and Paul Whiteman, July 26, 1926. Paul Whiteman Collection, Williams College.
38. "New Acts This Week, 'Crosby and Rinker'," *Variety*, October 6, 1926, 56.
39. "Whiteman Over $80,000 This Week At Paramount; $76,791 Last Wk.," *Variety*, February 16, 1927, 7. The feature was Warner Bros.' *The Third Degree* (1926), Michael Curtiz's first American film.
40. "Paul Whiteman to Play 44 Weeks for $528,000," *Billboard*, July 16, 1927, 30.
41. Berrett, *Louis Armstrong & Paul Whiteman: Two Kings of Jazz*, 88.
42. Whiteman and McBride, *Jazz*, 242.
43. James F. Gillespie, with Wesley Stout, "Hot Music," *Saturday Evening Post*, March 19, 1932, 86.
44. "Whiteman's Delay," *Variety*, May 16, 1928, 53.
45. Agreement between Paul Whiteman and Universal Pictures Corporation, October 18, 1928. Courtesy of Richard Koszarski.

Chapter 2

1. Carl Laemmle, "This Business of Motion Pictures," *Film History* 3, no. 1 (1989): 49. [Laemmle's article, prepared by the studio in 1927, remained unpublished until 1989.] Robert Cochrane invested $2,500 in October 1906 for a share of the company.
2. Laemmle, "This Business of Motion Pictures," 61.
3. William H. Swanson, Cross Examination, *United States of America, petitioner, vs. Motion Picture Patents Co., et al., defendants*, District Court of the United States, for the Eastern District of Pennsylvania, Record, Vol. II, 655.
4. May 1914 letter from David Horsley to Robert Grau, quoted in Robert Grau, *The Theatre of Science: A Volume of Progress and Achievement in the Motion Picture Industry* (New York: Broadway Publishing Company, 1914), 41
5. "$750,000 Picture Stock Sale by Universal Film Faction," *Variety*, October 10, 1914, 1.
6. "Carl Laemmle and R. H. Cochrane Buy Out P. A. Powers," *Motion Picture News*, March 27, 1920, 2879.
7. "Universal City Opened," *Moving Picture World*, March 27, 1915, 1908. For a thorough account of the opening day, see Robert S. Birchard, "The Road to Universal City," *American Cinematographer* 86, no. 7 (July 2005): 70-77.
8. Advertisement, "An Open Letter to All Film Manufacturers," *Moving Picture World*, September 11, 1915, 1767.
9. Hal Mohr, interview with Richard Koszarski, June 11, 1973. Courtesy of Richard Koszarski.
10. William A. Johnston, "'Uncle Carl' of the Films," *Motion Picture News*, November 30, 1929, 28.
11. Griffith Park is a 4,000-acre municipal park in a mountainous area near Burbank that has long been popular with filmmakers.
12. Lenore Coffee, *Storyline: Recollections of a Hollywood Screenwriter* (London: Cassell & Company Ltd., 1973), 83.
13. Herbert Cruikshank, "The Crown Prince of Hollywood," *Motion Picture Classic*, December 1928, 80.
14. Robert H. Cochrane, letter to Bosley Crowther, 1950s, quoted in Mark A. Vieira, *Irving Thalberg: Boy Wonder to Producer Prince* (Berkeley: University of California Press, 2010), 7.
15. "Thalberg's Rise to Fame Won Title of 'Boy Wonder'," *Los Angeles Times*, September 15, 1936, 5.
16. Grace Kingsley, "Flashes: Thalberg to East," *Los Angeles Times*, April 22, 1921, III4. Similar gossip about the anticipated marriage appeared in *Variety*.
17. Coffee, *Storyline*, 83.
18. Richard Koszarski, *Von: The Life and Films of Erich von Stroheim* (New York: Limelight Editions, 2001), 86.
19. Robert S. Birchard, *Early Universal City* (Charleston, SC: Arcadia, 2009), 7. See also: "Motion Pictures and Poultry Both Produced at One Great Plant," *Pacific Poultrycraft*, August 1925, 10.
20. Fay Wray, in William M. Drew, *At the Center of the Frame* (Lanham, MD: Vestal Press, 1999), 69.
21. "Managing Unhealthy," *Variety*, March 18, 1925, 29.
22. "Plenty of Kidding at Laemmle's Dinner," *Variety*, March 24, 1926, 35.
23. "Financial Statements," *The Film Daily 1928 Year Book* (New York: The Film Daily), 803-29. The companies had different fiscal years, but

the results are broadly comparable. The figures for Paramount, Loew's, and Fox include the companies' theater holdings.

24. "Convention Hopes Are Realized at Milwaukee," *Exhibitors Trade Review*, May 23, 1925, 22.
25. "'U' to Merge Chain and Picture Corp.," *Motion Picture News*, September 23, 1927, 919.
26. "U Wants Moss to Take Back Colony," *Variety*, November 14, 1928, 18.
27. William A. Johnston, "An Editor on Broadway," *Motion Picture News*, May 1, 1926, 2000.
28. Richard Koszarski, *Universal Pictures: 65 Years* (New York: The Museum of Modern Art, 1977), 11-12.
29. "3,200 Using Service," *Film Daily*, October 14, 1925, 1.
30. Robert H. Cochrane, to Federal Trade Commission, quoted in Howard T. Lewis, *The Motion Picture Industry* (New York: D. Van Nostrand Company, Inc., 1933), 152.
31. "Stars' Box Office Values," *Variety*, January 6, 1926, 1, 26. Two years later Laura La Plante had moved ahead of Reginald Denny in the list, with the addition of Jean Hersholt and Conrad Veidt, and the departure of Peters and Valli. See also: "Leading Film Stars of '27," *Variety*, January 4, 1928, 1, 8, 9.
32. Joseph Schildkraut, *My Father and I* (New York: Viking Press, 1959), 192.
33. Eugene Zukor, interviewed in Neal Gabler, *An Empire of Their Own: How the Jews Invented Hollywood* (New York: Crown Publishers, Inc., 1988), 39.
34. "Eugene Zukor Made Assistant to President of Famous Players," *Exhibitors Herald and Motography*, August 9, 1919, 67.
35. "Carl Laemmle Definitely on Road to Recovery, Universal is Advised," *Motion Picture News*, July 24, 1926, 302.
36. "Carl Laemmle to Train Son in All Branches of Film Business," *Universal Weekly*, December 11, 1926, 12.
37. Phil M. Daly, "And That's That!," *Film Daily*, July 30, 1926, 5.
38. "'Collegians' Proving So Popular That New Series is Planned," *Universal Weekly*, November 13, 1926, 27.
39. "Laemmle Buys Ince's Estate, Dias Dorados," *Variety*, May 5, 1926, 4.
40. Patsy Ruth Miller, in William M. Drew, *Speaking of Silents: First Ladies of the Screen* (Vestal, NY: Vestal Press, 1989), 153.
41. Jim Tully, "I'll Give a Million Dollars for a New Star," *New Movie Magazine*, June 1933, 34.
42. Richard Koszarski interviewed Junior in 1972. See: Richard Koszarski, "'It's No Use to Have an Unhappy Man': Paul Fejos at Universal," *Film History* 17, no. 2/3 (2005): 235.
43. Paul Fejos, Reminiscences of Paul Fejos: Oral History, 1963, 50-51. Special Collections, Columbia University Libraries.
44. *Lonesome*, in "What the Picture Did For Me," *Exhibitors Herald-World*, March 9, 1929, 70. Stacy W. Osgood, Kenwood theatre, Chicago, Illinois. General Patronage.
45. "Fox Recalls Tone Truck Upon Finding U Has Secretly Made Sound Picture," *Variety*, September 5, 1928, 5.
46. "Young Laemmle, Pop Away, Fires Oldtimers, Relatives and Proteges," *Variety*, February 13, 1929, 5.
47. Fejos, Reminiscences, 52.
48. Paul Fejos, "Illusion on the Screen," *New York Times*, May 26, 1929, X3.
49. Fejos, "Illusion on the Screen," X3.
50. Tully, "I'll Give a Million Dollars for a New Star," 34; "Welsh and Heath Resign; Junior Laemmle Is Boss," *Motion Picture News*, June 1, 1929, 1823; "Laemmle to Go Abroad; Junior to Head Studio," *Exhibitors Herald-World*, June 29, 1929, 150.

Chapter 3

1. By comparison, only five pictures from Universal's recently concluded 1927–28 season cost over $200,000—the most expensive was E. A. Dupont's *Love Me and the World Is Mine* (1928), at $329,578—and only two of these films narrowly scraped past $200,000 in profit. Universal Financial Records, 1927–1928. Courtesy of Richard Koszarski.
2. Agreement between Paul Whiteman and Universal Pictures Corporation, October 18, 1928. Courtesy of Richard Koszarski. The contract also stated that "Mr. Whiteman and his band will provide at his and their expense, street clothes, tuxedo and afternoon outfits if necessary for any characters or roles to be portrayed by him and/or his band during the term of the employment under this agreement." This stipulation would come back to haunt them a year after the film was eventually released. A syndicated Associated Press story reported that Universal filed a suit against Whiteman in 1931 to regain a $1,500 expenditure the studio had paid toward the band members' 22 tuxedos used in the film. "Film Company Sues Whiteman for $1,500," *Appleton Post-Crescent* [Wisconsin], Associated Press syndicated article, August 4, 1931, 4
3. After deducting overhead and distribution expenses, *Melody of Love* made $79,517 in profit. Universal Financial Records, 1928–1929. Courtesy of Richard Koszarski.
4. "Universal Sound Stages Are Marvels of Science," *Universal Weekly*, December 29, 1928, 1.
5. Miles Kreuger, *Show Boat: The Story of a Classic American Musical* (New York: Oxford University Press, 1977), 83. Kreuger documents that this contractual payment was to be divided among multiple participants: producer Florenz Ziegfeld (5/13ths), composer Jerome Kern (3/13ths), writer Edna Ferber (3/26ths), lyricist Oscar Hammerstein II (5/26ths), and music publisher T. B. Harms (1/13th). Additionally, 15% of the net profits above $125,000 would also be split among the participants.
6. "Whiteman To Name Own Sum For Second Talkie For U," *Billboard*, November 17, 1928, 19.
7. "Paul Whiteman Slated for Concert Broadcast Before Starting 'King of Jazz' for Universal," *Universal Weekly*, February 9, 1929, 12.
8. "Whiteman To Name Own Sum For Second Talkie for U," *Billboard*, November 17, 1928, 19.
9. "Whiteman's Carnegie Scene for His U Talker," *Variety*, December 19, 1928, 5.
10. Contract amendment between Paul Whiteman and Universal Pictures Corporation, January 10, 1929. Paul Whiteman Collection, Williams College Archives & Special Collections.
11. Agreement between Paul Whiteman and Lennen & Mitchell, Inc., January 8, 1929. Paul Whiteman Collection, Williams College Archives & Special Collections.
12. Paul Schofield, "The King of Jazz," synopsis, undated, *Universal Catalog of Library Properties*. Motion Picture, Broadcasting and Recorded Sound Division (MBRS), Library of Congress.
13. "Whiteman To Name Own Sum For Second Talkie for U," *Billboard*, November 17, 1928, 19.
14. L. Wolfe Gilbert, "Dream World" lyrics, Ferde Grofé Collection, Music Division, Library of Congress. Copyrighted by L. Wolfe Gilbert & Mabel Wayne, May 11, 1929; L. Wolfe Gilbert, "Forever and a Day" lyrics, Ferde Grofé Collection, Music Division, Library of Congress. Copyrighted by L. Wolfe Gilbert & Mabel Wayne, March 15, 1929.
15. Night letter from New York to Carl Laemmle Sr., March 20, 1929. Courtesy of Richard Koszarski.
16. Telegram from the Coast, March 21, 1929. Courtesy of Richard Koszarski.
17. Telegram from New York to Carl Laemmle Sr., March 22, 1929. Courtesy of Richard Koszarski.
18. Universal's screen test of George Gershwin doesn't appear to have happened. Telegram from the Coast to Werner Straus, March 27, 1929. Courtesy of Richard Koszarski.
19. C. J. Tevlin, General Statistics Department, "Statistics on Feature Releases," RKO Radio Pictures, Inc., June 1952. Courtesy of Richard Jewell.
20. Seymour Stern, "Magyar Genius Given Chance at Universal," *New York Herald Tribune*, January 20, 1929, F3.
21. Paul Fejos, Reminiscences of Paul Fejos: Oral History, 1963, 54-55. Special Collections, Columbia University Libraries.
22. Carl Laemmle Sr., telegram to [Sydney] Singerman, May 2, 1929; Werner Straus, night letter to Coast, May 3, 1929; Carl Laemmle Sr., telegram to Werner Straus, May 18, 1929; Lou B. Metzger, telegram to Mrs. Straus, May 20, 1929; Lou B. Metzger, telegram to Mrs. Straus, May 20, 1929. All courtesy of Richard Koszarski.
23. "The Critics Look At Fejos," *Universal Weekly*, April 27, 1929, 14.
24. "Jazz King Reaches Coast," *Universal Weekly*, June 22, 1929, 6.
25. Abel Green, "Whiteman-Old Gold Special Bunch Ride De Luxe—50 Aboard and Happy," *Variety*, May 29, 1929, 31, 38.
26. Abel Green, "With the Whiteman Special," *Variety*, June 5, 1929, 57.
27. "Noted Band Leader Arrives," *Los Angeles Times*, June 7, 1929, A13.
28. Philip K. Scheuer, "That 'Rhapsody in Blue': It's Still Whiteman's Tour de Force; Jazz King Won't Comment on 'Acting' for the Talkies," *Los Angeles Times*, June 16, 1929, C12.
29. Grace Kingsley, "Olga Steck With Universal," *Los Angeles Times*, June 5, 1929, A12; "Noted Band Leader Arrives," *Los Angeles Times*, June 7, 1929, A13.
30. "Gigantic 'King of Jazz' Set," *Universal Weekly*, August 10, 1929, 9.
31. Muriel Babcock, "King of Jazz Lacks Throne," *Los Angeles Times*, August 18, 1929, 13.
32. "Original Story Chosen for Whiteman's 'King of Jazz,'" *Universal City Club Bulletin*, July 20, 1929, 13. Beinecke Rare Book & Manuscript Library, Yale University Libraries.
33. Evidence suggests the 1928 James Ashmore Creelman play *The Jazz King* was consulted by the Universal scenario department. A synopsis for the play is listed in the *Universal Catalog of Library Properties*. The play was later made into a film by Paramount Pictures in 1932, under the title *Dancers in the Dark*.
34. "Whiteman Leaves To Make U. Film," *Billboard*, June 1, 1929, 21.
35. Edward T. Lowe, Jr. (screenplay) and Frank M. Dazey (author), "The King of Jazz," synopsis,

undated, *Universal Catalog of Library Properties*. Motion Picture, Broadcasting and Recorded Sound Division (MBRS), Library of Congress.

36. Scheuer, "That 'Rhapsody in Blue'," C12.
37. Helen Louise Walker, "Jazz King Who Won't Act," *Film Weekly*, August 5, 1929, 10.
38. Scheuer, "That 'Rhapsody in Blue'," C12.
39. "Soundproof Bungalow Built for Jazz King," *Universal Weekly*, July 27, 1929; Grace Kingsley, "A Wedding and Whiteman Lodge," *Los Angeles Times*, August 25, 1929, J5; Nelson B. Bell, "Behind the Screens," *Washington Post*, June 29, 1929, 9.
40. Kurt Dieterle, Interview with Floyd Levin, January 18, 1990, 29. Kurt Dieterle Papers, Williams College Archives & Special Collections.
41. Bill Swigert, "Along the Coast," *Variety*, July 17, 1929, 81.
42. "Mary Nolan to be Guest at WMAL," *Washington Post*, August 6, 1929, 10.
43. Mayme Ober Peak, "Junior Laemmle, at 21, Is Proving He's More Than Son of Boss," *Boston Globe*, September 1, 1929, A34.
44. Fejos, Reminiscences, 55.
45. "Not Romantic Lover; Band First, Says Paul," *Variety*, August 14, 1929, 4.
46. Fejos, Reminiscences, 55.
47. "Whiteman Film, Revue In Form, Is Now Set," *Variety*, July 17, 1929, 5.
48. "Theatre, Vaudeville and Melody," *Hollywood Filmograph*, July 27, 1929, 14.
49. Abel Green, "Words About Music," *Variety*, July 3, 1929, 96.
50. "Not Romantic Lover, Band First, Says Paul," *Variety*, August 14, 1929, 4.
51. Babcock, "King of Jazz Lacks Throne," *Los Angeles Times*, August 18, 1929, 13.
52. Carl Laemmle Jr., telegram to Lou B. Metzger, July 29, 1929. Courtesy of Richard Koszarski.
53. "Whiteman on Pay And More Delays May Mean Shorts," *Billboard*, August 3, 1929, 20.
54. "Bars Paul Whiteman From Equity Benefit," *New York Times*, August 1, 1929, 19.
55. "Rhythm Boy [sic] on Bill at Orpheum," *Los Angeles Times*, July 26, 1929, 9; "Special Concert," *Los Angeles Times*, July 6, 1929, 3.
56. Kurt Dieterle, quoted in Philip R. Evans and Linda K. Evans, Bix: *The Leon Bix Beiderbecke Story* (Bakersfield, CA: Prelike Press, 1998), 473.
57. "Venuti Will Recover," *Variety*, August 14, 1929, 57.
58. Herbert S. Weil, "Latest American News," *Melody Maker*, December 1, 1929, 1137.
59. "Killed in Crash," *Variety*, August 7, 1929, 227.
60. Grace Kingsley, "A Wedding and Whiteman Lodge!" *Los Angeles Times*, August 25, 1929, J5.
61. Peak, "Junior Laemmle, at 21, Is Proving He's More Than Son of Boss," *Boston Globe*, September 1, 1929, A34.
62. Made for a total world cost of $1,769,973, *Broadway* would eventually return only $1,348,050 in worldwide revenue—a net loss of $421,923 for the studio. Universal Financial Records, 1929–1930. Courtesy of Richard Koszarski.
63. "U's Next Big One," *Variety*, August 7, 1929, 188.
64. Hal Mohr, Interview with Richard Koszarski, June 11, 1973. Courtesy of Richard Koszarski.
65. Fejos, Reminiscences, 57. For more on the departure of Paul Fejos from Universal, see Richard Koszarski, "'It's No Use to Have an Unhappy Man': Paul Fejos at Universal," *Film*

History 17, no. 2/3 (2005): 234-40.

Chapter 4

1. Marjorie Farnsworth, *The Ziegfeld Follies* (New York: Bonanza Books, 1956), 25-28; Thomas H. Gressler, "John Murray Anderson: Director of Revues" (unpublished PhD dissertation, Kent State University, 1973), 21-23.
2. John Murray Anderson, *Out Without My Rubbers* (New York: Library Publishers, 1954), 62.
3. Robert Baral, "Pre-Beatnik Greenwich Village and Murray Anderson's Follies," *Variety*, January 6, 1960, 263.
4. Anderson, *Out Without My Rubbers*, 62-63; "Greenwich Village Follies," *Billboard*, September 13, 1919, 91.
5. Gilbert Seldes, "A Revue Reviewed," *Vanity Fair*, January 1923. Reprinted, retitled "A Tribute to Florenz Ziegfeld," in Gilbert Seldes, *The 7 Lively Arts* (New York and London: Harper & Brothers, 1924), 131.
6. Gressler, "John Murray Anderson" (unpublished PhD dissertation, 1973), 102.
7. Anderson, *Out Without My Rubbers*, 41, 49.
8. "Cabarets," *Variety*, April 13, 1917, 16.
9. *New York American* and *Evening World* reviews, quoted in "The Crowning Achievement in Modern Revue," *Variety*, November 2, 1917, 60.
10. Gordon Whyte, "Varied Career of John Murray Anderson," *Billboard*, April 3, 1920, 32.
11. "Inside Stuff on Legit," *Variety*, April 2, 1920, 15; Anderson, *Out Without My Rubbers*, 67.
12. Edward H. Smith, "What's Amiss in the American Theater?," *The World Magazine*, New York World, August 15, 1920, 10.
13. Colgate Baker, "'Greenwich Village Follies,' And John Murray Anderson, the Miracle Man," *New York Review*, September 16, 1922.
14. Colgate Baker, "'What's in a Name?' New Art in Musical Comedy & John Murray Anderson," *New York Review*, April 10, 1920.
15. "Inside Stuff on Legit," *Variety*, April 2, 1920, 15.
16. "$85,000 in Name Show," *Variety*, March 5, 1920, 12.
17. Robert Baral, *Revue: A Nostalgic Reprise of the Great Broadway Period* (New York: Fleet Publishing Corp., 1962), 222.
18. "Best Sellers in Sheet Music," *Variety*, January 7, 1925, 40.
19. "Operetta Vogue Displacing Revues on Broadway's Winter Schedule," *Variety*, January 21, 1925, 19.
20. Anderson, *Out Without My Rubbers*, 76.
21. Herman Rosse, "The Super-deLuxe Mammoth Motion Picture Palace," *Theatre Arts Monthly* 10, no. 11 (November 1926): 763.
22. Anderson, *Out Without My Rubbers*, 97-98.
23. "Theatre Attendance Record Here Broken," *Boston Globe*, October 18, 1925, A16.
24. Libbey, "House Reviews: Met., Boston," *Variety*, October 21, 1925, 32.
25. "Metropolitan," *Variety*, November 11, 1925, 36.
26. *Film Year Book 1927* (New York: The Film Daily, 1927), 665.
27. F. P. Presentations Produced in N. Y.; 20 Weeks of Travel-Acts in Them Also," *Variety*, December 16, 1925, 29.
28. "Publix Greatest Employers of Stage Talent in America," *Publix Opinion*, April 16, 1928, 1.
29. James Dietrich, interview with Diane and Richard Koszarski, 1976. Courtesy of Richard Koszarski.
30. "Everybody Goes to Markert," full-page advertisement, *Variety*, December 5, 1928, 46.
31. Kenneth Macgowan, *The Theatre of Tomorrow*

(New York: Boni and Liveright, 1921), 121.
32. Sheldon Cheney, "Hermann Rosse's Stage Designs," *Theatre Arts Magazine* 5, no. 2 (April 1921): 148.
33. "Presentation Costs," *Variety*, March 10, 1926, 35.
34. "Jazz Rhapsody at Metropolitan," *Boston Globe*, March 16, 1926, 22.
35. "Rhapsody in Jazz," reviewed at the Rivoli, New York, *Variety*, March 10, 1926, 36.
36. "Murray Anderson's Rhapsody in Jazz Howard Offering," *Atlanta Constitution*, May 30, 1926, C5.
37. "Rhapsody in Jazz," *Variety*, March 10, 1926, 36.
38. "Murray Anderson's Rhapsody in Jazz," *Atlanta Constitution*, May 30, 1926, C5.
39. Edited excerpts from Herman Rosse, "The Super-deLuxe Mammoth Motion Picture Palace," *Theatre Arts Monthly* 10, no. 11 (November 1926): 763-66.
40. "The Garden of Kama," *Variety*, January 27, 1926, 36.
41. "The Grecian Urn," *Variety*, May 19, 1926, 19.
42. "Publix Allows Option on Charlot to Lapse," *Variety*, August 24, 1927, 5.
43. "Publix Using Big Names," *Variety*, June 23, 1926, 5.
44. Abel., "Film House Reviews: Paramount," *Variety*, February 16, 1927, 23.
45. Abel., "Film House Reviews: Paramount," *Variety*, June 8, 1927, 21.
46. Sime., "Film House Reviews: Paramount," *Variety*, June 15, 1927, 28.
47. "Paul Whiteman To Play 44 Weeks For $528,000," *Billboard*, July 16, 1927, 30; "Publix Dropping Unit Shows on Entire Circuit of Houses," *Billboard*, July 9, 1927, 84.
48. "Bigger and Better," *Publix Opinion*, December 10, 1927, 3.
49. 'Highlights' Boasts Great Entertainment," *Publix Opinion*, December 24, 1927, 1.
50. Anderson would return to Publix for several months in the spring of 1929, between his productions of *Hello Daddy!* (1929) and *Murray Anderson's Almanac* (1929).
51. "John Murray Anderson Quits Publix Concern," *Billboard*, November 17, 1928, 18.
52. Carlton Winckler, interview with Thomas H. Gressler, December 23, 1971. Quoted in Gressler, "John Murray Anderson" (unpublished PhD dissertation, 1973), 70, 74.
53. "The Magic Rug," Publix Unit Show Manual No. 32, William S. Kenly Collection, The Museum of Modern Art Department of Film Special Collections, New York.
54. Carlton Winckler, Gressler interview, 1971, in Gressler, "John Murray Anderson" (unpublished PhD dissertation, 1973), 160.
55. John Murray Anderson, "Seventy Per Cent Comedy," unidentified periodical, [August 1929], John Murray Anderson clipping file, New York Public Library for the Performing Arts.
56. Libbey, "Out-of-Town Reviews: Almanac," *Variety*, August 7, 1929, 226.
57. Wilfred J. Riley, "Murry [sic] Anderson's Almanac," *Billboard*, August 24, 1929, 7
58. Libbey, "Out-of-Town Reviews: Almanac," *Variety*, August 7, 1929, 226.
59. Riley, "Murry [sic] Anderson's Almanac," *Billboard*, August 24, 1929, 7.
60. Anderson, *Out Without My Rubbers*, 117.
61. Anderson, *Out Without My Rubbers*, 118.

Chapter 5

1. Scott Eyman, *Print the Legend: The Life and Times of John Ford* (New York: Simon & Schuster, 1999), 98.

2. Metzger had entered the film business in 1910 in Oregon, as a film inspector for the Portland sub-distributor for the Laemmle Film Service, and he originated the Complete Film Service contract when he was manager of Universal's Kansas City Exchange. "Know Your Sales Leaders," *Exhibitors Herald and Moving Picture World*, February 25, 1928, 20.

3. Carl Laemmle Jr., telegram to L. B. Metzger, September 14, 1929. Courtesy of Richard Koszarski.

4. Edwin Schallert, "Revues Stir Controversy," *Los Angeles Times*, March 9, 1930, B11.

5. John Murray Anderson, New York, letter to Carl Laemmle Jr., Universal City, September 21, 1929. Paul Whiteman Collection, Williams College.

6. Robert H. Cochrane, telegram to Coast, September 5, 1929. Courtesy of Richard Koszarski.

7. L. B. Metzger, telegram to Carl Laemmle Jr., September 6, 1929. Courtesy of Richard Koszarski.

8. Agreement between Paul Whiteman and Universal Pictures Corporation, October 18, 1928. Courtesy of Richard Koszarski. "Mr. Whiteman hereby reserves and retains unto himself all of the musical compositions written by or for him ... for the picture to be produced hereunder and the right to convey the same to any publishing company of his selection..."

9. Carl Laemmle Jr., telegram to L. B. Metzger, September 14, 1929. Courtesy of Richard Koszarski.

10. "Gershwin Reminiscences," *Variety*, July 14, 1937, 53. The contract between Universal and Harms, Inc., was signed on October 3, 1929.

11. John Murray Anderson, New York, letter to Carl Laemmle Jr., Universal City, September 21, 1929. Paul Whiteman Collection, Williams College.

12. Ruth Morris, "Uncommon Chatter: 'Show of Shows' Expensive," *Variety*, November 27, 1929, 53.

13. *King of Jazz* is entirely Technicolor. *Happy Days* is black & white, photographed in Fox's Grandeur "wide film" process as well as 35mm. It received only two first-run engagements in Grandeur; most of the world saw a normal 35mm version. The others have sequences in Technicolor.

14. "A Director's Ambitions," *New York Times*, May 11, 1930, 122.

15. John Murray Anderson, New York, letter to Carl Laemmle Jr., Universal City, September 21, 1929. Paul Whiteman Collection, Williams College.

16. Mayme Ober Peak, "Junior Laemmle, at 21, Is Proving That He's More Than Son of Boss," *Boston Globe*, September 1, 1929, A34.

17. John Murray Anderson, *Out Without My Rubbers* (New York: Library Publishers, 1954), 121.

18. Paul Fejos, Reminiscences of Paul Fejos: Oral History, 1963, 50-51. Special Collections, Columbia University Libraries, 56. In an interview with Catherine Wunscher published in the March 1954 issue of *Films In Review*, Fejos provides this account: "As I was finishing *Broadway*, Carl Laemmle Jr. told me they had Paul Whiteman's band under contract but no story in which the band could be used. After two months we evolved a big revue which I directed under the title *King of Jazz*." Fejos also claimed to have

directed *King of Jazz* in other interviews.

19. M. F. Murphy, interoffice communication to Mr. Rosse, Universal Pictures, October 12, 1929. Herman Rosse Collection, Williams College.

20. Carl Laemmle Jr., telegram to L. B. Metzger, September 14, 1929. Courtesy of Richard Koszarski.

21. Anderson, *Out Without My Rubbers*, 128.

22. The list of ideas and the sketches are in the Herman Rosse Collection, Williams College.

23. Universal, letter to Wynn Holcomb, October 15, 1929. Courtesy of Richard Koszarski. Holcomb was to receive $1,000 and the cost of transportation to California for his work on the scrapbook and the cartoon.

24. Will Friedwald, "A Little More Modernistic - Animating Paul Whiteman," *Mindrot. The Animated Film Quarterly*, no. 10, April 20,1978, 23.

25. Harry Ruskin, *Comedy Is a Serious Business* (Chicago: The Dramatic Publishing Company, 1974), 12.

26. Ruskin, 20.

27. Herman Rosse, undated letter to family, translated from Dutch. Herman Rosse Collection, Williams College.

28. Cecilia Ager, "Hollywood Styles," *Variety*, November 27, 1929, 53. Cecilia Ager was the wife of *King of Jazz* songwriter Milton Ager.

29. "'King of Jazz Revue' Placed in Production," *Universal Weekly*, November 30, 1929, 1, 31.

30. Ray Rennahan, AFI Oral History with Charles Higham, June 5, 1972, transcript, Louis B. Mayer Library, American Film Institute.

31. Charles Strickfaden and Ken Darby, *From Ragtime to Rock: Rambling Recollections of the Jazz Era*, 1981. Unpublished. Quoted in Don Rayno, *Paul Whiteman: Pioneer in American Music, Vol. I: 1890-1930* (Lanham, MD: Scarecrow Press, 2003), 243.

32. "Whiteman Imports White," *Variety*, November 27, 1929, 65. James Dietrich identified White as being from Victor Recording.

33. Edwin Schallert, "Jazz King Will Turn Comedian," *Los Angeles Times*, December 1, 1929, B13.

34. James Dietrich, interview with Diane and Richard Koszarski, 1976. Courtesy of Richard Koszarski.

35. Harry Lang, "He Didn't Know How!," *Photoplay*, June 1930, 75.

36. Lang, "He Didn't Know How!," 75.

37. Thanks to Mark Cantor for directing our attention to this.

38. "A Director's Ambitions," *New York Times*, May 11, 1930, 122.

39. *The Case of Sergeant Grischa* was the third most costly film on RKO's program for the 1929–30 season, after *Rio Rita* (1929) and *Hit the Deck* (1930). RKO ledger courtesy of Richard B. Jewell. At First National, the anti-war flying picture *The Dawn Patrol* (1930) started filming in February 1930, and opened in July.

40. Carl Laemmle, "The Boy," *Photoplay*, September 1934, 38.

41. "All Quiet on the Western Front," *Billboard*, May 10, 1930, 22.

42. "Report of the Technicolor Art Department's Activities during the shooting of Manhattan Parade," November 24, 1931. André Durenceau folder, Natalie Kalmus Papers, Margaret Herrick Library, Academy of Motion Picture Arts and Sciences.

43. AFI and ASC Seminar with Ray Rennahan, Center for Advanced Film Studies, American Film Institute, May 7, 1977.

44. "Report of the Technicolor Art Department's Activities during the shooting of Manhattan Parade," November 24, 1931.

45. James Dietrich, interview with Diane and Richard Koszarski, 1976.

46. Notes, November 4-5, 1929, Natalie Kalmus Papers, Margaret Herrick Library, Academy of Motion Picture Arts and Sciences.

47. Notes, November 8, 1929, Natalie Kalmus Papers, Margaret Herrick Library, Academy of Motion Picture Arts and Sciences.

48. Herman Rosse, undated letter to family, translated from Dutch. Herman Rosse Collection, Williams College.

49. John W. Dodds, *The Several Lives of Paul Fejos: A Hungarian-American Odyssey* (New York: Wenner-Gren Foundation, 1973), 45.

50. Colgate Baker, "'Greenwich Village Follies,' And John Murray Anderson, the Miracle Man," *New York Review*, September 16, 1922.

51. "Coast Notes," *Variety*, November 27, 1929, 28.

52. "Mary Loses to Jeanette," *The Free Press*, January 19, 1930. Clipping in Whiteman Collection, Williams College.

53. "Mary Loses to Jeanette."

54. Notes, November 8, 1929, Natalie Kalmus Papers.

55. Robert McKay, e-mail correspondence with David Pierce, October 4, 2015.

56. Philip K. Scheuer, "Jazz Spectacle Sets Pace in Novelties," *Los Angeles Times*, April 13, 1930, B11.

57. Letter agreement, Universal Pictures Corporation with George Gershwin, October 3, 1929. Gershwin Collection, Library of Congress.

58. Anderson, *Out Without My Rubbers*, 123.

59. "Hollywood Tunes," *Exhibitors Herald-World*, November 2, 1929, 59.

60. Anderson, *Out Without My Rubbers*, 123.

61. Notes, November 19, 1929, Natalie Kalmus Papers, Margaret Herrick Library, Academy of Motion Picture Arts and Sciences.

62. Anderson, *Out Without My Rubbers*, 124.

63. G. A. Cave, interoffice communication to F. R. Oates, February 8, 1930. Technicolor Corporate Archive, George Eastman Museum.

64. James Dietrich, interview with Diane and Richard Koszarski, 1976.

65. "News of the Cafes," *Los Angeles Times*, November 13, 1929, A12.

66. Myra Nye, "Society of Cinemaland: 'Big U' Night," *Los Angeles Times*, November 24, 1929, 27.

67. "Oriental," dateline January 19, *Variety*, January 23, 1929, 42.

68. Herman Rosse, undated letter to family, translated from Dutch. Herman Rosse Collection, Williams College.

69. James Dietrich, interview with Diane and Richard Koszarski, 1976.

70. "Fox, Metro and U Set Studio Lay-off Period of 4 Wks. - Big Money Saving," *Variety*, November 20, 1929, 6.

71. "In a Pinch," *Variety*, November 27, 1929, 7.

72. "RKO Buys U. Films," *Billboard*, October 12, 1929, 22.

73. "Inside Stuff - Pictures," *Variety*, August 20, 1930, 57; Universal Annual Reports for 1929, 1930. Courtesy of Richard Koszarski.

74. "Publix-U Deal Set," *Variety*, November 6, 1929, 7. The deal did not close.

75. Universal Annual Reports for 1929, 1930. Courtesy of Richard Koszarski.

76. "Consolidated Gets Universal Lab at Fort Lee, N.J.," *Film Daily*, December 27, 1929, 1.

77. "Consol. Seeks Control," *Hollywood Reporter*, January 16, 1933, 1.

78. "News from the Dailies about Hollywood," *Variety*, March 26, 1930, 30.

79. Anderson, *Out Without My Rubbers*, 128.

80. "3 Whiteman Men Hurt," *Variety*, January 1, 1930, 57.

81. Richard Barrios, *A Song in the Dark: The Birth of the Musical Film* (New York: Oxford University Press, 1995) 186.

82. George Gershwin, "Our New National Anthem," *Theatre Magazine*, August 1925.

83. Ray Rennahan, AFI Oral History with Charles Higham, June 5, 1972, transcript, Louis B. Mayer Library, American Film Institute.

84. "Huge Pivoting Bandstand Is Innovation by Rosse in *King of Jazz* Sets," *Exhibitors Herald-World*, February 15, 1930, 27.

85. Leonard Maltin, *The Art of the Cinematographer: A Survey and Interviews with Five Masters* (New York: Dover Publications, 1978), 86.

86. Nell O'Day, letter to Robert McKay, June 21, 1977. Courtesy of Robert McKay.

87. "A Director's Ambitions," *New York Times*, May 11, 1930, 122.

88. Anderson, *Out Without My Rubbers*, 124.

89. Carl Laemmle, "The Boy," *Photoplay*, September 1934, 94.

90. George J. Mitchell, "Making All Quiet on the Western Front," *American Cinematographer*, September 1985, 38.

91. Lewis Milestone, interview with Kevin Brownlow, 1970. Courtesy of Kevin Brownlow.

92. Lewis Milestone, interview with Kevin Brownlow, 1970.

93. Anderson, *Out Without My Rubbers*, 124.

94. Edwin Schallert, "Revues Stir Controversy," *Los Angeles Times*, March 9, 1930, B11.

95. Thomas H. Gressler, "John Murray Anderson: Director of Revues" (unpublished PhD dissertation, Kent State University, 1973), 166.

96. Gressler, 168.

97. "Out-of-Town Reviews - Almanac," *Variety*, August 7, 1929, 226.

98. Mary Fanton Roberts, "An Essentially American Producer at Last - John Murray Anderson," *The Touchstone*, November 1920, 94.

99. Filmed at the same time that *King of Jazz* was in production were *Bride of the Regiment* (an atypical nine weeks in production), *Bright Lights* (four weeks), and *Viennese Nights* (five weeks). For details, see Technicolor's production schedules for 1929 and 1930, in James Layton and David Pierce, *The Dawn of Technicolor: 1915-1935* (Rochester: George Eastman House, 2015), 244.

100. "Santa Claus," *Motion Picture News*, March 1, 1930, 14.

101. John W. Dodds, *The Several Lives of Paul Fejos*, 46 fn.

Chapter 6

1. "Out-of-Town Reviews," *Variety*, August 7, 1929, 226.

2. Charles Irwin was the house M. C. at the Publix-owned Capitol Theater in Detroit. He also regularly appeared at the Paramount Theatre in New York and many other Publix houses around the country. In 1929 Irwin hosted the John Murray Anderson prologue "Say It With Music." He appeared in a 1928 Vitaphone short called *The Debonair Humorist*, as well as several early M-G-M sound shorts. "Publix Signs Chas. Irwin For 3 Years in Detroit," *Billboard*, January 8, 1927, 36; "Talking Shorts," *Variety*, June 20,

1928, 27; "Whiting and Burt Do M-G-M Shorts," *Billboard*, November 3, 1928, 26; "Paramount," *Variety*, April 24, 1929, 39.

3. "All Color Cartoon in King of Jazz Latest Talking Picture Development," *Universal Weekly*, March 29, 1930, 9.

4. Will Friedwald, "A Little More Modernistic - Animating Paul Whiteman," *Mindrot. The Animated Film Quarterly*, no. 10, April 20,1978, 22.

5. Joe Adamson, *The Walter Lantz Story: with Woody Woodpecker and Friends* (New York: G. P. Putnam's Sons, 1985), 81-82.

6. But this was not the first color cartoon. That distinction goes to *The Debut of Thomas Cat* (1920), photographed in Brewster Color.

7. "Paul Whiteman Concert," *Variety*, November 4, 1925, 23.

8. "Warning! Paul Whiteman has protected his stage idea and title 'Meet the Boys,'" *Variety*, September 16, 1925, 50.

9. "Hot Lips," "Linger Awhile," and "Nola" were recorded by the band in 1922, 1923, and 1929 respectively. "Wild Cat" was recorded by Joe Venuti and Eddie Lang in 1927.

10. "Bridal Veil Number in King of Jazz," *Universal Weekly*, April 5, 1930, 10.

11. Nell O'Day, letter to Robert McKay, June 21, 1977. Courtesy of Robert McKay. Although O'Day remembers this being filmed, a study of the original sound discs reveals the waltz was never included in the general release version.

12. James Dietrich, interview with Diane and Richard Koszarski, 1976. Courtesy of Richard Koszarski.

13. "Mississippi Mud" was also written by Harry Barris, with lyrics by James Cavanaugh. It was recorded three times by The Rhythm Boys between July 1927 and February 1928.

14. *King of Jazz* songs and dialogue continuity, 1930, Motion Picture Scripts Collection, New York State Archives.

15. Notes from the 1930 continuity, courtesy of Richard Koszarski; *King of Jazz* copyright deposit description, published May 17, 1930, received May 24, 1930, Copyright Office, Library of Congress.

16. From Charles Irwin's introduction to the scene.

17. The same "And then the war broke out!" joke is used at the conclusion of the Vitaphone short *Jack White with The Montrealers* (1929).

18. The Brox Sisters were much in demand at this time. After earning a reputation on Broadway in successive runs of the *Music Box Revue* in the mid-1920s, they appeared in several early sound shorts for Vitaphone, M-G-M, and Universal, and also helped to immortalize "Singin' In the Rain" in *The Hollywood Revue of 1929*.

19. C. B. Paine, Memo to Adolph Schimel, March 31, 1930. Courtesy of Richard Koszarski.

20. "Universal Moviegrams," *Universal Weekly*, June 21, 1930, 1.

21. "Straight Dance Bands Without Chance With Only Straight Music," *Variety*, June 9, 1926, 41.

22. "Paul Whiteman's Concert," *Variety*, October 10, 1928, 53.

23. Rivoli Program, week beginning March 7, 1926, Leo Morgan Papers, New York Public Library for the Performing Arts.

24. "The American Stage," *The Stage*, August 4, 1927, 17.

25. "The Giant Piano," *Variety*, October 6, 1926, 55.

26. "Smarty," *Variety*, October 26, 1927, 51.

27. "81st St.," *Variety*, April 15, 1921, 20.

28. *Hollywood Filmograph*, November 9, 1929.

29. "Mabel Wayne Scores Again in King of Jazz," *Universal Weekly*, March 22, 1930, 14.

30. *King of Jazz* copyright description, received May 24, 1930, Library of Congress.

31. "Universal Signs Al Norman for King of Jazz Revue," *Universal Weekly*, November 23, 1929, 10.

32. "Dancing Feet," *Variety*, January 25, 1928, 33.

33. "Paul Small, 45, Stage Producer," *New York Herald Tribune*, August 7, 1954, 10.

34. Colgate Baker, "Greenwich Village Follies," *The New York Review*, September 16, 1922.

35. Leslie had performed as an "old-time vocalist" for several seasons in Franker Wood and Bunee Wyde's "All Right Eddie" vaudeville act in the early 1920s and in 1923 in *Earl Carroll's Vanities*. He also teamed with John Murray Anderson on the *Greenwich Village Follies*.

36. Bing Crosby, *Call Me Lucky* (New York: Simon and Schuster, 1953), 102.

37. "Cabarets: Ziegfeld's Midnight Frolic," *Variety*, October 20, 1916, 18.

38. Sheet music: Sigmund Romberg and Jean Schwartz, "America's Popular Song," *The Passing Show of 1919* (New York & Detroit: Jerome H. Remick & Co., 1919).

39. Jack F. Murray, "Metropolitan Baffles Description," *Billboard*, October 24, 1925, 89; Mordaunt Hall, "A Kiss For Cinderella," *New York Times*, December 25, 1925, 10.

40. "Says F-P-L Puts Feature Production in Shorts," *Film Daily*, June 9, 1929, 6.

41. "John Murray Anderson rec'd $1,000.00 for MELTING POT routine from Para. F.L. Corp. who gave permission for its use in KING OF JAZZ." Quoted from *Universal Catalog of Library Properties*. Motion Picture, Broadcasting and Recorded Sound Division (MBRS), Library of Congress.

42. The Melting Pot number was filmed in January 1930, midway through the production. It was likely "Shadows" was written as a production number, hence its inclusion in the finale, but the number was never filmed.

43. Several scene stills exist of Paul Howard's dance routine from "A Bench in the Park" at the USC Cinematic Arts Library.

44. Paul Whiteman and Mary Margaret McBride, *Jazz* (New York: J. H. Sears & Company, Inc., 1926), 3.

46. Whiteman and McBride, *Jazz*, 9. Whiteman and McBride, *Jazz*, 15-16.

47. Gilbert Seldes, "American Music in the Concert Hall," Paul Whiteman Souvenir Program, Transcontinental Concert Tour, 1928–29, New York Public Library for the Performing Arts.

Chapter 7

1. Lewis Milestone, interview with Kevin Brownlow, 1970. Courtesy of Kevin Brownlow.

2. Florabel Muir, "Carl Laemmle Grooms 3 Big Wows for 1930," *New York Daily News*, reprinted in *Universal Weekly*, January 4, 1930, 22.

3. Edwin Schallert, "'Ghosting' Songs Now Favored," *Los Angeles Times*, January 19, 1930, B13.

4. Coral Clyee, "Jazz Talkie by Whiteman a Revelation in Sound," *New York Morning Telegraph*, reprinted in *Universal Weekly*, February 15, 1930, 18.

5. Rose Kearin to F. W. Murnau, May 13, 1930. Courtesy of Kevin Brownlow. Director F. W. Murnau was out of the country filming *Tabu* (1931), and Kearin, Murnau's secretary, wrote

this letter relating a conversation with Edgar G. Ulmer to keep Murnau current with activities in Hollywood. Ulmer had worked on Murnau's *Sunrise* (1927).

6. Advertisement, *All Quiet on the Western Front*, *Variety*, April 30, 1930, 23.
7. Edwin Schallert, "War Shown in Stern Reality," *Los Angeles Times*, April 22, 1930, A9.
8. "Disappointments on Coast Last Wk - Western Front Made Big Showing, $22,000 at $1.50 Top," *Variety*, April 30, 1930, 9.
9. "Greasing the Breaks," *Motion Picture News*, June 21, 1930, 17. Reprinted in "The Breaks," *Talking Screen*, July 1930, 17.
10. "Trailers as Aid to Salesmen Tried by Paramount and 'U'," *Motion Picture News*, January 18, 1930, 30. Eight prints of each title were made, and then sent around from one exchange to another. The use of in-house promotional trailers had been initiated by Paramount for the Technicolor operetta *The Vagabond King*.
11. "Laemmle Urges Tents to Foil 'Monopoly'," *Motion Picture News*, May 3, 1930, 26, 26C.
12. "Plan 40 Tent Roadshows for Paul Whiteman Film," *Film Daily*, April 17, 1930, 1.
13. "Roxy Theatre Books Seven Universal Specials," *Universal Weekly*, April 12, 1930, 13.
14. "Universal Executives Discuss Foreign Films," *Motion Picture News*, May 3, 1930, 26.
15. "Universal Un-Conventionalities," *Motion Picture News*, May 3, 1930, 26A.
16. Ginger Rogers, *Ginger: My Story* (New York: HarperCollins, 1991), 61.
17. Advertisement, *All Quiet on the Western Front*, *Universal Weekly*, May 10, 1930, 1.
18. "30 Ticket Steerers Pinched at Central," *Variety*, May 14, 1930, 59.
19. Treasurer, Universal, letter to Arthur A. Jones, Comptroller, Roxy Theater, New York, May 1930. Courtesy of Richard Koszarski.
20. "Based on the premise that color films affect full reproduction from soundtracks, Metro has been running a separate sound track for its specials at the Astor." "Inside Stuff - Pictures," *Variety*, February 19, 1930, 52.
21. Sime, "King of Jazz," *Variety*, May 7, 1930, 31.
22. "Gershwin Plays His Rhapsody," *New York Sun*, May 7, 1930, 43.
23. Sime, "Film House Reviews, Roxy," *Variety*, May 7, 1930, 55.
24. Quoted in "King of Jazz at Roxy Proclaimed Magnificent," *Universal Weekly*, May 24, 1930, 10.
25. Advertisement, "King of Jazz," *New York Times*, May 9, 1930, 27.
26. Sime, "Film House Reviews, Roxy," *Variety*, May 7, 1930, 55.
27. Edwin C. Stein, "Whiteman's King of Jazz Triumphs at the Roxy," *Brooklyn Standard Union*, May 5, 1930, 6.
28. "King of Jazz Universal All-Color," *Inside Facts of Stage and Screen*, May 3, 1930, 4.
29. [J. W.] Alicoate, "Paul Whiteman in King of Jazz," *Film Daily*, May 4, 1930, 1.
30. P. S. Harrison, "The King of Jazz," *Harrison's Reports*, May 17, 1930, 79.
31. John S. Cohen Jr., "The New Photoplays," *New York Sun*, May 3, 1930, 7.
32. Edwin Schallert, "'Ghosting' Songs Now Favored," *Los Angeles Times*, January 19, 1930, B13.
33. "King of Jazz Universal All-Color," *Inside Facts of Stage and Screen*, May 3, 1930, 4.
34. Llewellyn Miller, "The King of Jazz Opens; Revue is Spectacular," *Los Angeles Record*, April 19, 1930.
35. Leonard Troland, interoffice communication to George A. Cave, December 11, 1929. Technicolor Corporate Archive, George Eastman Museum.
36. Herbert T. Kalmus, interoffice communication to Leonard Troland, April 26, 1930. Technicolor Corporate Archive, George Eastman Museum.
37. "Inside Stuff - Pictures," *Variety*, April 30, 1930, 55.
38. Mordaunt Hall, "Murray Anderson's Sparkling Film: Pastel Shaded King of Jazz Possesses Wonderful Photography and Smart Skits," *New York Times*, May 11, 1930, 121.
39. Marguerite Tazelaar, "On the Screen: King of Jazz - Roxy," *New York Herald Tribune*, May 3, 1930, 8.
40. Leonard Troland, interoffice communication to J. A. Ball, May 13, 1930. Technicolor Corporate Archive, George Eastman Museum.
41. "Unemployment and Opposition Banged Minn. Houses Last Week," *Variety*, March 19, 1930, 8.
42. "$19,100 Best in K.C.; Pan Stock-Film $14,300," *Variety*, January 29, 1930, 13.
43. "Not a Revue," Variety, April 16, 1930, 10.
44. Advertisement, "Paramount Theatre," *Los Angeles Times*, April 24, 1930, A17.
45. "Movietone Follies Gagged for S.F. Booking; Big Draw," *Inside Facts of Stage and Screen*, June 28, 1930, 7. The Los Angeles engagement was titled *Svenson's Big Night*. It is not clear if the change was made to the prints, or just the advertising.
46. "Jazz King in King of Jazz Here at Last," *Washington Post*, May 4, 1930, A2; Nelson B. Bell, "Behind the Screens," *Washington Post*, May 3, 1930, 11.
47. "3 H.O. Films in Wash. Didn't Help 1st Runs," *Variety*, May 21, 1930, 10.
48. Nelson B. Bell, "Some Random Observations on Films Past and Current," *Washington Post*, May 25, 1930, A2.
49. Sime, "King of Jazz," *Variety*, May 7, 1930, 31.
50. Movietone was 1.33:1 in photography and 1.17:1 in projection. Vitaphone was 1.33:1 in photography and projection.
51. F. H. Richardson, "Sound Pictures: Sound-Silent Picture Outline," *Exhibitors Herald and Moving Picture World*, November 3, 1928, 33.
52. Lester Cowan, "Camera and Projector Apertures in Relation to Sound-on-Film Pictures," *Journal of the Society of Motion Picture Engineers*, January 1930, 108-121.
53. "No U.S. Film Monopoly; Mr. Cochran Declares It Impossible; Limited Output with World Appeal," *Daily Telegraph*, June 12, 1930, 8.
54. "The Week on the Screen; The 'Talkies' Progress," *Manchester Guardian*, June 21, 1930, 12.
55. "King of Jazz," *The Bioscope*, June 18, 1930, 23.
56. See: Ivan Patrick Gore, "Cabaret: Thames Riviera," *The Stage*, July 17, 1930, 5; "King of Jazz Carnival: Giant Thames Riviera Show," *The Bioscope*, July 9, 1930, 28; Recordist [pseud.], "On the Sound Track," *The Bioscope*, July 23, 1930, 19. Admission for the afternoon only was 5 shillings, the entire event with entertainment plus dinner was 30 shillings, or one pound ten shillings, roughly $7.50 at the 1930 exchange rate.
57. "Speedy RCA: Royalty View King of Jazz," *Kinematograph Weekly*, July 24, 1930, 39.
58. "All Quiet Completes Six Months Played to Over a Million," *Kinematograph Weekly*, October 23, 1930, 18.
59. "Universal May Lease London Moss Houses," *Variety*, July 16, 1930, 7, 42; "Talkies for
60. All: Universal's Plan for Silent Exhibitors," *Kinematograph Weekly*, July 17, 1930, 53. "All Quiet Pre-Releases; A Protest to Universal," *Kinematograph Weekly*, September 18, 1930, 51.
61. H. E. W., "Orchestra & Talkie Music; A Study in Contrast," *Daily Telegraph*, October 21, 1930, 8.
62. G. A. Atkinson, "The First Film About Football," *Sunday Express*, September 28, 1930, 4.
63. "King of Jazz: Mr. Paul Whiteman's New Film," *The Times* (London), October 10, 1930, 10.
64. Including *King of Jazz*, 38% of Universal's revenue from the 1930-31 season came from foreign (outside the U.S. and Canada). At M-G-M, for the same season, foreign revenue was 35% of total revenue.
65. P. S. Harrison, "What the 1930-31 MGM Pictures Did for the Independent Exhibitors," *Harrison's Reports*, August 22, 1931, 136.
66. P. S. Harrison, "X-Raying the 1930-31 Products - Last Article," *Harrison's Reports*, October 11, 1930, 161, 164.
67. "Remarks of Mr. Carl Laemmle at the Sales Convention of Universal Pictures Corporation, St. Moritz Hotel, New York City, Friday, May 8, 1931," 14. Courtesy of Richard Koszarski.
68. "Remarks of Mr. Carl Laemmle at the Sales Convention of Universal Pictures Corporation," 20.

Chapter 8

1. Average Figures Drawn from Universal Financial Records, 1926–1928. Courtesy of Richard Koszarski.
2. Paul Kohner, Interview with Richard Koszarski, August 14, 1974. Courtesy of Richard Koszarski. Lupita Tovar and Pancho Kohner, *Lupita Tovar:*
3. *The Sweetheart of México: A Memoir. As told to her son Pancho Kohner* ([Bloomington, IN]: Xlibris Corp., 2011), 51.
4. *Lupita Tovar Kohner: An Oral History*, interviewed by Larry Ceplair, June 2-9, 2005. Center for Oral History Research, University of California Los Angeles.
5. Chapin Hall, "Stars Are Dimmed," *New York*
6. *Times*, March 22, 1931, X5. Frederick Kohner, *The Magician of Sunset Boulevard: The Improbable Life of Paul Kohner, Hollywood Agent* (Palos Verdes, CA: Morgan Press, 1977), 57.
7. Tovar and Kohner, *Lupita Tovar*, 56.
8. The foreign versions of the studio's Slim Summerville comedies cost as little as $6,000, compared to $22,000 and up for the English-language equivalents. *Shooting Record of Pictures 1930-1931-1932*, Universal Collection, Cinematic Arts Library, University of Southern California.
9. "České verse," *Hollywood*, July 1930, 1.
10. Outtakes of Sôjin's introductions for *Happy Days* survive in the Fox Movietone News collection at the University of South Carolina (Columbia).
11. "Paramount on Parade Is Now Made in Japanese," *Hollywood Filmograph*, July 19, 1930, 15. An image of Suisei Matsui in costume for *Paramount on Parade* can be seen here: "Shuffled But Not Lost," *Picture Play Magazine*, January 1931, 71.
12. "In 16 Versions," *Variety*, January 29, 1930, 7.
13. Frederick Kohner, *The Magician of Sunset Boulevard*, 59.
14. *Shooting Record of Pictures 1930-1931-1932*, Universal Collection, Cinematic Arts Library,

University of Southern California.

15. Interestingly, although *The Last Performance* was released in Europe in both German and Hungarian dubbed versions, the U.S. domestic release was silent.

16. The foreign versions ran approximately 82 minutes, versus 103 minutes for the domestic U.S. version. Unique music cues were prepared to accompany the opening titles and introductions of each edition. The Hungarian version, for example, opened with Franz Liszt's *Hungarian Rhapsody* and the *Marche Hongroise* by Hector Berlioz.

17. Edited excerpts from Tetsu Komai, "How I Got to Be the Moderator for King of Jazz," *Kinema Junpo*, February 21, 1931. Translated by Shota Ogawa and Daisuke Kawahara.

18. Unidentified Czech publication, September 1930, Antonín Vaverka scrapbooks, Národní filmový archiv. Translated by Anna Batistová.

19. "Release Shipments 1924-1951," Technicolor Corporate Archive, George Eastman Museum. Technicolor's records conflict with information found in Universal's files. According to Universal, either 203 or 218 prints were ordered in total for the 1930 release. Information courtesy of Richard Koszarski.

20. Notes on the Spanish continuity for *King of Jazz*, 1976, Courtesy of Richard Koszarski. Thanks to archivist Scott MacQueen for clarification of Technicolor's positive assembly practices at this time.

21. Of course the ultimate arbiter of how these prints were seen at venues across the world was the projectionist. Although the foreign release prints were full-aperture, in most cases they were likely projected through a narrower Movietone aperture plate. The surviving French print at the Gosfilmofond archive in Russia features an opening title centered for full aperture, although the rest of the titles in the film are centered for Movietone sound projection.

22. Britain was the fifth-largest international market for American films in 1926, although for six non-consecutive years during the 1920s it was the primary market. Kristin Thompson, *Exporting Entertainment: America in the World Film Market, 1909-34* (London: BFI Publishing, 1985), 127, 139.

23. *Cinema Year Book of Japan 1936-1937* (Tokyo: Sanseido, 1937), 114, as quoted in Thompson, *Exporting Entertainment*, 143. It is important to note that only 5.7% of all films released in Japan in 1930 were in sound, and only 8.4% the following year. Because of the slower adoption of sound production in Japan, it is not surprising that many early sound releases in that country were American.

24. Domestically, *El Rey del Jazz* began playing at Spanish-language theaters in the United States in August 1930. The film played at the Teatro Palace in San Antonio, Texas, the week beginning August 22, 1930.

25. Information courtesy of Carlos Roberto de Souza.

26. The film in question was *L'uomo più allegro di Vienna* (Italy, 1925), released in France in 1927.

27. *Nytid*, February 3, 1931. Translated by Natalie Snoyman.

28. "Ao Cahir do Panno," *Caderno Unico*, October 11, 1930, 13. Translated by Gloria Diez.

29. Antonín Vaverka's striking resemblance to the Austrian Emperor Franz Joseph did land him notable parts in Universal's *Merry-Go-Round* (1923) and Erich von Stroheim's *The Wedding March* (1928).

30. Frederick Kohner, *The Magician of Sunset Boulevard*, 59.

31. Frederick Kohner, *The Magician of Sunset Boulevard*, 61. According to Mr. Veroslav Haba, Curator of American Film at the Národní filmový archiv, who has listened to the Czech audio, Vaverka's performance is "old-fashioned in syntax and accent," but is not "as bad as stated" by Dr. Janowsky. Veroslav Haba, e-mail correspondence with James Layton, November 6, 2015.

32. *Telegraf*, September 5, 1930, Antonín Vaverka scrapbooks, Národní filmový archiv.

33. *Studio*, no. 8, October 1930, 243. Translated by Anna Batistová.

34. Antonín Vaverka, *Mé vzpomínky od zlaté Prahy až po americké hvězdy* [*My Memories from Golden Prague to American Stars*], undated, Antonín Vaverka Collection, Národní filmový archiv. Translated by Anna Batistová.

35. Richard Barrios, *A Song in the Dark: The Birth of the Musical Film*, 2nd edition (New York: Oxford University Press, 2010), 332.

36. Information courtesy of Carlos Roberto de Souza.

37. "Jazzkungen kommer," *Folkets Dagblad Politiken*, September 28, 1930. Translated by Natalie Snoyman.

38. Swedish version, Greta Granstedt, apparently struggled to "attempt to speak the language of her ancestors." *Aftonbladet*, September 30, 1930. Translated by Natalie Snoyman.

39. Universal Financial Records, 1930–1931. Courtesy of Richard Koszarski.

40. Frederick Kohner, *The Magician of Sunset Boulevard*, 57.

Chapter 9

1. Carl Laemmle, "Universal's New Production Policy," *Film Daily*, June 16, 1930, 3. The *All Quiet* sequel would eventually be made as *The Road Back* in 1937.

2. Figures drawn from Universal Financial Records, 1930–1931. Courtesy of Richard Koszarski. Unlike its competitors, especially Paramount, Universal was not encumbered by debt from buying theaters at the height of the market, that subsequently lost much of their value.

3. Contract between Universal Pictures Corporation and John Murray Anderson, May 2, 1930, courtesy of Richard Koszarski; "Anderson Signs With U; Whiteman Film Is Reason," *Motion Picture News*, April 26, 1930, 31; "Buying Anderson Contract," *Motion Picture News*, August 16, 1930, 23.

4. "John Murray Anderson Assigned Dramatic Story," *Film Daily*, November 2, 1930, 2; "Reviving Anderson," *Variety*, April 8, 1931, 2.

5. Notes from Memo from H. H. Zehner to Miss Hughes, June 22, 1931, courtesy of Richard Koszarski.

6. Instead, the studio concentrated on the horror genre, and had considerable success with the likes of *Dracula*, *Frankenstein* (1931), and *The Mummy* (1932).

7. James F. Gillespie, with Wesley Stout, "Hot Music," *Saturday Evening Post*, March 19, 1932, 86.

8. "What the Picture Did for Me," Motion Picture Herald, July 8, 1933, 48; "What the Picture Did for Me," *Motion Picture Herald*, August 26, 1933, 93.

9. "What the Picture Did for Me," *Motion Picture Herald*, September 2, 1933, 52. Cozy Theatre, Winchester, Indiana; "What the Picture Did for Me," *Motion Picture Herald*, August 5, 1933, 49.

10. "Inside Stuff — Pictures," *Variety*, July 11, 1933, 51.

11. "What the Picture Did for Me," *Motion Picture Herald*, November 11, 1933, 52. Genesco Theatre, Genesco, Illinois; "What the Picture Did for Me," *Motion Picture Herald*, September 16, 1933, 59. Mission Theatre, Menard, Texas.

12. "Theatre Receipts," *Motion Picture Herald*, November 11, 1933, 40; "Theatre Receipts," *Motion Picture Herald*, December 23, 1933, 54.

13. "World Revenue Report by Picture, 1932/1933 Product, Domestic Revenue Through Week Ending October 30, 1937 (Final Report)," Universal Corporate Archive. Courtesy Dr. Jan-Christopher Horak.

14. "New Company Gets Option to Buy Universal Pictures for $5,500,000," *Motion Picture Herald*, November 9, 1935, 23.

15. For details of this remarkable commitment, see Udo Bayer, "Laemmle's List: Carl Laemmle's Affidavits for Jewish Refugees," *Film History* 10, no. 4 (1998): 501-21.

16. Reminiscences of Samson Raphaelson, June 1959, 6. Columbia Center for Oral History, Columbia University, New York.

17. Peter Bogdanovich, *Who the Devil Made It* (New York: Alfred A. Knopf, 1997), 575.

18. Rupert Neate, "Rupert Murdoch's son James to take the reins at 21st Century Fox," *Guardian* (London), June 16, 2015. Even though the Murdoch family only owned 12% of the company, they had 40% of the voting rights.

19. Universal offered several other titles from the 1929/30 period in its "Show-at-Home" 16mm library, although they were presented in silent release versions only. These included *Broadway*, *Captain of the Guard*, *Czar of Broadway* (1930), *Melody Lane* (1929), and *Skinner Steps Out* (1929). "Universal Pictures Corp. Show-At-Home Movie Library 16mm," 1936, David Bradley Collection, Lilly Library, Indiana University, Bloomington.

20. Melvin Sattler, letter to Mrs. Paul Whiteman, October 12, 1971. Business and photograph files, Paul Whiteman Collection, Williams College.

21. It was and still is customary to destroy most film prints after their exhibition life has ended, although in the 1930s it was common that a few prints might remain in film exchanges to service bookings. The studios themselves maintained library reference copies of the majority of sound releases, although these would not have been available for public screenings. Outside of a few popular titles and those that played on television, many films of this period effectively remained out of circulation after their initial release.

22. "Beginnings of the American Musical," unsigned program note, National Film Theatre, "Song and Dance" series, [October 1954], BFI Reuben Library.

23. A brief account of the 1965 screening is given in Fred Reynolds, *Road to Hollywood: The Bing Crosby Films Book*, 2nd edition, revised & enlarged (Gateshead [England]: John Joyce & Son, 1986), 16. Additional information from Thomas Christensen, Curator, Danish Film Institute, e-mail correspondence with James Layton, September 16, 2015. Because of the content of this print, it is believed to originate from the 1930 general release version, or some undocumented variant of it.

24. *FIAF Annual Report*, 1965, FIAF files, Special Collections, The Museum of Modern Art

Department of Film.

25. Minutes, XXIst Congress and General Meeting, June 21-26, 1965, FIAF files, Special Collections, The Museum of Modern Art Department of Film; "Vzkřísili jsme Kréle jazzu," *Kino*, September 9, 1965, 10. Translated by Anna Batistová.

26. This nitrate print is now at Gosfilmofond of Russia, undoubtedly the result of an exchange between FIAF member archives.

27. "Vzkřísili jsme Kréle jazzu," *Kino*, September 9, 1965, 10.

28. Information courtesy of Veroslav Haba, Curator of American Film, Národní filmový archiv, e-mail correspondence with James Layton, November 6, 2015. The French nitrate print was copied onto Orwocolor negative film, and a new soundtrack negative was produced from the sound discs. An Orwocolor projection print was then produced from these negatives via two printing passes. Further information on these archival elements can be found in Appendix VIII of this book.

29. A black & white copy of this reconstruction was acquired by the American Film Institute from the Staatliches Filmarchiv in 1970, and was deposited at the Library of Congress. This print does not appear to have ever been shown publicly.

30. "Profiles: Film Resource," *New Yorker*, November 20, 1989, 60, 62. This origin story was consistently told by film historian and collector William K. Everson.

31. Philip Jenkinson, letter to David Bradley, November 1, 1970. David Bradley Collection, Lilly Library, Indiana University, Bloomington;Edward Watz, e-mail correspondence with James Layton, July 12, 2015. Watz used to work for Raymond Rohauer, who later acquired the print.

32. Philip Jenkinson, letter to David Bradley, April 5, 1969. David Bradley Collection, Lilly Library, Indiana University. The three reels Jenkinson refers to are 16mm. It appears that the original 35mm print he copied was made accessible to Jenkinson for a short time, and was never owned by him.

33. Philip Jenkinson, letter to David Bradley, December 30, 1969. David Bradley Collection, Lilly Library, Indiana University.

34. William K. Everson, *King of Jazz* program note, Theodore Huff Memorial Film Society, September 22, 1969. William K. Everson Collection, Department of Cinema Studies, Tisch School of the Arts, New York University.

35. "'27-'33 Medium Rare: Ten Retrospective Selections from the American Film Institute Collection at the Library of Congress," New York Film Festival program supplement, September 25-27, 1970, 5. Courtesy of Scott MacQueen.

36. Richard Koszarski, "The King of Jazz," in Richard Koszarski, George Lobell, and Richard Corliss, "Lost & Found," *Film Comment*, Spring 1971, 70-74.

37. Leonard Feather, "Movie Review: King of Jazz to Screen," *Los Angeles Times*, October 9, 1970, F14.

38. "Hal Mohr's THE WEDDING MARCH will be shown tonight in place of his long-lost film, THE KING OF JAZZ," Los Angeles County Museum of Art announcement, October 10, 1970. James Layton Collection.

39. David Shepard, e-mail correspondence with James Layton, November 15, 2015.

40. Philip Jenkinson, letter to David Bradley, November 1, 1970. David Bradley Collection, Lilly Library, Indiana University.

41. Information courtesy of Scott MacQueen, e-mail correspondence with James Layton, September 18, 2015.

42. This video master was also shown on Irish television several times throughout the 1970s, and turned up again on Channel 4 on Christmas Eve in 1987, the last time *King of Jazz* was screened on British television.

Chapter 10

1. In 1986 Philip Jenkinson charged £708 (16 pence per foot plus 15% tax, the equivalent of $1,035 in 1986, or close to $2,300 in 2016) to make a new 16mm reversal print of *King of Jazz* for U.S. collector Robert McKay. Philip Jenkinson, letter to Robert McKay, April 10, 1986. Courtesy of Robert McKay.

2. Rohauer kept no paperwork related to this transaction. It is likely he acquired the print after Philip Jenkinson copied it. This would make the acquisition date 1969 or later.

3. Ed Watz, e-mail correspondence with James Layton, July 12, 2015.

4. John Baxter, "The Silent Empire of Raymond Rohauer," *The Times Magazine* (London), January 19, 1975; William K. Everson, "Raymond Rohauer: King of the Film Freebooters," *Grand Street* No. 49: Hollywood (Summer 1994): 188-196.

5. Kevin Brownlow, "On the Trail of the Unknown Chaplin," *American Film*, September 1984, 28.

6. George Willeman, e-mail correspondence with James Layton, April 26, 2016.

7. The Vitaphone Project was founded in 1991 by Ron Hutchinson, John Newton, Sherwin Dunner, and Vince Giordano as a not-for-profit organization to unite collectors with archives and studios. To date the Project has raised more than $350,000 to support the restoration of more than 150 early sound shorts and 12 features. The Project has helped locate and document over 6,000 Vitaphone discs in private hands worldwide.

8. This test was screened at The Reel Thing Technical Symposium in Hollywood in August 2015. The footage was introduced by Richard Dayton and Eric Aijala of YCM.

9. Ron Hutchinson, e-mail correspondence with James Layton, April 2, 2016.

10. Stephen C. Leggett, e-mail correspondence with David Pierce, April 30, 2016.

11. "Cinema with the Right Stuff Marks 2013 National Film Registry," Library of Congress press release, December 18, 2013. https://www.loc.gov/today/pr/2013/13-216.html

12. Peter Schade, conference call with James Layton and David Pierce, April 14, 2016.

13. Emily Wensel, conference call with James Layton and David Pierce, April 14, 2016.

14. Schade, conference call, April 14, 2016.

15. Since this collection of Universal nitrate moved to the UCLA Film & Television Archive in 2010, several important rediscoveries have been made. These discoveries include unearthing the original camera negative for the two-color Technicolor masked-ball sequence from the silent 1925 version of *The Phantom of the Opera*, and James Whale's original cut of *The Road Back* (1937), the sequel to *All Quiet on the Western Front* that was re-edited before release to add more comedy.

16. The five features that have survived with two-color Technicolor camera negatives intact are *Toll of the Sea* (missing the final reel, 1922), *The Black Pirate* (as second and third takes from foreign release negatives, 1926), *Follow Thru* (1930), *Whoopee!* (foreign negative, 1930), and *King of Jazz* (shortened reissue negative, 1930). Additionally, several shorts exist as negatives, mostly cartoons, and some color-insert sequences for otherwise black & white features.

17. Of the 371 films made entirely or partially using two-color Technicolor, only 124 survive in some form. For more information, see James Layton and David Pierce, *The Dawn of Technicolor, 1915–1935* (Rochester, NY: George Eastman House, 2015).

18. The source of this destruction rumor has yet to be confirmed by any original documentation.

19. When staff at YCM Laboratories inspected the positive protection elements made by Universal in the 1970s, they discovered that the green master was printed upside down, which resulted in the action running backwards. Information courtesy of Eric Aijala, e-mail correspondence with James Layton, May 8, 2016.

20. Ken Tom, conference call with James Layton and David Pierce, April 14, 2016.

21. A 2,000 ft. reel of two-color Technicolor negatives equates to approximately 11 minutes of printed screen time.

22. Ken Tom, conference call, April 14, 2016.

23. These three scenes can still be viewed on the old VHS release of *King of Jazz*.

24. Schade, conference call, April 14, 2016.

25. Seanine Bird, conference call, April 14, 2016.

26. Schade, conference call.

27. Bird, conference call.

28. The complicated restoration of *Lost Horizon* (1937) was "the culmination of 13 years of detective work" by preservationist Robert Gitt, first under the auspices of the American Film Institute, and later at the UCLA Film & Television Archive, where the work was completed in 1986. Historian Ronald Haver oversaw the 1983 reconstruction of *A Star Is Born* (1954) after he discovered and pieced together 20 minutes of footage (out of 27 minutes) that had been cut from the film following its initial release. This original release version was pieced together using segments of film stored in 200 cans found in a Warner Bros. storage bunker, along with stills for the footage that was not found. Stephen Farber, "Cuts in Film 'Lost Horizon' Restored," *New York Times*, September 3, 1986, C19; "Ronald Haver, 54; Was Film Restorer of 'A Star Is Born,'" *New York Times*, May 21, 1993, B8.

29. Conversely, sometimes picture elements survive, but the audio does not. A good example is the 2003 restoration of Sergio Leone's *The Good, the Bad, and the Ugly* (1966), which premiered in its Italian version at 180 minutes, but was originally released in the U.S. at 162 minutes. John Kirk's restoration for M-G-M required actors Clint Eastwood and Eli Wallach to record new audio for the dialogue in these previously deleted scenes.

30. Bird, conference call.

31. Schade, conference call.

32. Tom, conference call.

33. Bird, conference call.

34. Schade, conference call.

35. Bird, conference call.

36. Schade, conference call.

37. Bird, conference call.

IMAGE CREDITS

BBC Photo Library: 225

Billy Rose Theatre Division, New York Public Library for the Performing Arts, Astor, Lenox and Tilden Foundations: 77 (left), 88, 90 (right)

Gary Chapman: 78

Pete Comandini: 54

Deutsche Kinemathek: 200

Doyle New York: 157

Michael Feinstein/photo by James Kendi: 222

Michael Feinstein/photo by Mark Vieira: 176

Mark Forer: 193

Jack Fulton Family/Matías Bombal: 29, 62, 110, 122

Galerie Bassenge: 165 (left)

George Eastman Museum: 64 (top), 150, 183, 189, 210 (top)

Gosfilmofond: 204, 207, 210 (bottom)

Harry Ransom Center, The University of Texas at Austin: 190

Heritage Auctions: 48 (right), 53 (right)

HLC Properties, Ltd.: 31

Ron Hutchinson: 199

The Institute of the American Musical: 134, 135

Pancho Kohner: 202

Richard Koszarski: 4, 39, 55, 160, 171, 172, 178 (left), 185, 188, 216, 226, 229 (left), 269, 271 (top)

James Layton: 41, 77 (right), 94, 95, 195, 218, 220, 228, 229 (right)

Library of Congress National Audio-Visual Conservation Center: 234

Library of Congress, George Gershwin Collection: 23, 24, 26, 28

Library of Congress, Prints & Photographs Division, George Grantham Bain Collection: 20, 47

Neil Lipes: 70

Margaret Herrick Library, Academy of Motion Picture Arts and Sciences, Bison Archives Photographs collected by Marc Wanamaker: 197

Margaret Herrick Library, Academy of Motion Picture Arts and Sciences, Core Collection, Production Files: p. 270 (bottom right)

John McElwee: 100, 198

Robert McKay: 64 (bottom), 112 (right), 113, 123 (bottom), 143, 208, 212, 227, 268

Peter Mintun: 19, 34

Media History Digital Library: 49, 59, 60, 63, 99, 124, 140 (top), 180, 182, 184, 186 (bottom), 187, 219, 221

Museo Nazionale del Cinema: 209

The Museum of Modern Art: front end pages, 36, 38, 42, 43, 44, 46, 48 (left), 50, 51, 52, 53 (left), 56, 58, 68, 69, 71, 73, 89 (bottom), 92, 101, 102, 117, 129, 132, 145, 146 (top), 154 (top), 159 (bottom), 165 (right), 191, 231

Národní filmový archiv: 213, 224

National Library of Sweden: 211

NBCUniversal: 108 (top), 109, 111, 112 (left), 115, 116, 120, 123 (top), 128 (bottom), 131, 136, 140 (bottom), 146 (bottom), 149 (bottom), 151, 152, 161, 163, 164, 167 (bottom), 169, 173 (bottom), 194, 230, 238, 239, 240, 241, 242, 243, 244, 245, 246, 270 (all ill. except bottom right), 271 (bottom)

NBCUniversal/photo by Julian Antos: 237

The New York Public Library Digital Collections: 76, 79

New York State Archives, Motion Picture Scripts Division: 148

David Pierce: 40 (top)

Ronald Grant Archive: 108 (bottom)

William H. Rosar: 137

Svenska Filminstitutets bibliotek: 214

Karl Thiede: 45, 66 (left)

University of South Carolina, Moving Image Research Collections: 203

The University of Southern California Cinematic Arts Library, Film Stills Collection: 108 (middle), 265, 272

The University of Southern California Digital Library: 40 (bottom)

The University of Texas at Arlington Libraries, Special Collections, Billy Burke Photograph Collection: 170

Frank van Nus: 61

Marc Wanamaker/Bison Archives: 66 (right), 67

Williams College Archives and Special Collections, Herman Rosse Collection: 2–3, 74, 80–81, 82, 83, 84, 85, 87, 89 (top), 91, 93, 96, 103, 105 (5), 106, 107, 114, 118–119, 127, 128 (top), 138–139, 141, 142, 144, 147, 149 (top), 153, 154 (bottom), 158, 159 (top), 167 (top), 168, 173 (top), 178 (right), 181, 266, 267

Williams College Archives and Special Collections, Paul Whiteman Collection: 16, 18, 22, 27, 30, 33, 35, 90 (left), 166

Milan Wolf/photo by Ivan Svoboda: 223

Joe Yranski: 125

INDEX